Waiting for Spring 5

Anashin

Waiting
for Spring
vol.5

Presented by
Anashin

CONTENTS

WAITING FOR SPRING

Harumatsu Bokura

Character & Story

To be like her role model Aya-chan, Mitsuki is determined to make some real friends in high school, but her days pass by without much success. She finds solace at the café where she works, but it doesn't stay a sanctuary for long... One day, the school's celebrities—the Elite Four Hotties of the basketball team— appear out of nowhere! Before she knows it, Mitsuki gets caught up in their silly hijinks. As she spends more time with the four of them, she begins to meet new people and make new friends, too. When she goes to a practice game to cheer the boys on, she is reunited with Aya-chan and is stunned to learn that her childhood best friend was actually a boy! What's more, he really wants to date her! The inter-high basketball preliminaries have begun, and everyone is getting serious—about love *and* basketball!

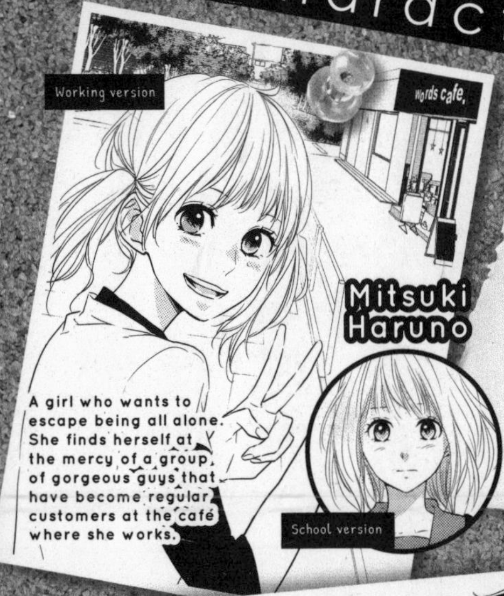
words cafe.

Working version

Mitsuki Haruno

A girl who wants to escape being all alone. She finds herself at the mercy of a group of gorgeous guys that have become regular customers at the café where she works.

School version

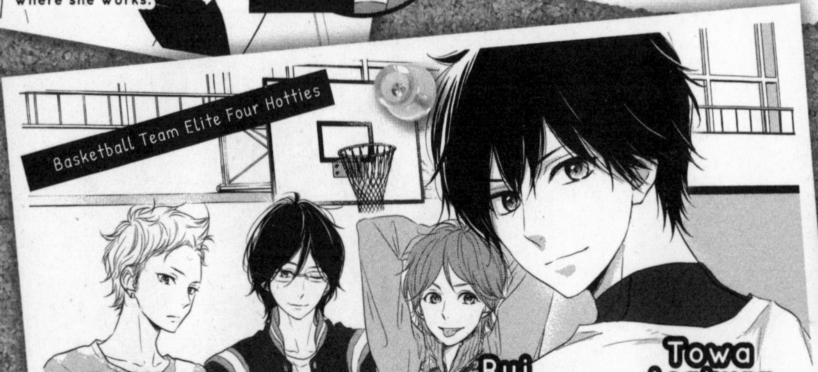

Basketball Team Elite Four Hotties

Towa Asakura

Mitsuki's classmate. He's quiet and a bit spacey, but he's always there to help her.

Rui Miyamoto

A first-year in high school. His innocent smile is adorable, but it hides a wicked heart?!

Kyōsuke Wakamiya

A second-year in high school. Mysterious and always cool-headed. He's like a big brother to everyone.

Ryūji Tada

A second-year. Comes off as a bad boy, but is rather naïve. He's crushing on the Boss's daughter, Nanase-san.

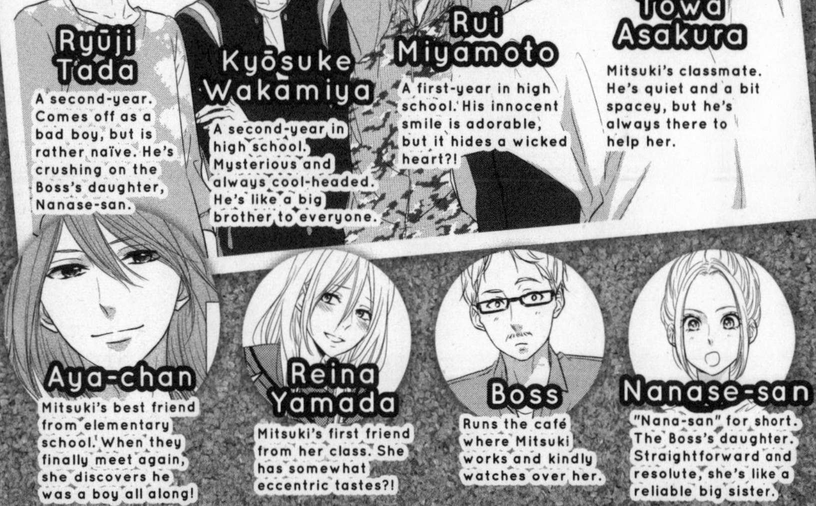

Aya-chan

Mitsuki's best friend from elementary school. When they finally meet again, she discovers he was a boy all along!

Reina Yamada

Mitsuki's first friend from her class. She has somewhat eccentric tastes?!

Boss

Runs the café where Mitsuki works and kindly watches over her.

Nanase-san

"Nana-san" for short. The Boss's daughter. Straightforward and resolute, she's like a reliable big sister.

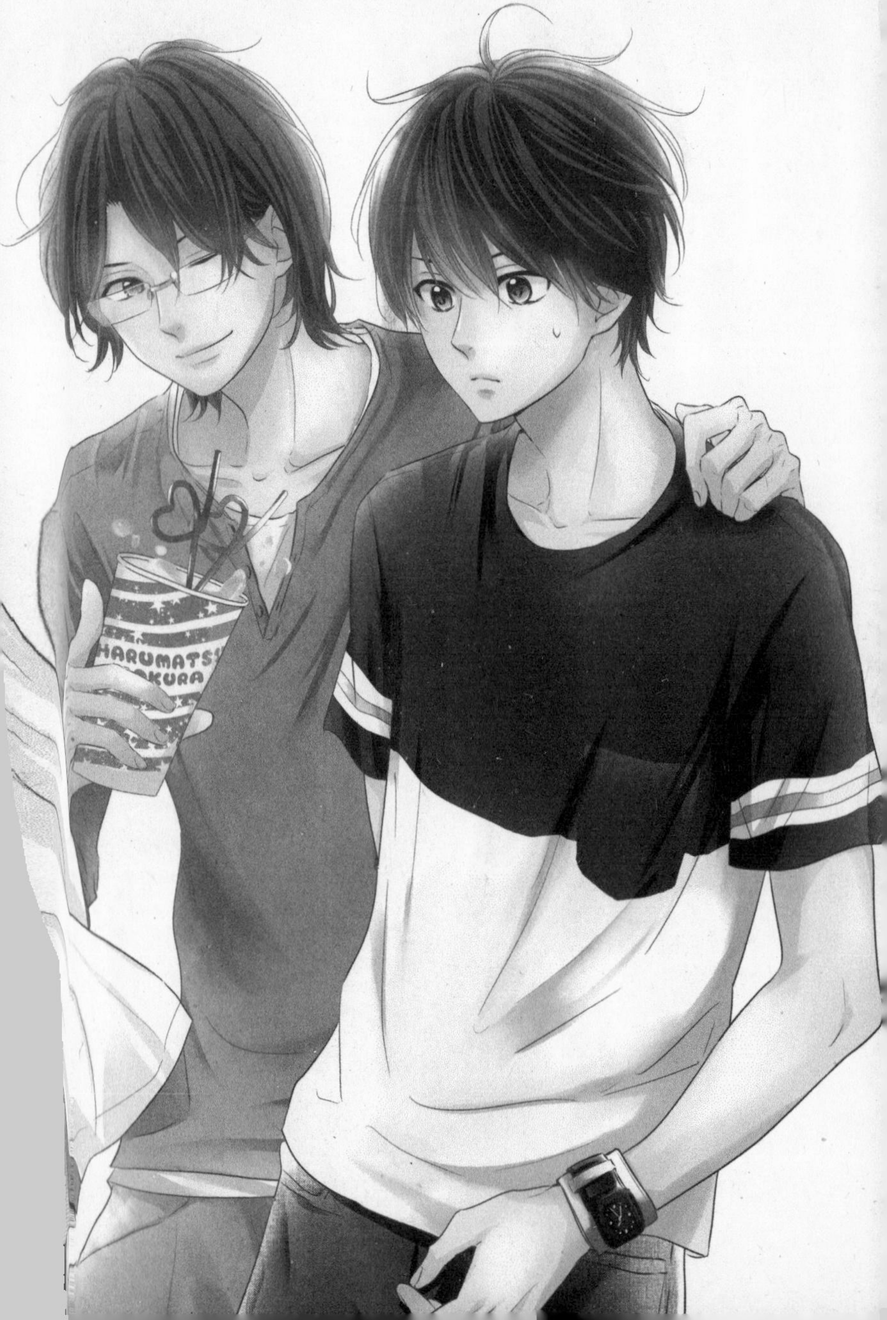

period 21: "Miracle Ferris Wheel"

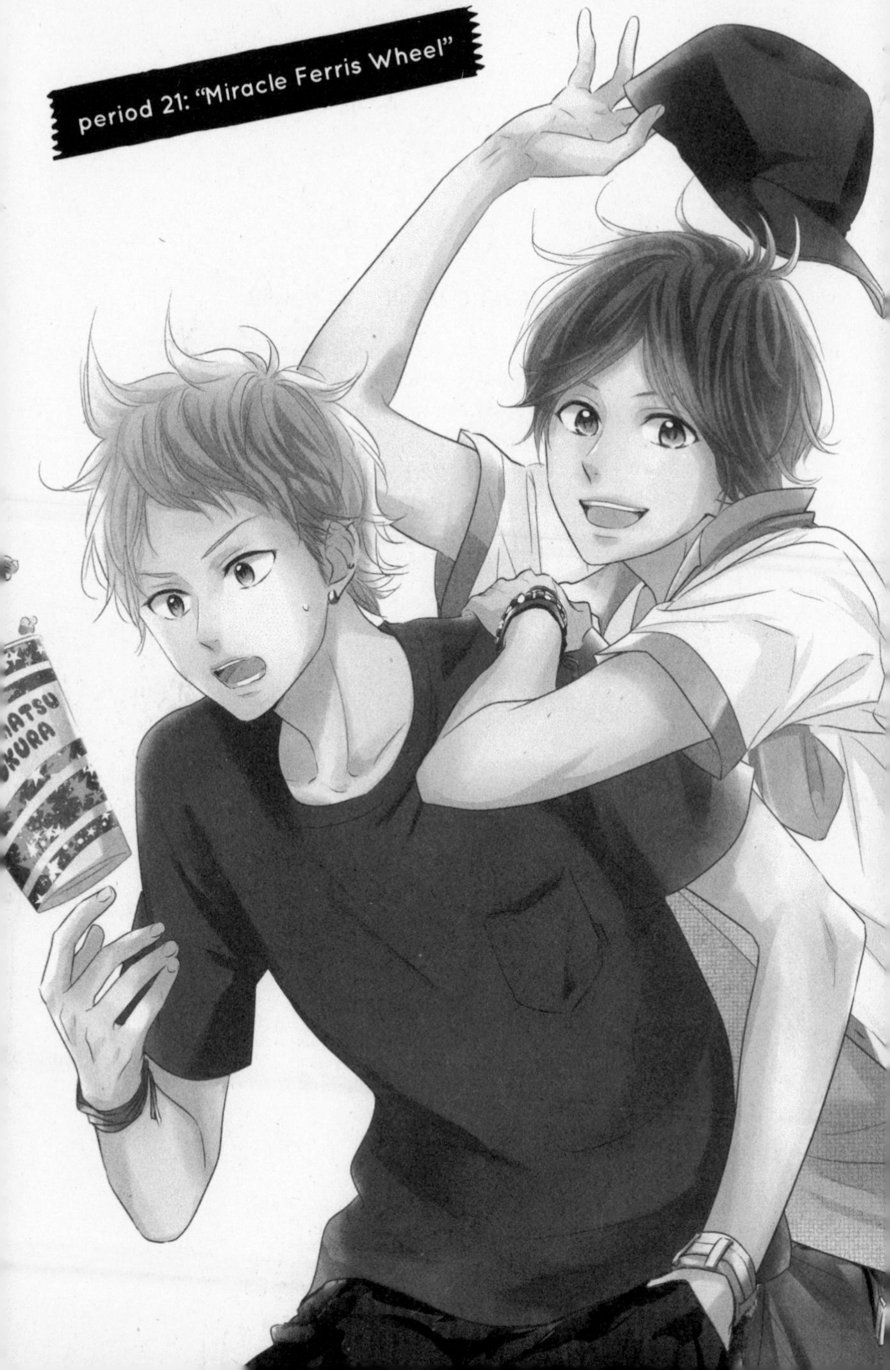

Hello!!
Anashin here!

Thank you so much for picking up Volume 5!

As I announced in Volume 4, this volume marks the beginning of books with only four chapters. Nevertheless, the number of pages per chapter has gone up slightly, and the release dates are coming a little sooner, so I hope you will continue to enjoy the series as you always have. (The amount of bonus material has gone up a little, too!)

That being said, I'm hoping to step it up and work even harder. I'm counting on your support! I hope you enjoy Volume 5. ☆

Aya-chan won the battle for the cover.
Sorry, Mitsuki.

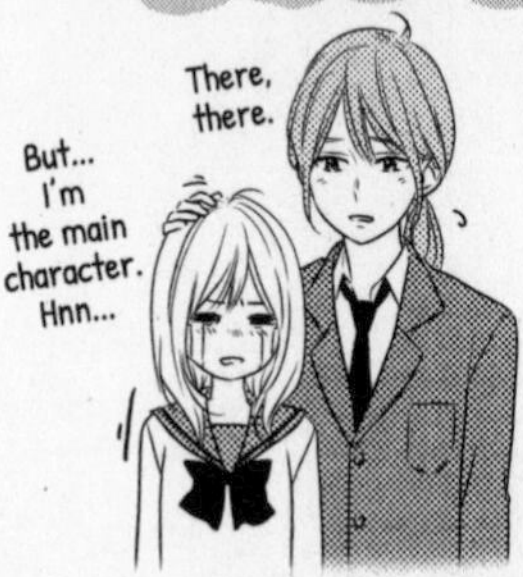
There, there.
But... I'm the main character. Hnn...

I'm not trying to pick on you. It's just that, considering what happens in this volume, Aya-chan was the only way to go. And so...

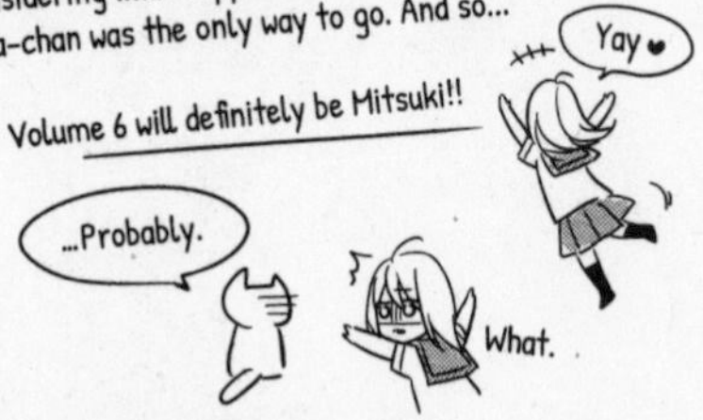
Yay
Volume 6 will definitely be Mitsuki!!
...Probably.
What.

Don't worry. It will be Mitsuki.

Please look forward to Volume 6, too.

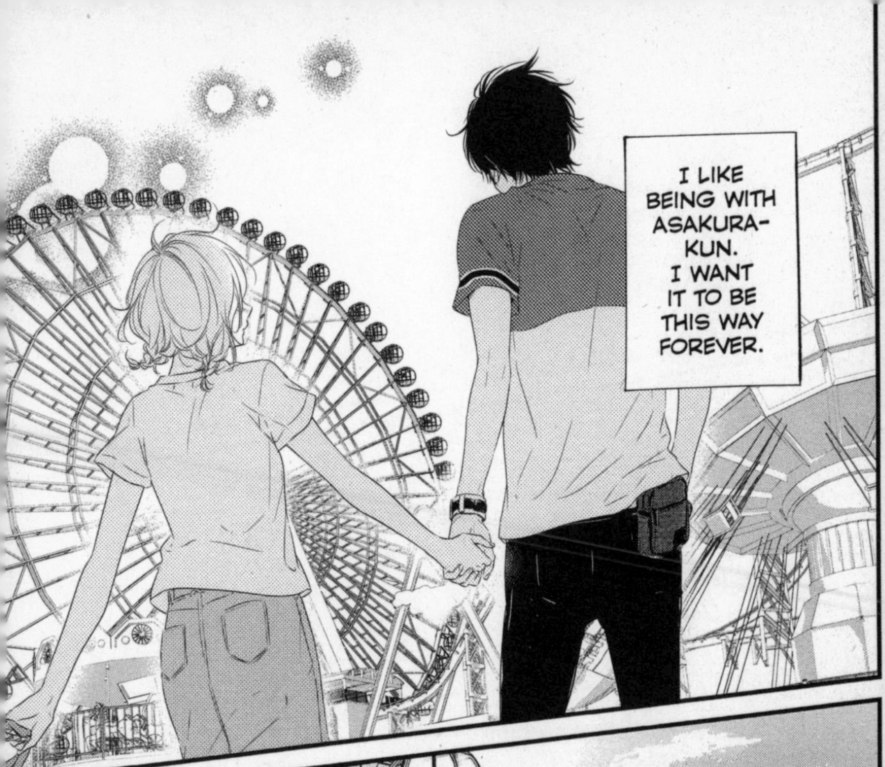
I LIKE BEING WITH ASAKURA-KUN. I WANT IT TO BE THIS WAY FOREVER.
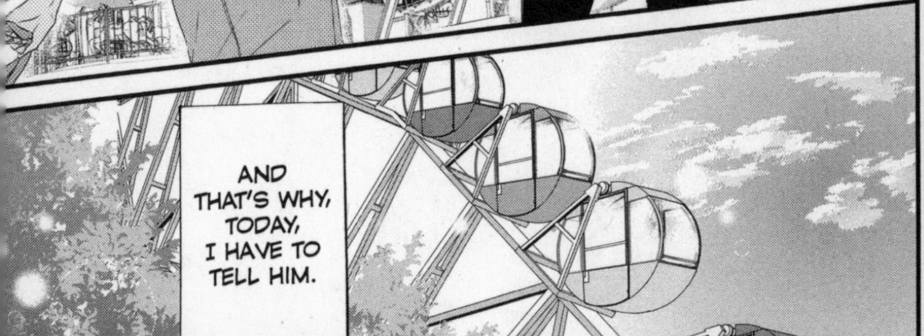
AND THAT'S WHY, TODAY, I HAVE TO TELL HIM.
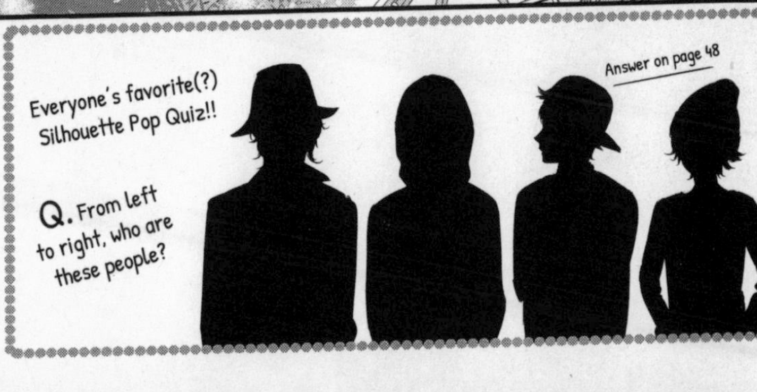
Everyone's favorite(?) Silhouette Pop Quiz!!
Answer on page 48
Q. From left to right, who are these people?

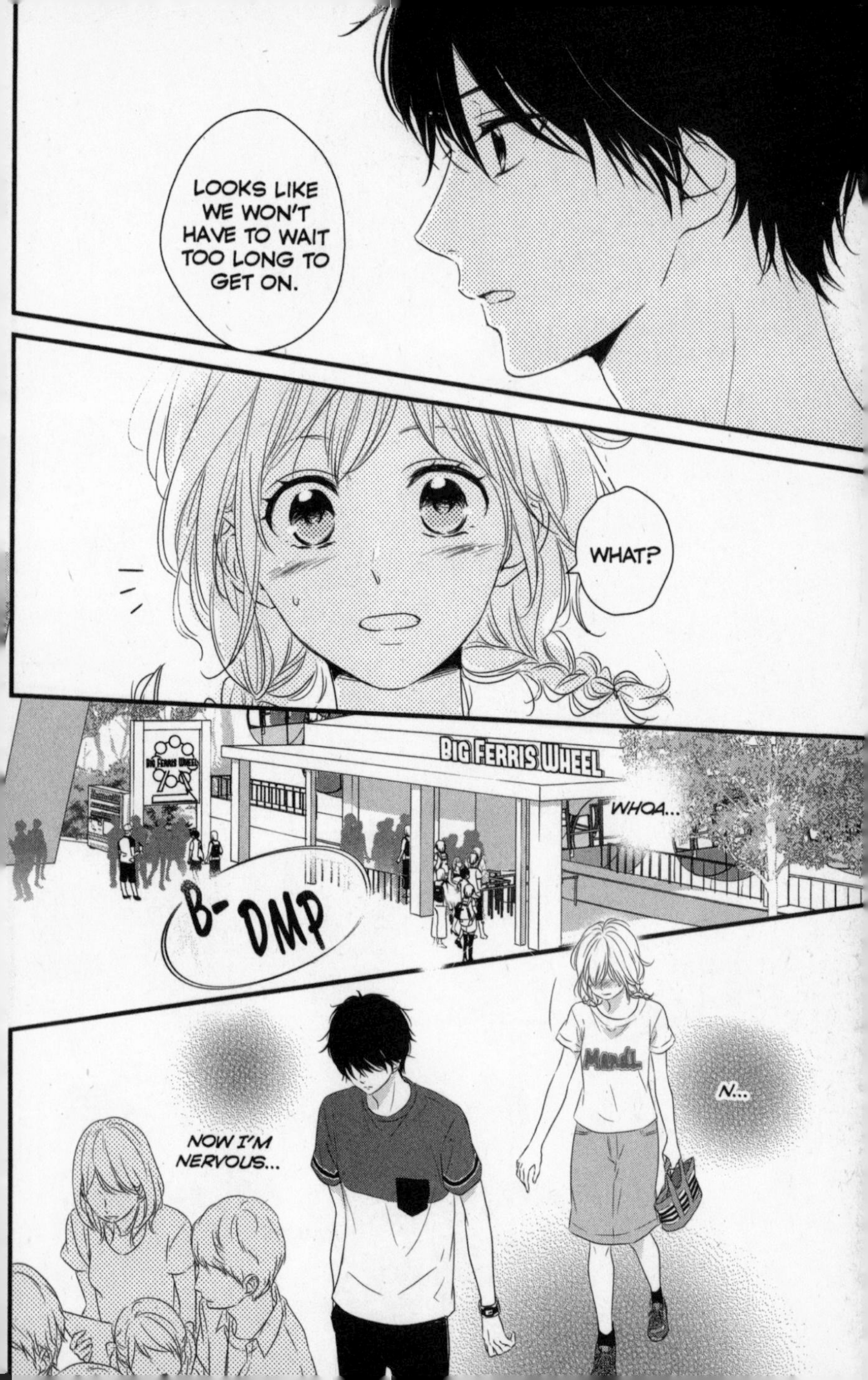
LOOKS LIKE WE WON'T HAVE TO WAIT TOO LONG TO GET ON.
WHAT?
BIG FERRIS WHEEL
WHOA...
B-DMP
N...
NOW I'M NERVOUS...

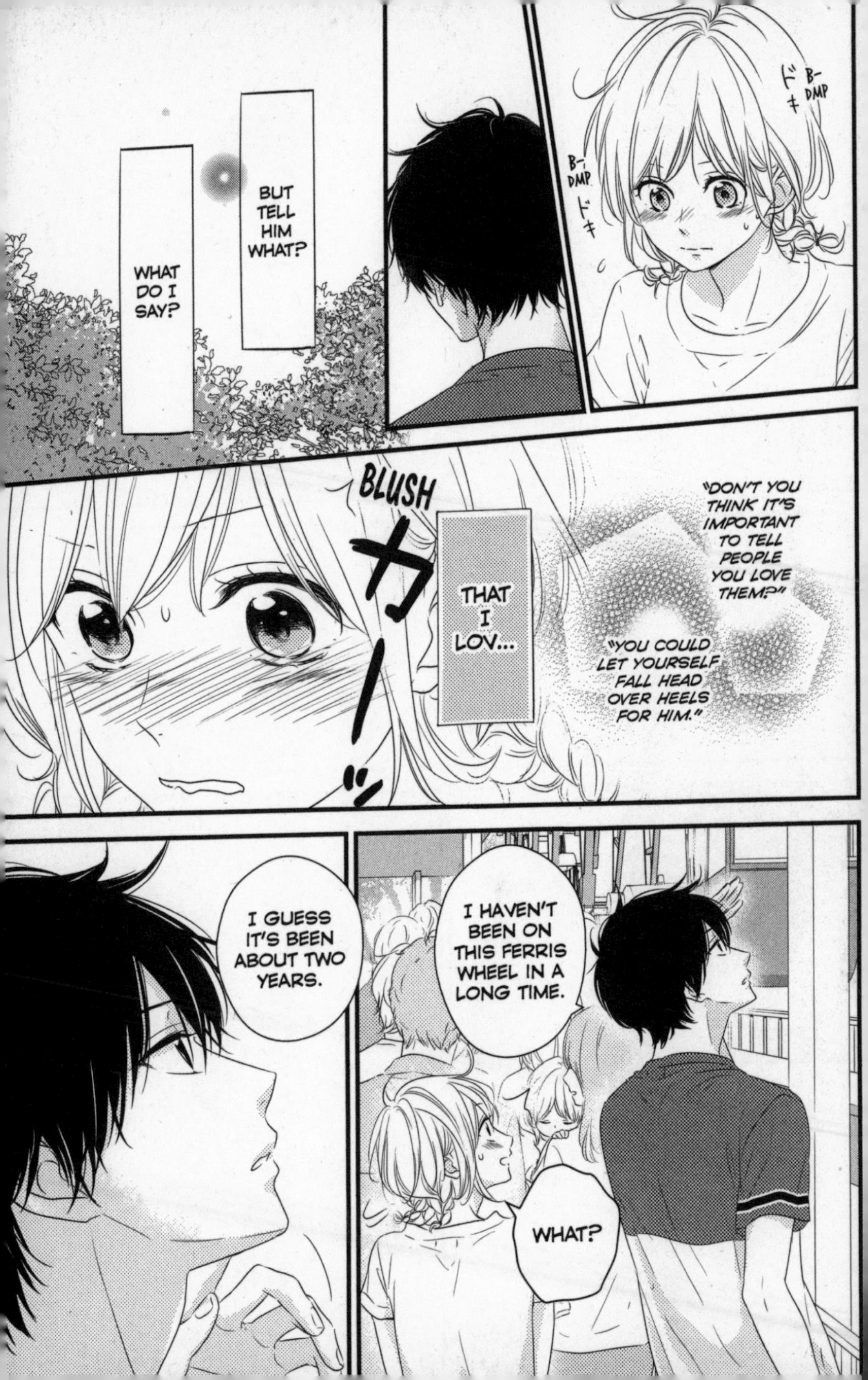
B-DMP ドキ
B-DMP ドキ
BUT TELL HIM WHAT?
WHAT DO I SAY?
"DON'T YOU THINK IT'S IMPORTANT TO TELL PEOPLE YOU LOVE THEM?"
"YOU COULD LET YOURSELF FALL HEAD OVER HEELS FOR HIM."
THAT I LOV...
BLUSH
カーッ
I HAVEN'T BEEN ON THIS FERRIS WHEEL IN A LONG TIME.
WHAT?
I GUESS IT'S BEEN ABOUT TWO YEARS.

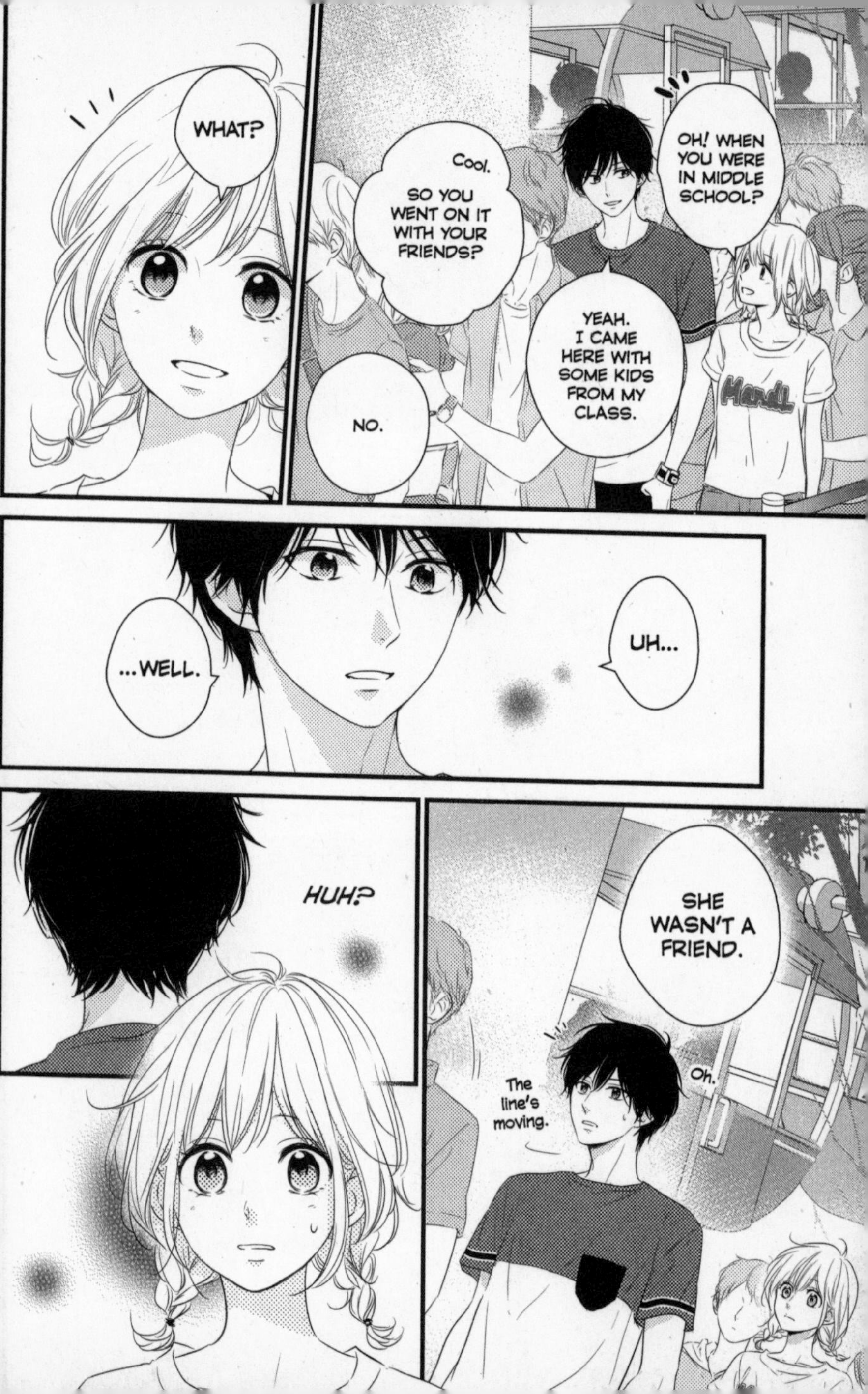
OH! WHEN YOU WERE IN MIDDLE SCHOOL?
YEAH. I CAME HERE WITH SOME KIDS FROM MY CLASS.
Cool.
SO YOU WENT ON IT WITH YOUR FRIENDS?
NO.
WHAT?
UH...
...WELL.
SHE WASN'T A FRIEND.
Oh.
The line's moving.
HUH?

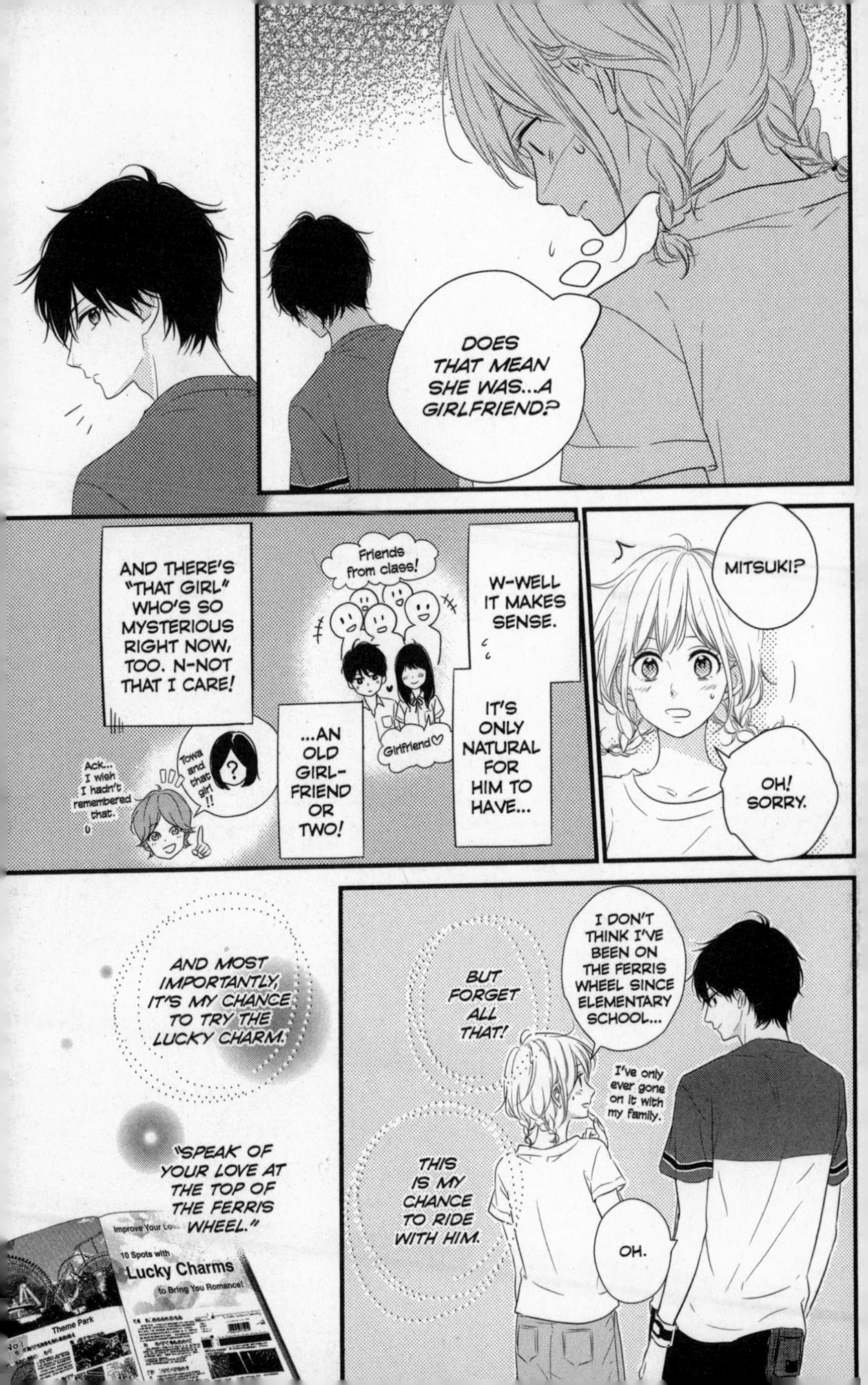
DOES THAT MEAN SHE WAS...A GIRLFRIEND?
MITSUKI?
OH! SORRY.
W-WELL IT MAKES SENSE.
IT'S ONLY NATURAL FOR HIM TO HAVE...
...AN OLD GIRL-FRIEND OR TWO!
Friends from class!
Girlfriend♡
AND THERE'S "THAT GIRL" WHO'S SO MYSTERIOUS RIGHT NOW, TOO. N-NOT THAT I CARE!
Towa and that girl!!
Ack... I wish I hadn't remembered that.
I DON'T THINK I'VE BEEN ON THE FERRIS WHEEL SINCE ELEMENTARY SCHOOL...
I've only ever gone on it with my family.
OH.
BUT FORGET ALL THAT!
THIS IS MY CHANCE TO RIDE WITH HIM.
AND MOST IMPORTANTLY, IT'S MY CHANCE TO TRY THE LUCKY CHARM.
"SPEAK OF YOUR LOVE AT THE TOP OF THE FERRIS WHEEL."
10 Spots with
Lucky Charms
to Bring You Romance!
Theme Park

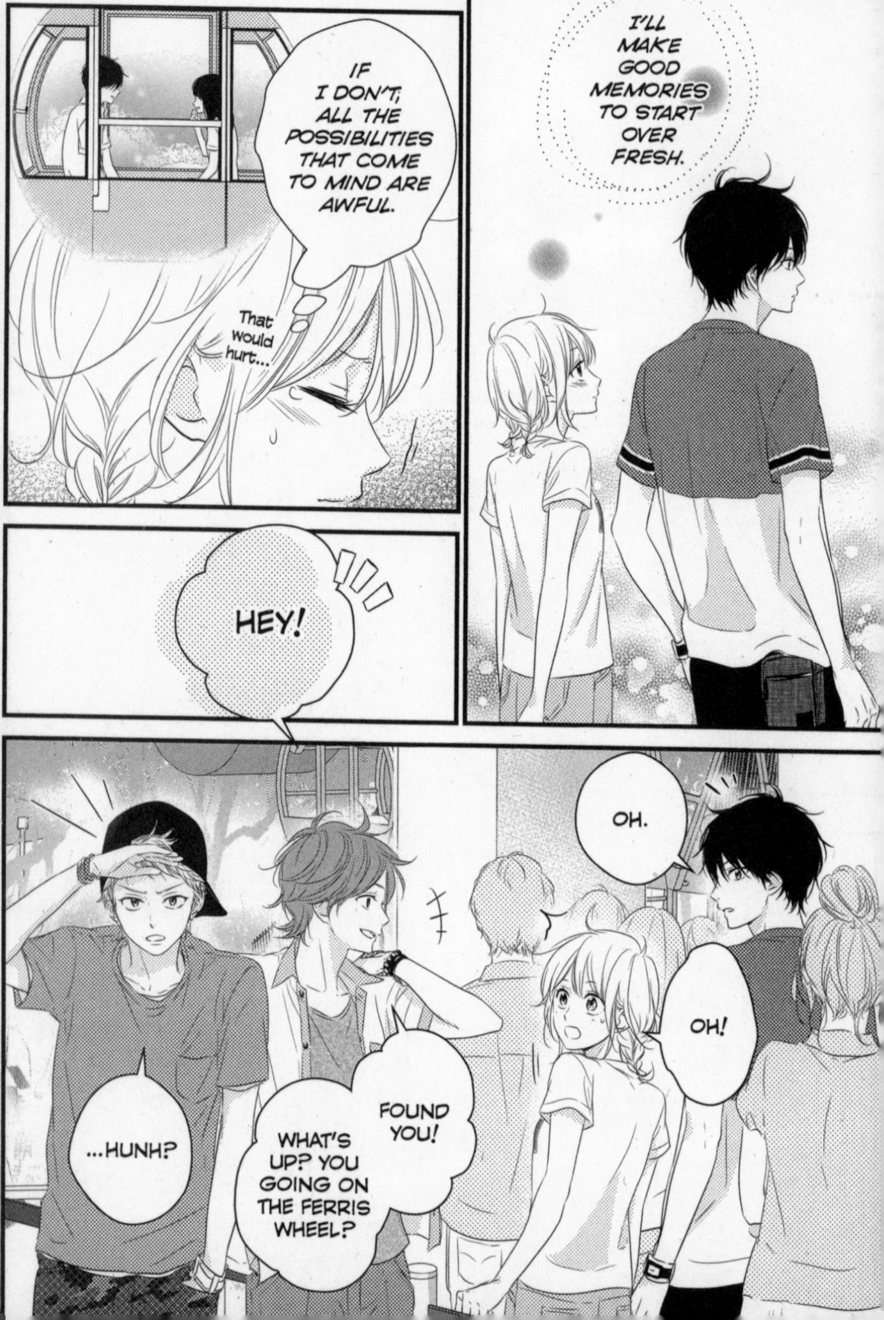
I'LL MAKE GOOD MEMORIES TO START OVER FRESH.
IF I DON'T, ALL THE POSSIBILITIES THAT COME TO MIND ARE AWFUL.
That would hurt...
HEY!
OH.
OH!
FOUND YOU!
WHAT'S UP? YOU GOING ON THE FERRIS WHEEL?
...HUNH?

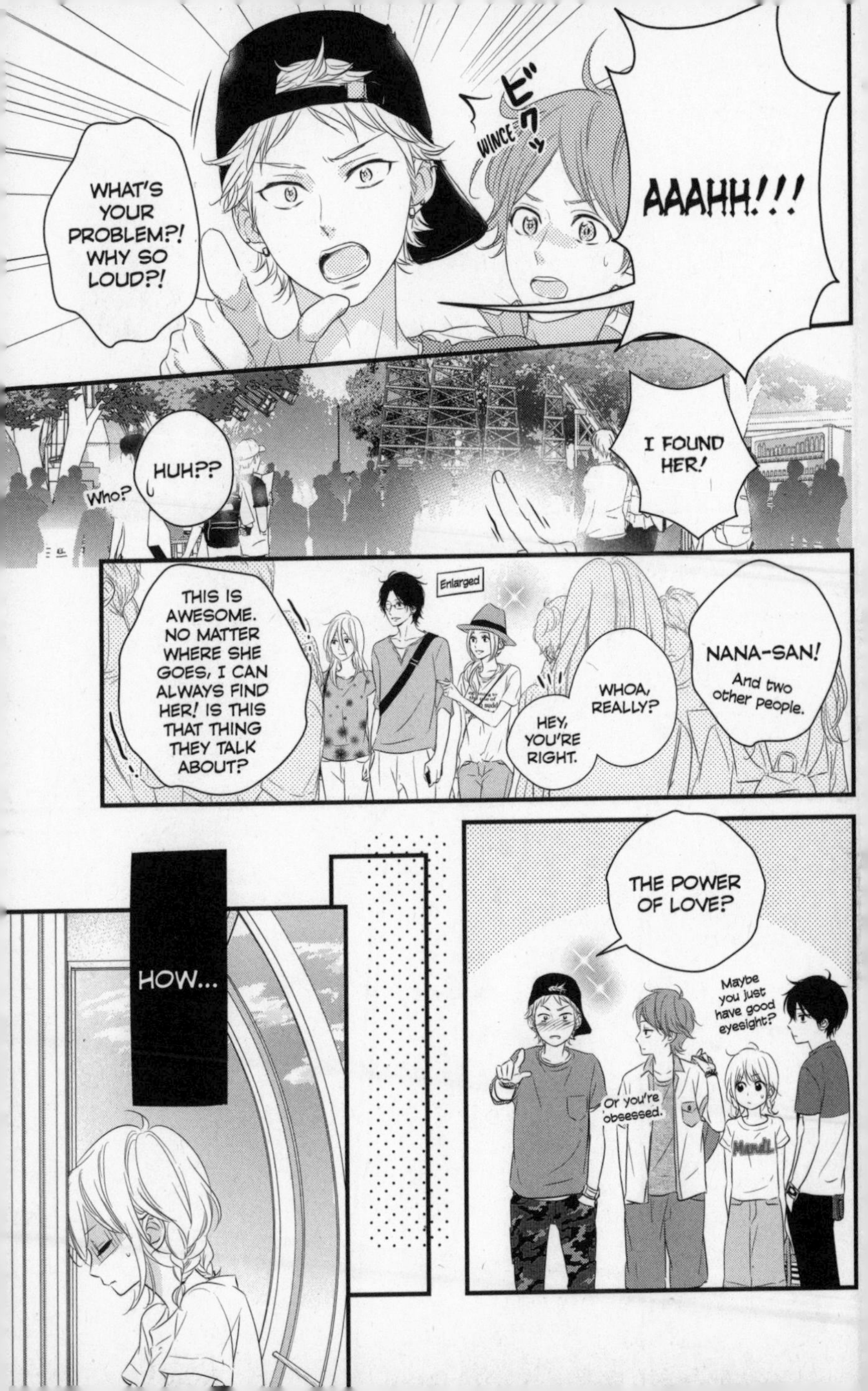
AAAHH!!!
ビクッ
WINCE
WHAT'S YOUR PROBLEM?! WHY SO LOUD?!
I FOUND HER!
HUH??
Who?
NANA-SAN!
And two other people.
WHOA, REALLY?
HEY, YOU'RE RIGHT.
Enlarged
THIS IS AWESOME. NO MATTER WHERE SHE GOES, I CAN ALWAYS FIND HER! IS THIS THAT THING THEY TALK ABOUT?
THE POWER OF LOVE?
Maybe you just have good eyesight?
Or you're obsessed.
HOW...

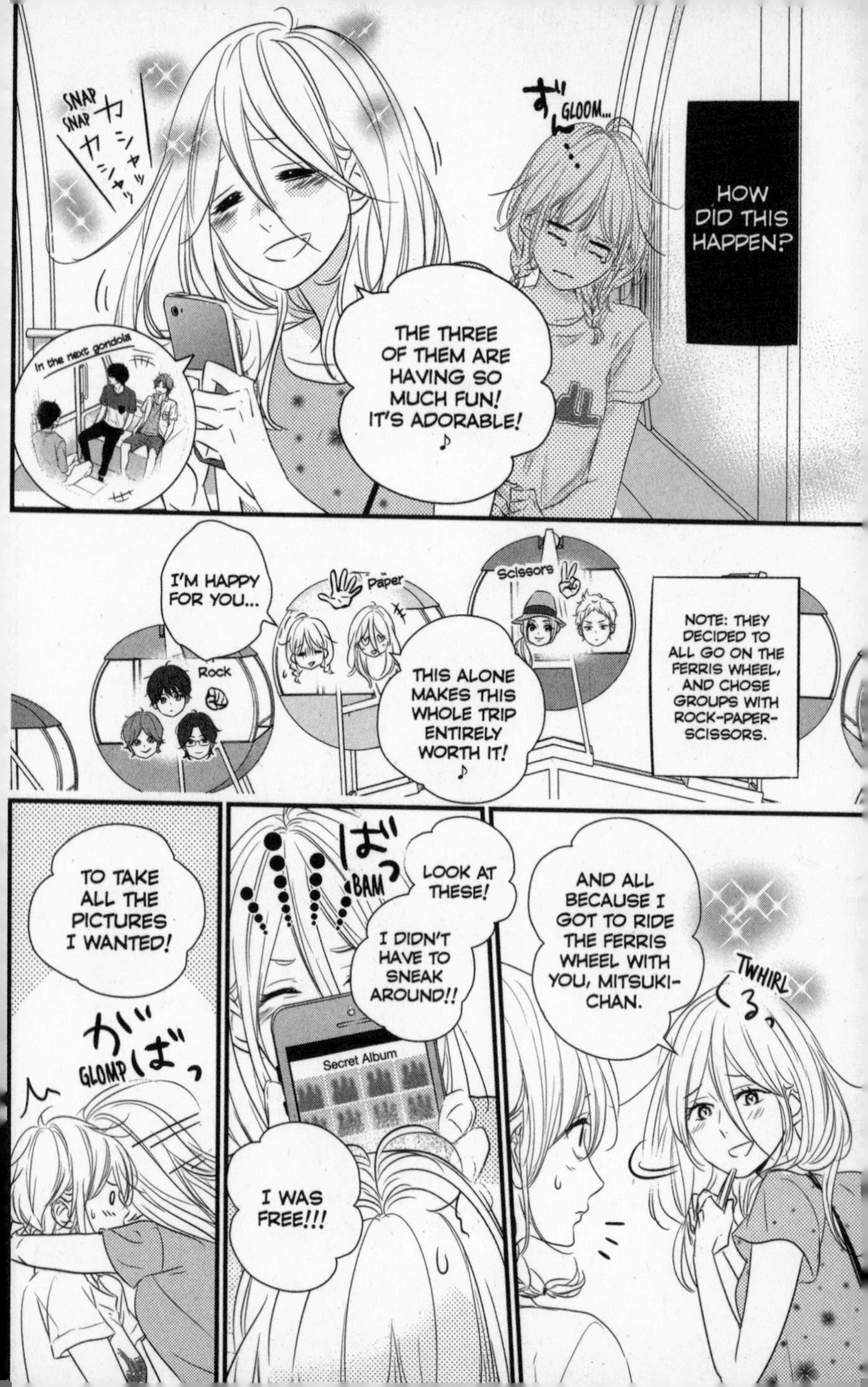

HOW DID THIS HAPPEN?
ずん GLOOM...
THE THREE OF THEM ARE HAVING SO MUCH FUN! IT'S ADORABLE! ♪
カシャッ カシャッ SNAP SNAP
In the next gondola
NOTE: THEY DECIDED TO ALL GO ON THE FERRIS WHEEL, AND CHOSE GROUPS WITH ROCK-PAPER-SCISSORS.
Scissors
Paper
THIS ALONE MAKES THIS WHOLE TRIP ENTIRELY WORTH IT! ♪
I'M HAPPY FOR YOU...
Rock
くるっ TWHIRL
AND ALL BECAUSE I GOT TO RIDE THE FERRIS WHEEL WITH YOU, MITSUKI-CHAN.
ばっ BAM
LOOK AT THESE!
I DIDN'T HAVE TO SNEAK AROUND!!
Secret Album
I WAS FREE!!!
TO TAKE ALL THE PICTURES I WANTED!
がばっ GLOMP

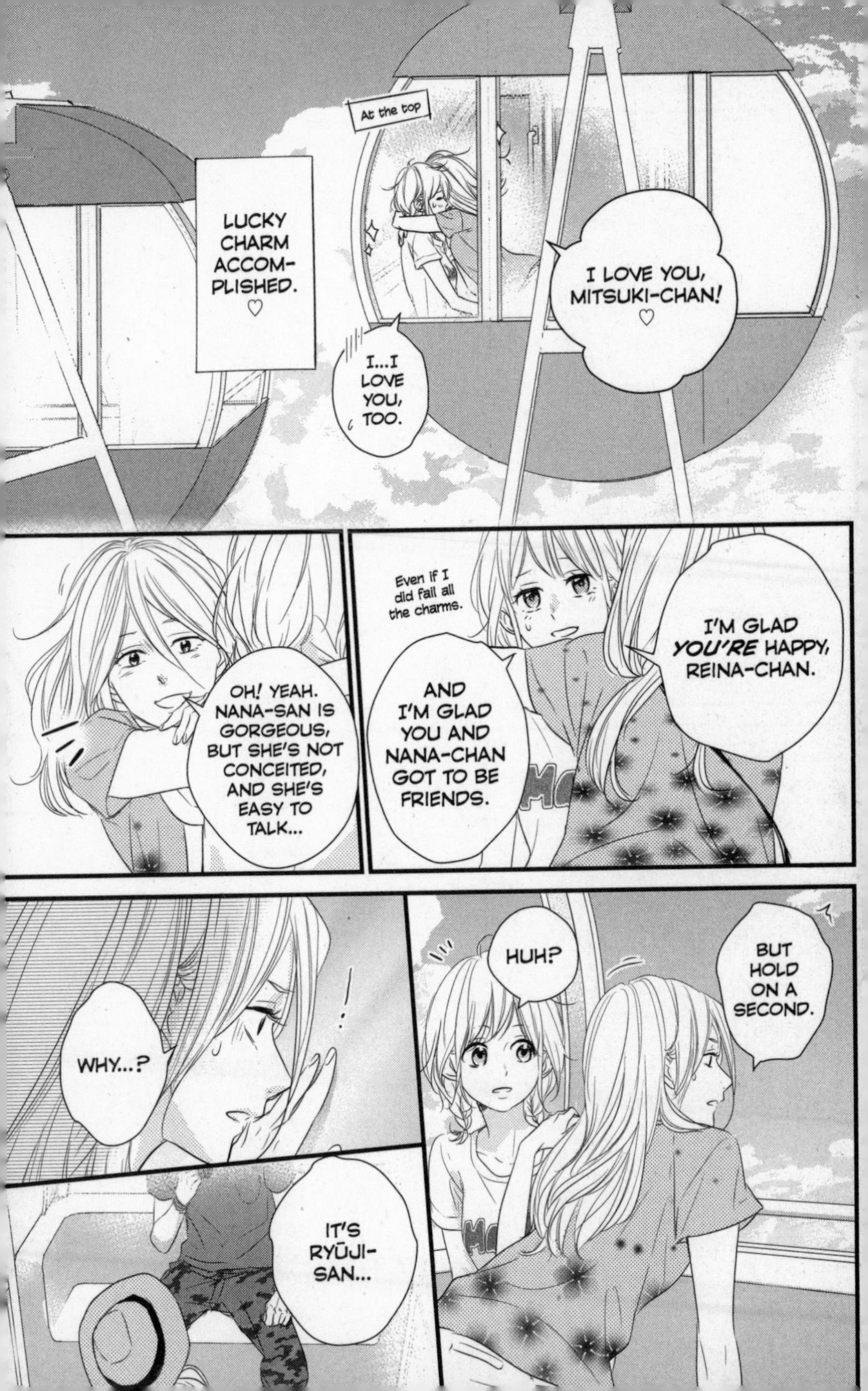
At the top
I LOVE YOU, MITSUKI-CHAN! ♡
LUCKY CHARM ACCOMPLISHED. ♡
I...I LOVE YOU, TOO.
I'M GLAD *YOU'RE* HAPPY, REINA-CHAN.
Even if I did fail all the charms.
AND I'M GLAD YOU AND NANA-CHAN GOT TO BE FRIENDS.
OH! YEAH. NANA-SAN IS GORGEOUS, BUT SHE'S NOT CONCEITED, AND SHE'S EASY TO TALK...
BUT HOLD ON A SECOND.
HUH?
WHY...?
IT'S RYŪJI-SAN...

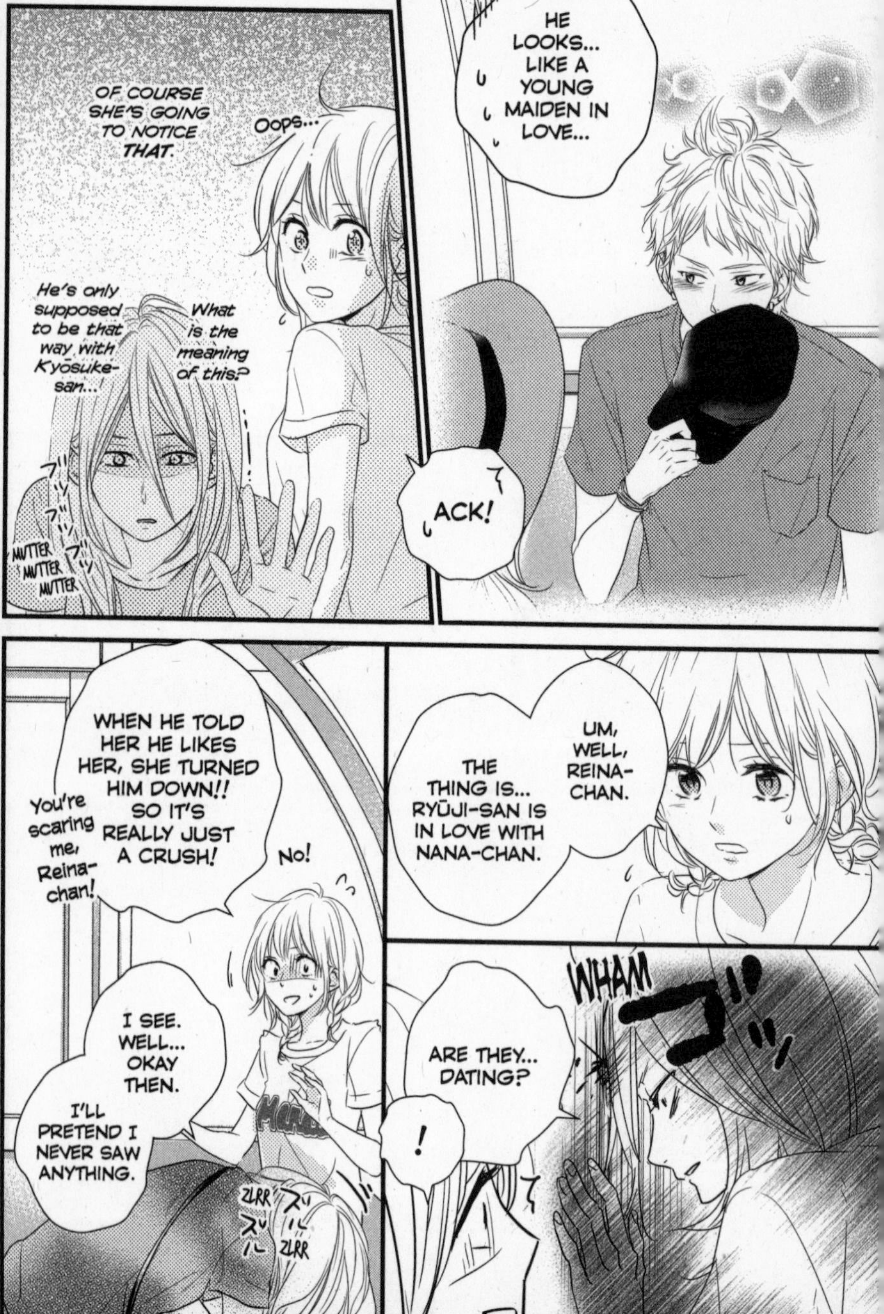

HE LOOKS... LIKE A YOUNG MAIDEN IN LOVE...
ACK!
Oops...
OF COURSE SHE'S GOING TO NOTICE **THAT**.
What is the meaning of this?
He's only supposed to be that way with Kyōsuke-san...
MUTTER MUTTER MUTTER
UM, WELL, REINA-CHAN.
THE THING IS... RYŪJI-SAN IS IN LOVE WITH NANA-CHAN.
WHAM
ARE THEY... DATING?
!
WHEN HE TOLD HER HE LIKES HER, SHE TURNED HIM DOWN!! SO IT'S REALLY JUST A CRUSH!
No!
You're scaring me, Reina-chan!
I SEE. WELL... OKAY THEN.
I'LL PRETEND I NEVER SAW ANYTHING.
ZLRR
ZLRR

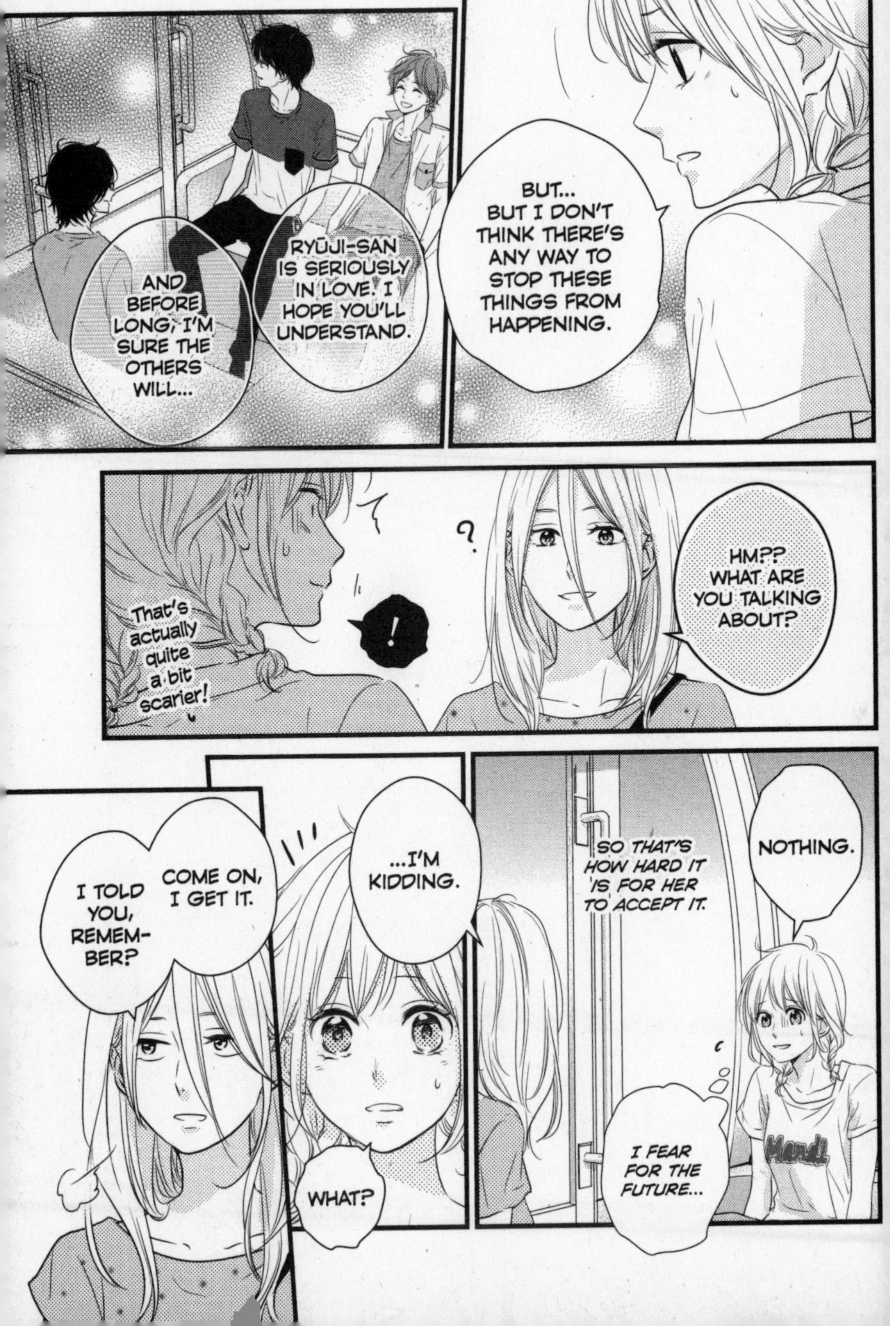
BUT... BUT I DON'T THINK THERE'S ANY WAY TO STOP THESE THINGS FROM HAPPENING.
RYŪJI-SAN IS SERIOUSLY IN LOVE. I HOPE YOU'LL UNDERSTAND.
AND BEFORE LONG, I'M SURE THE OTHERS WILL...
HM?? WHAT ARE YOU TALKING ABOUT?
!
That's actually quite a bit scarier!
NOTHING.
SO THAT'S HOW HARD IT IS FOR HER TO ACCEPT IT.
I FEAR FOR THE FUTURE...
...I'M KIDDING.
WHAT?
COME ON, I GET IT.
I TOLD YOU, REMEMBER?

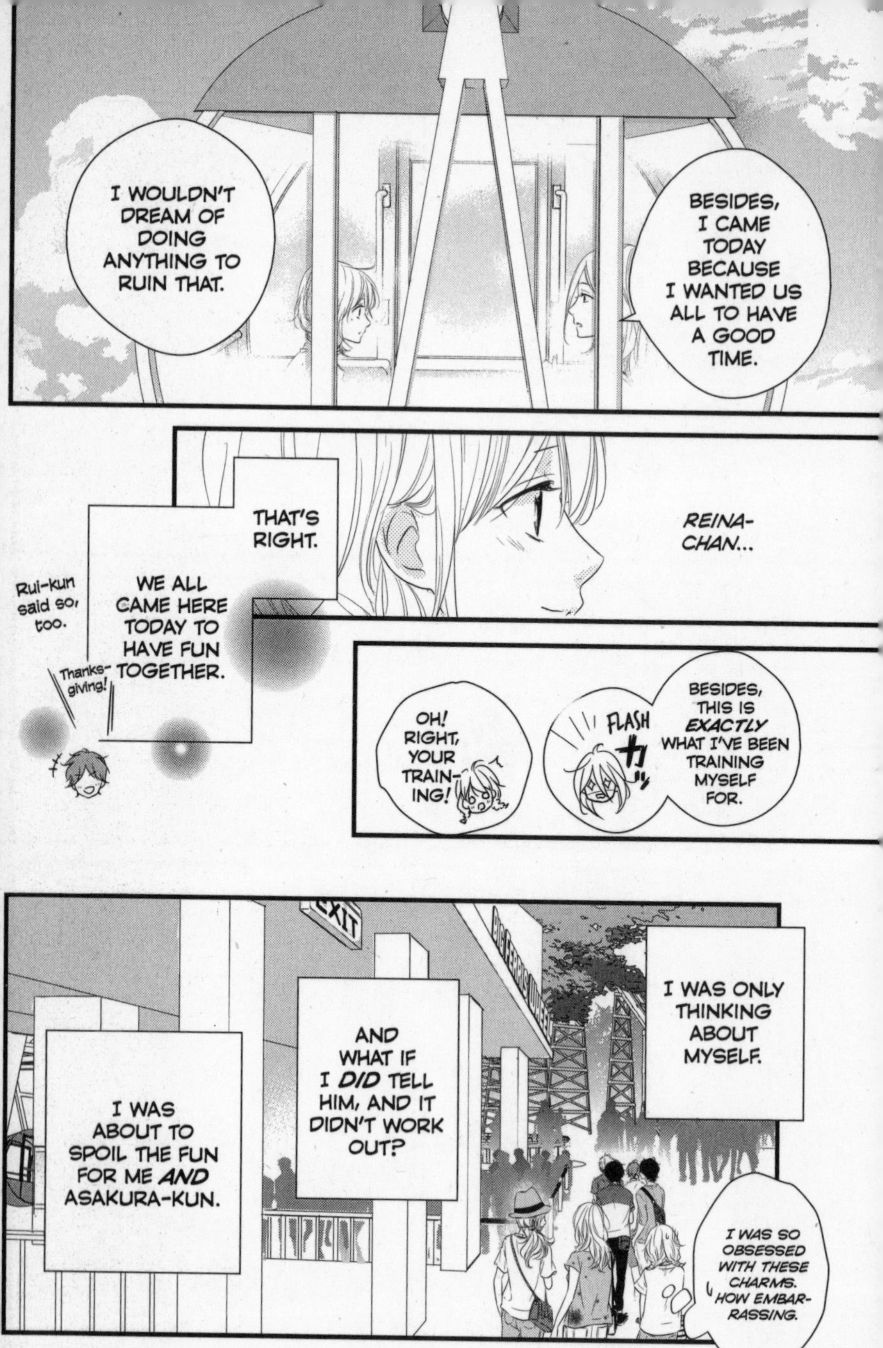
BESIDES, I CAME TODAY BECAUSE I WANTED US ALL TO HAVE A GOOD TIME.
I WOULDN'T DREAM OF DOING ANYTHING TO RUIN THAT.
REINA-CHAN...
THAT'S RIGHT.
WE ALL CAME HERE TODAY TO HAVE FUN TOGETHER.
Rui-kun said so, too.
Thanks-giving!
BESIDES, THIS IS EXACTLY WHAT I'VE BEEN TRAINING MYSELF FOR.
FLASH
OH! RIGHT, YOUR TRAINING!
EXIT
I WAS ONLY THINKING ABOUT MYSELF.
AND WHAT IF I DID TELL HIM, AND IT DIDN'T WORK OUT?
I WAS ABOUT TO SPOIL THE FUN FOR ME AND ASAKURA-KUN.
I WAS SO OBSESSED WITH THESE CHARMS. HOW EMBARRASSING.

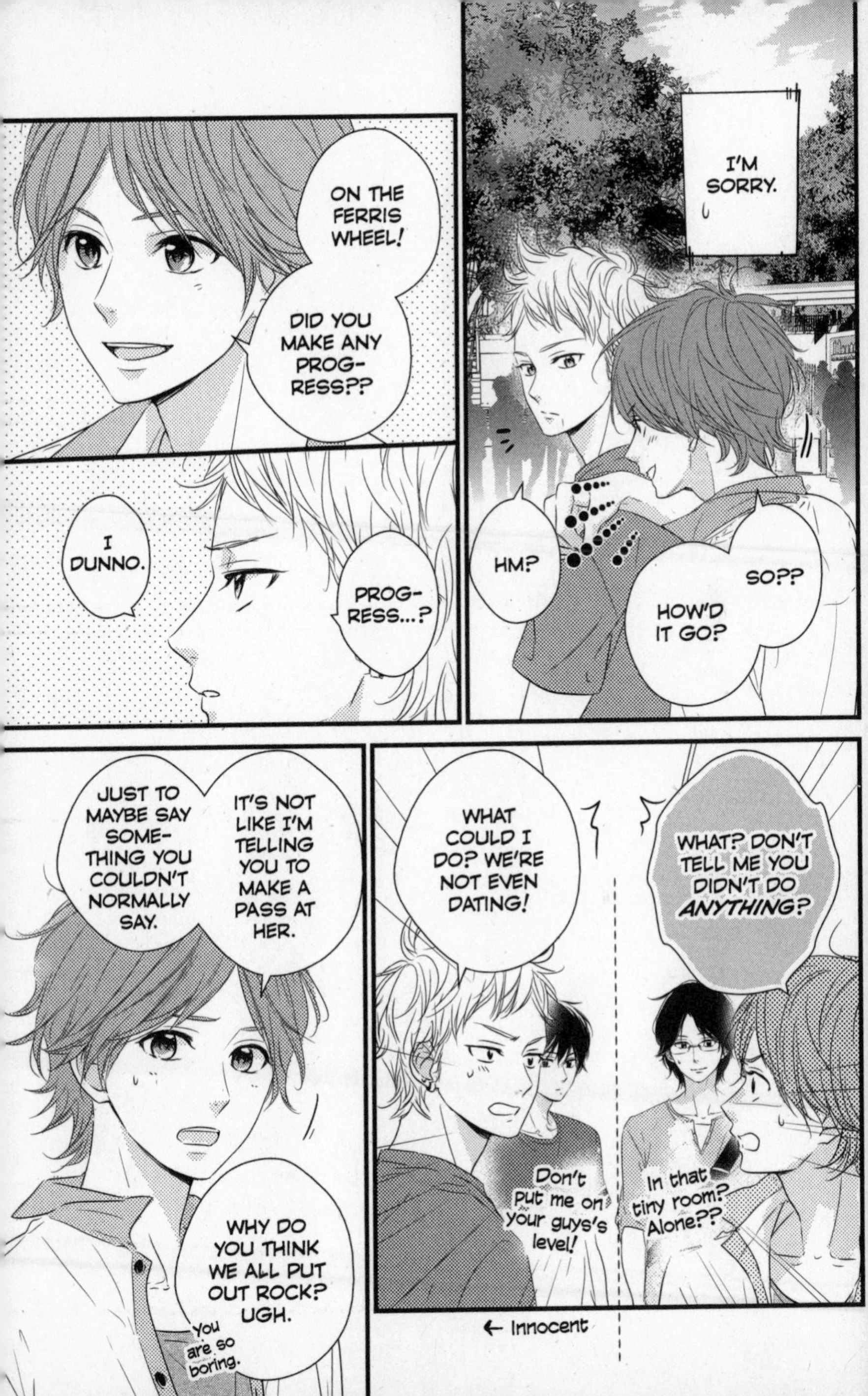
I'M SORRY.
SO?? HOW'D IT GO?
HM?
ON THE FERRIS WHEEL!
DID YOU MAKE ANY PROG-RESS??
PROG-RESS...?
I DUNNO.
WHAT? DON'T TELL ME YOU DIDN'T DO *ANYTHING*?
In that tiny room? Alone??
WHAT COULD I DO? WE'RE NOT EVEN DATING!
Don't put me on your guys's level!
← Innocent
IT'S NOT LIKE I'M TELLING YOU TO MAKE A PASS AT HER.
JUST TO MAYBE SAY SOME-THING YOU COULDN'T NORMALLY SAY.
WHY DO YOU THINK WE ALL PUT OUT ROCK? UGH.
You are so boring.

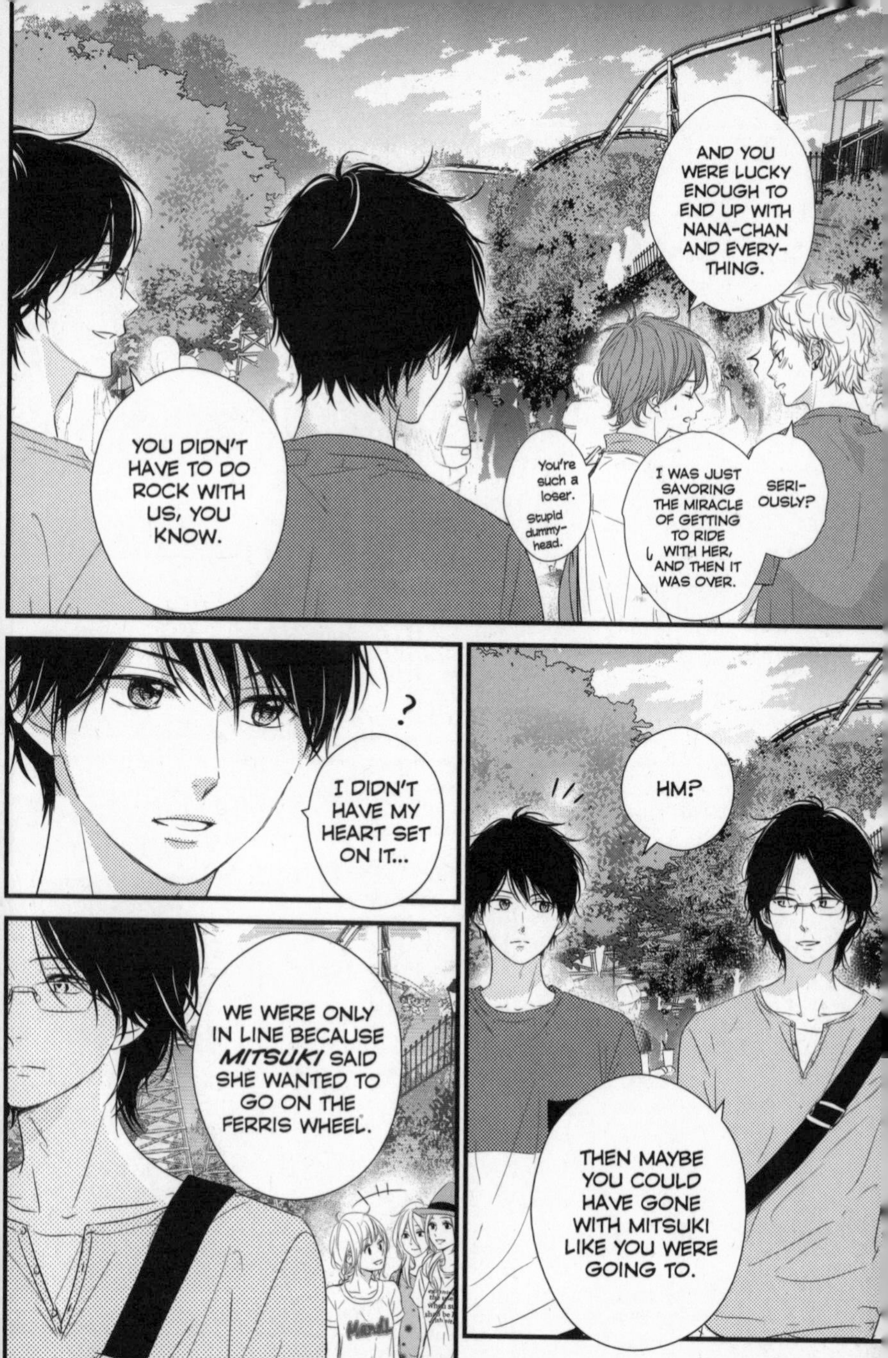
AND YOU WERE LUCKY ENOUGH TO END UP WITH NANA-CHAN AND EVERY-THING.
SERI-OUSLY?
I WAS JUST SAVORING THE MIRACLE OF GETTING TO RIDE WITH HER, AND THEN IT WAS OVER.
You're such a loser.
Stupid dummy-head.
YOU DIDN'T HAVE TO DO ROCK WITH US, YOU KNOW.
HM?
I DIDN'T HAVE MY HEART SET ON IT...
WE WERE ONLY IN LINE BECAUSE *MITSUKI* SAID SHE WANTED TO GO ON THE FERRIS WHEEL.
THEN MAYBE YOU COULD HAVE GONE WITH MITSUKI LIKE YOU WERE GOING TO.

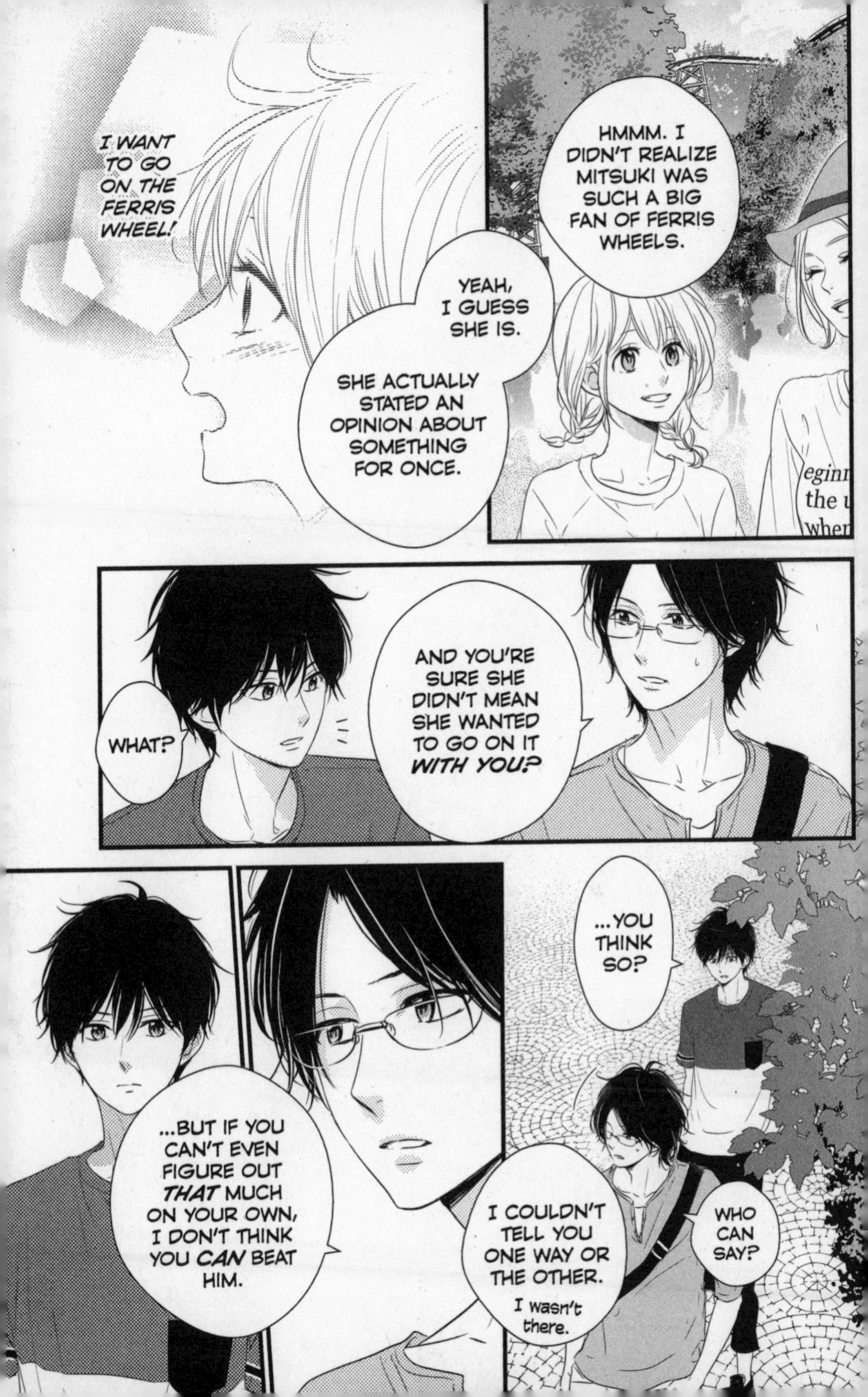
HMMM. I DIDN'T REALIZE MITSUKI WAS SUCH A BIG FAN OF FERRIS WHEELS.
YEAH, I GUESS SHE IS.
SHE ACTUALLY STATED AN OPINION ABOUT SOMETHING FOR ONCE.
I WANT TO GO ON THE FERRIS WHEEL!
AND YOU'RE SURE SHE DIDN'T MEAN SHE WANTED TO GO ON IT *WITH YOU?*
WHAT?
...YOU THINK SO?
WHO CAN SAY?
I COULDN'T TELL YOU ONE WAY OR THE OTHER.
I wasn't there.
...BUT IF YOU CAN'T EVEN FIGURE OUT *THAT* MUCH ON YOUR OWN, I DON'T THINK YOU *CAN* BEAT HIM.

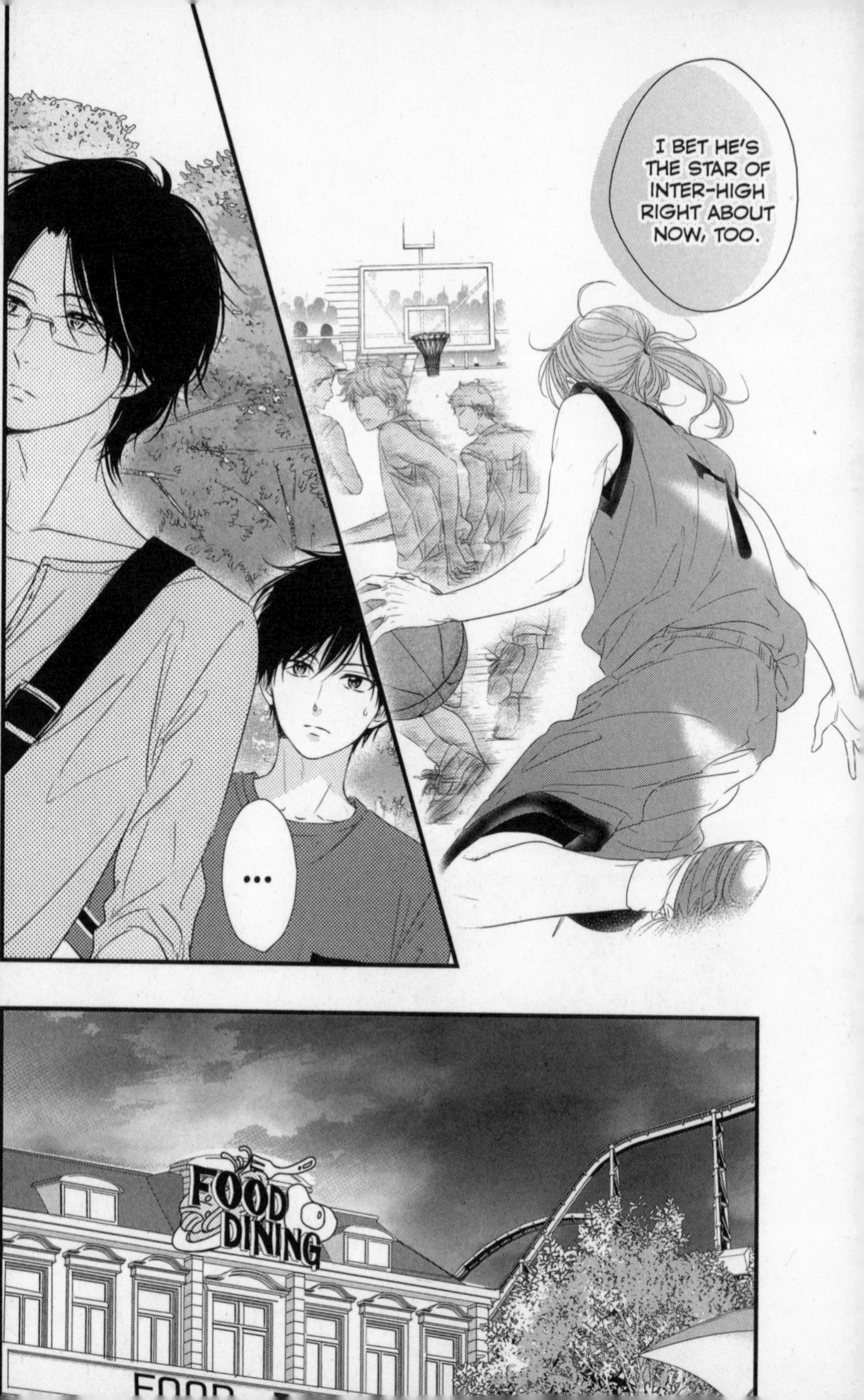
I BET HE'S THE STAR OF INTER-HIGH RIGHT ABOUT NOW, TOO.
...
FOOD DINING

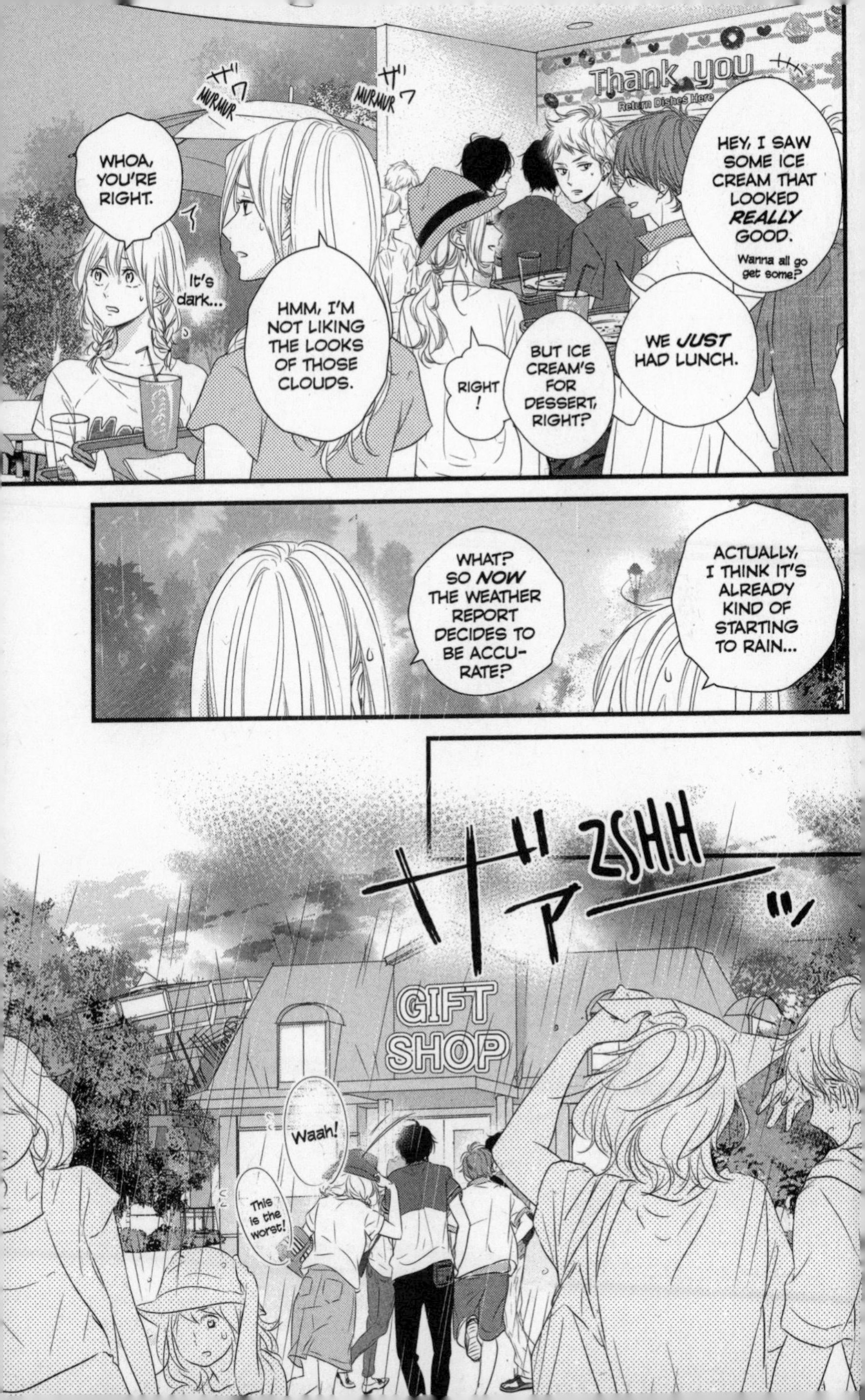
Thank you
Return Dishes Here
HEY, I SAW SOME ICE CREAM THAT LOOKED *REALLY* GOOD.
Wanna all go get some?
WE *JUST* HAD LUNCH.
BUT ICE CREAM'S FOR DESSERT, RIGHT?
RIGHT!
MURMUR
MURMUR
HMM, I'M NOT LIKING THE LOOKS OF THOSE CLOUDS.
WHOA, YOU'RE RIGHT.
It's dark...
ACTUALLY, I THINK IT'S ALREADY KIND OF STARTING TO RAIN...
WHAT? SO *NOW* THE WEATHER REPORT DECIDES TO BE ACCURATE?
ZSHH
GIFT SHOP
Waah!
This is the worst!

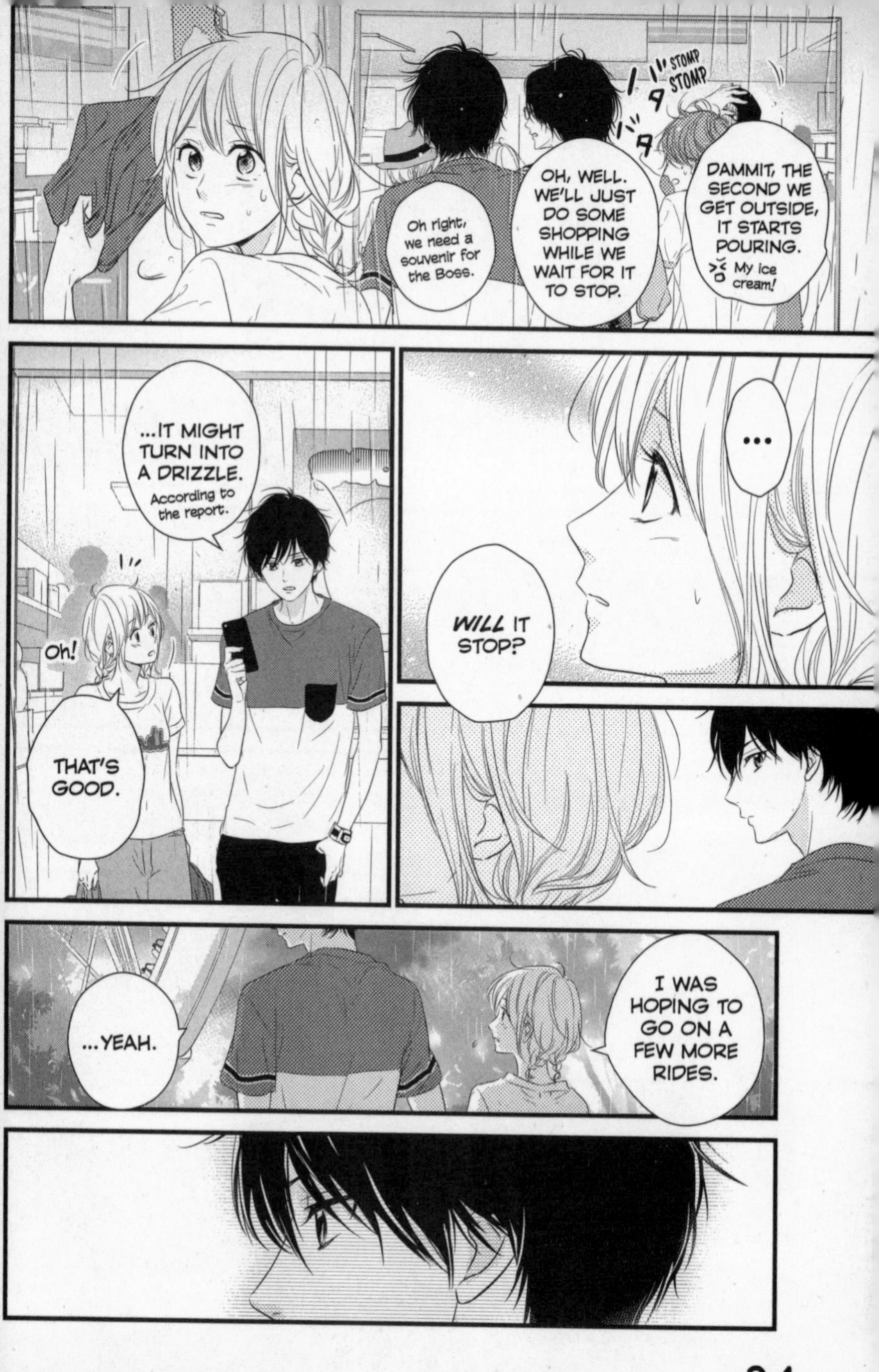
STOMP STOMP
DAMMIT, THE SECOND WE GET OUTSIDE, IT STARTS POURING.
My ice cream!
OH, WELL. WE'LL JUST DO SOME SHOPPING WHILE WE WAIT FOR IT TO STOP.
Oh right, we need a souvenir for the Boss.
...
WILL IT STOP?
...IT MIGHT TURN INTO A DRIZZLE.
According to the report.
Oh!
THAT'S GOOD.
I WAS HOPING TO GO ON A FEW MORE RIDES.
...YEAH.

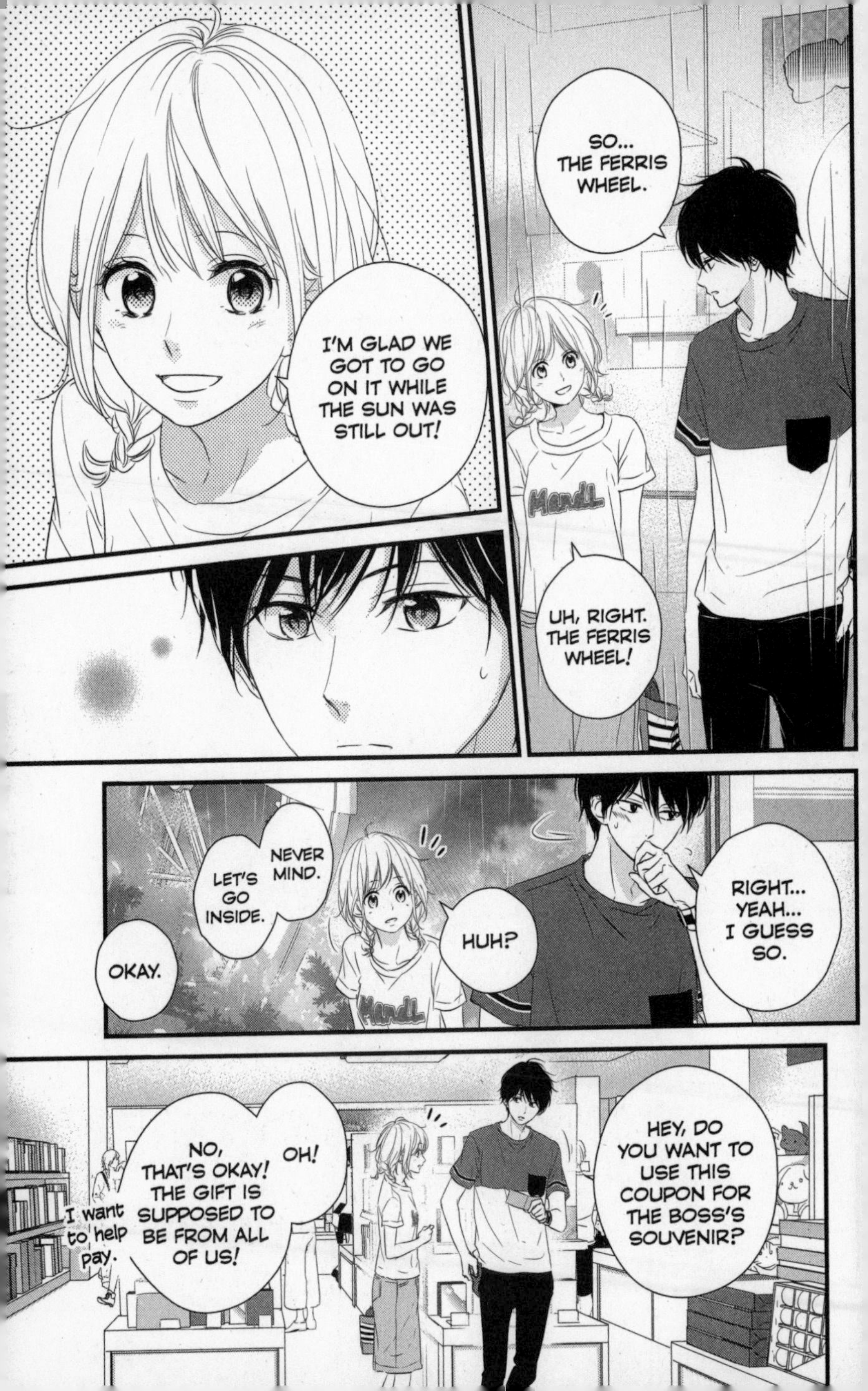
SO... THE FERRIS WHEEL.
UH, RIGHT. THE FERRIS WHEEL!
I'M GLAD WE GOT TO GO ON IT WHILE THE SUN WAS STILL OUT!
RIGHT... YEAH... I GUESS SO.
HUH?
NEVER MIND.
LET'S GO INSIDE.
OKAY.
HEY, DO YOU WANT TO USE THIS COUPON FOR THE BOSS'S SOUVENIR?
OH!
NO, THAT'S OKAY! THE GIFT IS SUPPOSED TO BE FROM ALL OF US!
I want to help pay.

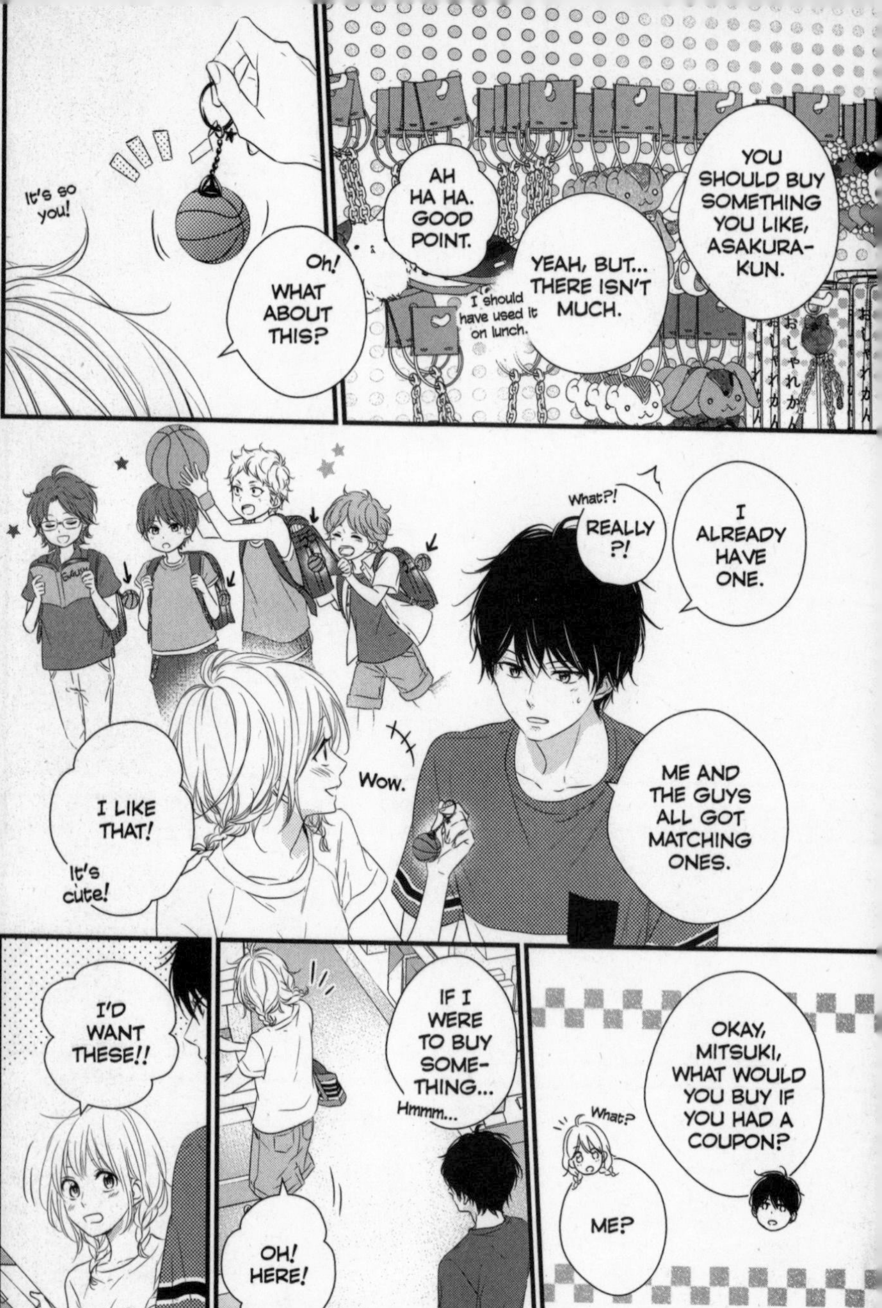
YOU SHOULD BUY SOMETHING YOU LIKE, ASAKURA-KUN.
YEAH, BUT... THERE ISN'T MUCH.
I should have used it on lunch.
AH HA HA. GOOD POINT.
Oh! WHAT ABOUT THIS?
It's so you!
I ALREADY HAVE ONE.
What?! REALLY?!
ME AND THE GUYS ALL GOT MATCHING ONES.
Wow.
I LIKE THAT!
It's cute!
OKAY, MITSUKI, WHAT WOULD YOU BUY IF YOU HAD A COUPON?
What?
ME?
IF I WERE TO BUY SOME-THING...
Hmmm...
OH! HERE!
I'D WANT THESE!!

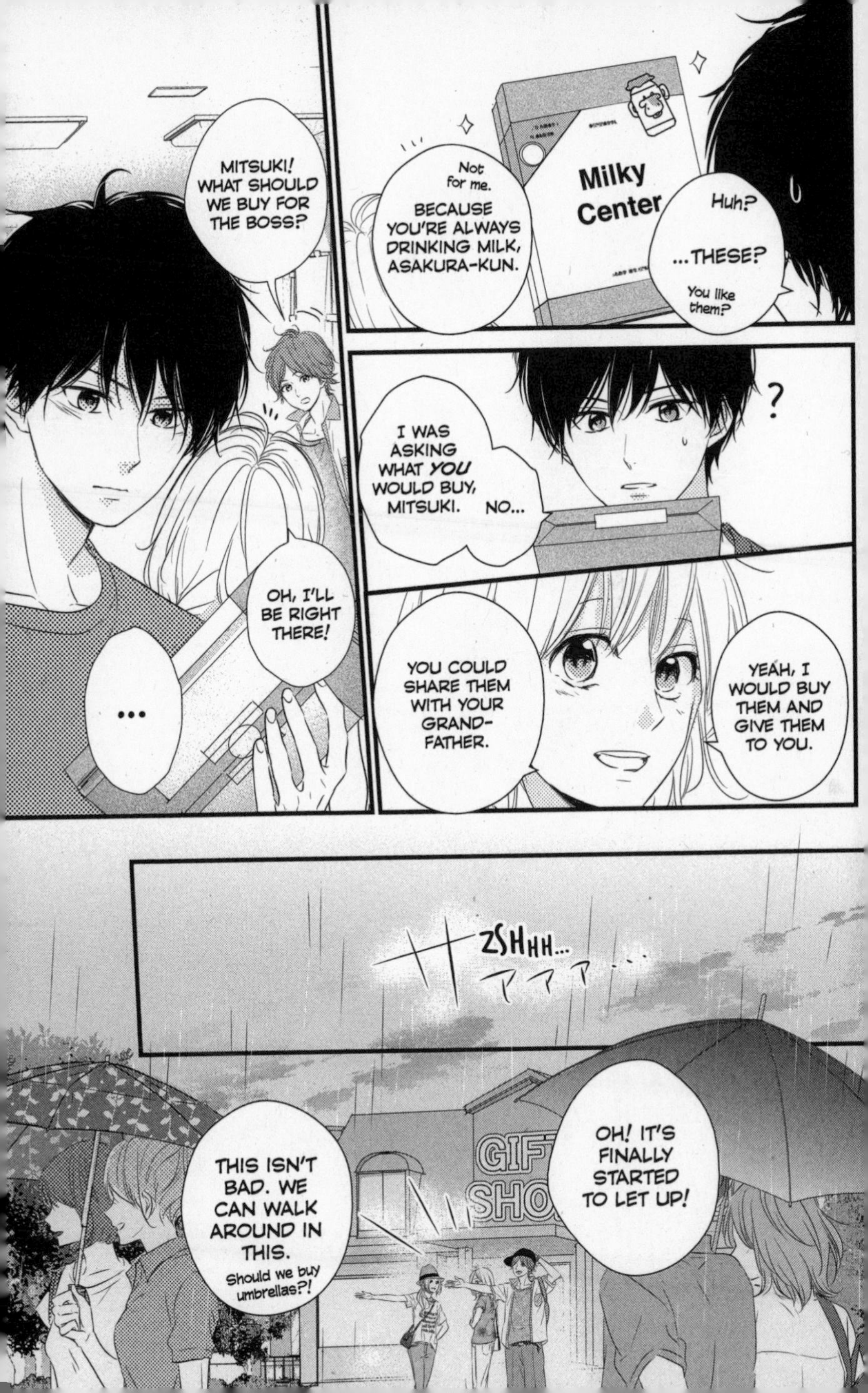
Huh?
...THESE?
You like them?
Milky Center
Not for me.
BECAUSE YOU'RE ALWAYS DRINKING MILK, ASAKURA-KUN.
?
I WAS ASKING WHAT *YOU* WOULD BUY, MITSUKI. NO...
YEAH, I WOULD BUY THEM AND GIVE THEM TO YOU.
YOU COULD SHARE THEM WITH YOUR GRANDFATHER.
MITSUKI! WHAT SHOULD WE BUY FOR THE BOSS?
OH, I'LL BE RIGHT THERE!
...
ZSHHH...
アアア
OH! IT'S FINALLY STARTED TO LET UP!
THIS ISN'T BAD. WE CAN WALK AROUND IN THIS.
Should we buy umbrellas?!

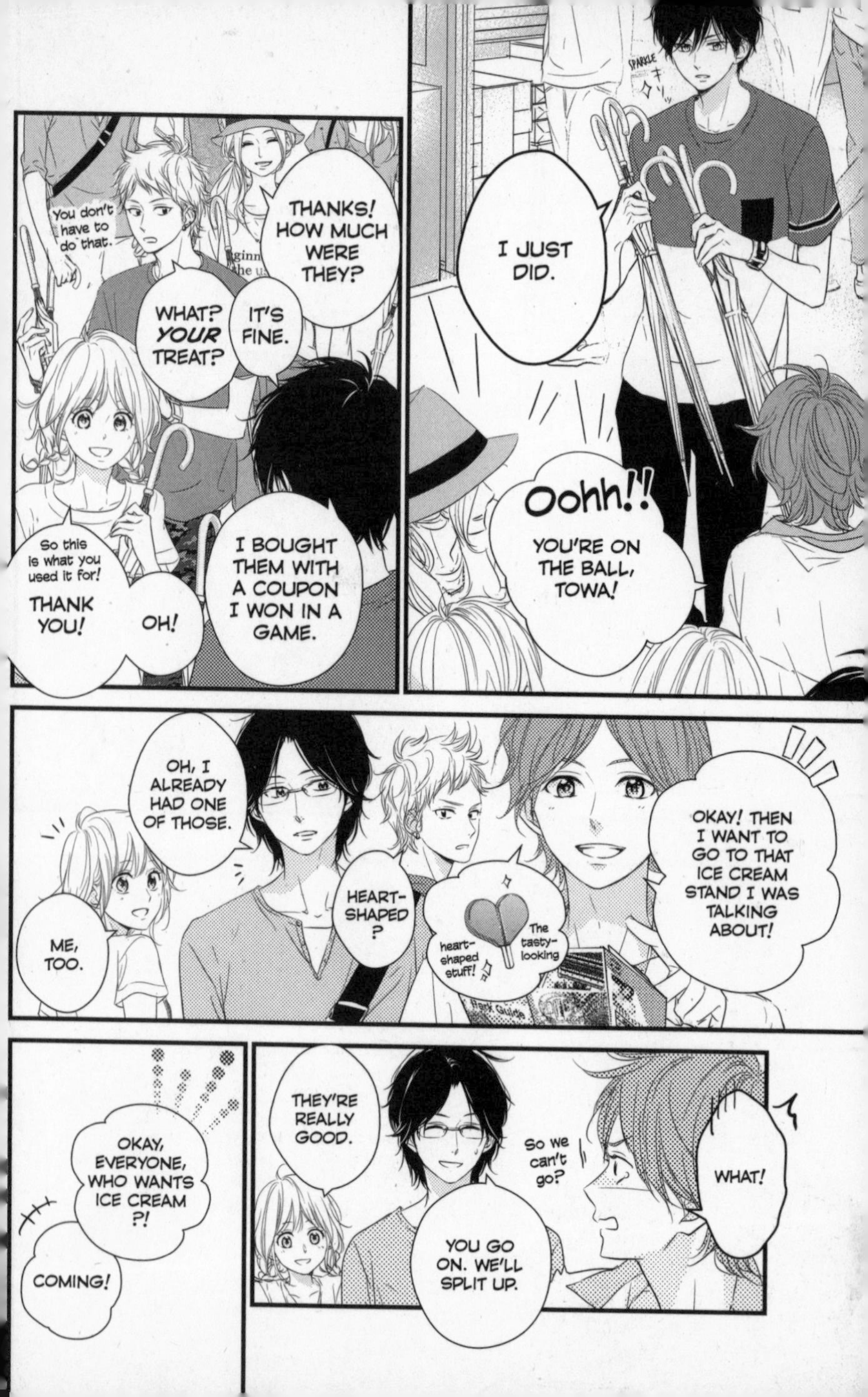

SPARKLE
I JUST DID.
Oohh!!
YOU'RE ON THE BALL, TOWA!
THANKS! HOW MUCH WERE THEY?
You don't have to do that.
IT'S FINE.
WHAT? *YOUR* TREAT?
I BOUGHT THEM WITH A COUPON I WON IN A GAME.
OH!
So this is what you used it for!
THANK YOU!
OKAY! THEN I WANT TO GO TO THAT ICE CREAM STAND I WAS TALKING ABOUT!
The tasty-looking heart-shaped stuff!
HEART-SHAPED?
OH, I ALREADY HAD ONE OF THOSE.
ME, TOO.
WHAT!
So we can't go?
THEY'RE REALLY GOOD.
YOU GO ON. WE'LL SPLIT UP.
OKAY, EVERYONE, WHO WANTS ICE CREAM?!
COMING!

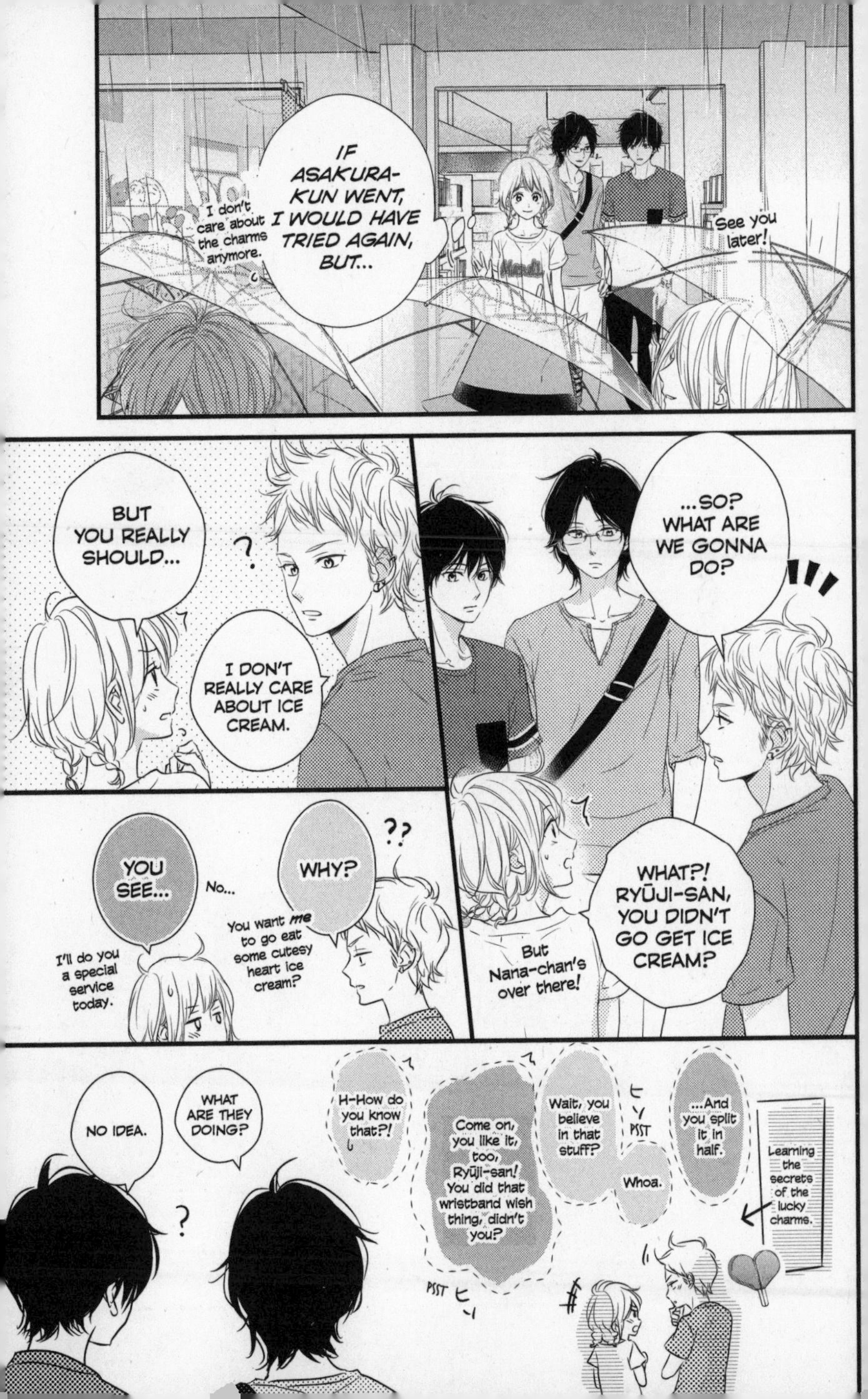
See you later!
IF ASAKURA-KUN WENT, I WOULD HAVE TRIED AGAIN, BUT...
I don't care about the charms anymore.
...SO? WHAT ARE WE GONNA DO?
WHAT?! RYŪJI-SAN, YOU DIDN'T GO GET ICE CREAM?
But Nana-chan's over there!
I DON'T REALLY CARE ABOUT ICE CREAM.
BUT YOU REALLY SHOULD...
WHY?
You want *me* to go eat some cutesy heart ice cream?
YOU SEE...
No...
I'll do you a special service today.
Learning the secrets of the lucky charms.
...And you split it in half.
Wait, you believe in that stuff?
PSST
Whoa.
Come on, you like it, too, Ryūji-san! You did that wristband wish thing, didn't you?
PSST
H-How do you know that?!
WHAT ARE THEY DOING?
NO IDEA.

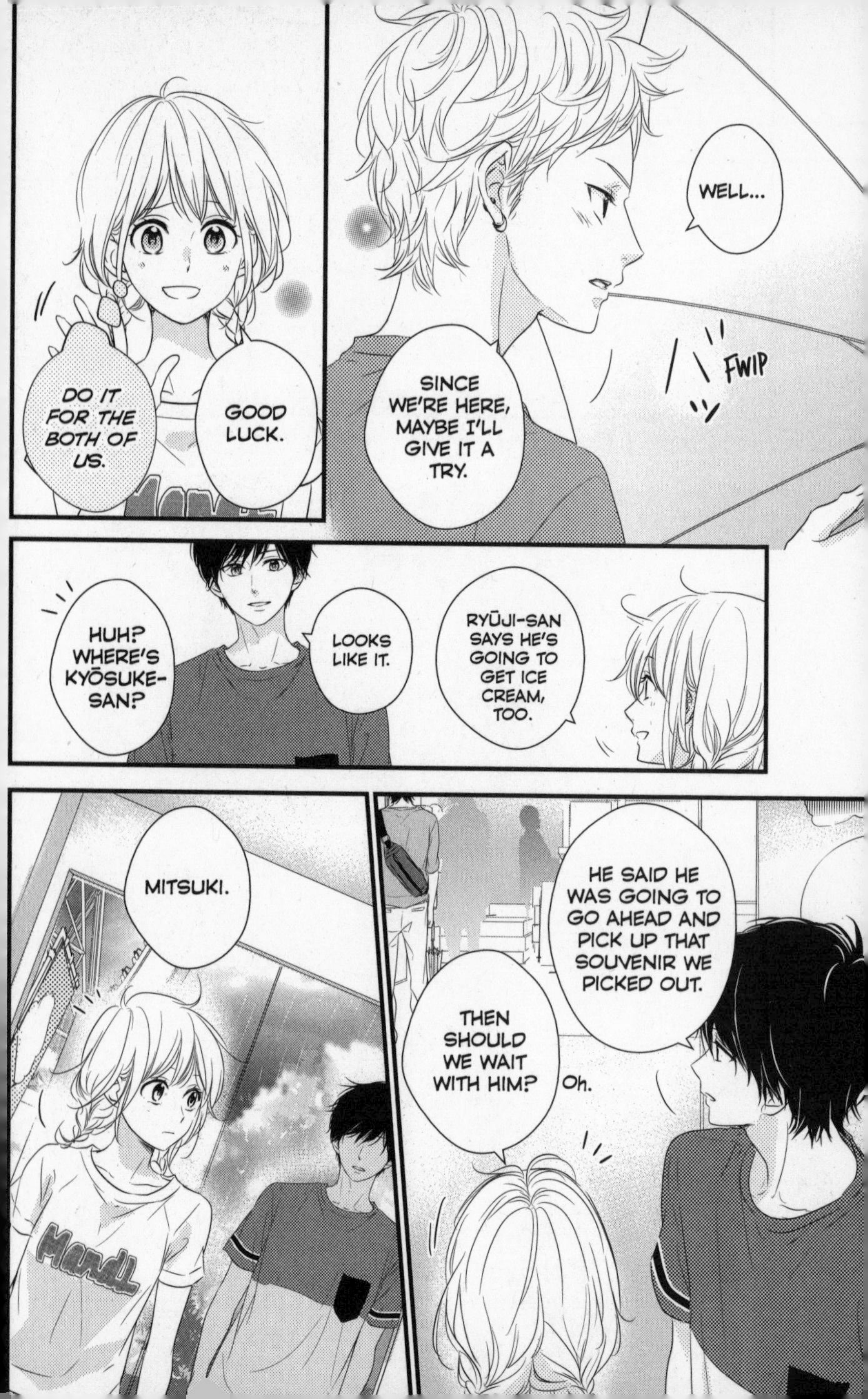
WELL...
SINCE WE'RE HERE, MAYBE I'LL GIVE IT A TRY.
FWIP
GOOD LUCK.
DO IT FOR THE BOTH OF US.
RYŪJI-SAN SAYS HE'S GOING TO GET ICE CREAM, TOO.
LOOKS LIKE IT.
HUH? WHERE'S KYŌSUKE-SAN?
HE SAID HE WAS GOING TO GO AHEAD AND PICK UP THAT SOUVENIR WE PICKED OUT.
Oh.
THEN SHOULD WE WAIT WITH HIM?
MITSUKI.

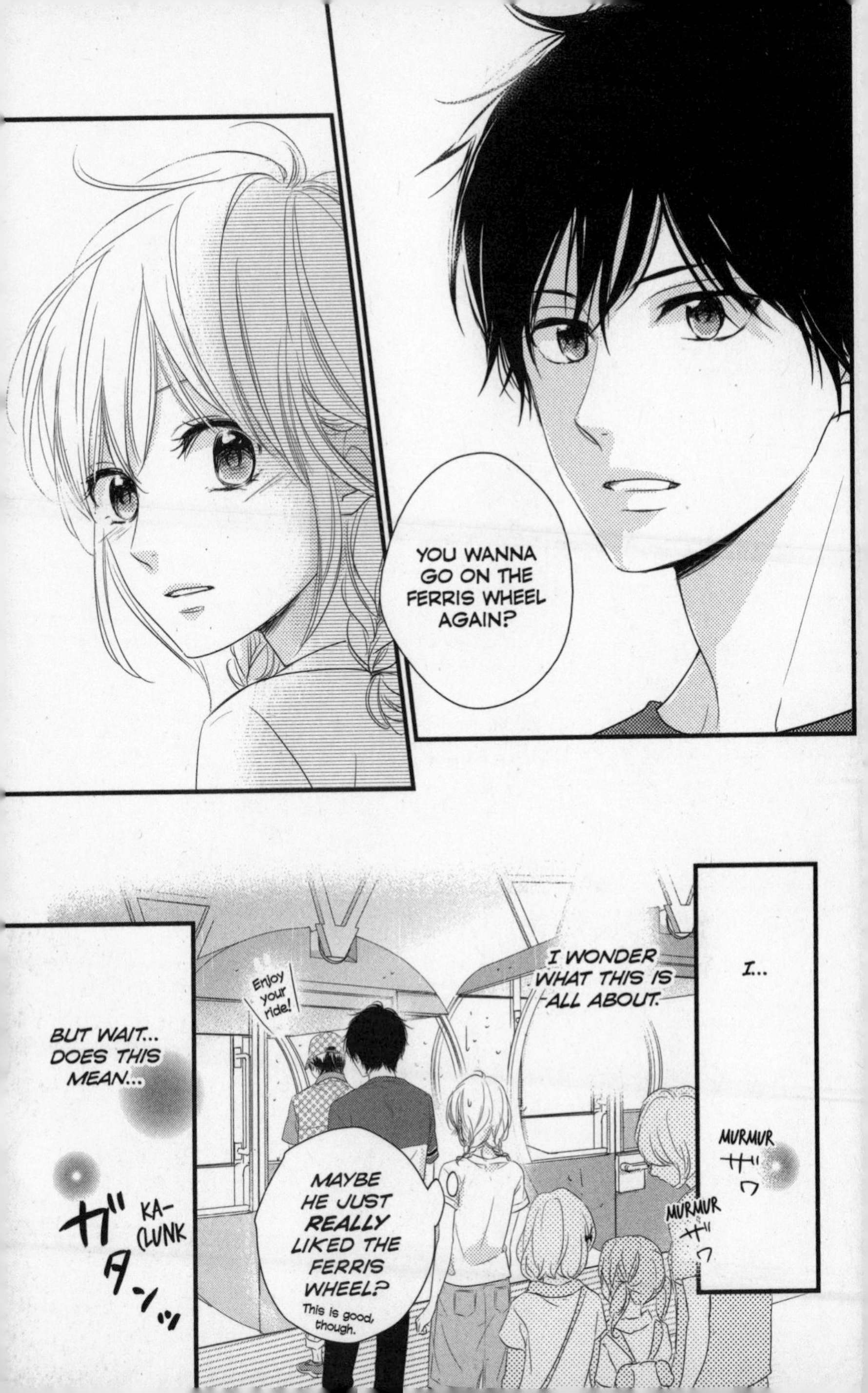

YOU WANNA GO ON THE FERRIS WHEEL AGAIN?
I...
I WONDER WHAT THIS IS ALL ABOUT.
Enjoy your ride!
MURMUR
MURMUR
BUT WAIT... DOES THIS MEAN...
MAYBE HE JUST REALLY LIKED THE FERRIS WHEEL?
This is good, though.
KA-CLUNK

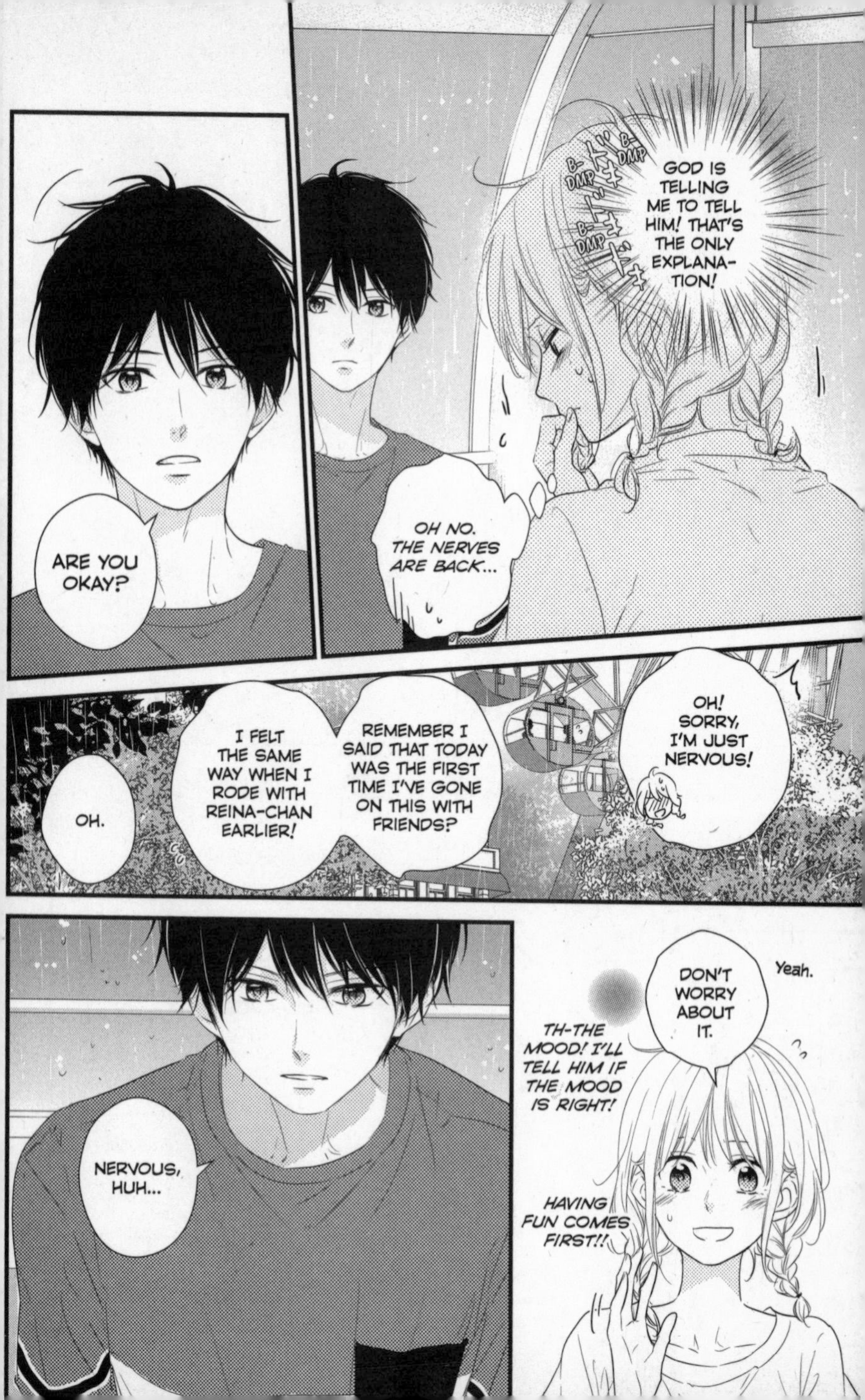
B-DMP
B-DMP
B-DMP
GOD IS TELLING ME TO TELL HIM! THAT'S THE ONLY EXPLANATION!
OH NO. THE NERVES ARE BACK...
ARE YOU OKAY?
OH! SORRY, I'M JUST NERVOUS!
REMEMBER I SAID THAT TODAY WAS THE FIRST TIME I'VE GONE ON THIS WITH FRIENDS?
I FELT THE SAME WAY WHEN I RODE WITH REINA-CHAN EARLIER!
OH.
DON'T WORRY ABOUT IT.
Yeah.
TH-THE MOOD! I'LL TELL HIM IF THE MOOD IS RIGHT!
HAVING FUN COMES FIRST!!
NERVOUS, HUH...

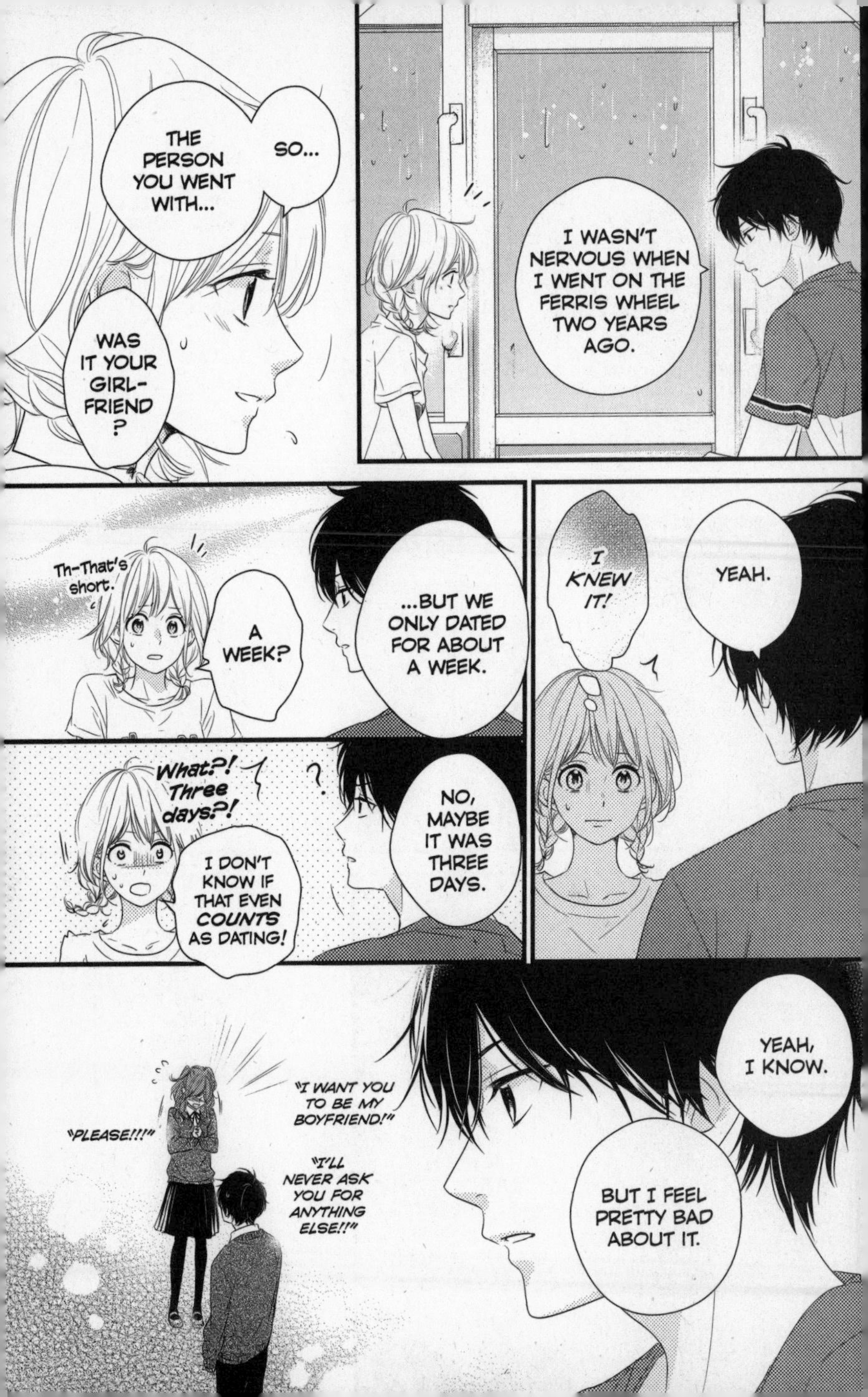
I WASN'T NERVOUS WHEN I WENT ON THE FERRIS WHEEL TWO YEARS AGO.
SO...
THE PERSON YOU WENT WITH...
WAS IT YOUR GIRLFRIEND?
YEAH.
I KNEW IT!
...BUT WE ONLY DATED FOR ABOUT A WEEK.
A WEEK?
Th-That's short.
NO, MAYBE IT WAS THREE DAYS.
What?! Three days?!
I DON'T KNOW IF THAT EVEN COUNTS AS DATING!
YEAH, I KNOW.
BUT I FEEL PRETTY BAD ABOUT IT.
"I WANT YOU TO BE MY BOYFRIEND!"
"PLEASE!!!"
"I'LL NEVER ASK YOU FOR ANYTHING ELSE!!"

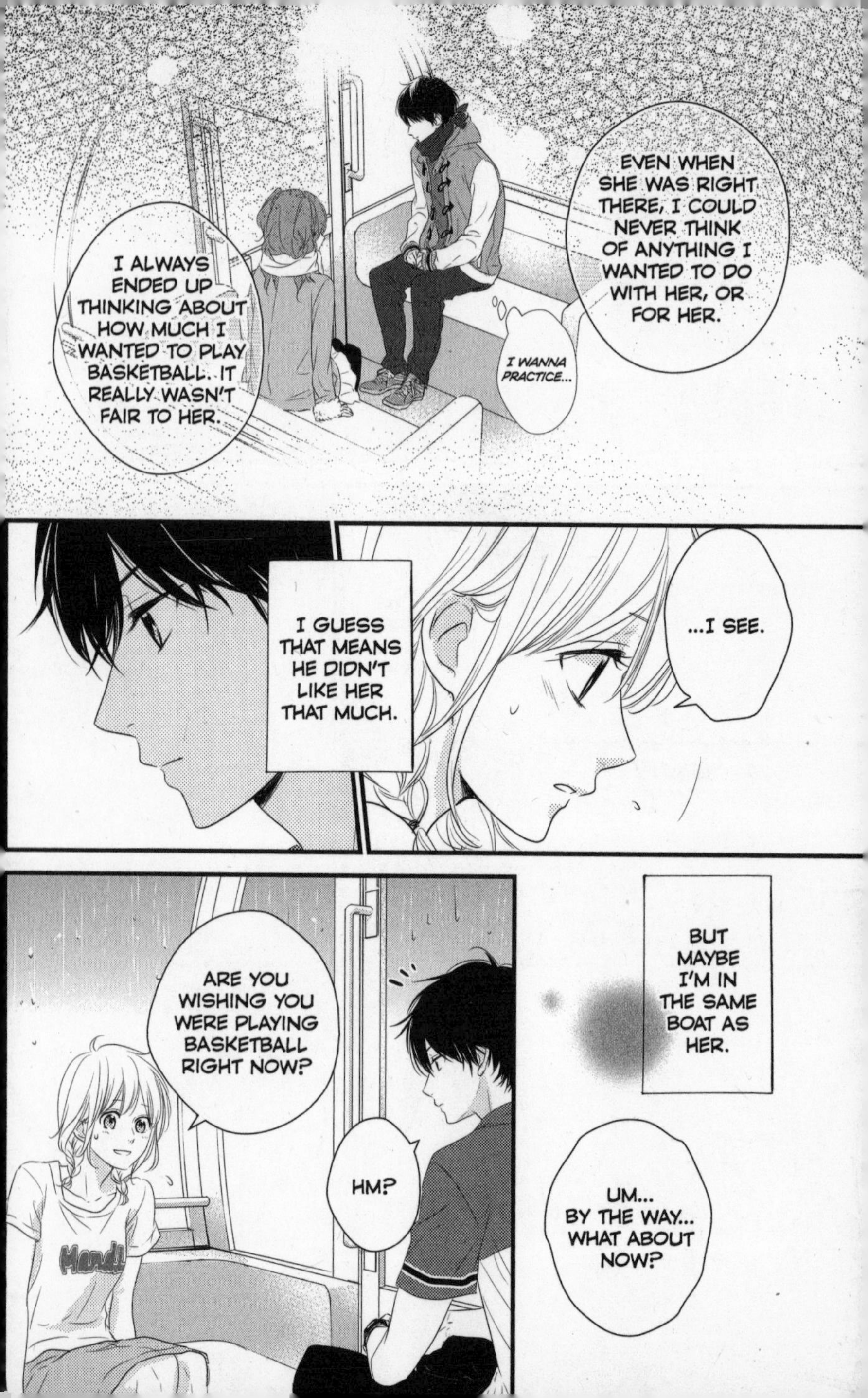
EVEN WHEN SHE WAS RIGHT THERE, I COULD NEVER THINK OF ANYTHING I WANTED TO DO WITH HER, OR FOR HER.
I WANNA PRACTICE...
I ALWAYS ENDED UP THINKING ABOUT HOW MUCH I WANTED TO PLAY BASKETBALL. IT REALLY WASN'T FAIR TO HER.
...I SEE.
I GUESS THAT MEANS HE DIDN'T LIKE HER THAT MUCH.
BUT MAYBE I'M IN THE SAME BOAT AS HER.
UM... BY THE WAY... WHAT ABOUT NOW?
ARE YOU WISHING YOU WERE PLAYING BASKETBALL RIGHT NOW?
HM?

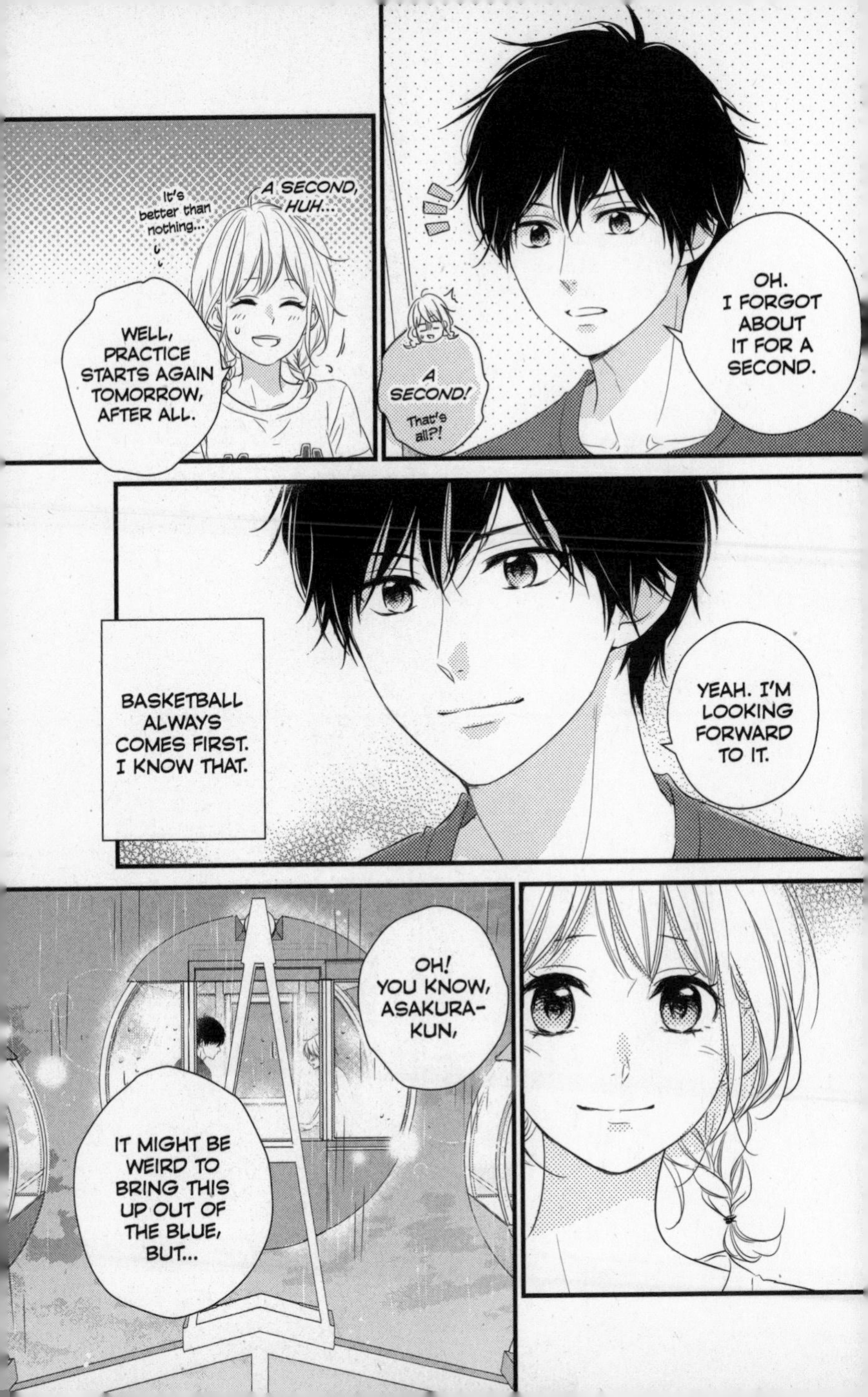
OH. I FORGOT ABOUT IT FOR A SECOND.
A SECOND! That's all?!
A SECOND, HUH...
It's better than nothing...
WELL, PRACTICE STARTS AGAIN TOMORROW, AFTER ALL.
YEAH. I'M LOOKING FORWARD TO IT.
BASKETBALL ALWAYS COMES FIRST. I KNOW THAT.
OH! YOU KNOW, ASAKURA-KUN,
IT MIGHT BE WEIRD TO BRING THIS UP OUT OF THE BLUE, BUT...

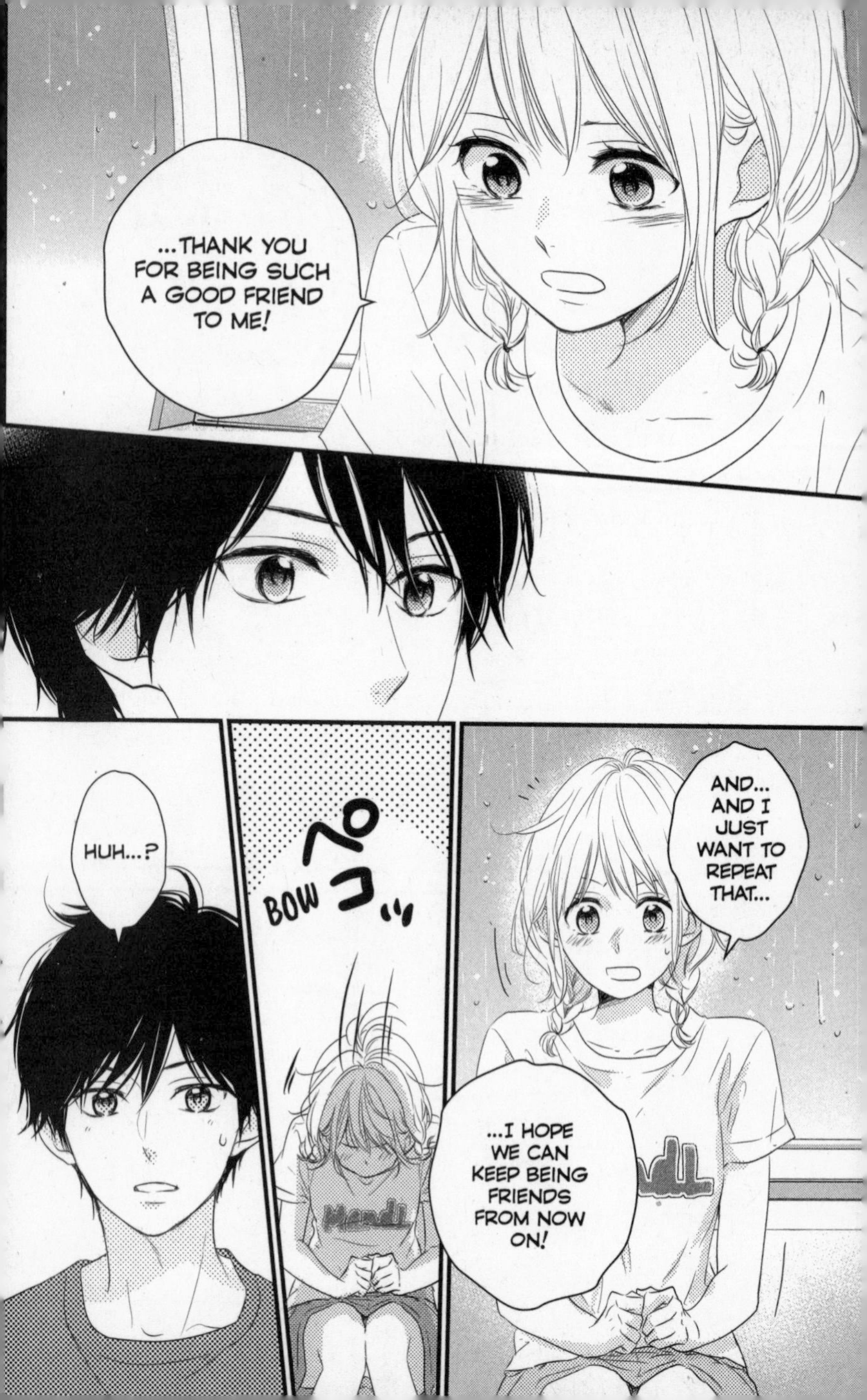
...THANK YOU FOR BEING SUCH A GOOD FRIEND TO ME!
AND... AND I JUST WANT TO REPEAT THAT...
...I HOPE WE CAN KEEP BEING FRIENDS FROM NOW ON!
ペコッ
BOW
HUH...?

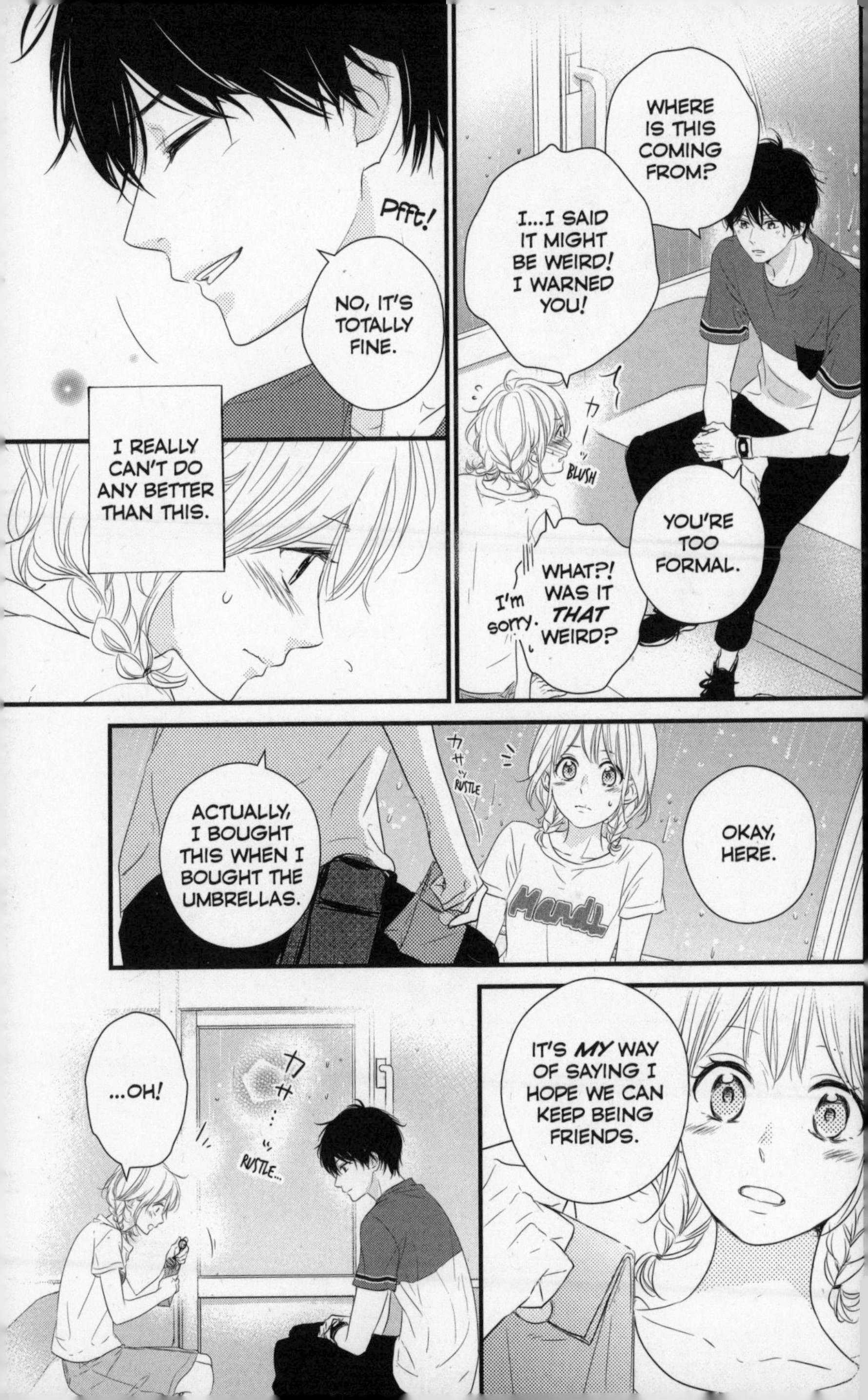
WHERE IS THIS COMING FROM?
I...I SAID IT MIGHT BE WEIRD! I WARNED YOU!
BLUSH
YOU'RE TOO FORMAL.
WHAT?! WAS IT *THAT* WEIRD?
I'm sorry.
Pfft!
NO, IT'S TOTALLY FINE.
I REALLY CAN'T DO ANY BETTER THAN THIS.
OKAY, HERE.
RUSTLE
ACTUALLY, I BOUGHT THIS WHEN I BOUGHT THE UMBRELLAS.
Mandi
IT'S *MY* WAY OF SAYING I HOPE WE CAN KEEP BEING FRIENDS.
...OH!
RUSTLE...

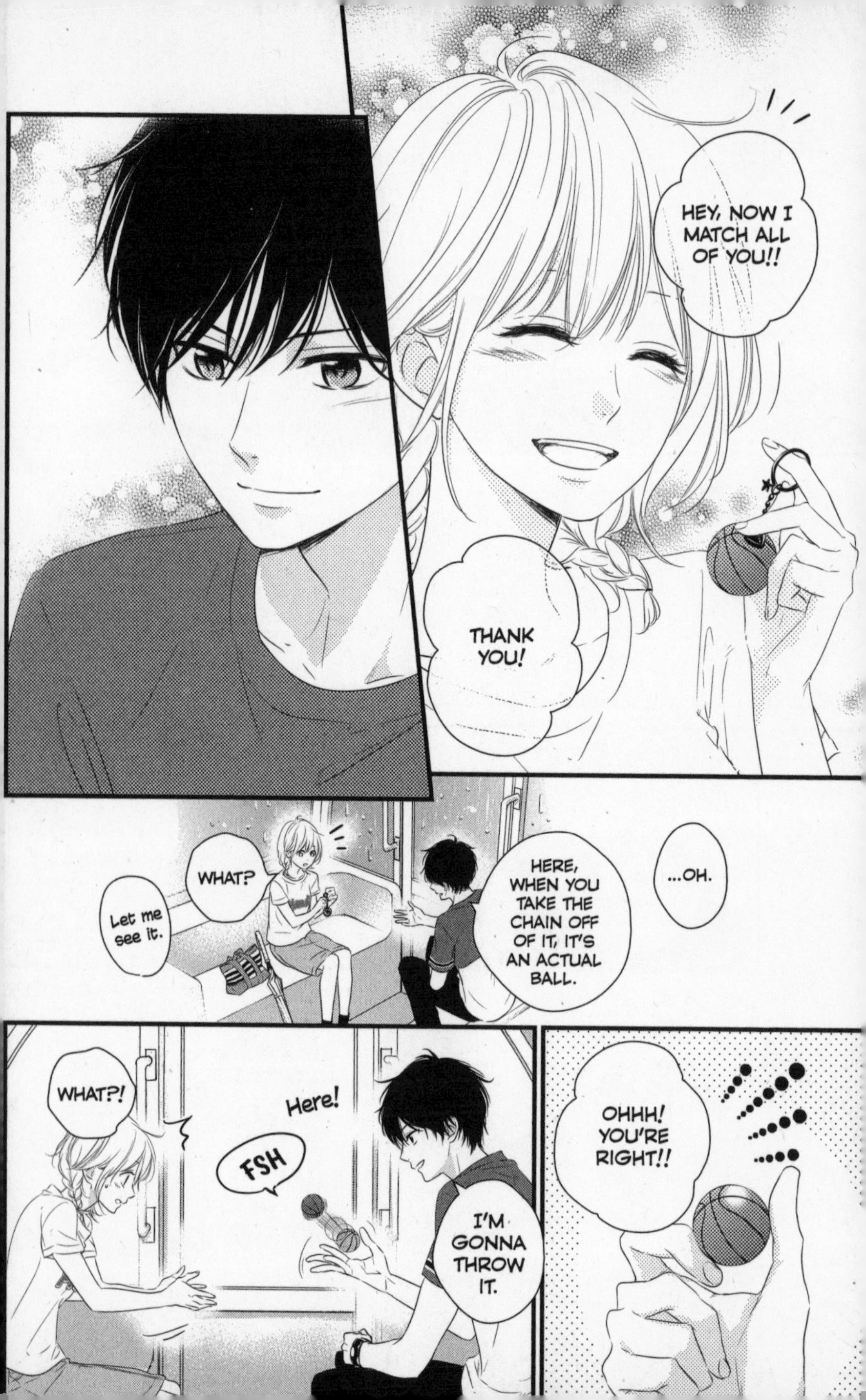
HEY, NOW I MATCH ALL OF YOU!!
THANK YOU!
...OH.
HERE, WHEN YOU TAKE THE CHAIN OFF OF IT, IT'S AN ACTUAL BALL.
WHAT?
Let me see it.
OHHH! YOU'RE RIGHT!!
I'M GONNA THROW IT.
WHAT?!
Here!
FSH

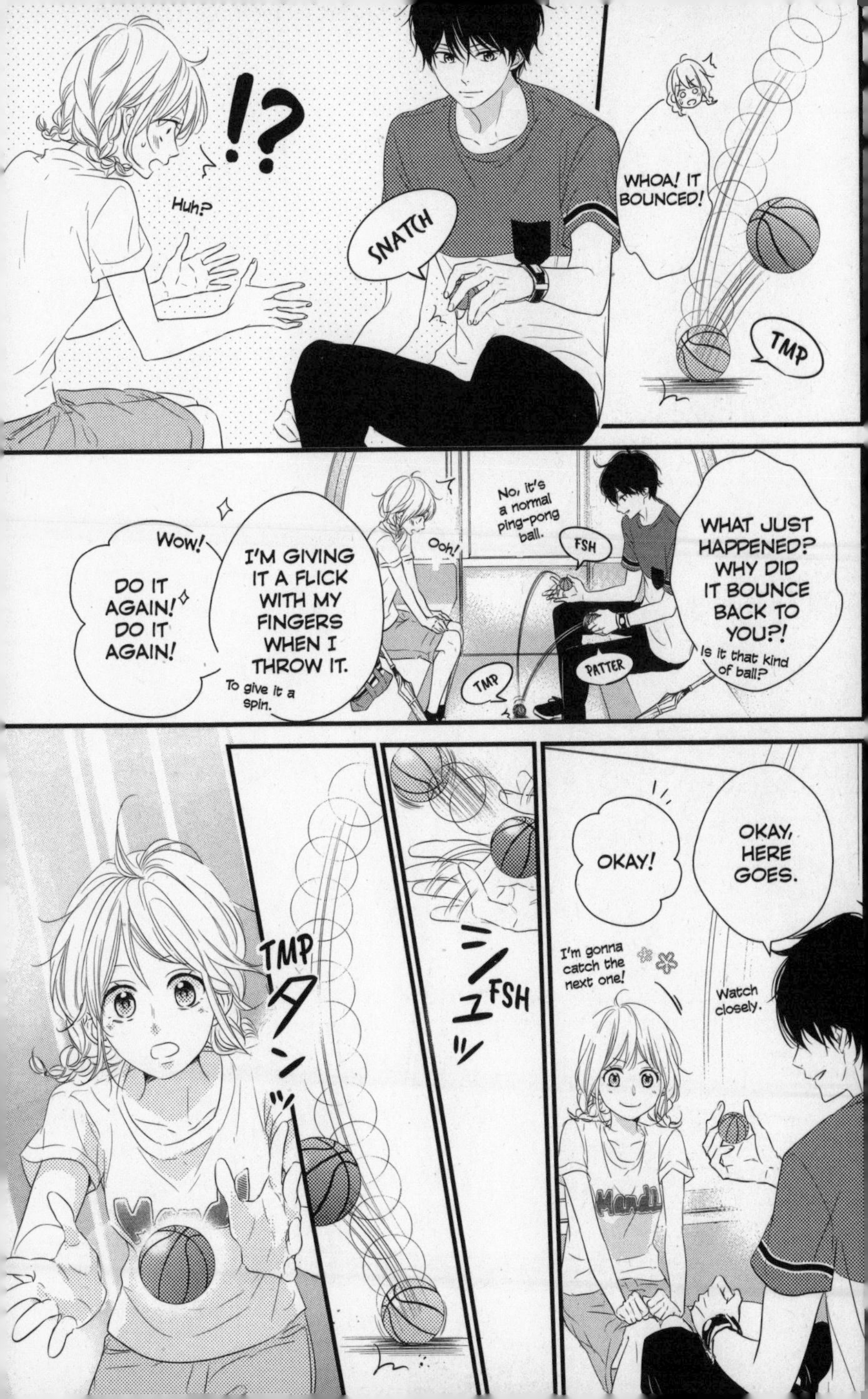
WHOA! IT BOUNCED!
TMP
!?
SNATCH
Huh?
WHAT JUST HAPPENED? WHY DID IT BOUNCE BACK TO YOU?!
Is it that kind of ball?
No, it's a normal ping-pong ball.
FSH
PATTER
Ooh!
TMP
I'M GIVING IT A FLICK WITH MY FINGERS WHEN I THROW IT.
To give it a spin.
Wow!
DO IT AGAIN! DO IT AGAIN!
OKAY, HERE GOES.
OKAY!
I'm gonna catch the next one!
Watch closely.
FSH
TMP

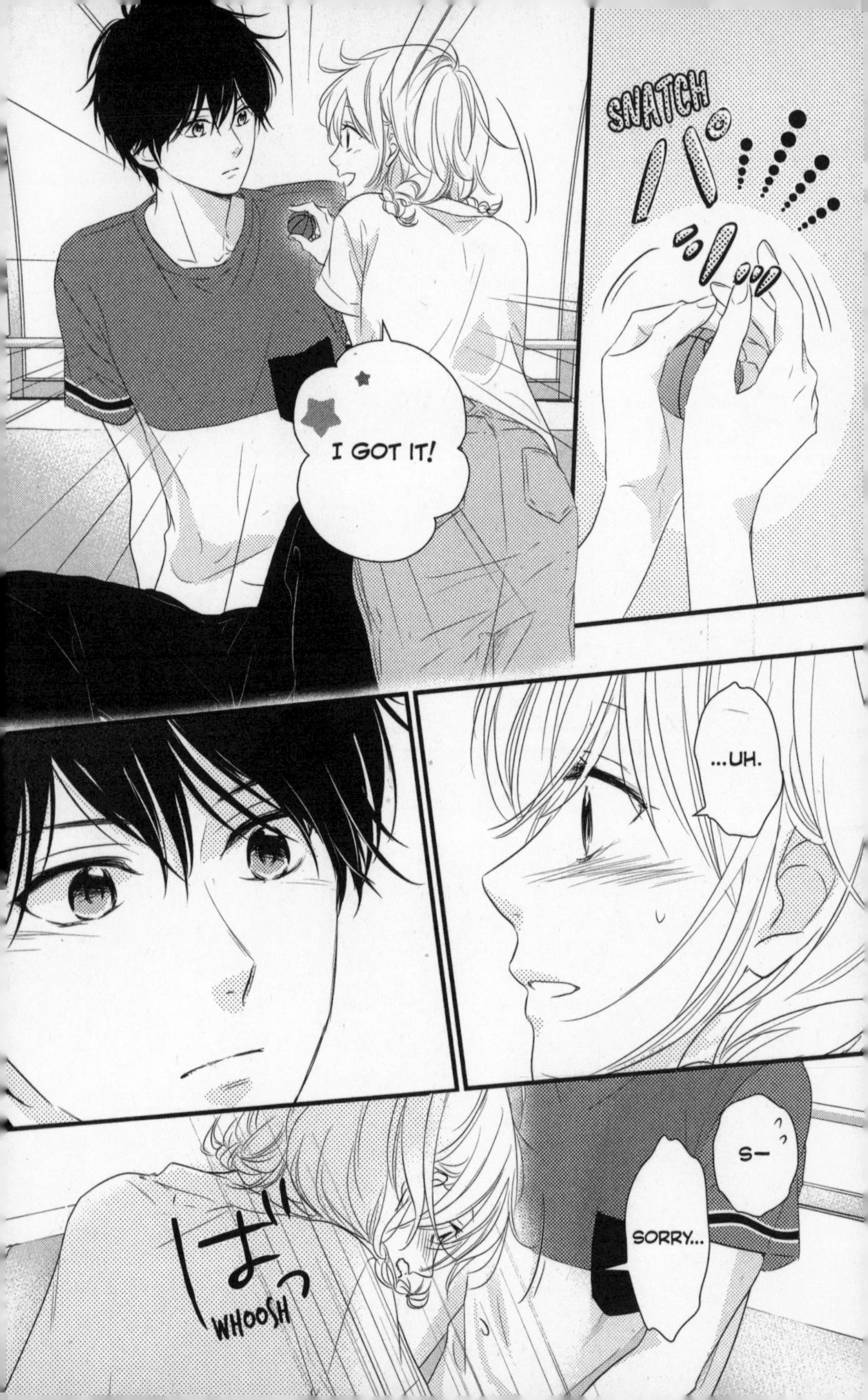
SNATCH
I GOT IT!
...UH.
S—
SORRY...
WHOOSH

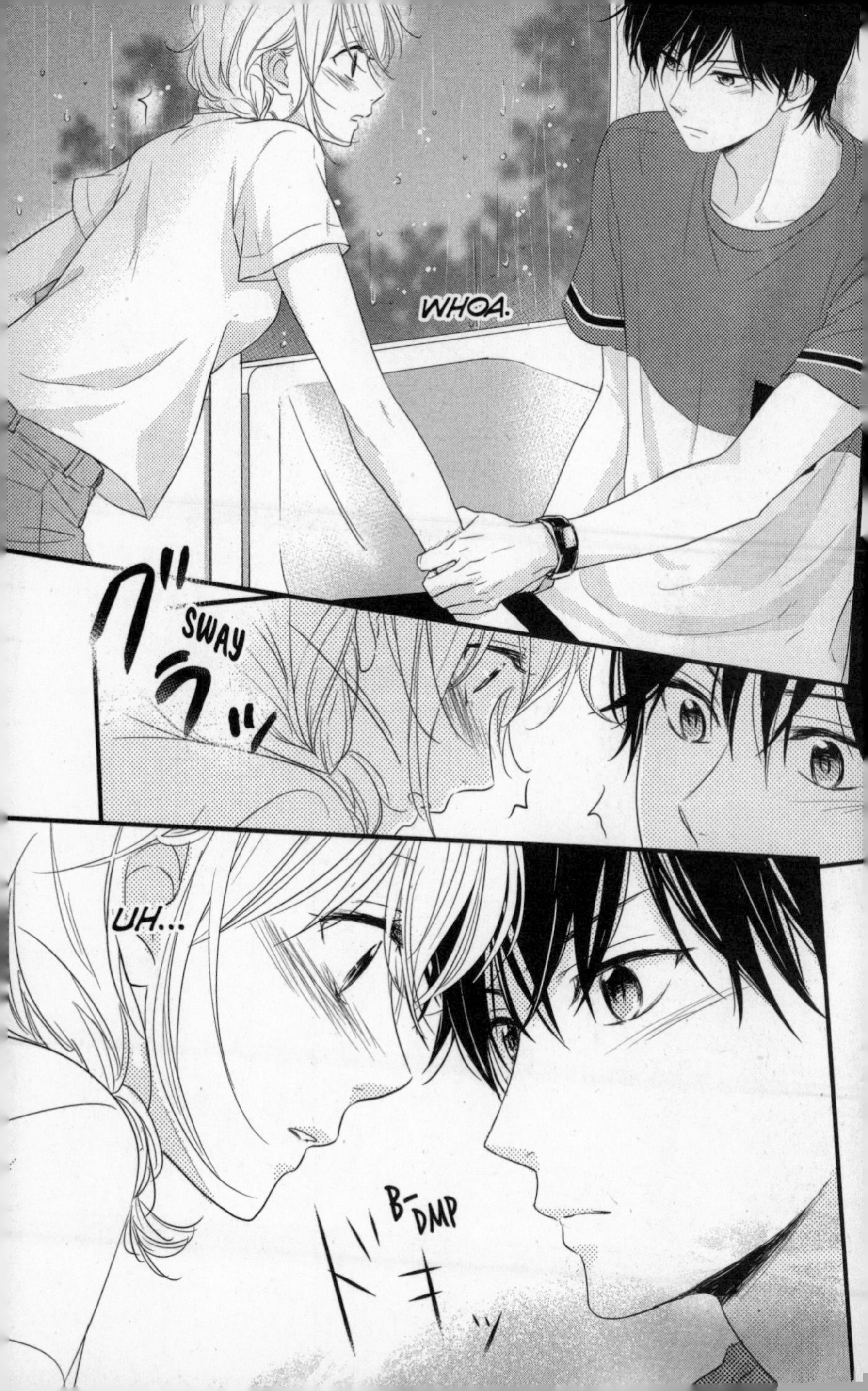
WHOA.
グラッ
SWAY
UH...
B-DMP
ドキッ

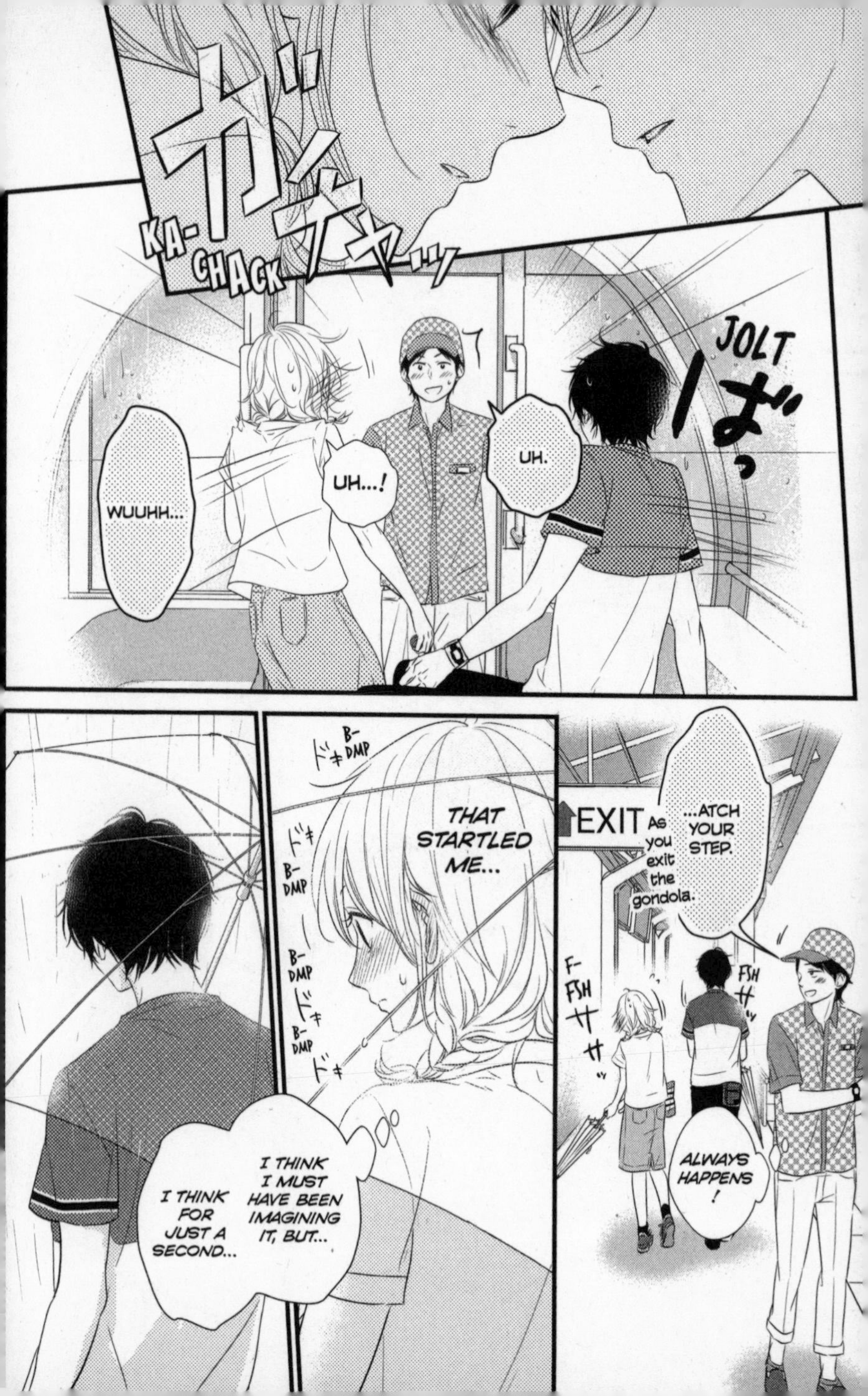
KA-CHACK
JOLT
UH.
UH...!
WUUHH...
...ATCH YOUR STEP.
As you exit the gondola.
EXIT
FSH
F-FSH
ALWAYS HAPPENS!
B-DMP
THAT STARTLED ME...
B-DMP
B-DMP
B-DMP
I THINK I MUST HAVE BEEN IMAGINING IT, BUT...
I THINK FOR JUST A SECOND...

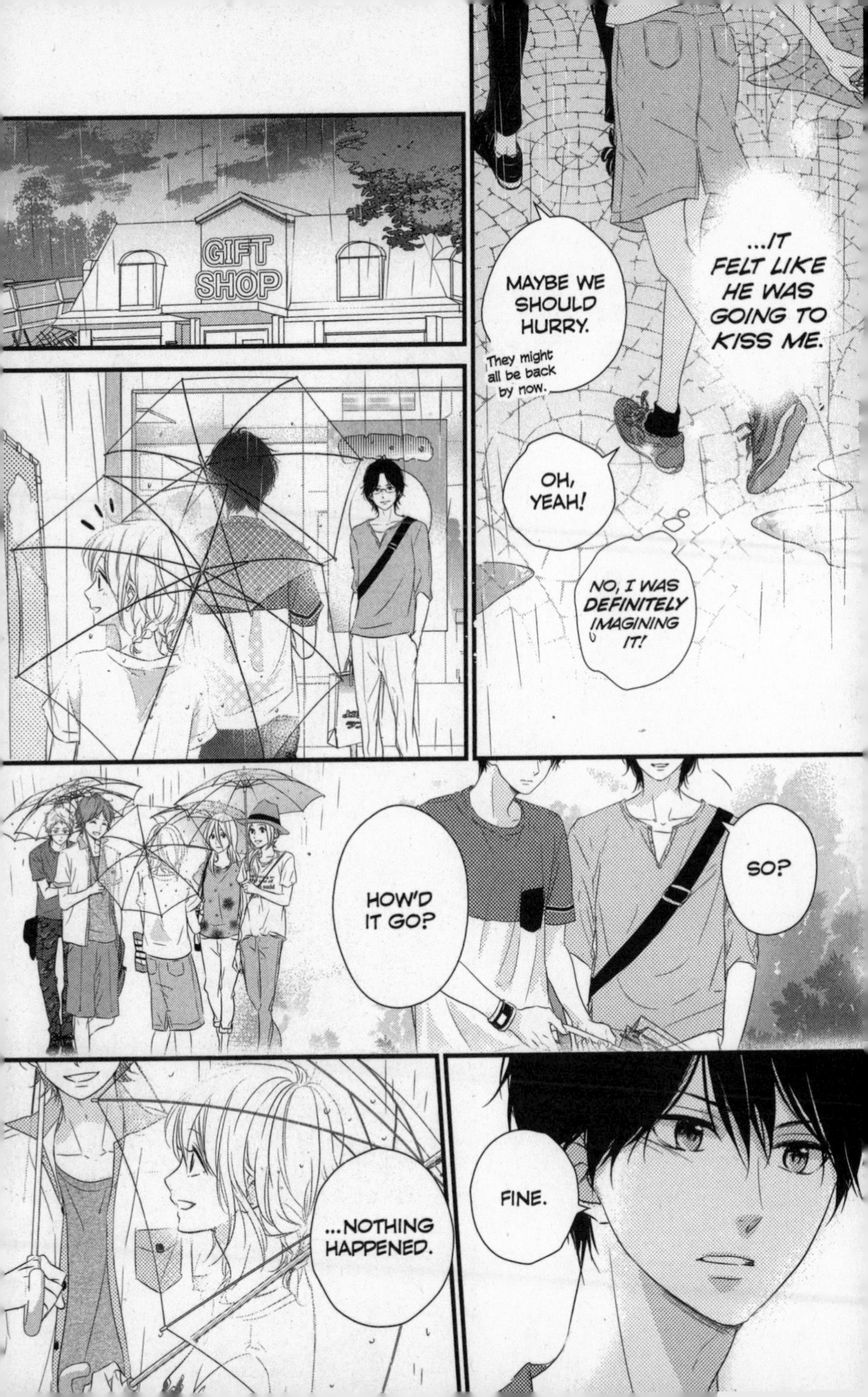
...IT FELT LIKE HE WAS GOING TO KISS ME.
MAYBE WE SHOULD HURRY.
They might all be back by now.
OH, YEAH!
NO, I WAS DEFINITELY IMAGINING IT!
GIFT SHOP
SO?
HOW'D IT GO?
FINE.
...NOTHING HAPPENED.

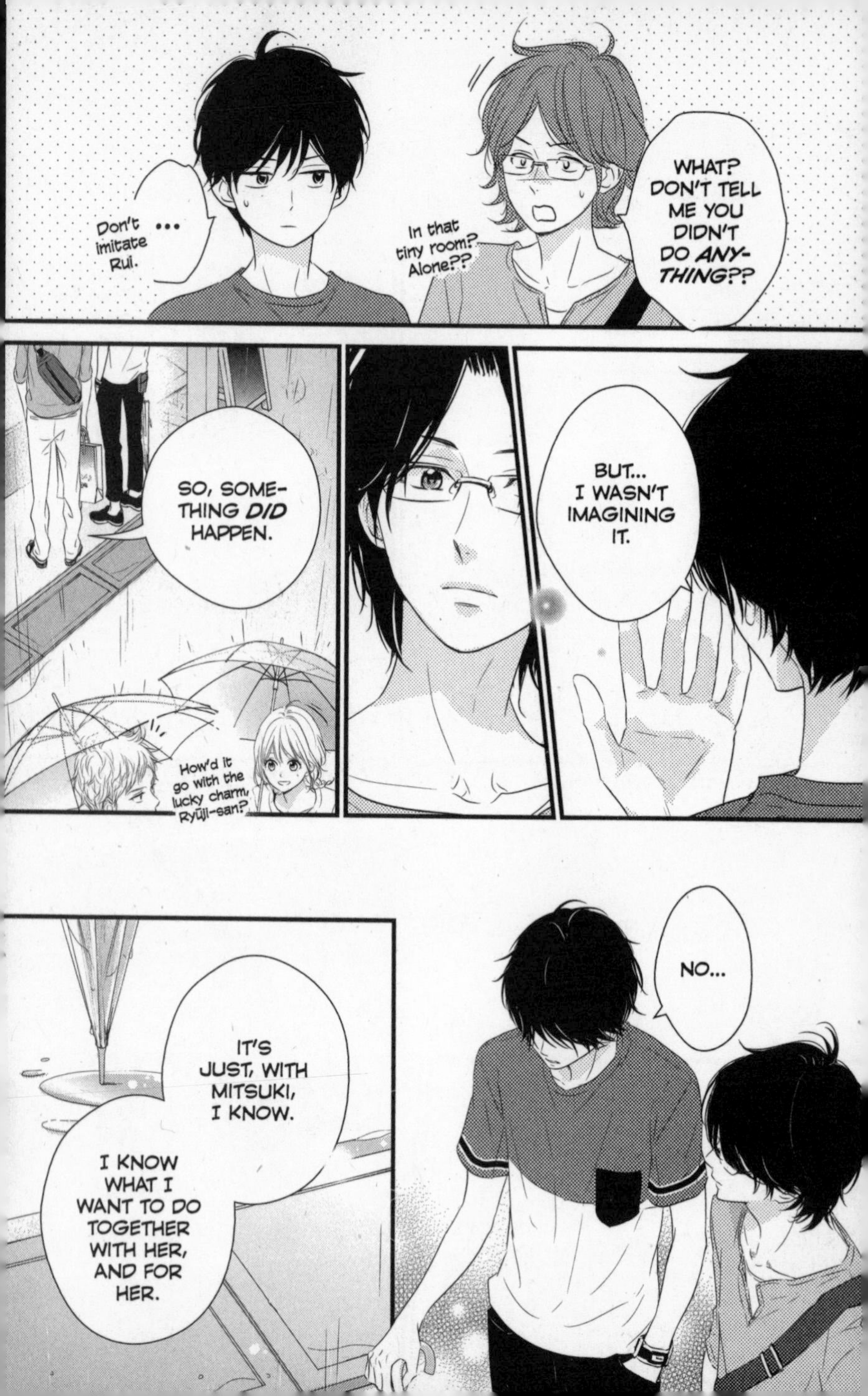
WHAT? DON'T TELL ME YOU DIDN'T DO *ANY-THING*??
In that tiny room? Alone??
... Don't imitate Rui.
BUT... I WASN'T IMAGINING IT.
SO, SOME-THING *DID* HAPPEN.
How'd it go with the lucky charm, Ryūji-san?
NO...
IT'S JUST, WITH MITSUKI, I KNOW.
I KNOW WHAT I WANT TO DO TOGETHER WITH HER, AND FOR HER.

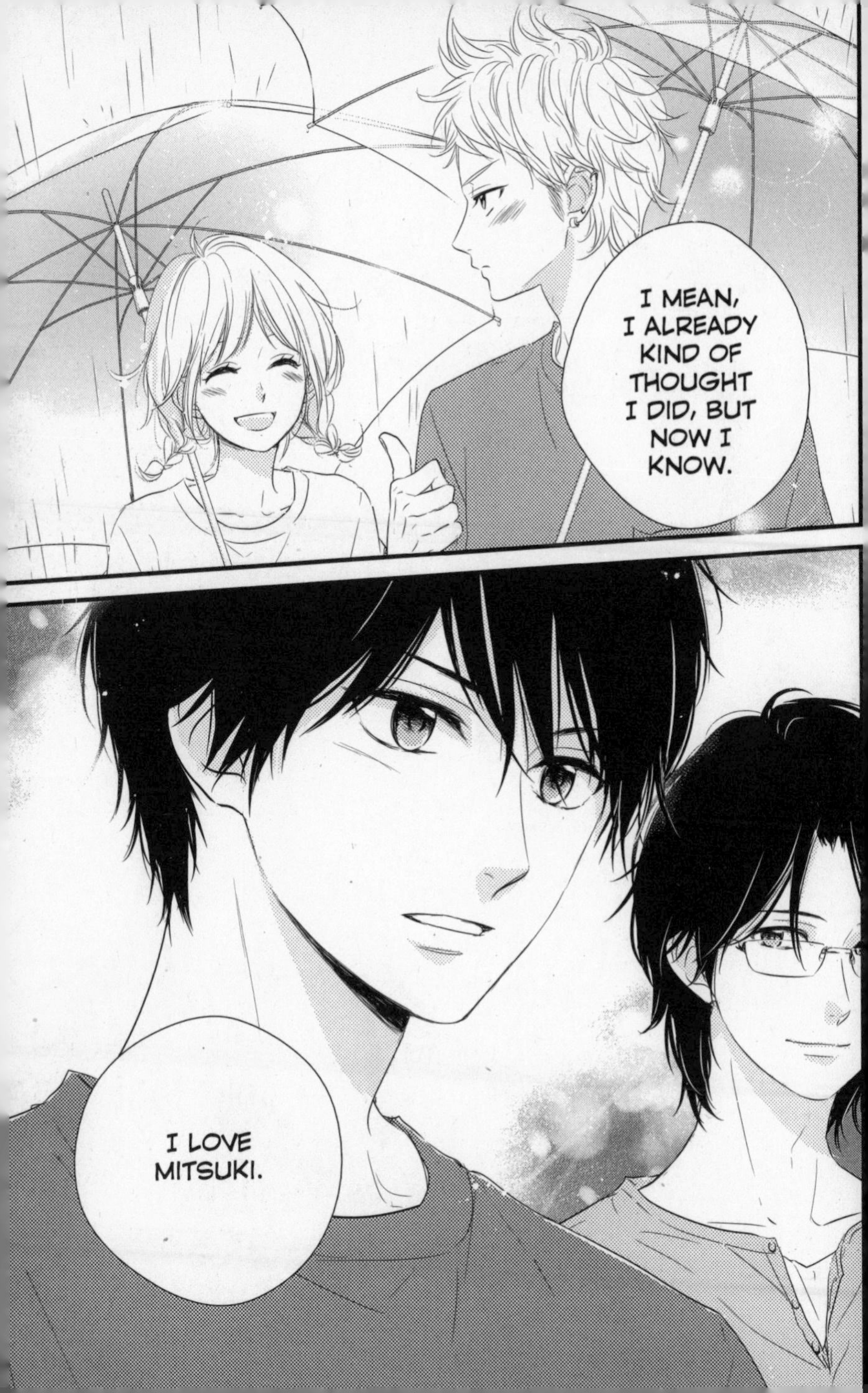
I MEAN, I ALREADY KIND OF THOUGHT I DID, BUT NOW I KNOW.
I LOVE MITSUKI.

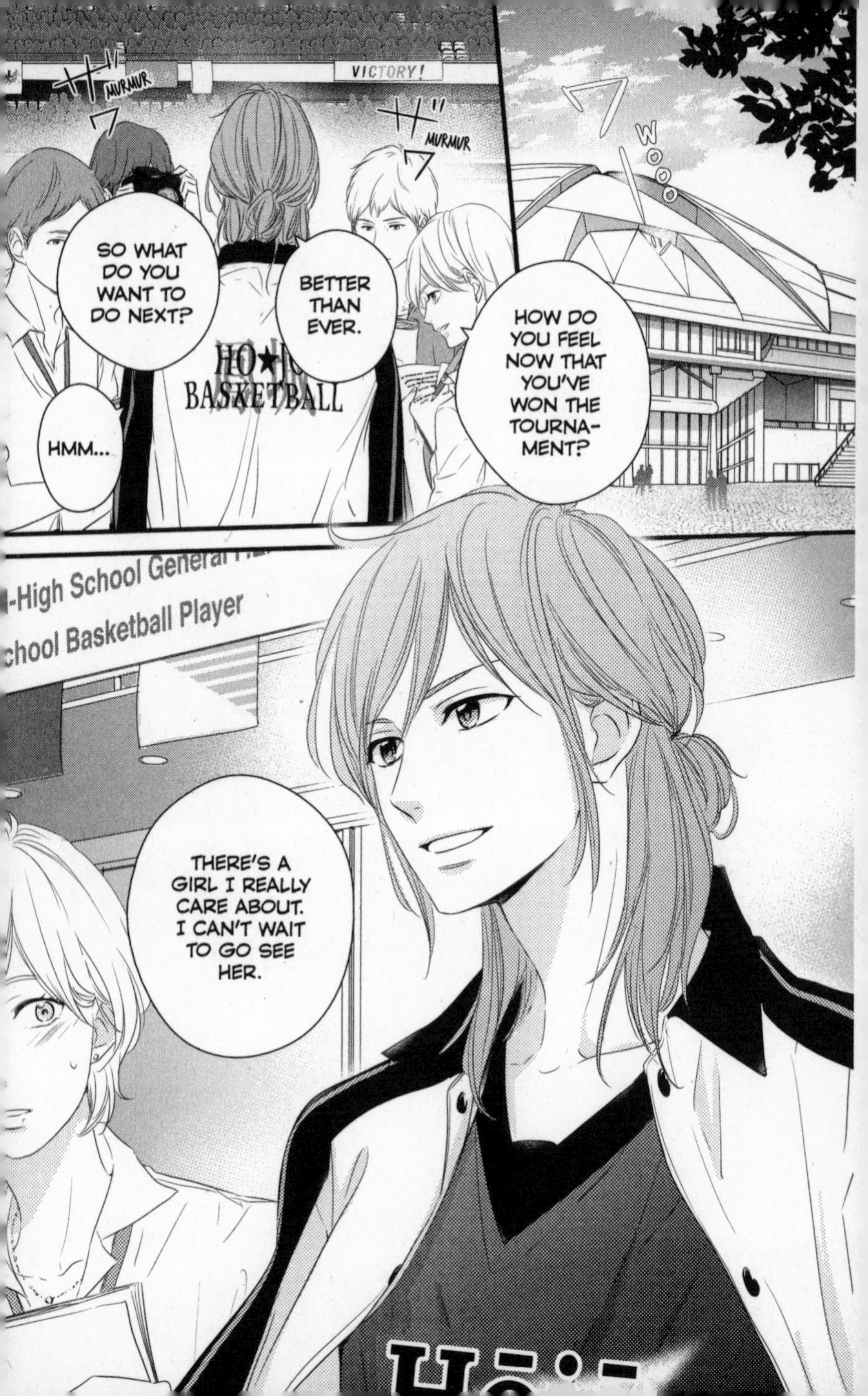
WOOO
HOW DO YOU FEEL NOW THAT YOU'VE WON THE TOURNA-MENT?
MURMUR
VICTORY!
MURMUR
BETTER THAN EVER.
SO WHAT DO YOU WANT TO DO NEXT?
HO★JO BASKETBALL
HMM...
-High School General
chool Basketball Player
THERE'S A GIRL I REALLY CARE ABOUT. I CAN'T WAIT TO GO SEE HER.

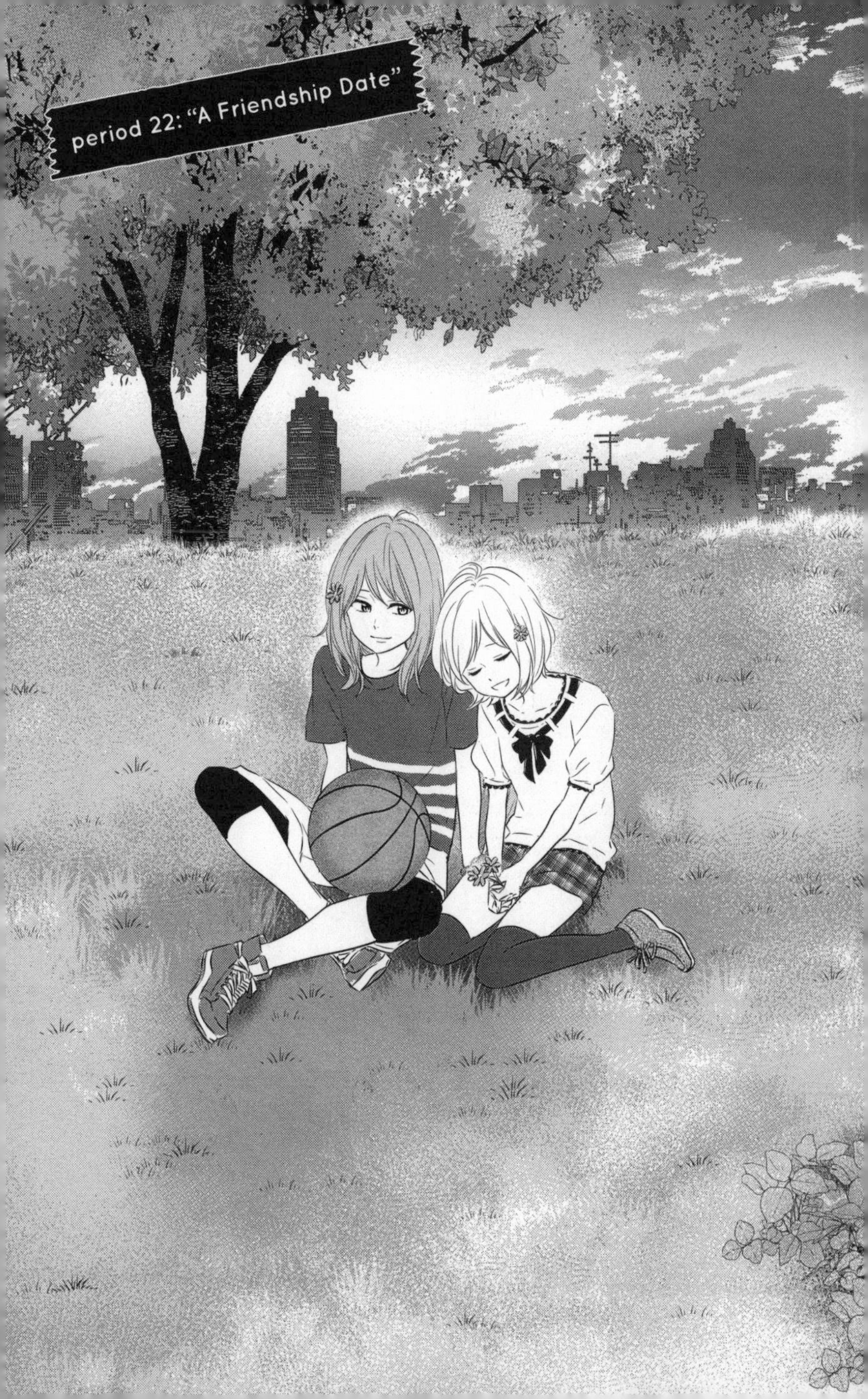
period 22: "A Friendship Date"

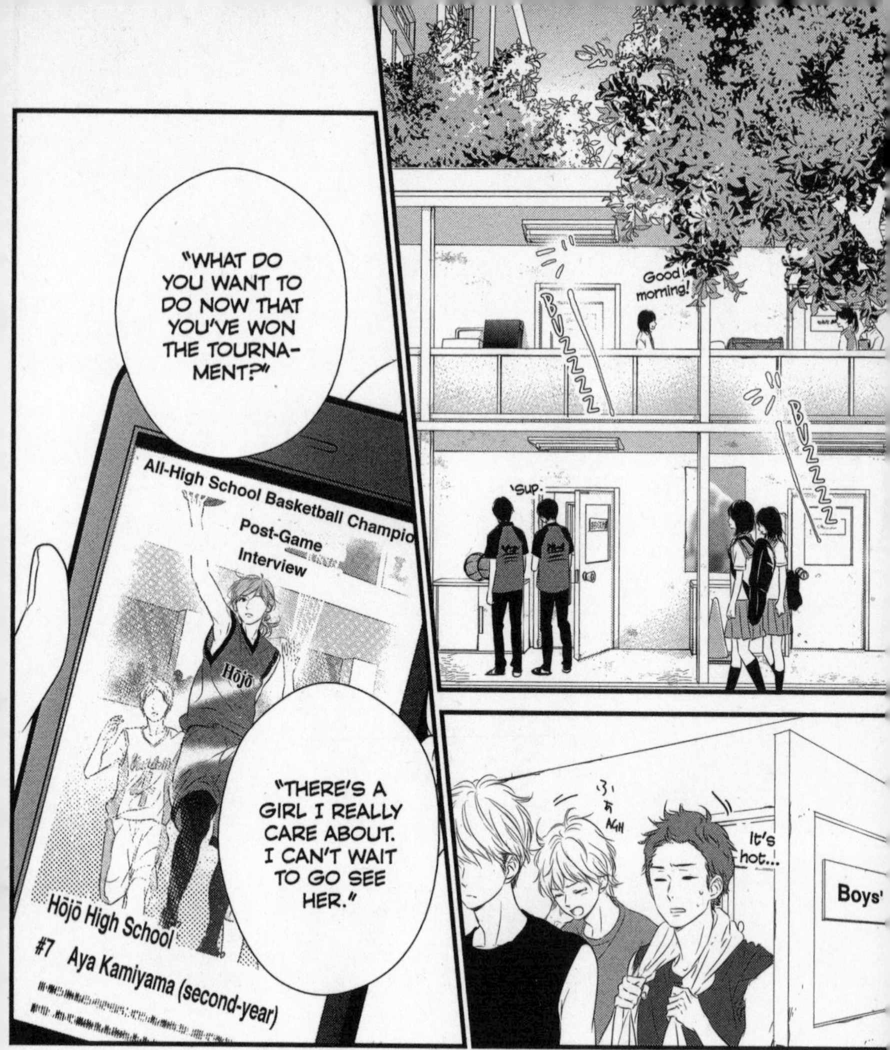
Good morning!
BUZZZZ
BUZZZZ
'Sup.
It's hot...
AGH
Boys'
"WHAT DO YOU WANT TO DO NOW THAT YOU'VE WON THE TOURNAMENT?"
All-High School Basketball Champio
Post-Game Interview
Hōjō
Hōjō High School
#7 Aya Kamiyama (second-year)
"THERE'S A GIRL I REALLY CARE ABOUT. I CAN'T WAIT TO GO SEE HER."

Answer to the Silhouette Pop Quiz

Shockingly! There were no twists this time! (ha ha)

Anyway, here's some random news. Towa's gotten taller recently. (178->180) [5'10''->5'11'']

Incidentally, Aya-chan is growing, too (179->181) [5'10.5''->5.11.5'']

He's still got you beat, Towa.

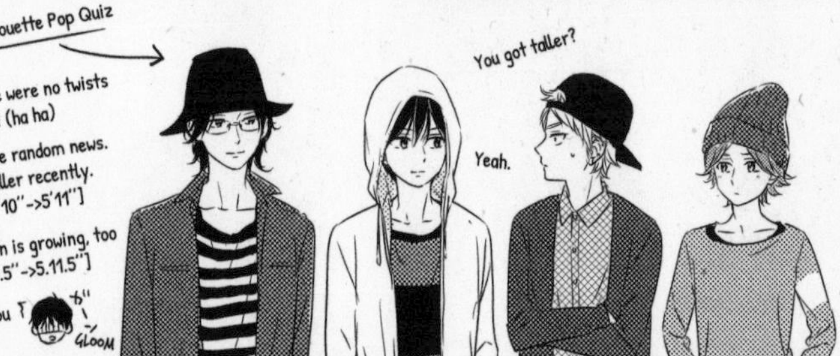
GLOOM
You got taller?
Yeah.

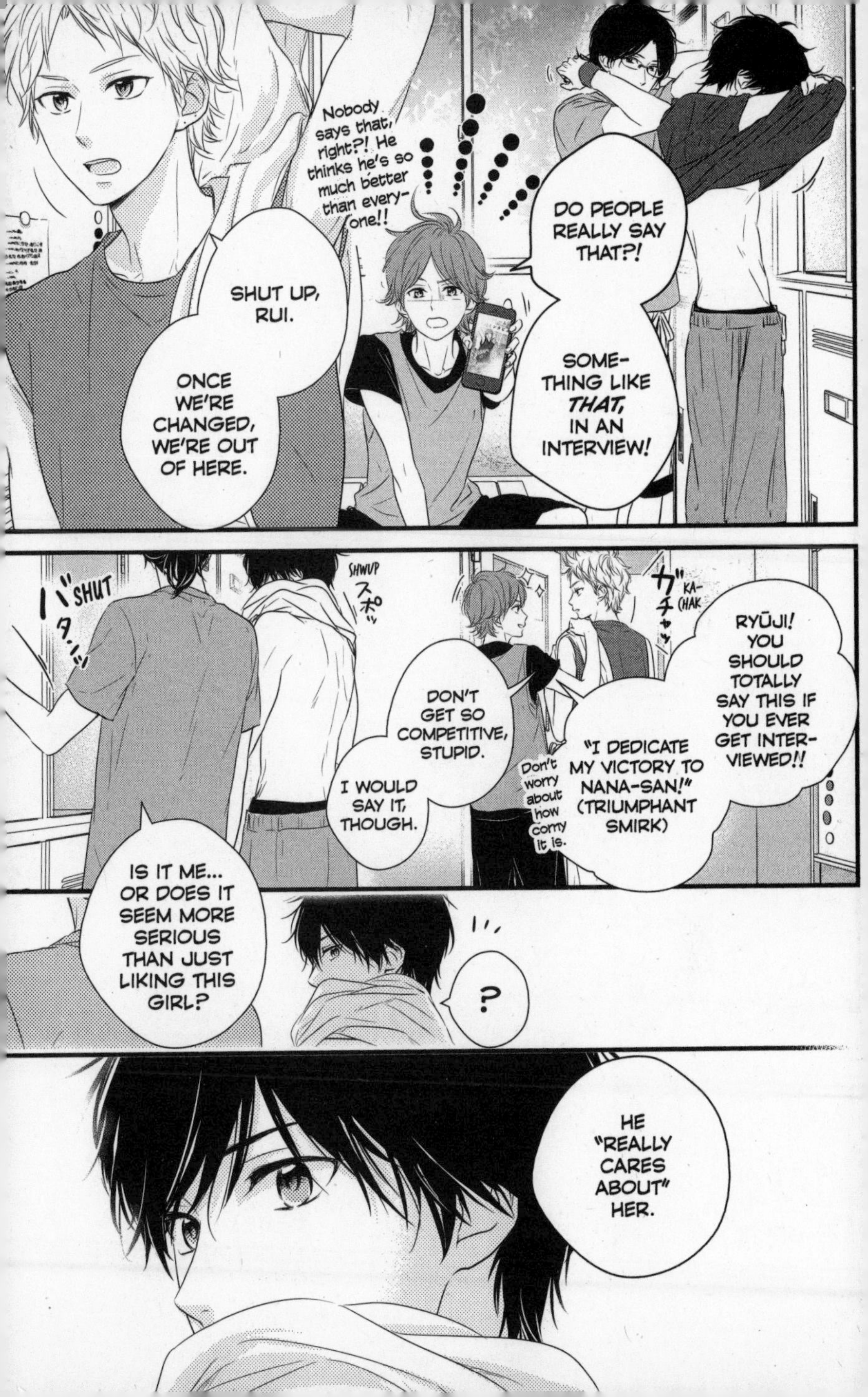
DO PEOPLE REALLY SAY THAT?!
SOME-THING LIKE *THAT,* IN AN INTERVIEW!
Nobody says that, right?! He thinks he's so much better than every-one!!
SHUT UP, RUI.
ONCE WE'RE CHANGED, WE'RE OUT OF HERE.
ガチャッ KA-CHAK
RYŪJI! YOU SHOULD TOTALLY SAY THIS IF YOU EVER GET INTER-VIEWED!!
"I DEDICATE MY VICTORY TO NANA-SAN!" (TRIUMPHANT SMIRK)
Don't worry about how corny it is.
DON'T GET SO COMPETITIVE, STUPID.
I WOULD SAY IT, THOUGH.
スポッ SHWUP
SHUT
?
IS IT ME... OR DOES IT SEEM MORE SERIOUS THAN JUST LIKING THIS GIRL?
HE "REALLY CARES ABOUT" HER.

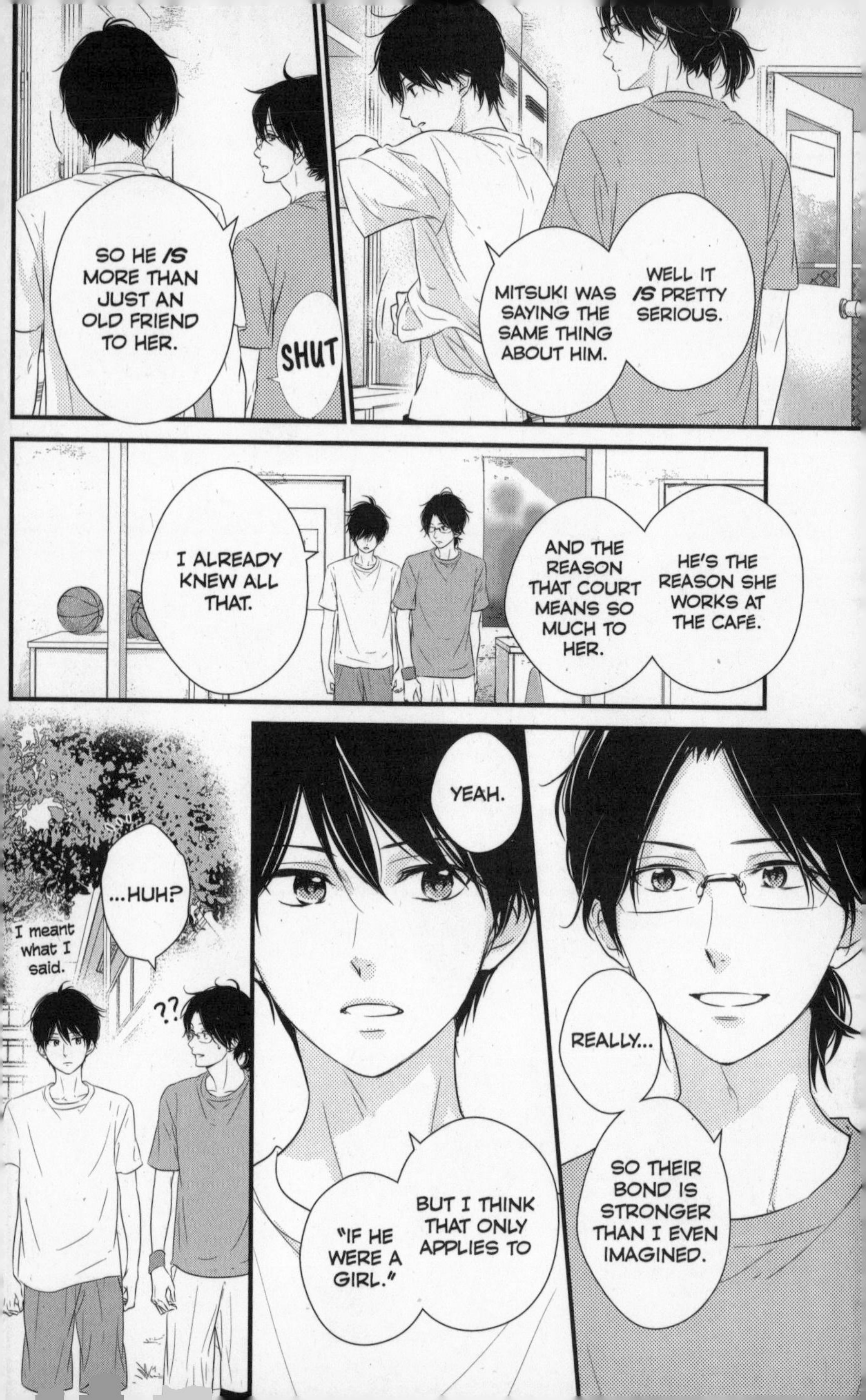
WELL IT IS PRETTY SERIOUS.
MITSUKI WAS SAYING THE SAME THING ABOUT HIM.
SO HE IS MORE THAN JUST AN OLD FRIEND TO HER.
SHUT
HE'S THE REASON SHE WORKS AT THE CAFÉ.
AND THE REASON THAT COURT MEANS SO MUCH TO HER.
I ALREADY KNEW ALL THAT.
REALLY...
SO THEIR BOND IS STRONGER THAN I EVEN IMAGINED.
YEAH.
BUT I THINK THAT ONLY APPLIES TO
"IF HE WERE A GIRL."
...HUH?
I meant what I said.
??

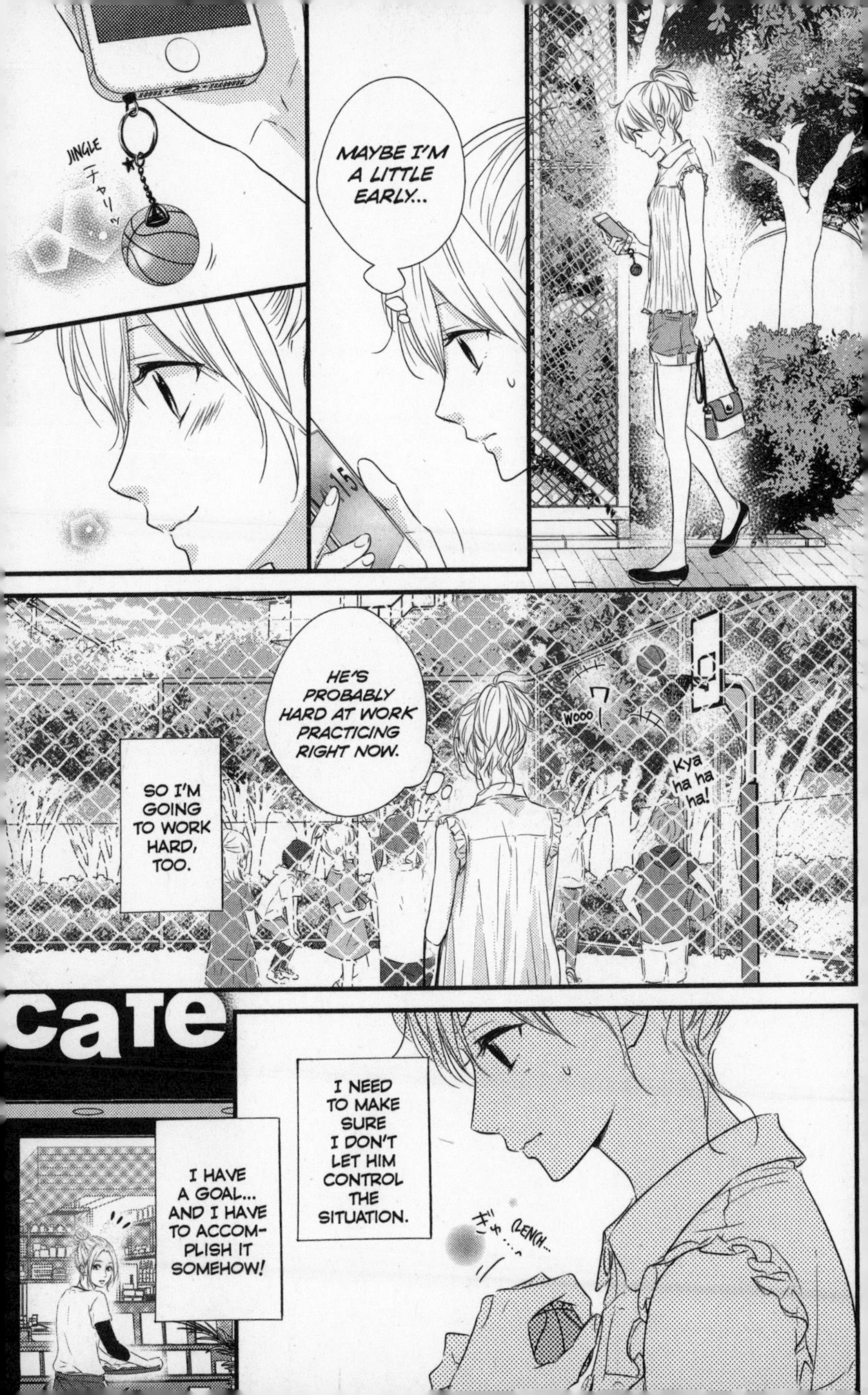

MAYBE I'M A LITTLE EARLY...
JINGLE
チャリッ
Kya ha ha ha!
WOOO!
ワ
HE'S PROBABLY HARD AT WORK PRACTICING RIGHT NOW.
SO I'M GOING TO WORK HARD, TOO.
I NEED TO MAKE SURE I DON'T LET HIM CONTROL THE SITUATION.
CLENCH...
ぎゅ…
cafe
I HAVE A GOAL... AND I HAVE TO ACCOMPLISH IT SOMEHOW!

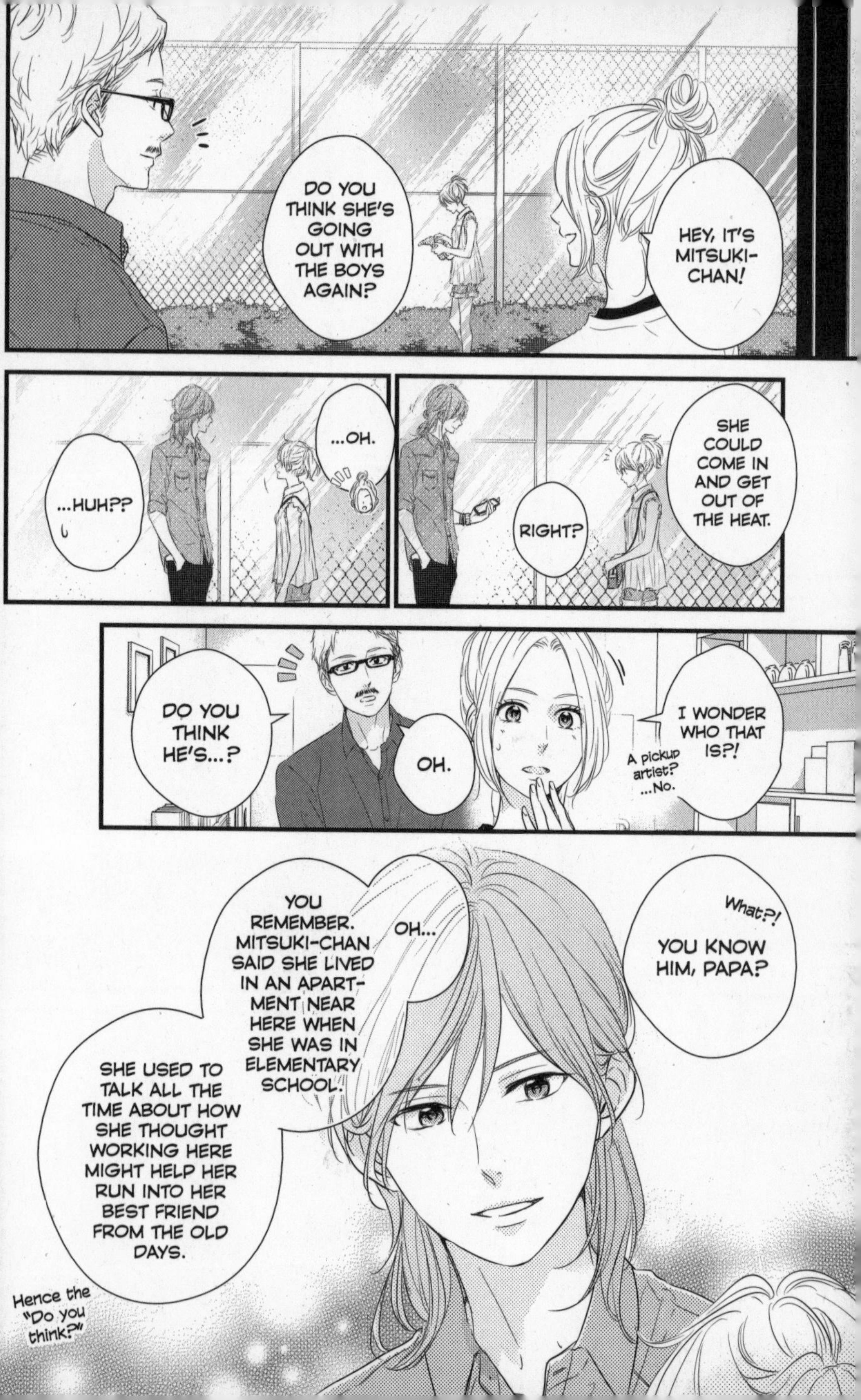
HEY, IT'S MITSUKI-CHAN!
DO YOU THINK SHE'S GOING OUT WITH THE BOYS AGAIN?
SHE COULD COME IN AND GET OUT OF THE HEAT.
RIGHT?
...OH.
...HUH??
I WONDER WHO THAT IS?!
A pickup artist? ...No.
OH.
DO YOU THINK HE'S...?
What?!
YOU KNOW HIM, PAPA?
OH...
YOU REMEMBER. MITSUKI-CHAN SAID SHE LIVED IN AN APARTMENT NEAR HERE WHEN SHE WAS IN ELEMENTARY SCHOOL.
SHE USED TO TALK ALL THE TIME ABOUT HOW SHE THOUGHT WORKING HERE MIGHT HELP HER RUN INTO HER BEST FRIEND FROM THE OLD DAYS.
Hence the "Do you think?"

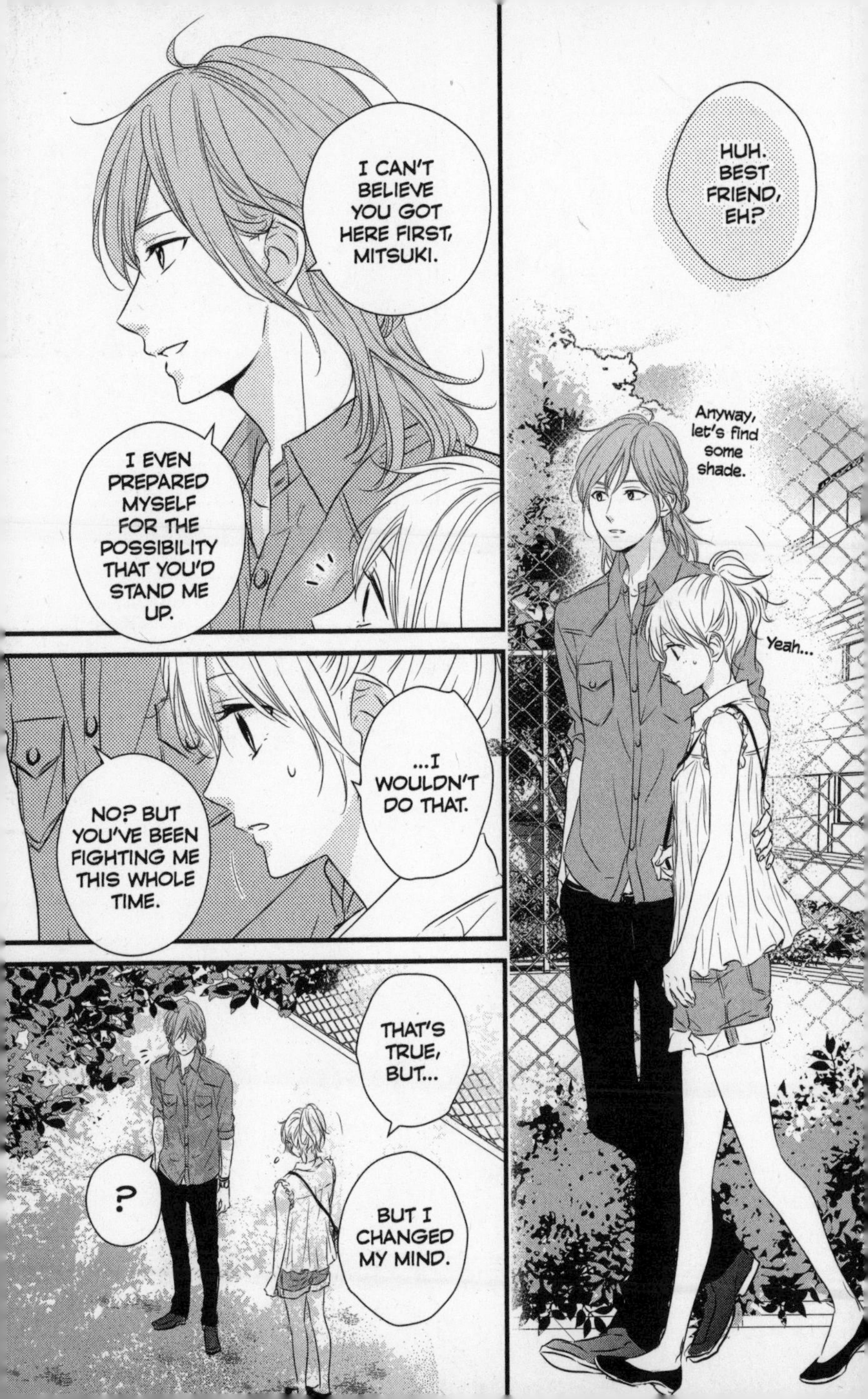
HUH. BEST FRIEND, EH?
Anyway, let's find some shade.
Yeah...
I CAN'T BELIEVE YOU GOT HERE FIRST, MITSUKI.
I EVEN PREPARED MYSELF FOR THE POSSIBILITY THAT YOU'D STAND ME UP.
...I WOULDN'T DO THAT.
NO? BUT YOU'VE BEEN FIGHTING ME THIS WHOLE TIME.
THAT'S TRUE, BUT...
BUT I CHANGED MY MIND.
?

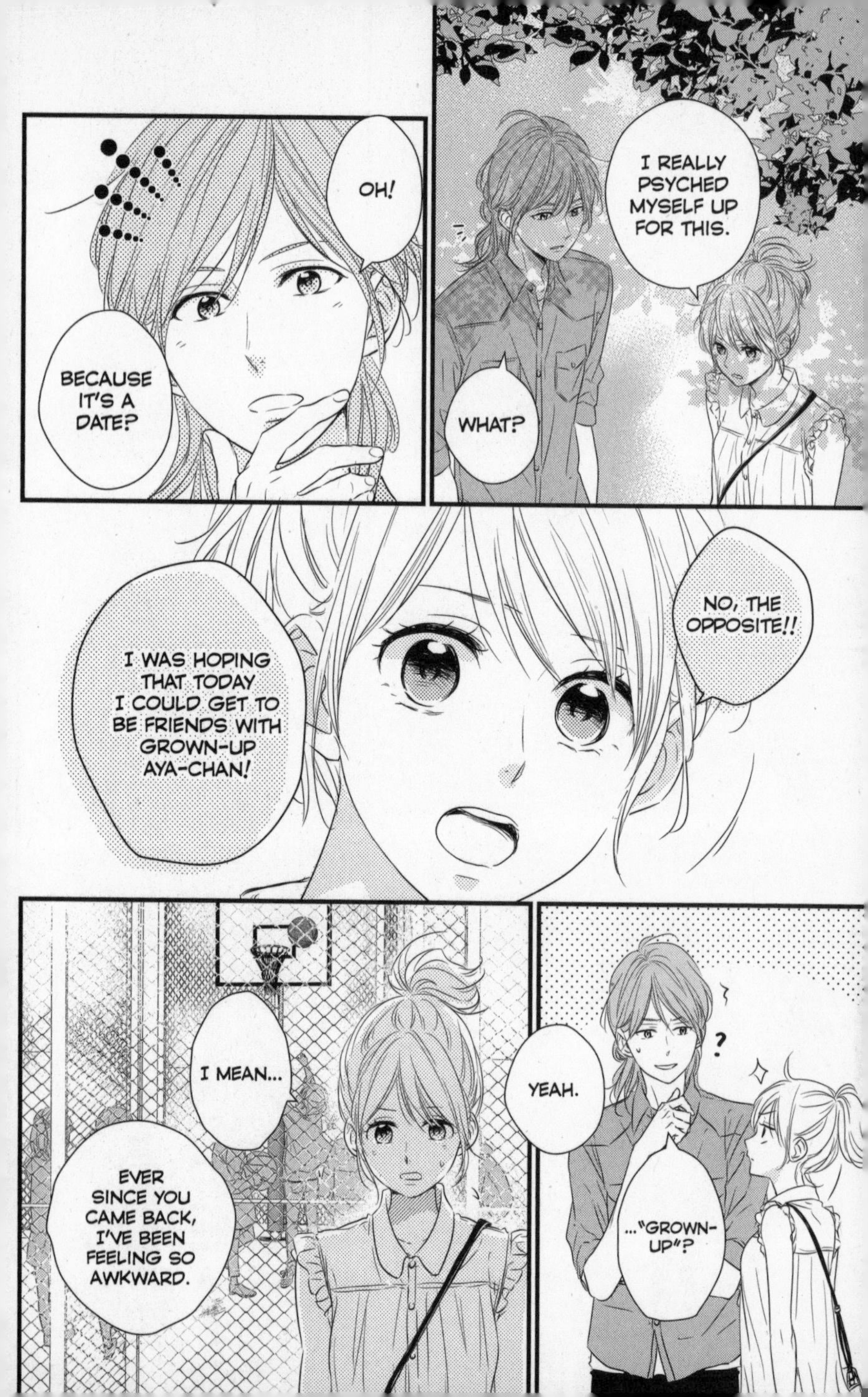

I REALLY PSYCHED MYSELF UP FOR THIS.
WHAT?
OH!
BECAUSE IT'S A DATE?
NO, THE OPPOSITE!!
I WAS HOPING THAT TODAY I COULD GET TO BE FRIENDS WITH GROWN-UP AYA-CHAN!
YEAH.
..."GROWN-UP"?
I MEAN...
EVER SINCE YOU CAME BACK, I'VE BEEN FEELING SO AWKWARD.

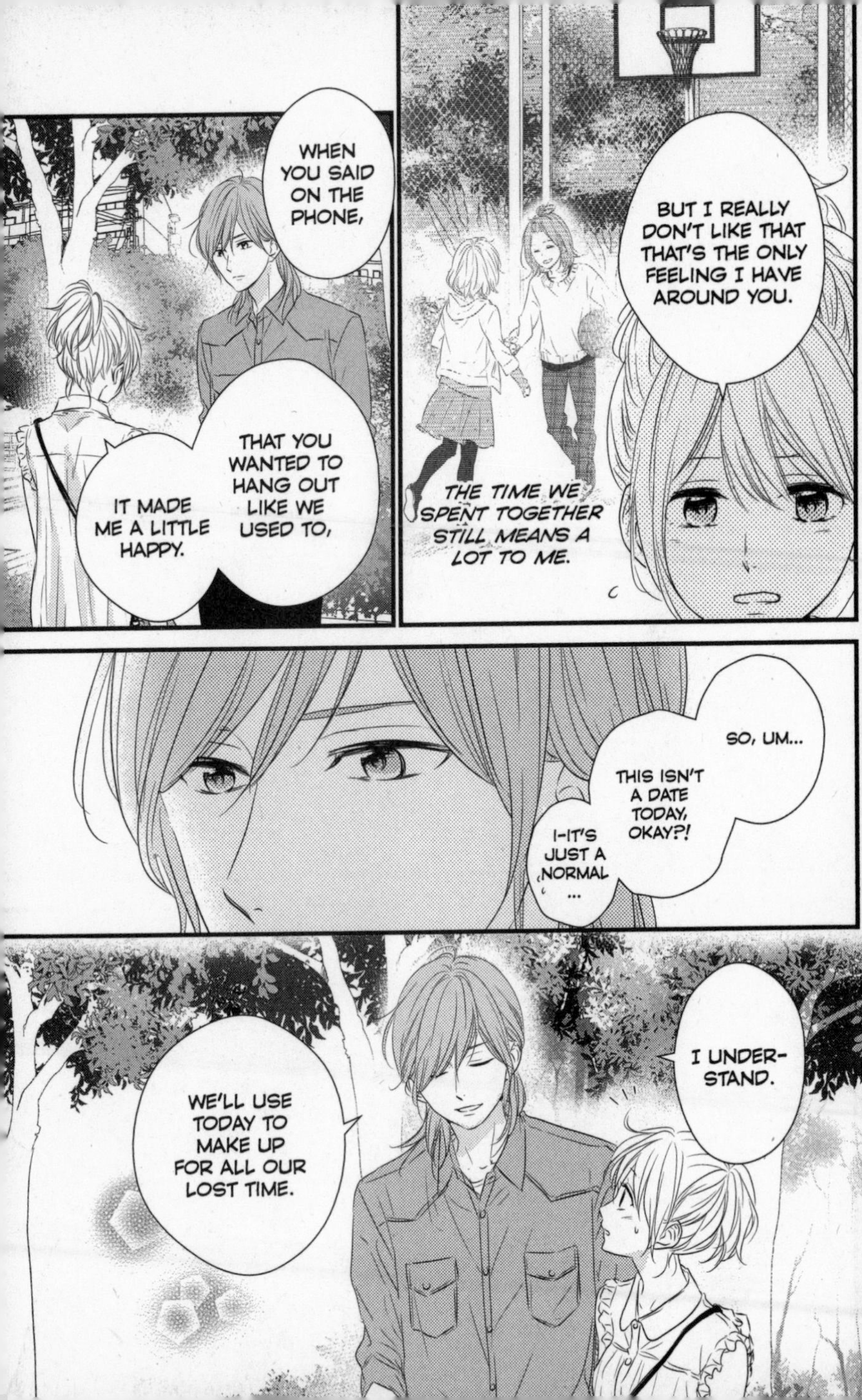
BUT I REALLY DON'T LIKE THAT THAT'S THE ONLY FEELING I HAVE AROUND YOU.
THE TIME WE SPENT TOGETHER STILL MEANS A LOT TO ME.
WHEN YOU SAID ON THE PHONE,
THAT YOU WANTED TO HANG OUT LIKE WE USED TO,
IT MADE ME A LITTLE HAPPY.
SO, UM...
THIS ISN'T A DATE TODAY, OKAY?!
I-IT'S JUST A NORMAL ...
I UNDER-STAND.
WE'LL USE TODAY TO MAKE UP FOR ALL OUR LOST TIME.

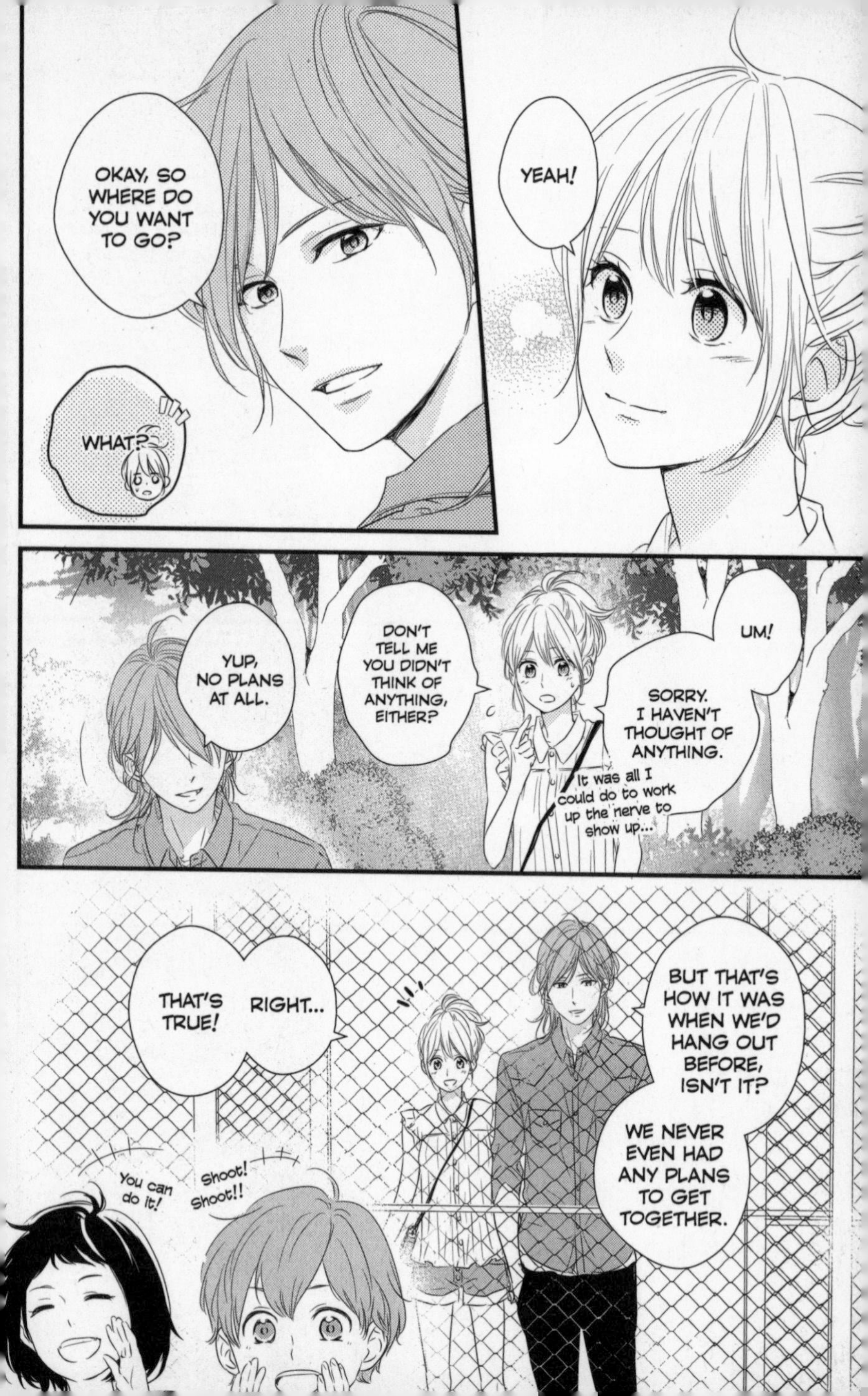
YEAH!
OKAY, SO WHERE DO YOU WANT TO GO?
WHAT?
UM!
SORRY. I HAVEN'T THOUGHT OF ANYTHING.
It was all I could do to work up the nerve to show up...
DON'T TELL ME YOU DIDN'T THINK OF ANYTHING, EITHER?
YUP, NO PLANS AT ALL.
BUT THAT'S HOW IT WAS WHEN WE'D HANG OUT BEFORE, ISN'T IT?
WE NEVER EVEN HAD ANY PLANS TO GET TOGETHER.
THAT'S TRUE! RIGHT...
Shoot! Shoot!!
You can do it!

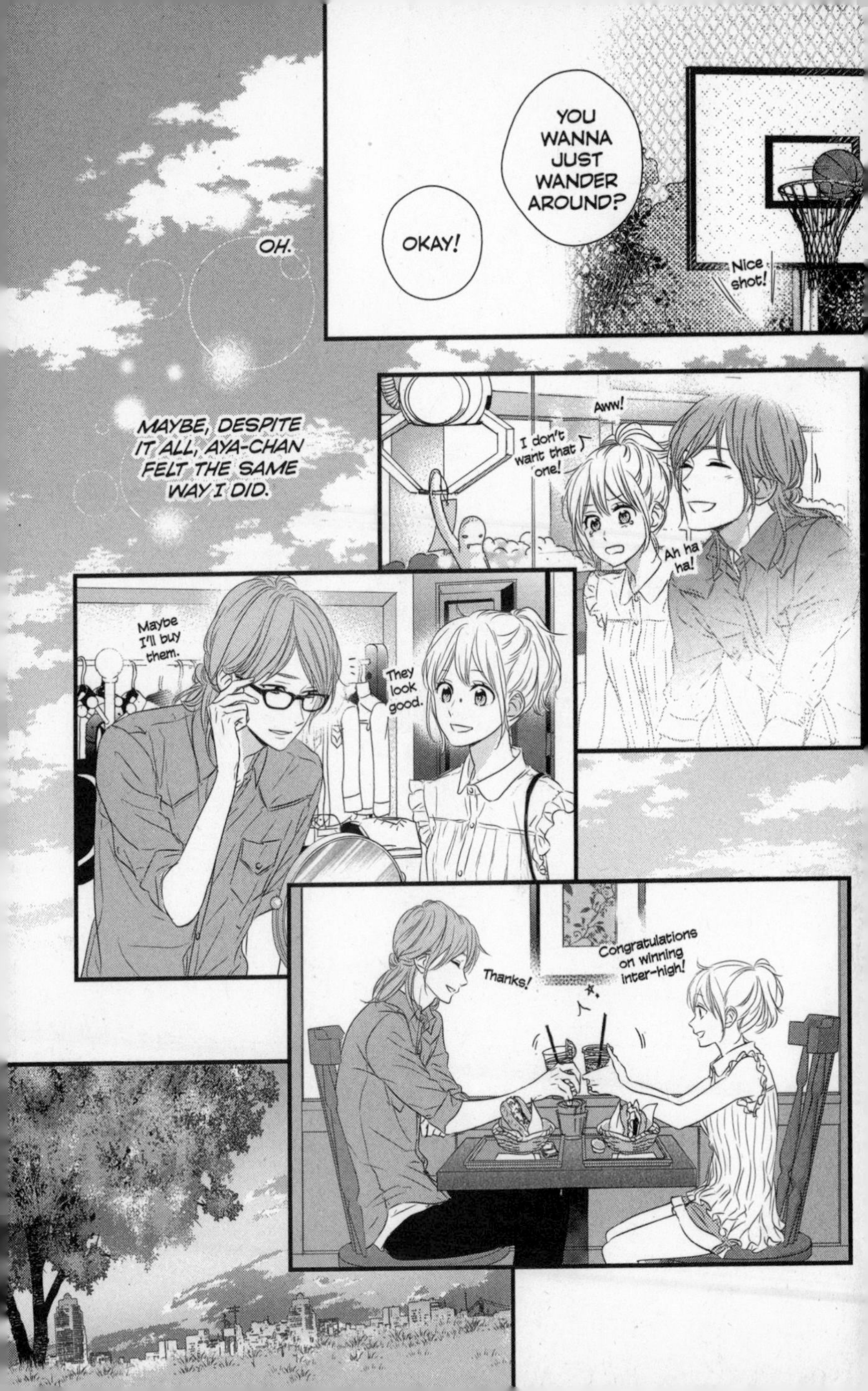
Nice shot!
YOU WANNA JUST WANDER AROUND?
OKAY!
OH.
MAYBE, DESPITE IT ALL, AYA-CHAN FELT THE SAME WAY I DID.
Aww!
I don't want that one! ♪
Ah ha ha!
They look good.
Maybe I'll buy them.
Congratulations on winning inter-high!
Thanks!

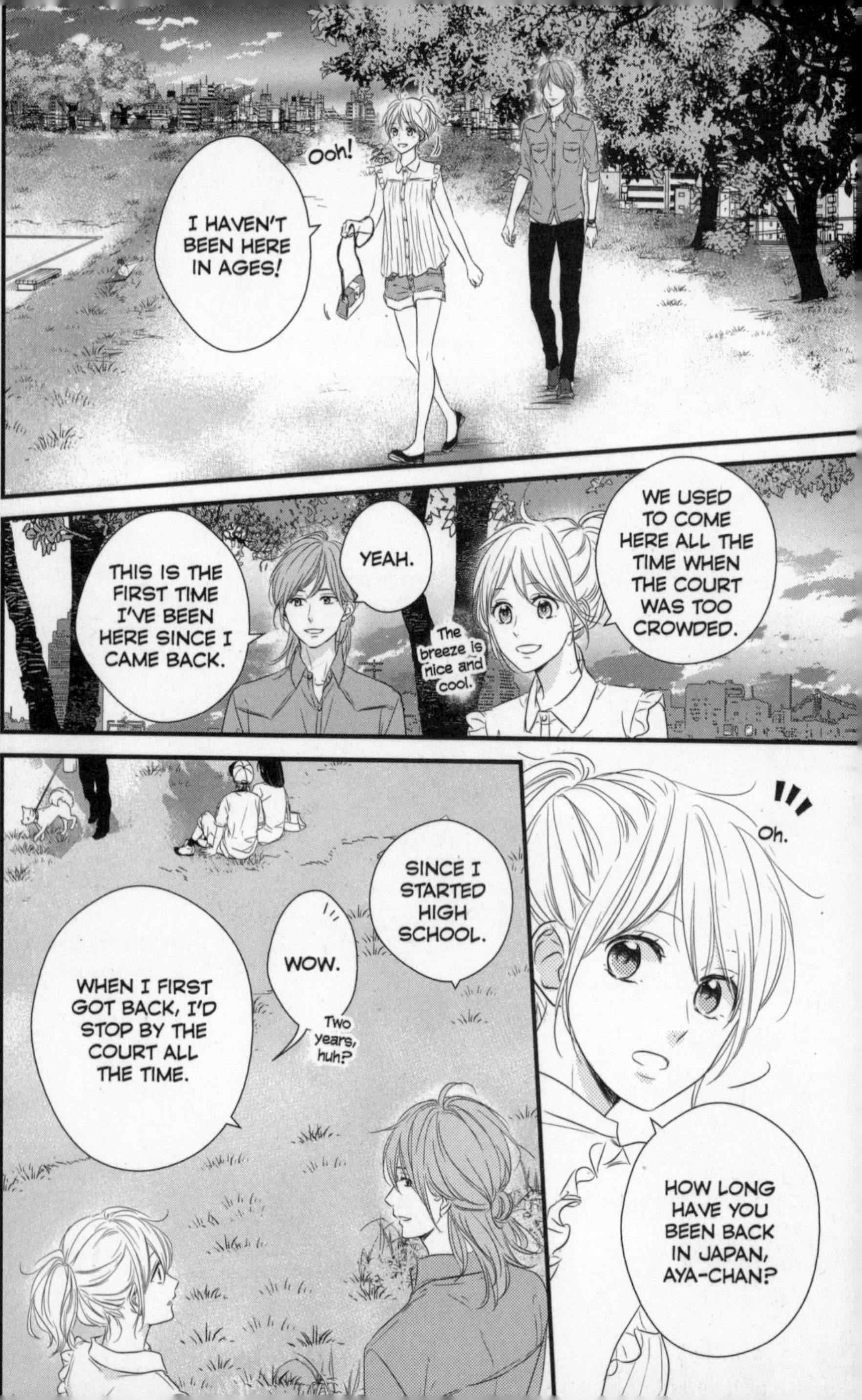
Ooh!
I HAVEN'T BEEN HERE IN AGES!
WE USED TO COME HERE ALL THE TIME WHEN THE COURT WAS TOO CROWDED.
The breeze is nice and cool.
YEAH.
THIS IS THE FIRST TIME I'VE BEEN HERE SINCE I CAME BACK.
Oh.
HOW LONG HAVE YOU BEEN BACK IN JAPAN, AYA-CHAN?
SINCE I STARTED HIGH SCHOOL.
WOW.
Two years, huh?
WHEN I FIRST GOT BACK, I'D STOP BY THE COURT ALL THE TIME.

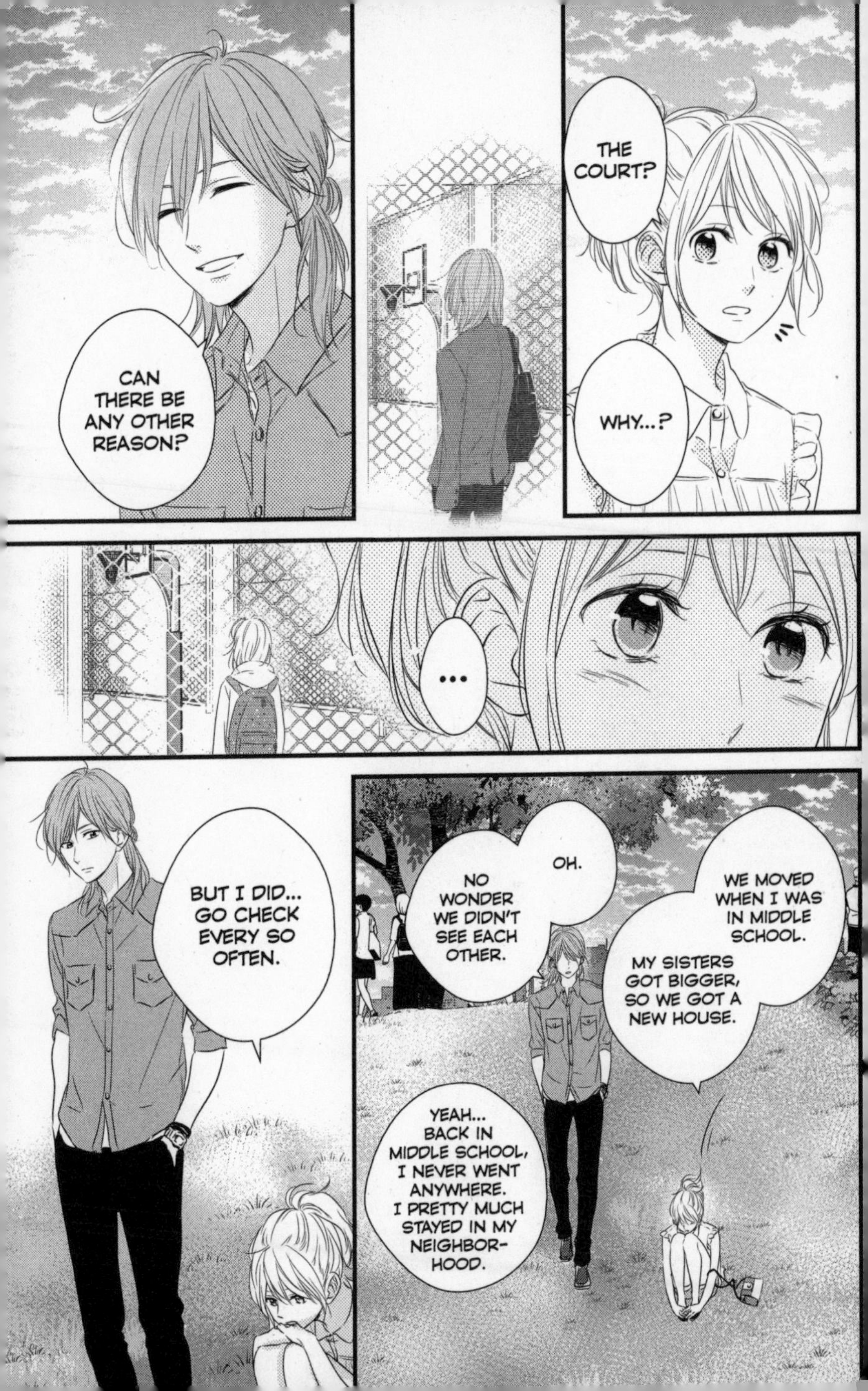
THE COURT?
WHY...?
CAN THERE BE ANY OTHER REASON?
...
WE MOVED WHEN I WAS IN MIDDLE SCHOOL.
MY SISTERS GOT BIGGER, SO WE GOT A NEW HOUSE.
OH.
NO WONDER WE DIDN'T SEE EACH OTHER.
YEAH... BACK IN MIDDLE SCHOOL, I NEVER WENT ANYWHERE. I PRETTY MUCH STAYED IN MY NEIGHBOR-HOOD.
BUT I DID... GO CHECK EVERY SO OFTEN.

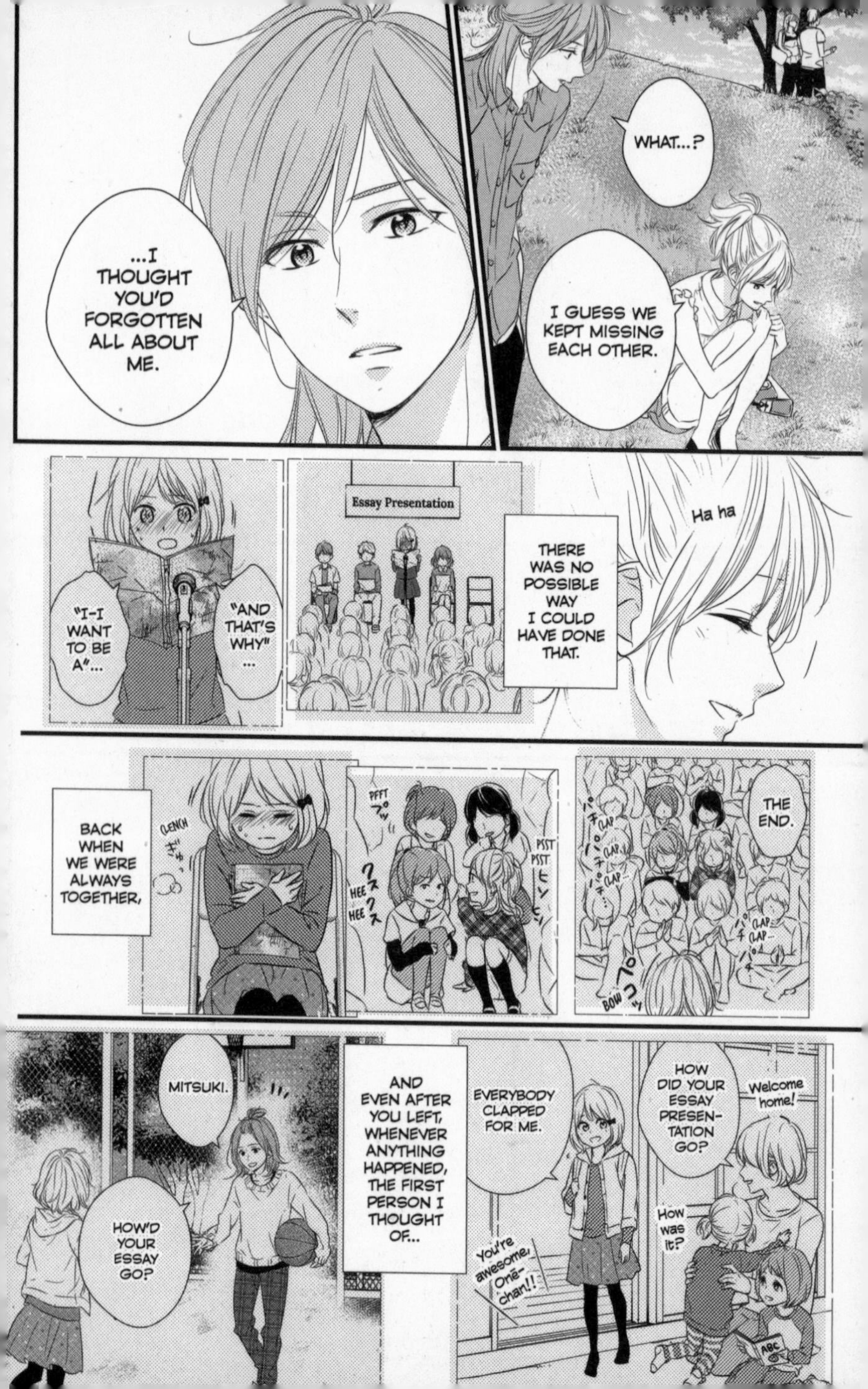
WHAT...?
I GUESS WE KEPT MISSING EACH OTHER.
...I THOUGHT YOU'D FORGOTTEN ALL ABOUT ME.
Ha ha
THERE WAS NO POSSIBLE WAY I COULD HAVE DONE THAT.
Essay Presentation
"AND THAT'S WHY"...
"I-I WANT TO BE A"...
THE END.
CLAP CLAP CLAP...
CLAP CLAP...
BOW
PSST PSST
PFFT
HEE HEE
CLENCH
BACK WHEN WE WERE ALWAYS TOGETHER,
Welcome home!
HOW DID YOUR ESSAY PRESENTATION GO?
How was it?
EVERYBODY CLAPPED FOR ME.
You're awesome, One-chan!!
AND EVEN AFTER YOU LEFT, WHENEVER ANYTHING HAPPENED, THE FIRST PERSON I THOUGHT OF...
MITSUKI.
HOW'D YOUR ESSAY GO?

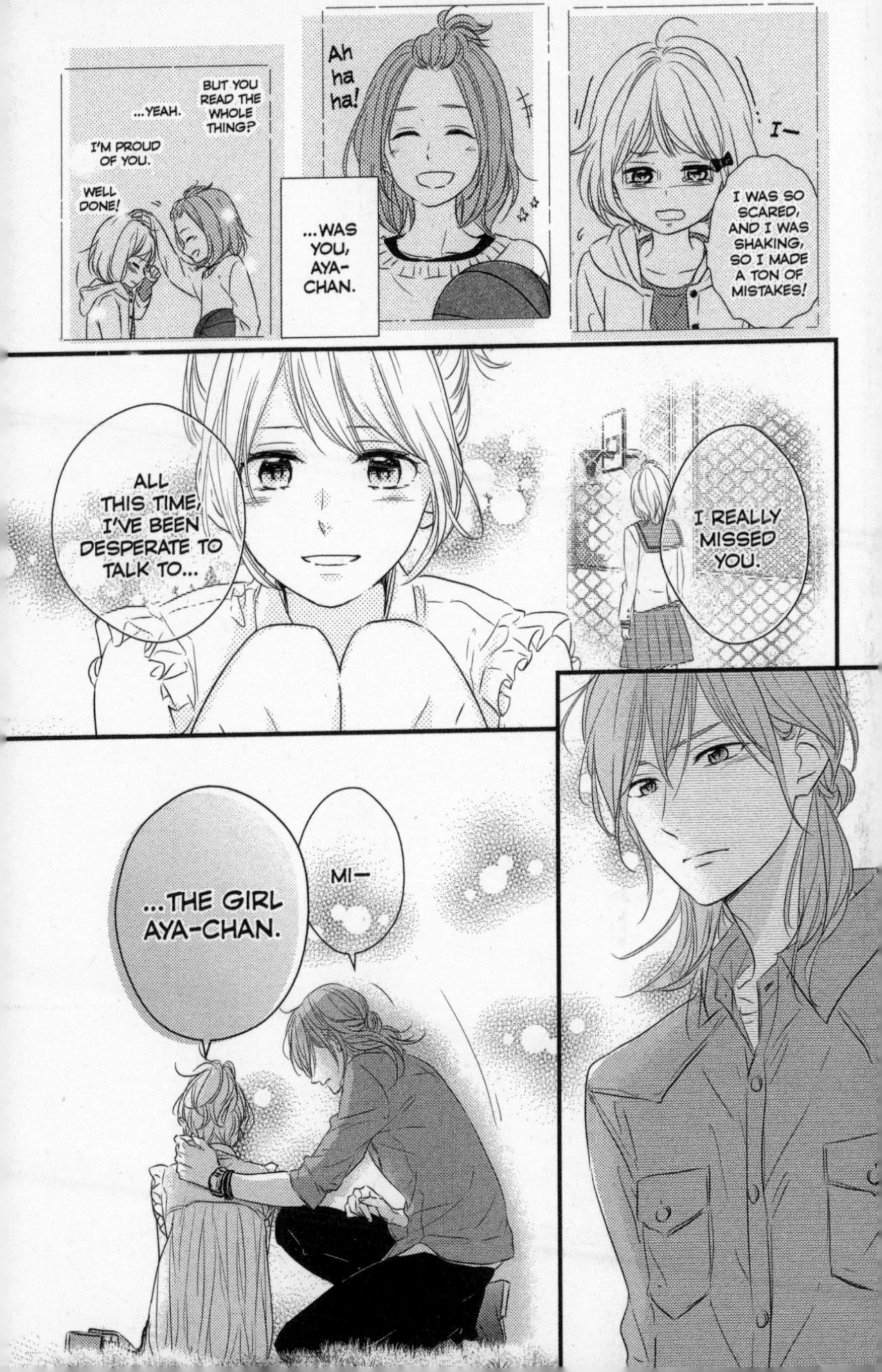
I—
I WAS SO SCARED, AND I WAS SHAKING, SO I MADE A TON OF MISTAKES!
Ah ha ha!
...WAS YOU, AYA-CHAN.
BUT YOU READ THE WHOLE THING?
...YEAH.
I'M PROUD OF YOU.
WELL DONE!
I REALLY MISSED YOU.
ALL THIS TIME, I'VE BEEN DESPERATE TO TALK TO...
MI—
...THE GIRL AYA-CHAN.

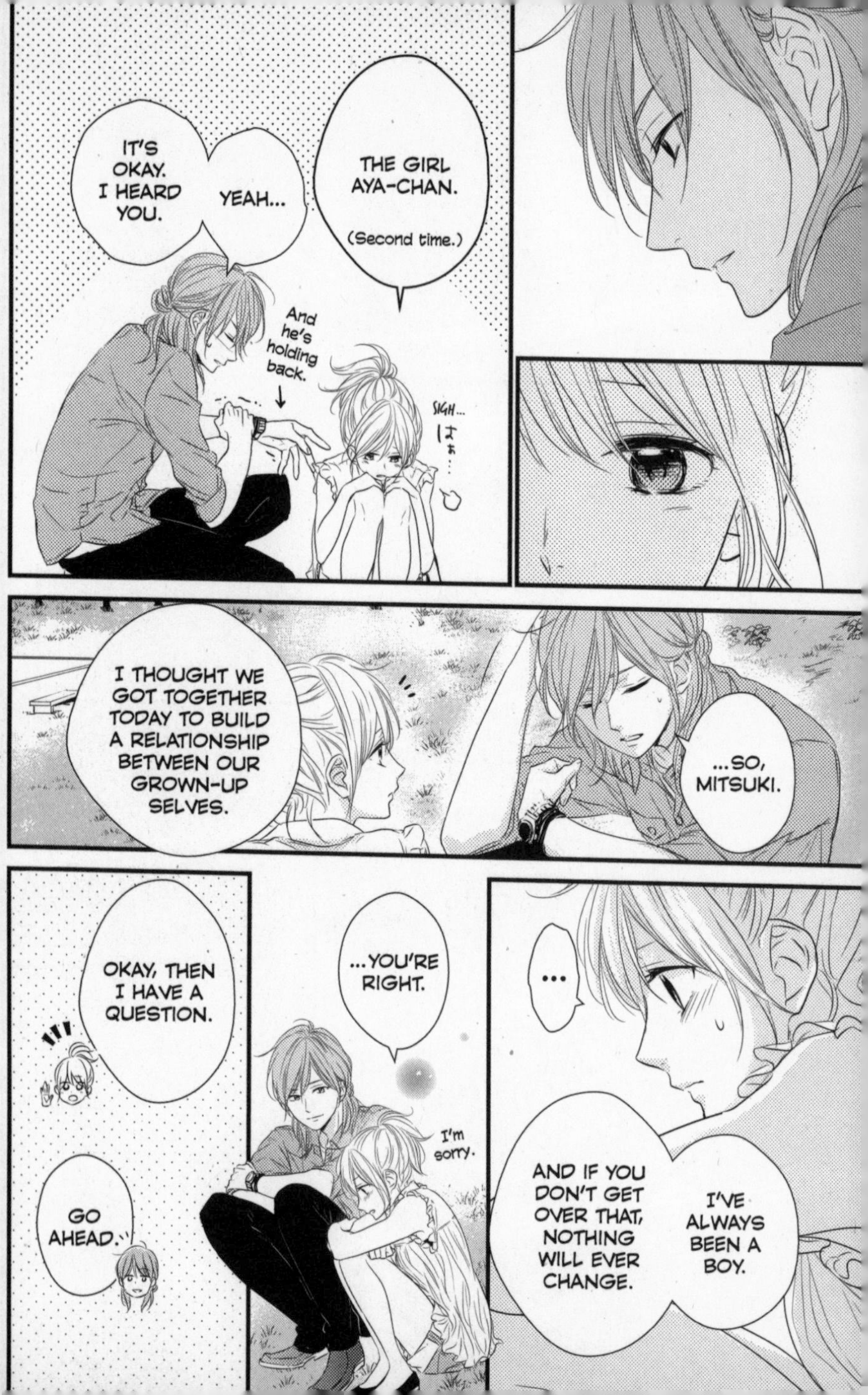
THE GIRL AYA-CHAN.
(Second time.)
YEAH...
IT'S OKAY. I HEARD YOU.
And he's holding back.
SIGH... はぁ…
...SO, MITSUKI.
I THOUGHT WE GOT TOGETHER TODAY TO BUILD A RELATIONSHIP BETWEEN OUR GROWN-UP SELVES.
...
I'VE ALWAYS BEEN A BOY.
AND IF YOU DON'T GET OVER THAT, NOTHING WILL EVER CHANGE.
...YOU'RE RIGHT.
I'm sorry.
OKAY, THEN I HAVE A QUESTION.
GO AHEAD.

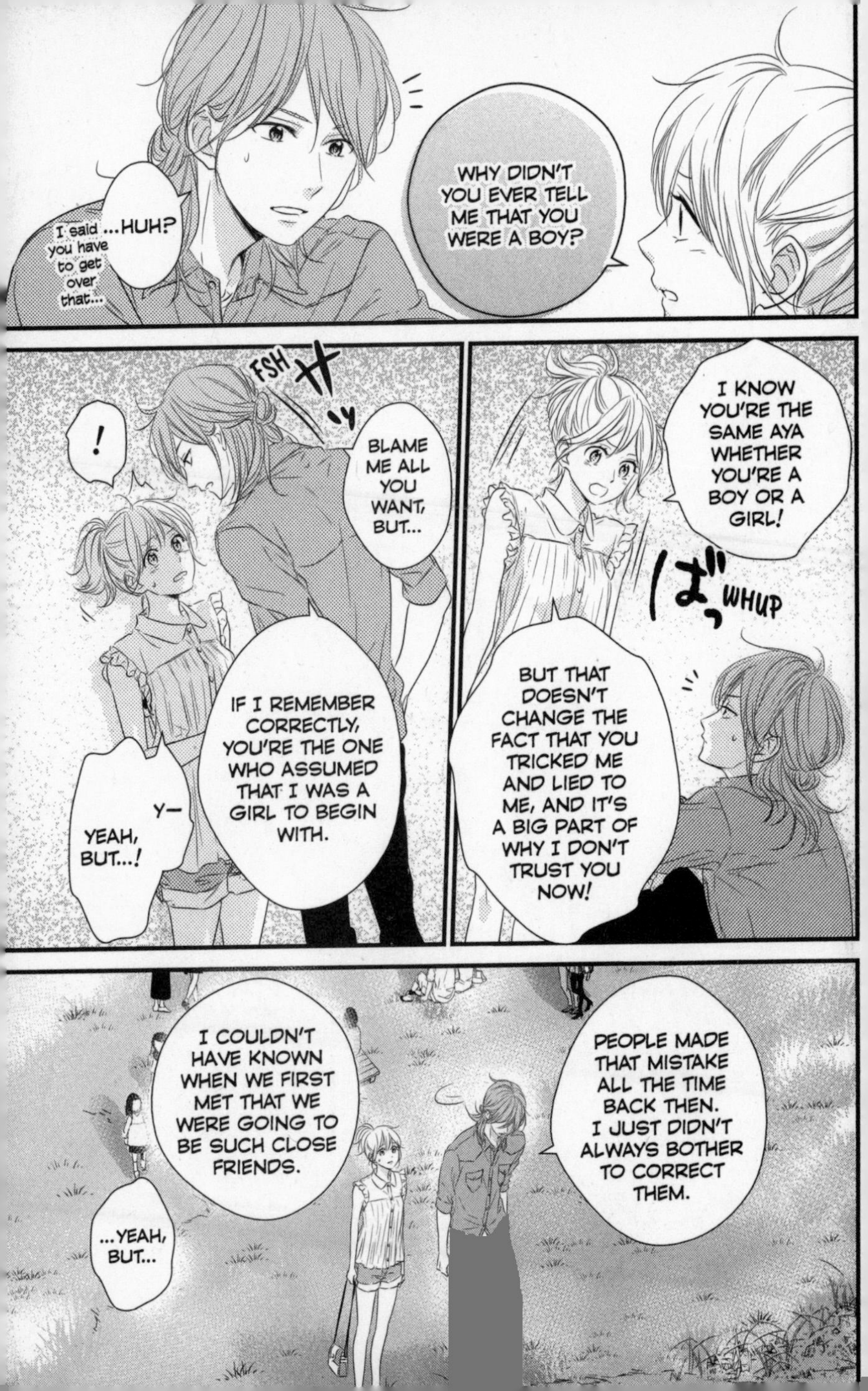
WHY DIDN'T YOU EVER TELL ME THAT YOU WERE A BOY?
...HUH?
I said you have to get over that...
I KNOW YOU'RE THE SAME AYA WHETHER YOU'RE A BOY OR A GIRL!
ばっ WHUP
BUT THAT DOESN'T CHANGE THE FACT THAT YOU TRICKED ME AND LIED TO ME, AND IT'S A BIG PART OF WHY I DON'T TRUST YOU NOW!
FSH
!
BLAME ME ALL YOU WANT, BUT...
IF I REMEMBER CORRECTLY, YOU'RE THE ONE WHO ASSUMED THAT I WAS A GIRL TO BEGIN WITH.
Y— YEAH, BUT...!
PEOPLE MADE THAT MISTAKE ALL THE TIME BACK THEN. I JUST DIDN'T ALWAYS BOTHER TO CORRECT THEM.
I COULDN'T HAVE KNOWN WHEN WE FIRST MET THAT WE WERE GOING TO BE SUCH CLOSE FRIENDS.
...YEAH, BUT...

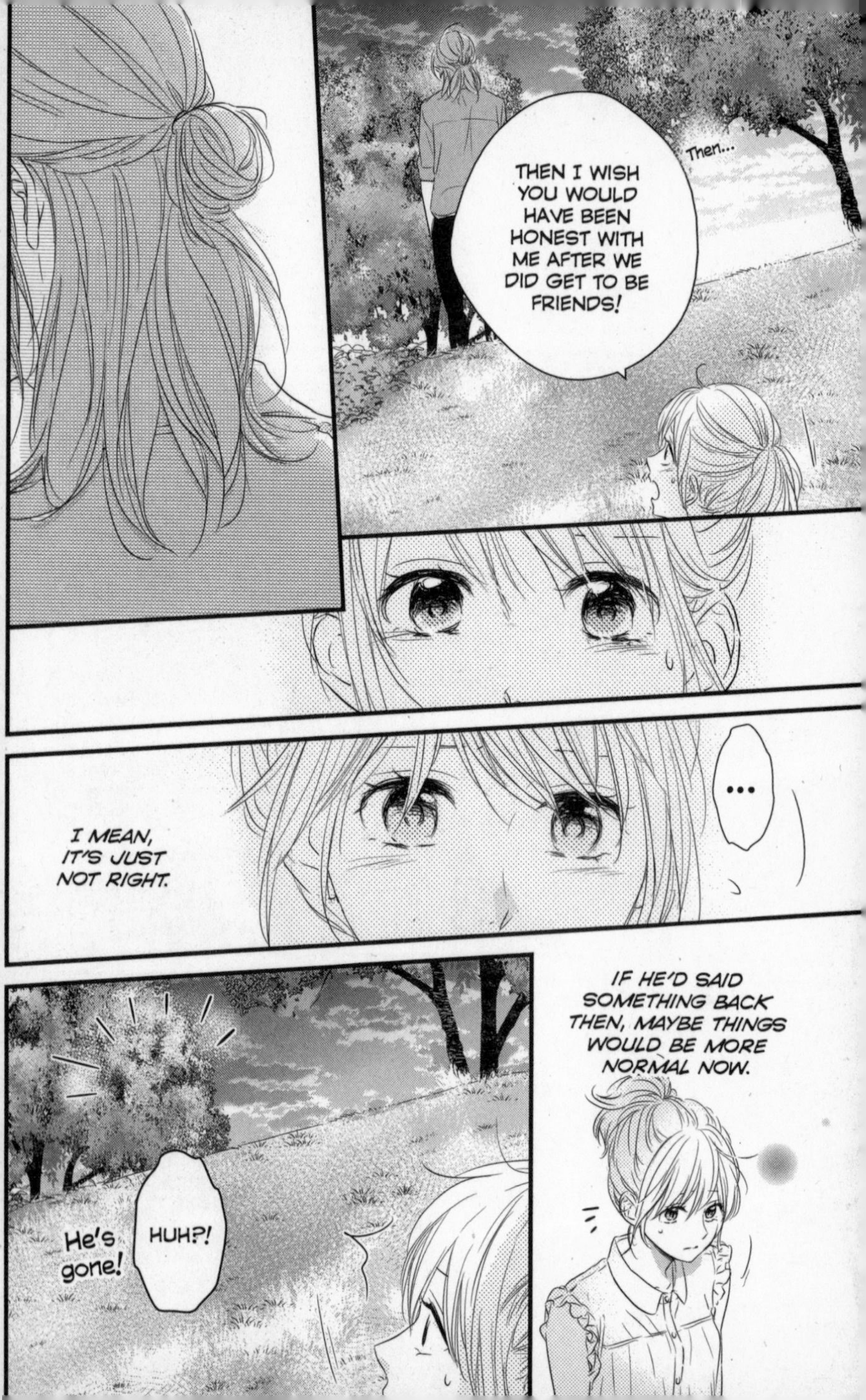
Then...
THEN I WISH YOU WOULD HAVE BEEN HONEST WITH ME AFTER WE DID GET TO BE FRIENDS!
...
I MEAN, IT'S JUST NOT RIGHT.
IF HE'D SAID SOMETHING BACK THEN, MAYBE THINGS WOULD BE MORE NORMAL NOW.
HUH?!
He's gone!

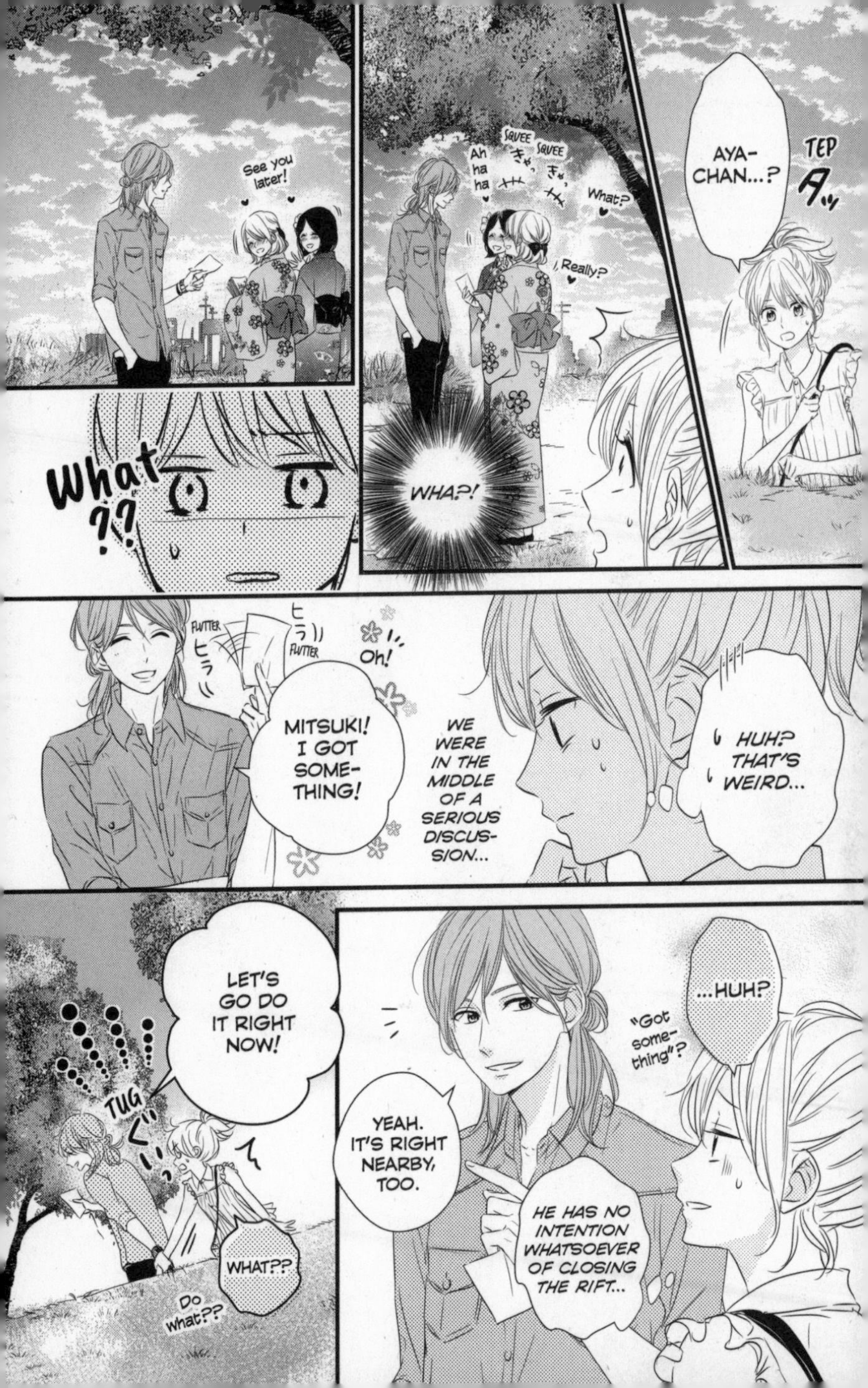

TEP
AYA-CHAN...?
Squee
Squee
What?
Ah ha ha
Really?
WHA?!
See you later!
What ??
HUH? THAT'S WEIRD...
Oh!
WE WERE IN THE MIDDLE OF A SERIOUS DISCUSSION...
FLUTTER
FLUTTER
MITSUKI! I GOT SOMETHING!
...HUH?
"Got something"?
YEAH. IT'S RIGHT NEARBY, TOO.
HE HAS NO INTENTION WHATSOEVER OF CLOSING THE RIFT...
LET'S GO DO IT RIGHT NOW!
TUG
WHAT??
Do what??

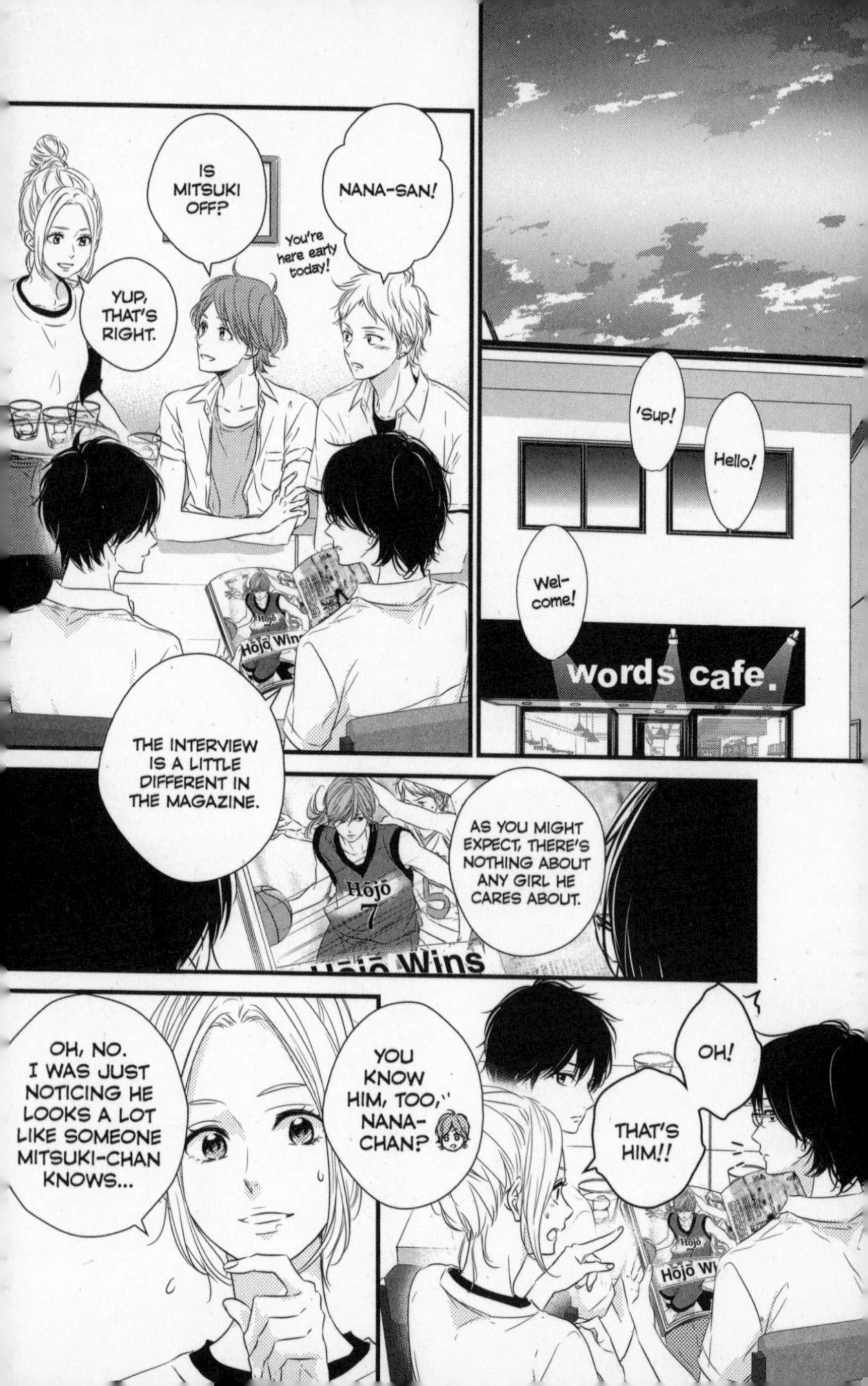
'Sup!
Hello!
Wel-come!
words cafe.
NANA-SAN!
You're here early today!
IS MITSUKI OFF?
YUP, THAT'S RIGHT.
Hōjō Wins
THE INTERVIEW IS A LITTLE DIFFERENT IN THE MAGAZINE.
AS YOU MIGHT EXPECT, THERE'S NOTHING ABOUT ANY GIRL HE CARES ABOUT.
Hōjō 7
OH!
THAT'S HIM!!
YOU KNOW HIM, TOO, NANA-CHAN?
OH, NO. I WAS JUST NOTICING HE LOOKS A LOT LIKE SOMEONE MITSUKI-CHAN KNOWS...

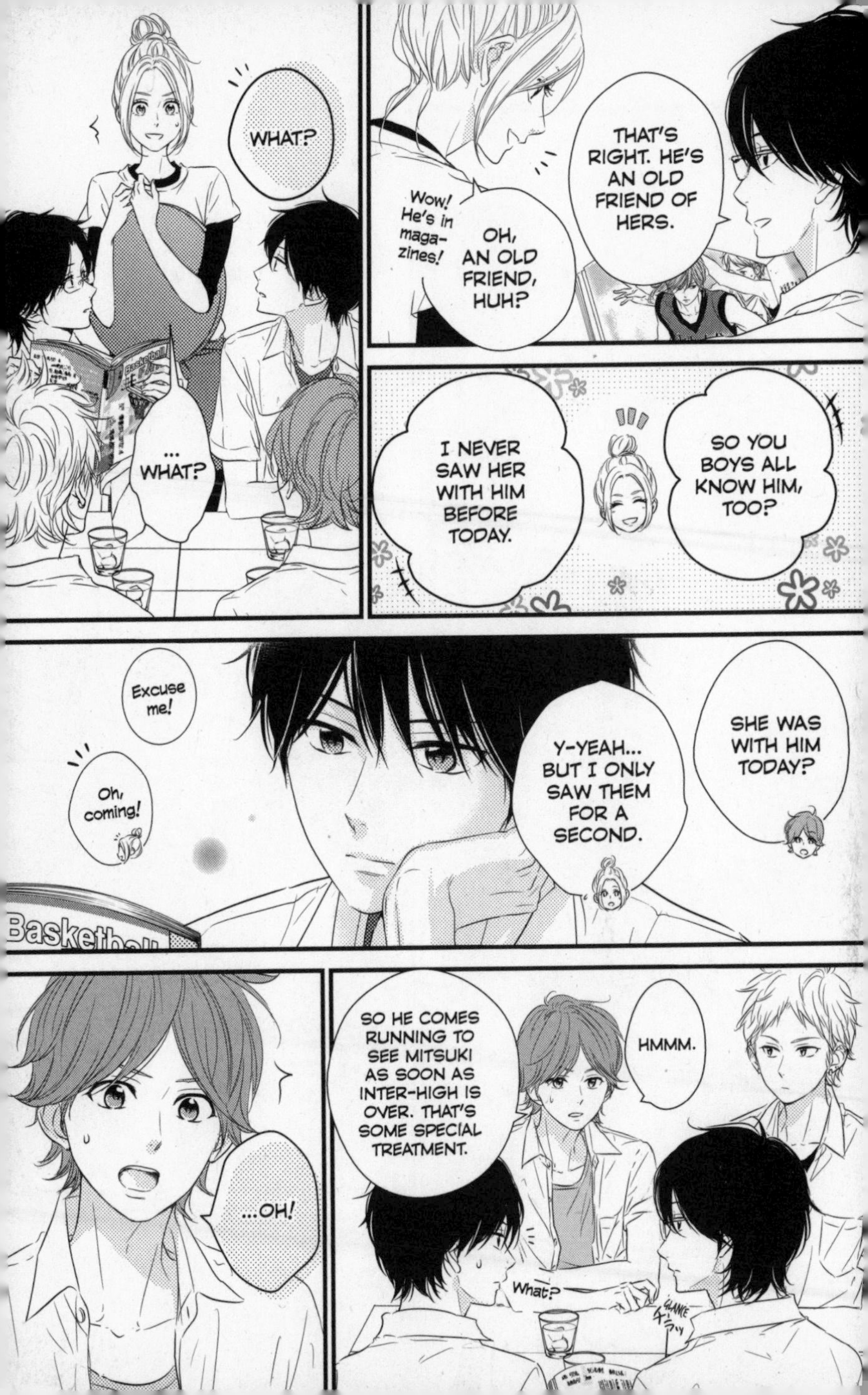
THAT'S RIGHT. HE'S AN OLD FRIEND OF HERS.
OH, AN OLD FRIEND, HUH?
Wow! He's in magazines!
SO YOU BOYS ALL KNOW HIM, TOO?
I NEVER SAW HER WITH HIM BEFORE TODAY.
WHAT?
... WHAT?
SHE WAS WITH HIM TODAY?
Y-YEAH... BUT I ONLY SAW THEM FOR A SECOND.
Excuse me!
Oh, coming!
HMMM.
SO HE COMES RUNNING TO SEE MITSUKI AS SOON AS INTER-HIGH IS OVER. THAT'S SOME SPECIAL TREATMENT.
What?
GLANCE
...OH!

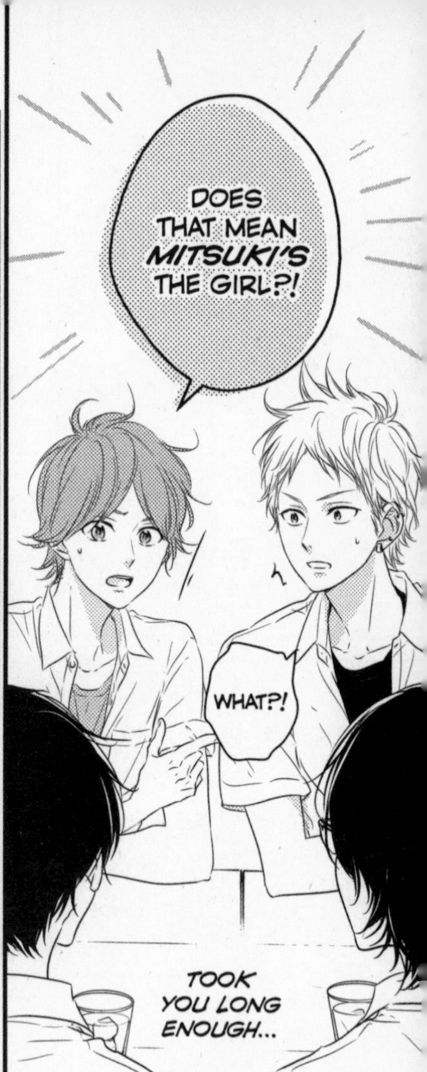
DOES THAT MEAN *MITSUKI'S* THE GIRL?!
WHAT?!
TOOK YOU LONG ENOUGH...
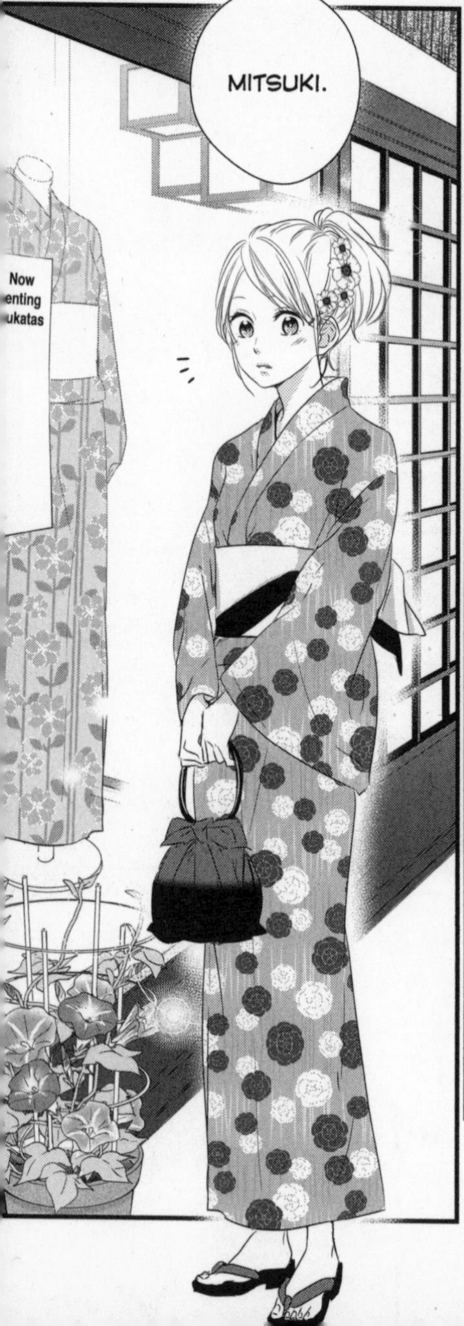
MITSUKI.
Now
enting
ukatas

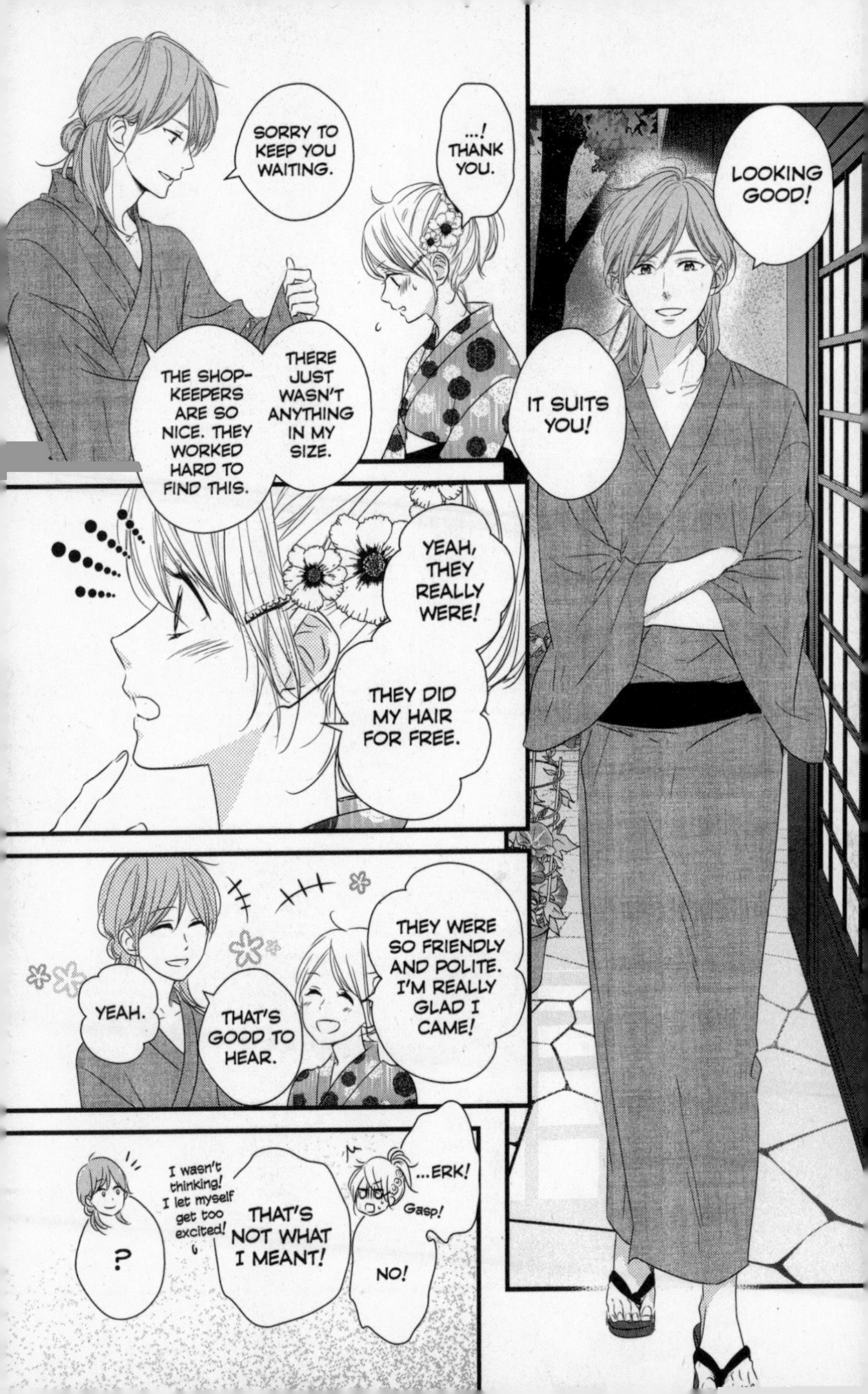
LOOKING GOOD!
IT SUITS YOU!
...! THANK YOU.
SORRY TO KEEP YOU WAITING.
THERE JUST WASN'T ANYTHING IN MY SIZE.
THE SHOP-KEEPERS ARE SO NICE. THEY WORKED HARD TO FIND THIS.
YEAH, THEY REALLY WERE!
THEY DID MY HAIR FOR FREE.
THEY WERE SO FRIENDLY AND POLITE. I'M REALLY GLAD I CAME!
THAT'S GOOD TO HEAR.
YEAH.
...ERK!
Gasp!
NO!
THAT'S NOT WHAT I MEANT!
I wasn't thinking! I let myself get too excited!
?

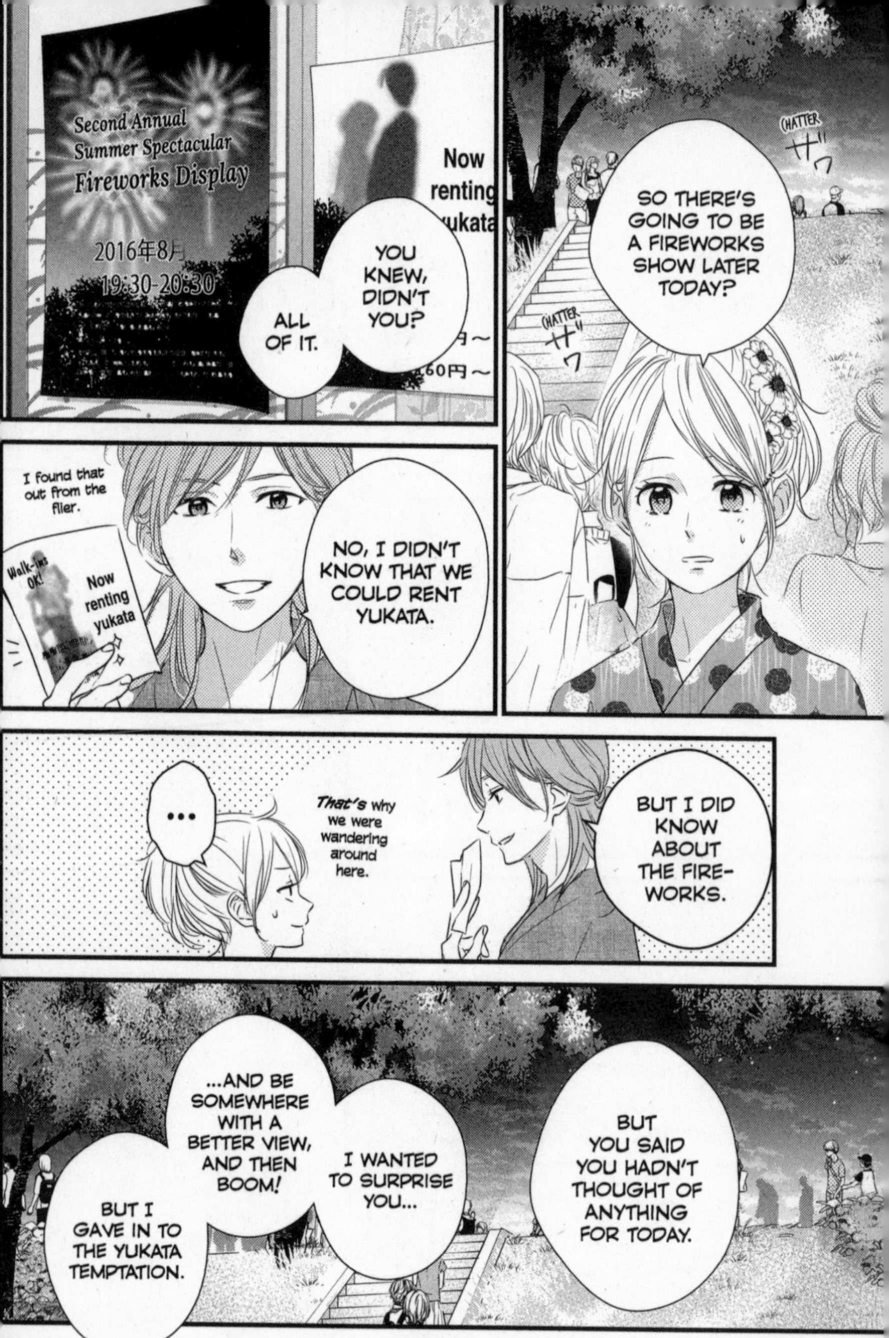
CHATTER ザワ
SO THERE'S GOING TO BE A FIREWORKS SHOW LATER TODAY?
CHATTER ザワ
Second Annual Summer Spectacular Fireworks Display
2016年8月
19:30-20:30
Now renting
ukata
YOU KNEW, DIDN'T YOU?
ALL OF IT.
NO, I DIDN'T KNOW THAT WE COULD RENT YUKATA.
I found that out from the flier.
Walk-ins OK!
Now renting yukata
BUT I DID KNOW ABOUT THE FIRE-WORKS.
That's why we were wandering around here.
...
BUT YOU SAID YOU HADN'T THOUGHT OF ANYTHING FOR TODAY.
I WANTED TO SURPRISE YOU...
...AND BE SOMEWHERE WITH A BETTER VIEW, AND THEN BOOM!
BUT I GAVE IN TO THE YUKATA TEMPTATION.

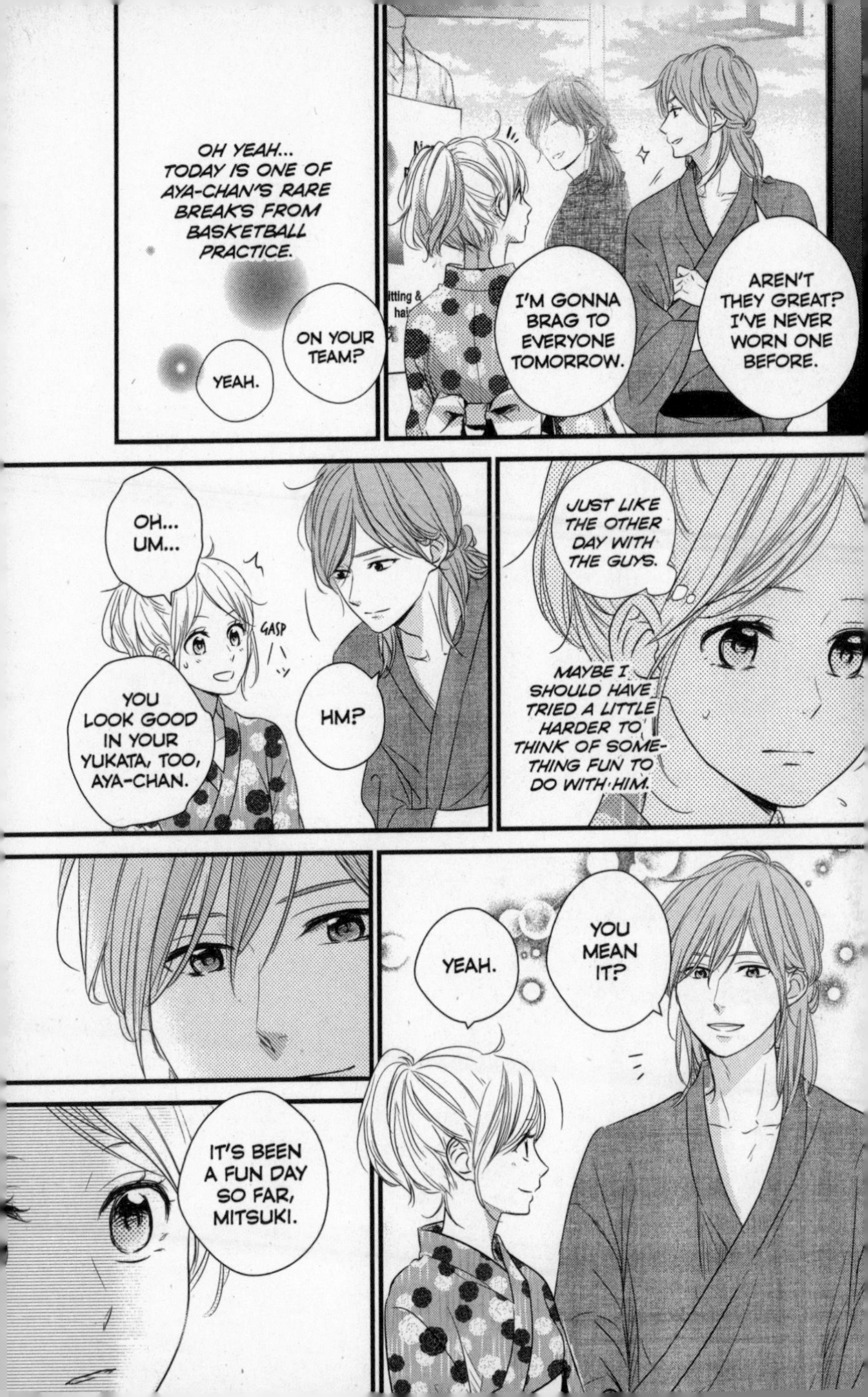
AREN'T THEY GREAT? I'VE NEVER WORN ONE BEFORE.
I'M GONNA BRAG TO EVERYONE TOMORROW.
OH YEAH... TODAY IS ONE OF AYA-CHAN'S RARE BREAKS FROM BASKETBALL PRACTICE.
ON YOUR TEAM?
YEAH.
JUST LIKE THE OTHER DAY WITH THE GUYS.
MAYBE I SHOULD HAVE TRIED A LITTLE HARDER TO THINK OF SOME-THING FUN TO DO WITH HIM.
OH... UM...
GASP
HM?
YOU LOOK GOOD IN YOUR YUKATA, TOO, AYA-CHAN.
IT'S BEEN A FUN DAY SO FAR, MITSUKI.
YOU MEAN IT?
YEAH.

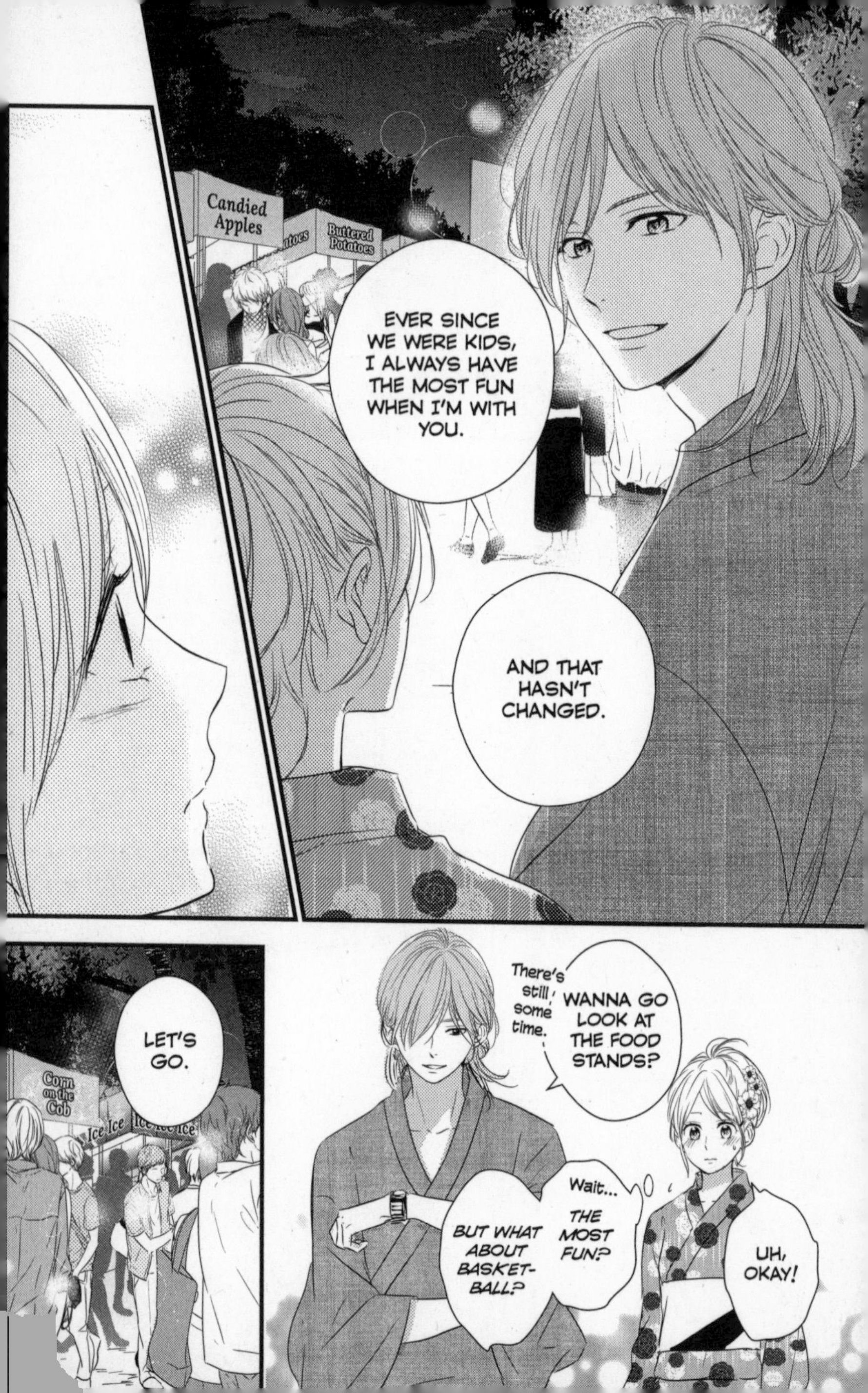
Candied Apples
Buttered Potatoes
EVER SINCE WE WERE KIDS, I ALWAYS HAVE THE MOST FUN WHEN I'M WITH YOU.
AND THAT HASN'T CHANGED.
WANNA GO LOOK AT THE FOOD STANDS?
There's still some time.
UH, OKAY!
Wait... THE MOST FUN?
BUT WHAT ABOUT BASKET-BALL?
LET'S GO.
Corn on the Cob
Ice Ice

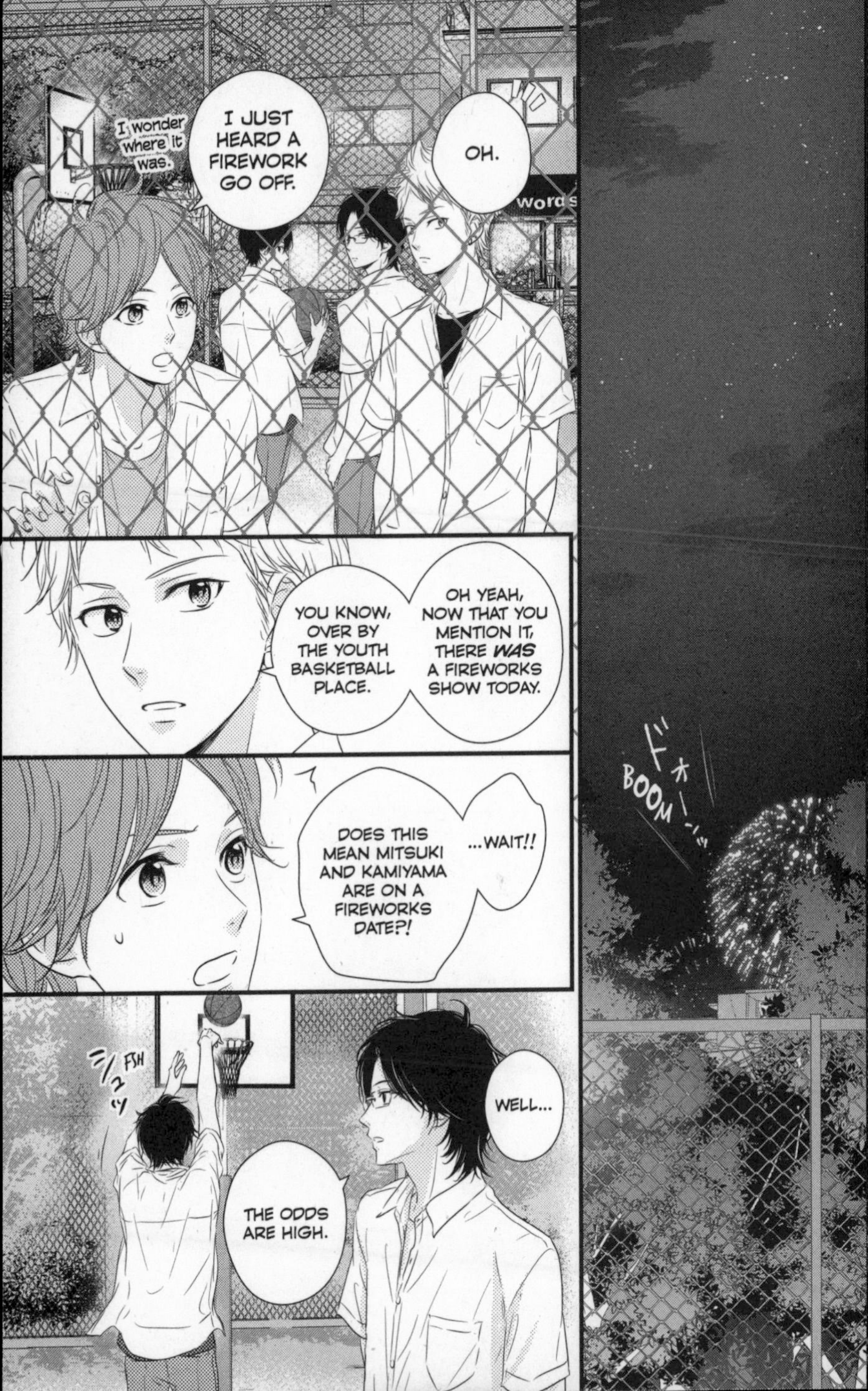
BOOM
OH.
I JUST HEARD A FIREWORK GO OFF.
I wonder where it was.
OH YEAH, NOW THAT YOU MENTION IT, THERE *WAS* A FIREWORKS SHOW TODAY.
YOU KNOW, OVER BY THE YOUTH BASKETBALL PLACE.
...WAIT!!
DOES THIS MEAN MITSUKI AND KAMIYAMA ARE ON A FIREWORKS DATE?!
FSH
WELL...
THE ODDS ARE HIGH.

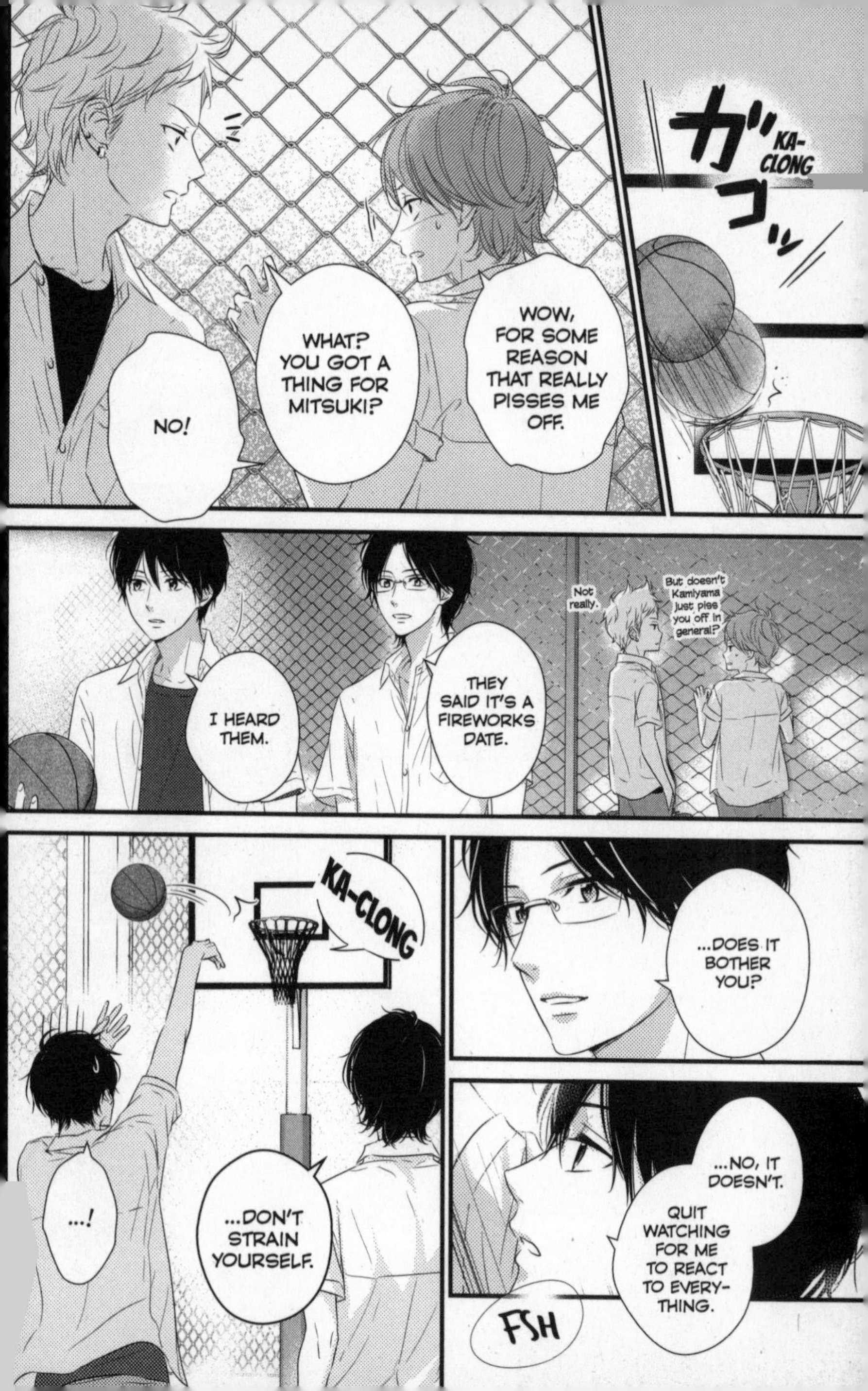
ガゴッ
KA-CLONG
WOW, FOR SOME REASON THAT REALLY PISSES ME OFF.
WHAT? YOU GOT A THING FOR MITSUKI?
NO!
But doesn't Kamiyama just piss you off in general?
Not really.
THEY SAID IT'S A FIREWORKS DATE.
I HEARD THEM.
...DOES IT BOTHER YOU?
...NO, IT DOESN'T.
QUIT WATCHING FOR ME TO REACT TO EVERY-THING.
FSH
KA-CLONG
...DON'T STRAIN YOURSELF.
...!

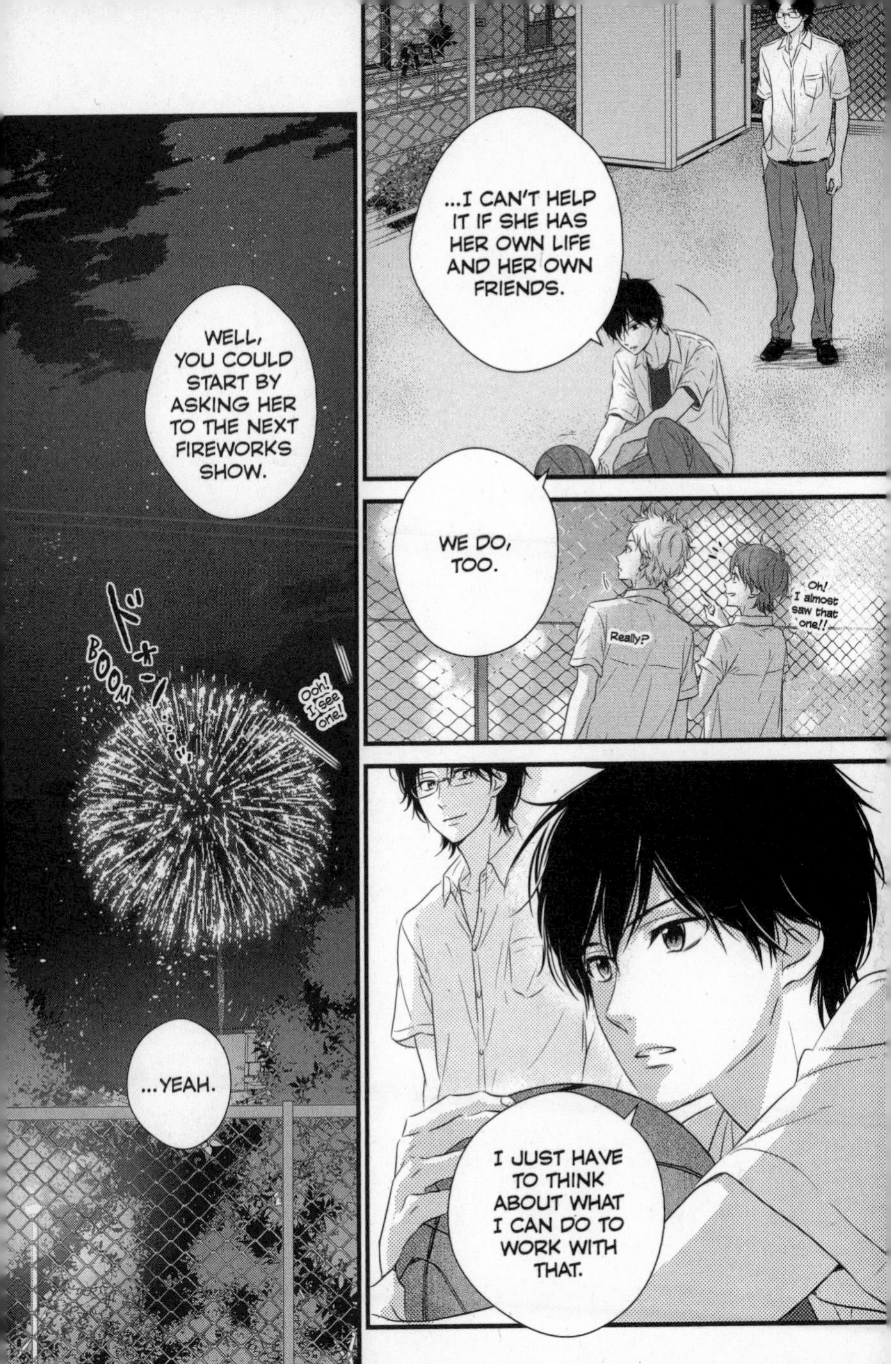
...I CAN'T HELP IT IF SHE HAS HER OWN LIFE AND HER OWN FRIENDS.
WE DO, TOO.
Oh! I almost saw that one!!
Really?
I JUST HAVE TO THINK ABOUT WHAT I CAN DO TO WORK WITH THAT.
WELL, YOU COULD START BY ASKING HER TO THE NEXT FIREWORKS SHOW.
BOOM
Ooh! I see one!
...YEAH.

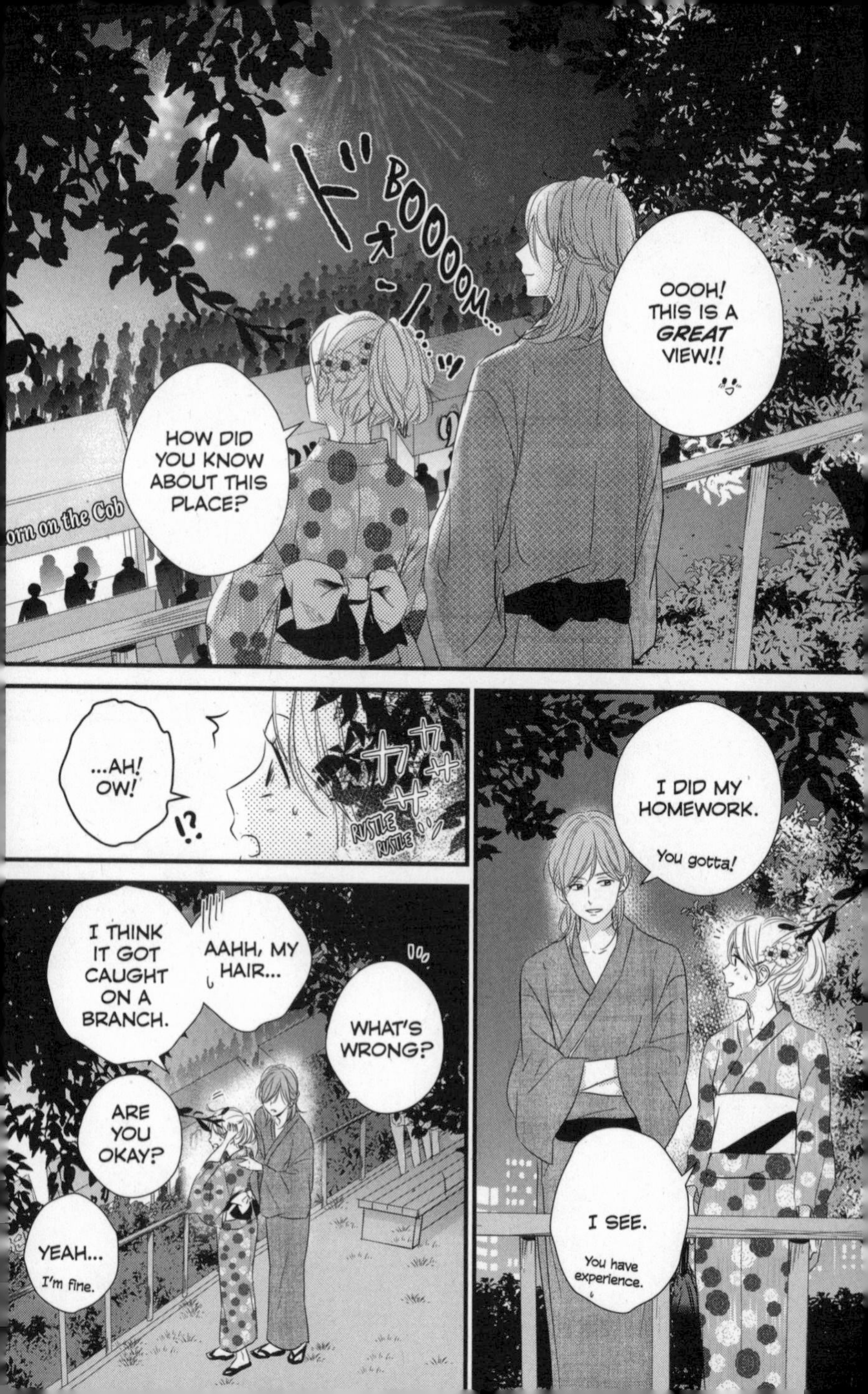
BOOOOM...
OOOH! THIS IS A GREAT VIEW!!
HOW DID YOU KNOW ABOUT THIS PLACE?
orn on the Cob
I DID MY HOMEWORK.
You gotta!
I SEE.
You have experience.
...AH! OW!
!?
RUSTLE RUSTLE
WHAT'S WRONG?
AAHH, MY HAIR...
I THINK IT GOT CAUGHT ON A BRANCH.
ARE YOU OKAY?
YEAH...
I'm fine.

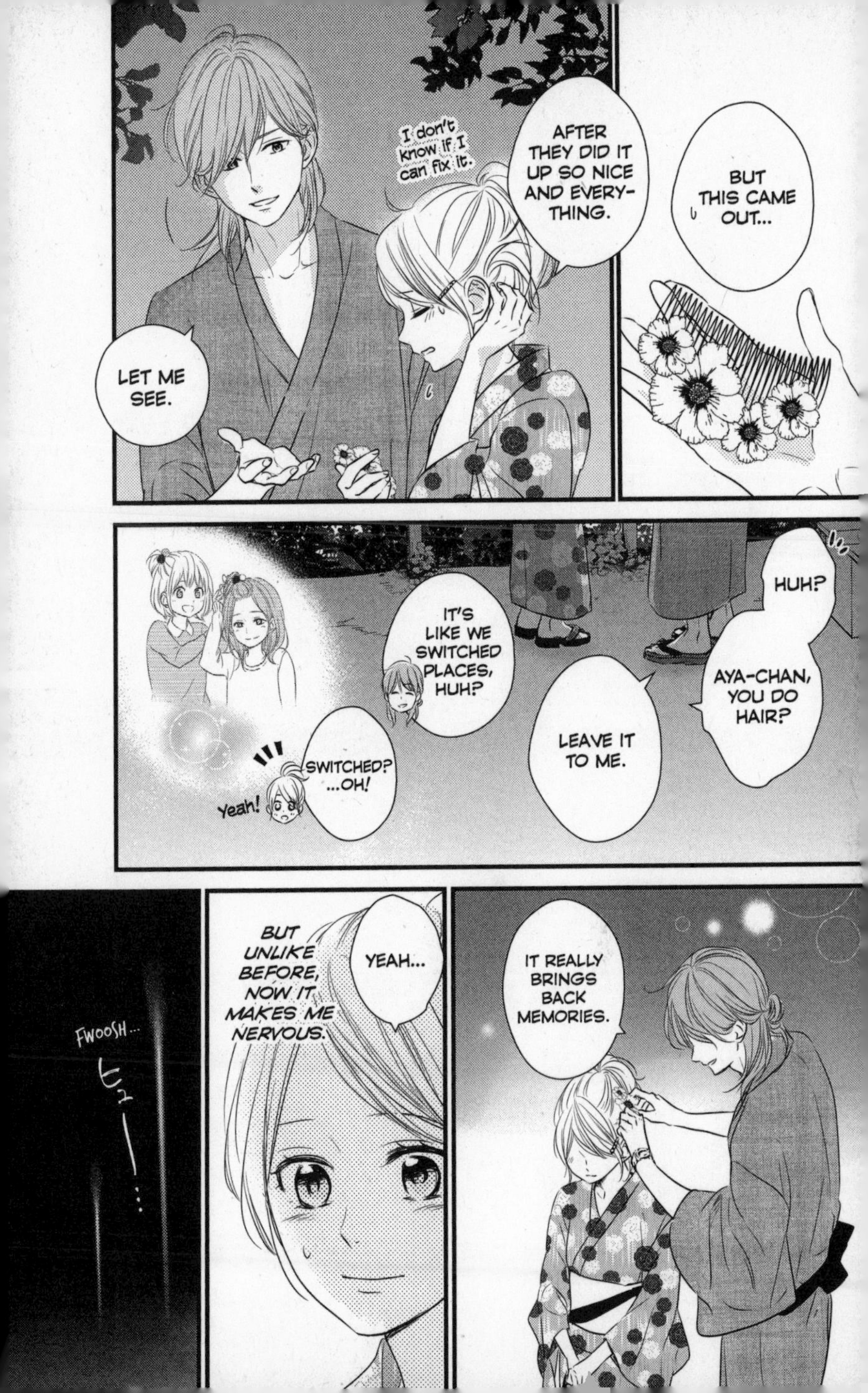
BUT THIS CAME OUT...
AFTER THEY DID IT UP SO NICE AND EVERYTHING.
I don't know if I can fix it.
LET ME SEE.
HUH?
AYA-CHAN, YOU DO HAIR?
LEAVE IT TO ME.
IT'S LIKE WE SWITCHED PLACES, HUH?
SWITCHED? ...OH!
Yeah!
IT REALLY BRINGS BACK MEMORIES.
YEAH...
BUT UNLIKE BEFORE, NOW IT MAKES ME NERVOUS.
FWOOSH...
ヒュー…

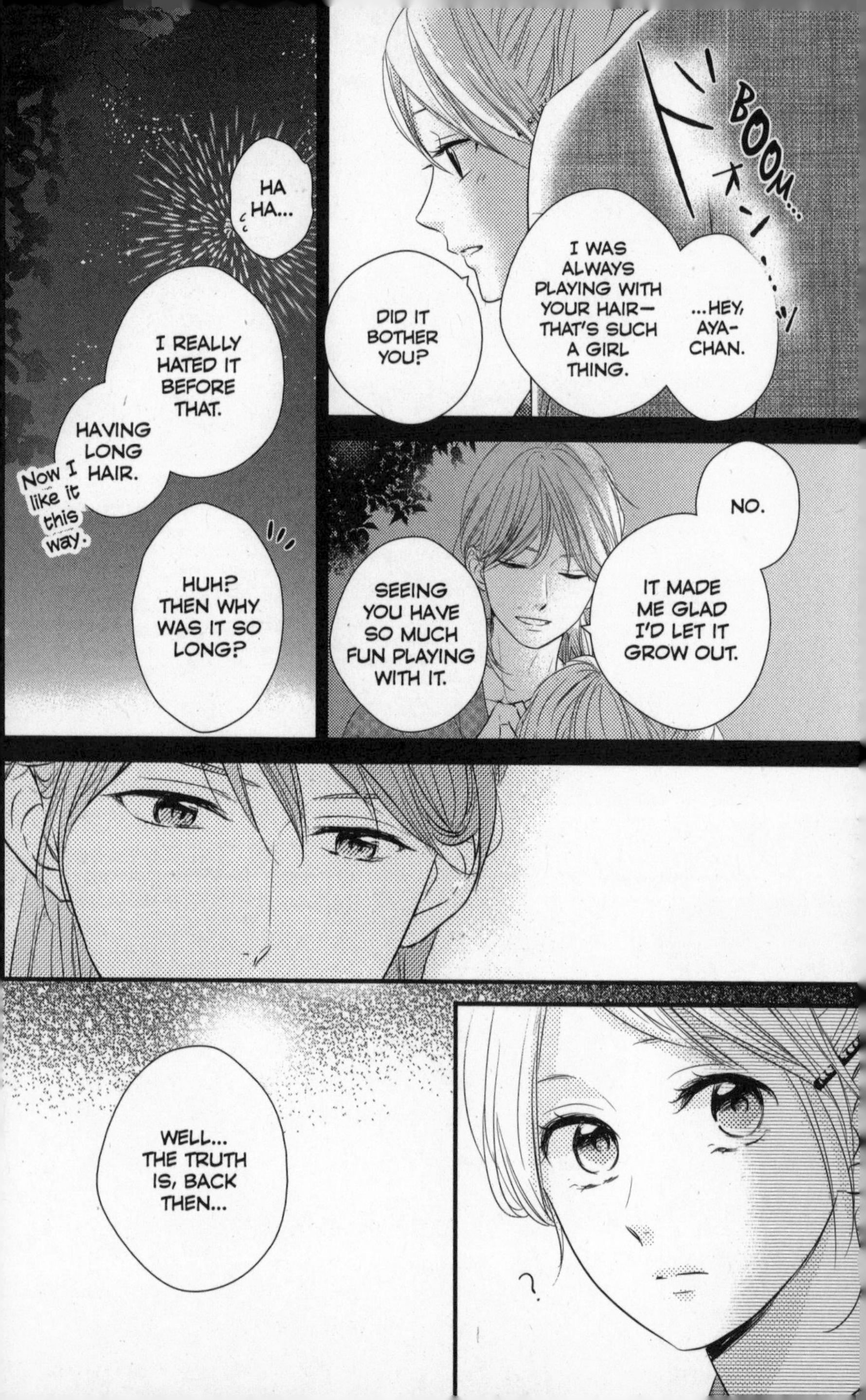
BOOM...
...HEY, AYA-CHAN.
I WAS ALWAYS PLAYING WITH YOUR HAIR—THAT'S SUCH A GIRL THING.
DID IT BOTHER YOU?
NO.
IT MADE ME GLAD I'D LET IT GROW OUT.
SEEING YOU HAVE SO MUCH FUN PLAYING WITH IT.
HA HA...
I REALLY HATED IT BEFORE THAT.
HAVING LONG HAIR.
Now I like it this way.
HUH? THEN WHY WAS IT SO LONG?
?
WELL... THE TRUTH IS, BACK THEN...

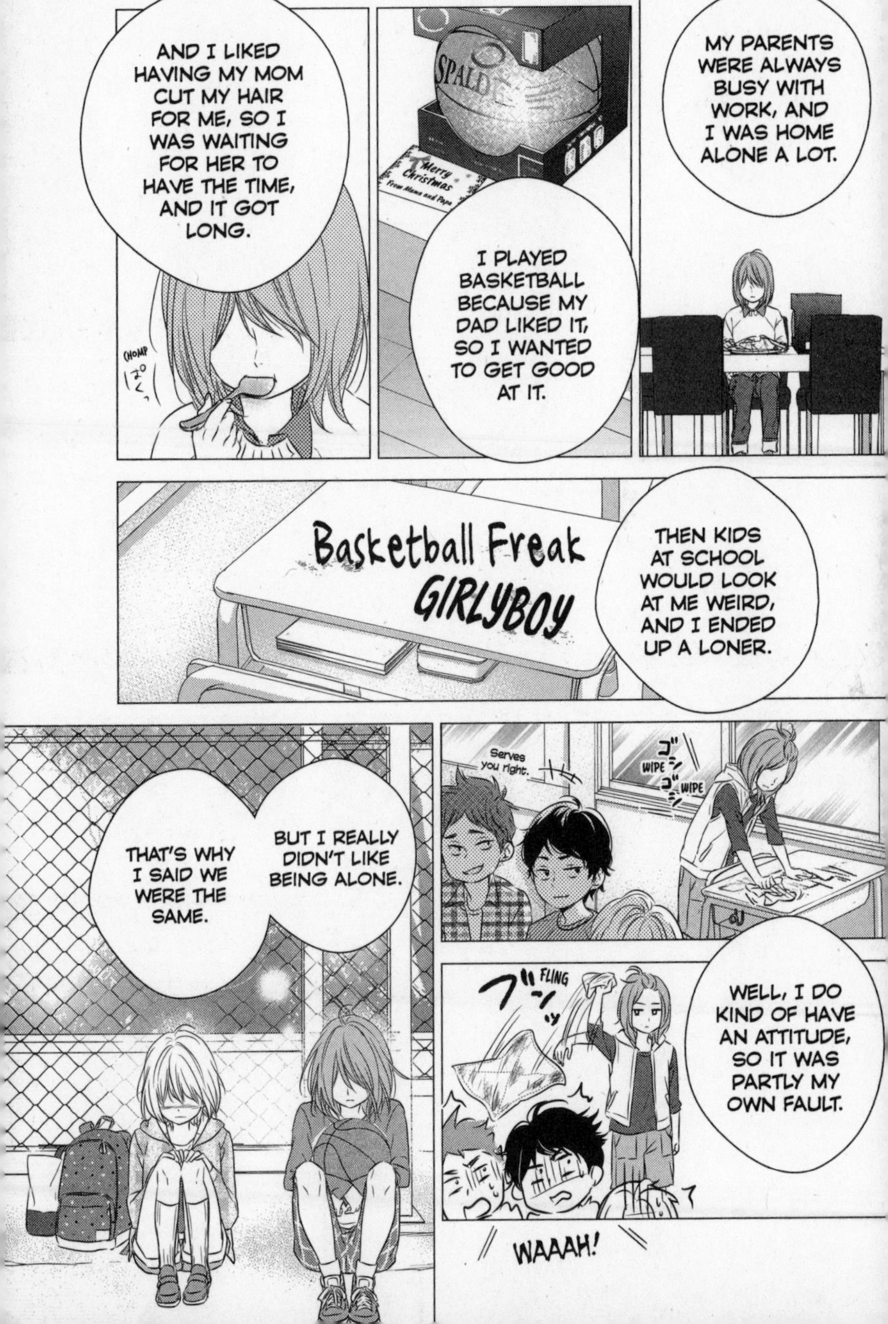
MY PARENTS WERE ALWAYS BUSY WITH WORK, AND I WAS HOME ALONE A LOT.
Merry Christmas
From Mama and Papa
I PLAYED BASKETBALL BECAUSE MY DAD LIKED IT, SO I WANTED TO GET GOOD AT IT.
AND I LIKED HAVING MY MOM CUT MY HAIR FOR ME, SO I WAS WAITING FOR HER TO HAVE THE TIME, AND IT GOT LONG.
CHOMP
THEN KIDS AT SCHOOL WOULD LOOK AT ME WEIRD, AND I ENDED UP A LONER.
Basketball Freak
GIRLYBOY
WIPE
WIPE
Serves you right.
WELL, I DO KIND OF HAVE AN ATTITUDE, SO IT WAS PARTLY MY OWN FAULT.
FLING
WAAAH!
BUT I REALLY DIDN'T LIKE BEING ALONE.
THAT'S WHY I SAID WE WERE THE SAME.

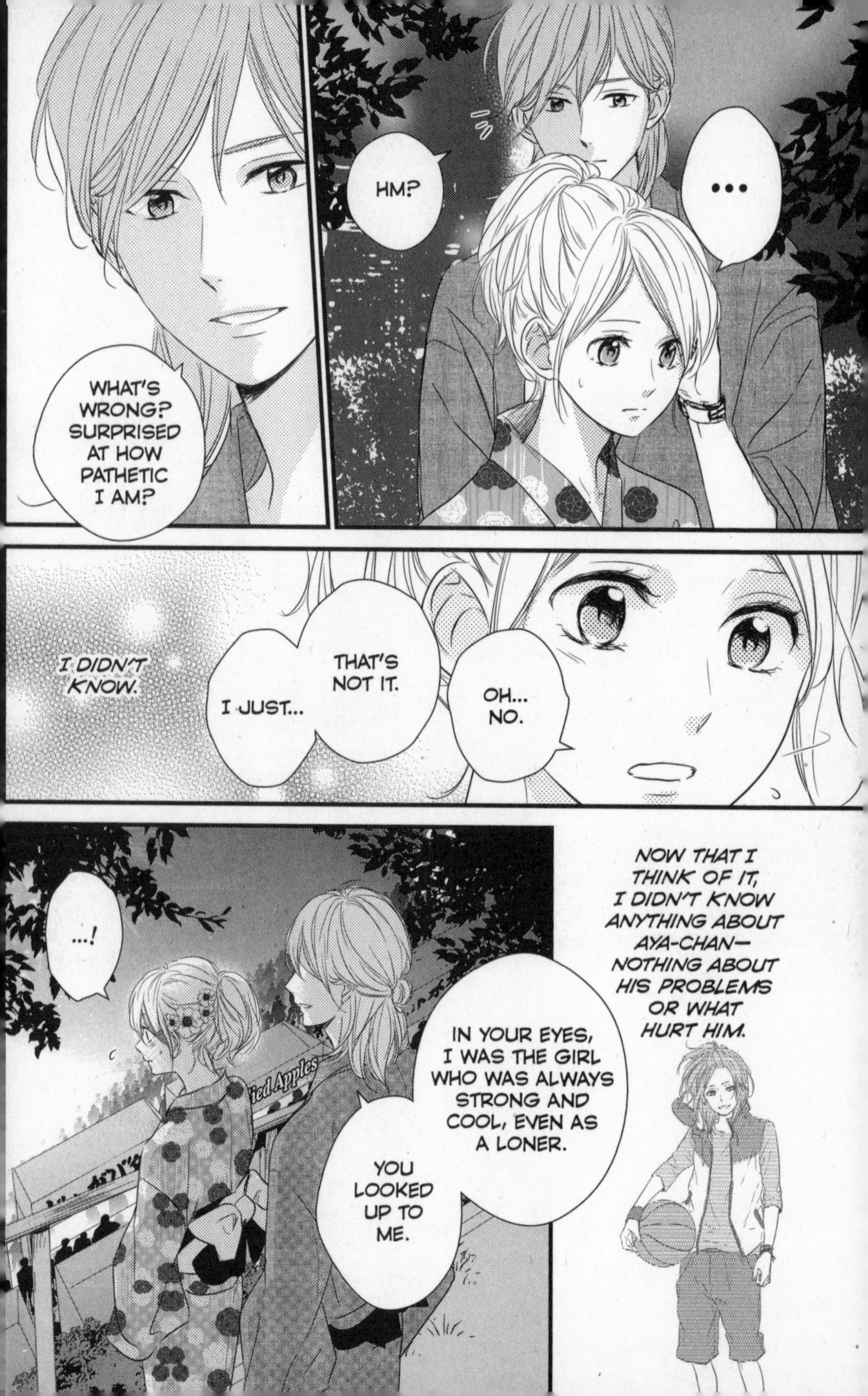
...
HM?
WHAT'S WRONG? SURPRISED AT HOW PATHETIC I AM?
OH... NO.
THAT'S NOT IT.
I JUST...
I DIDN'T KNOW.
NOW THAT I THINK OF IT, I DIDN'T KNOW ANYTHING ABOUT AYA-CHAN— NOTHING ABOUT HIS PROBLEMS OR WHAT HURT HIM.
IN YOUR EYES, I WAS THE GIRL WHO WAS ALWAYS STRONG AND COOL, EVEN AS A LONER.
YOU LOOKED UP TO ME.
...!
ied Apples

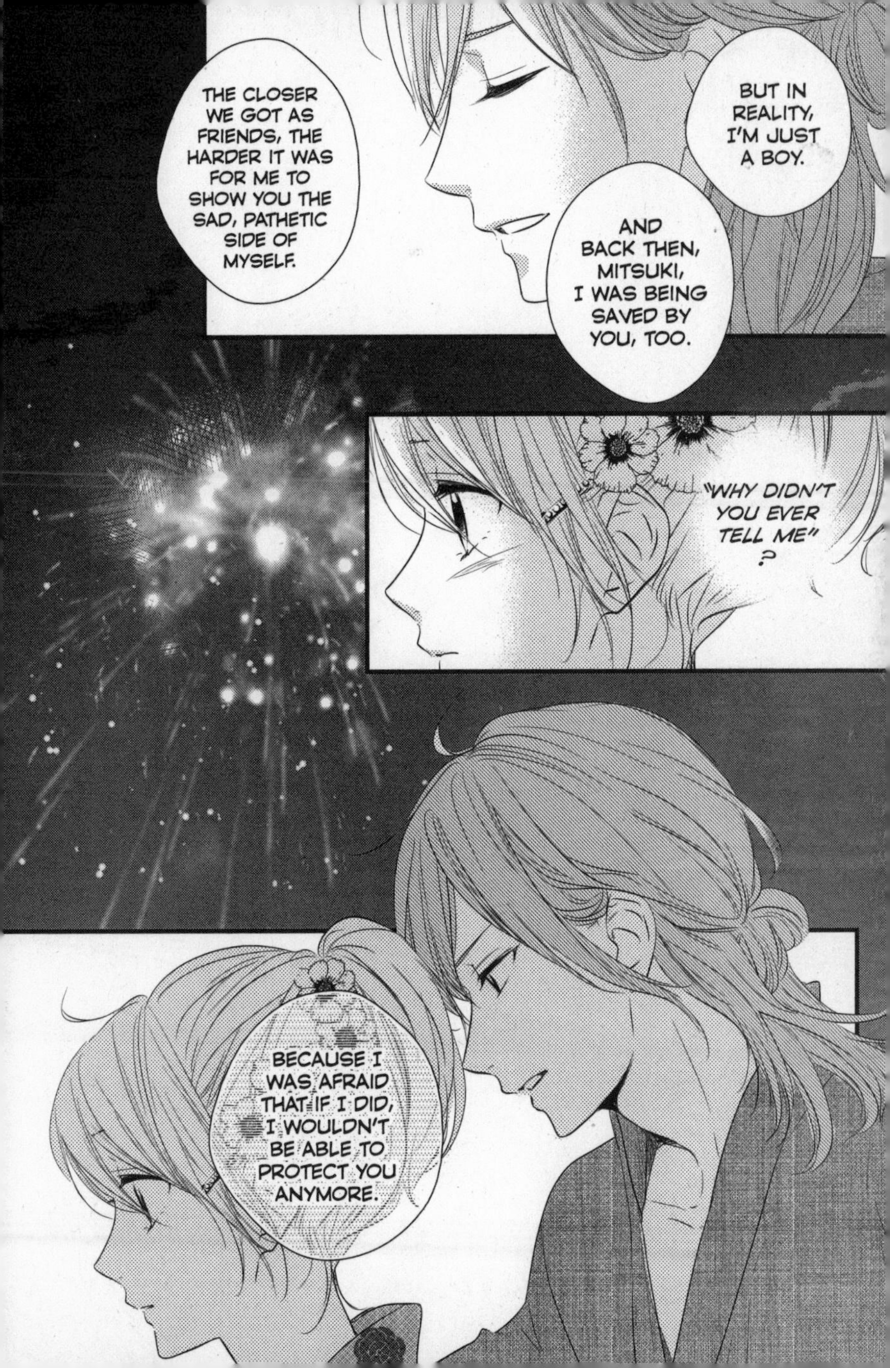
BUT IN REALITY, I'M JUST A BOY.
AND BACK THEN, MITSUKI, I WAS BEING SAVED BY YOU, TOO.
THE CLOSER WE GOT AS FRIENDS, THE HARDER IT WAS FOR ME TO SHOW YOU THE SAD, PATHETIC SIDE OF MYSELF.
"WHY DIDN'T YOU EVER TELL ME"?
BECAUSE I WAS AFRAID THAT IF I DID, I WOULDN'T BE ABLE TO PROTECT YOU ANYMORE.

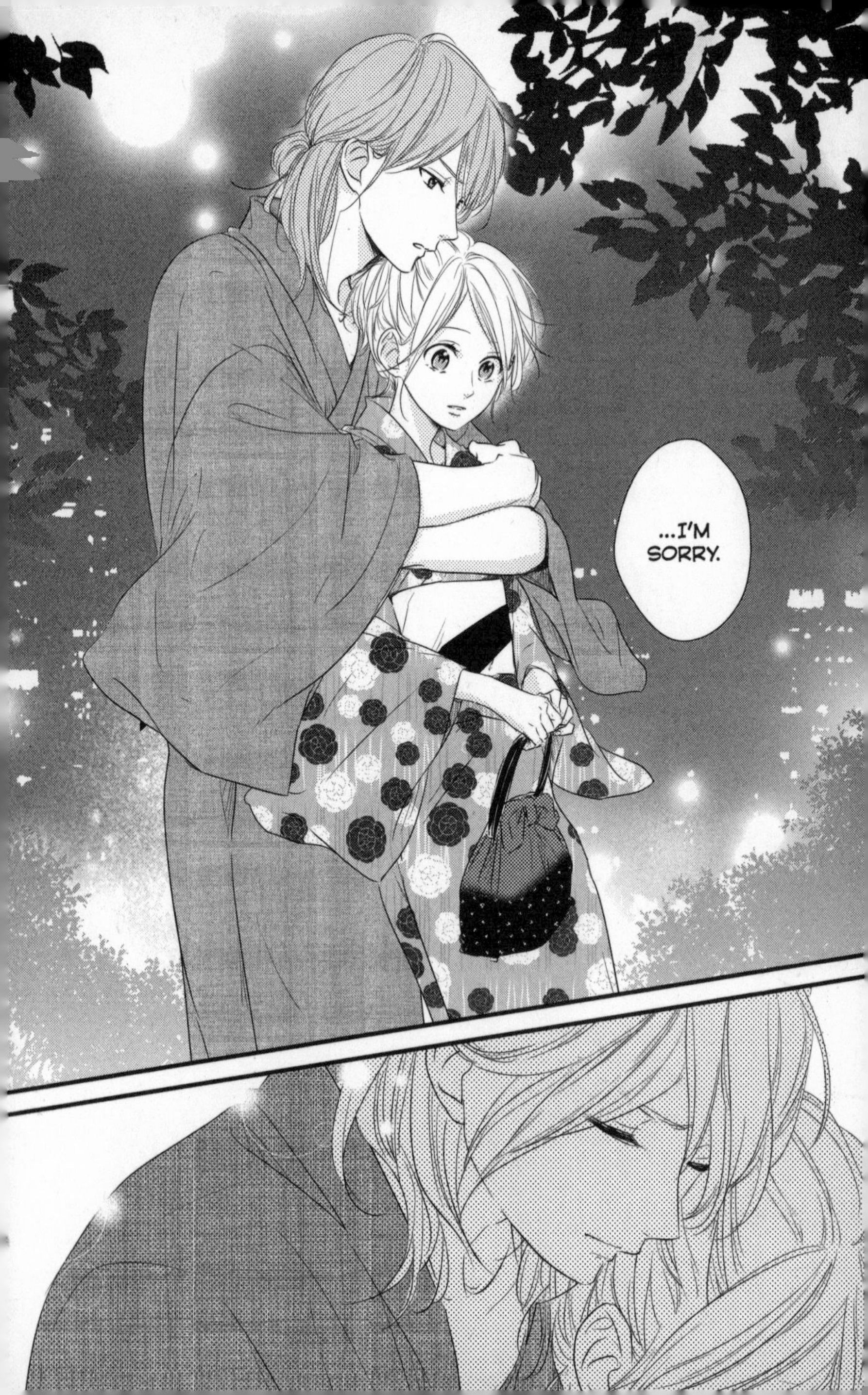
...I'M SORRY.

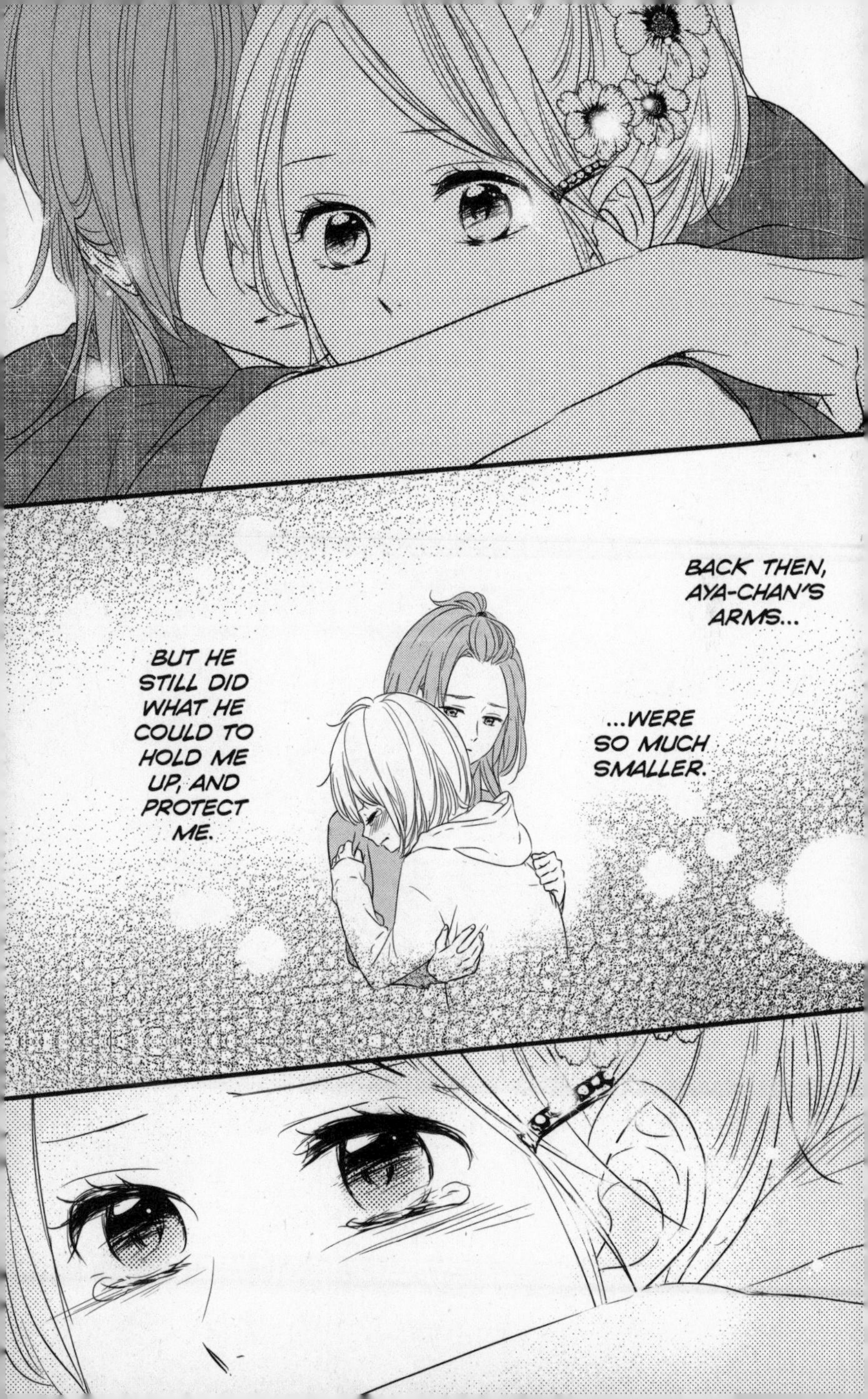
BACK THEN, AYA-CHAN'S ARMS...
...WERE SO MUCH SMALLER.
BUT HE STILL DID WHAT HE COULD TO HOLD ME UP, AND PROTECT ME.

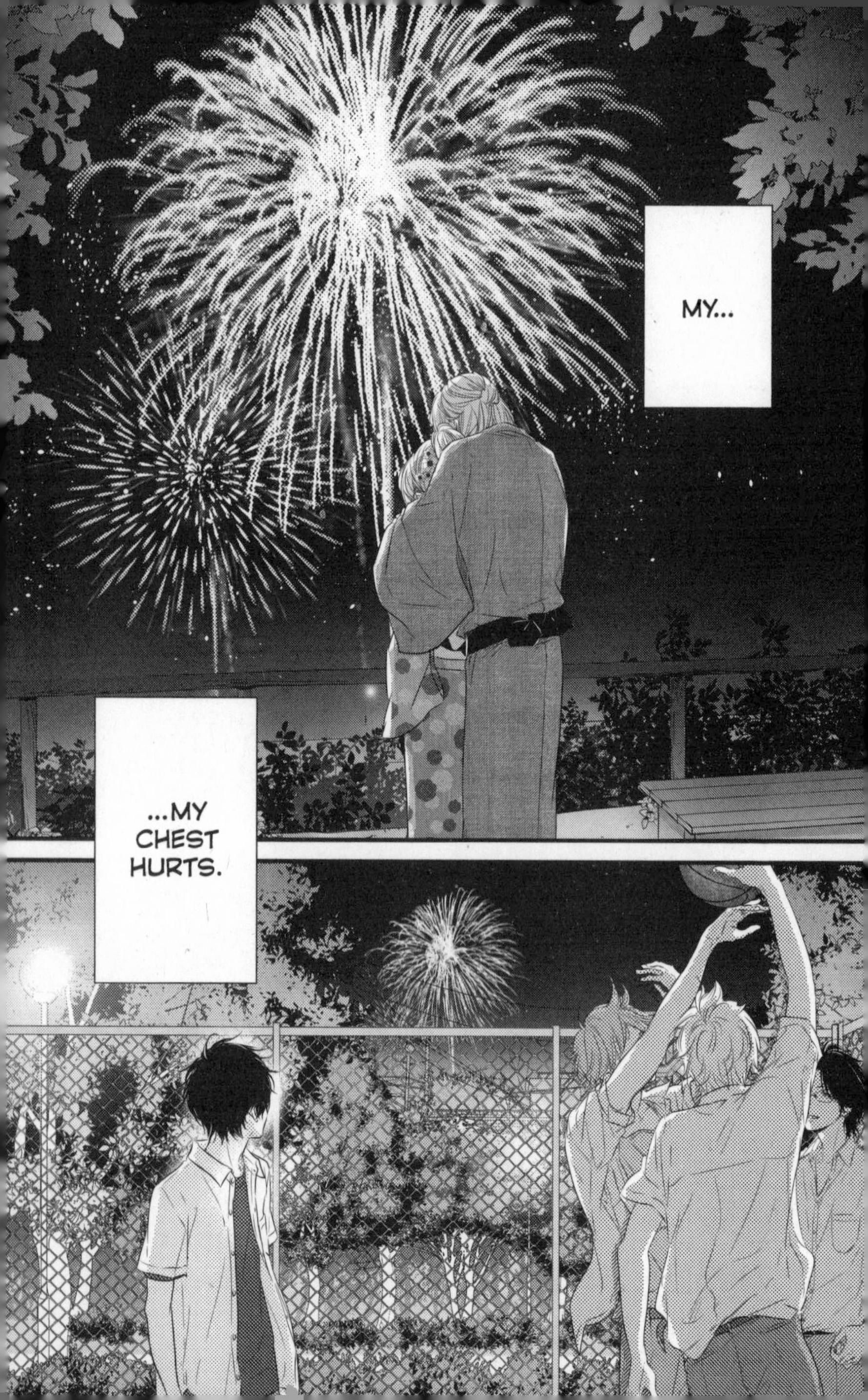
MY...
...MY CHEST HURTS.

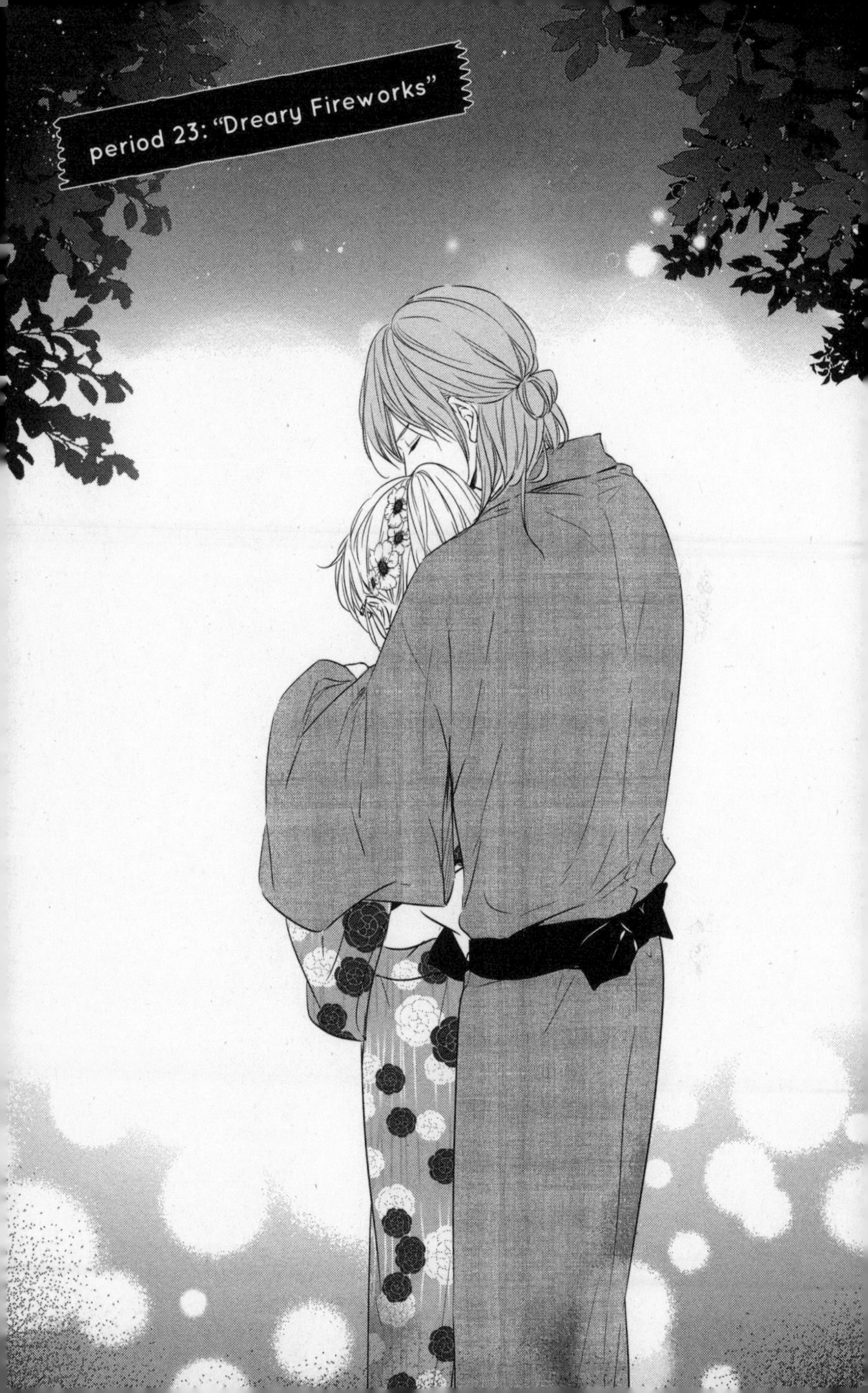
period 23: "Dreary Fireworks"

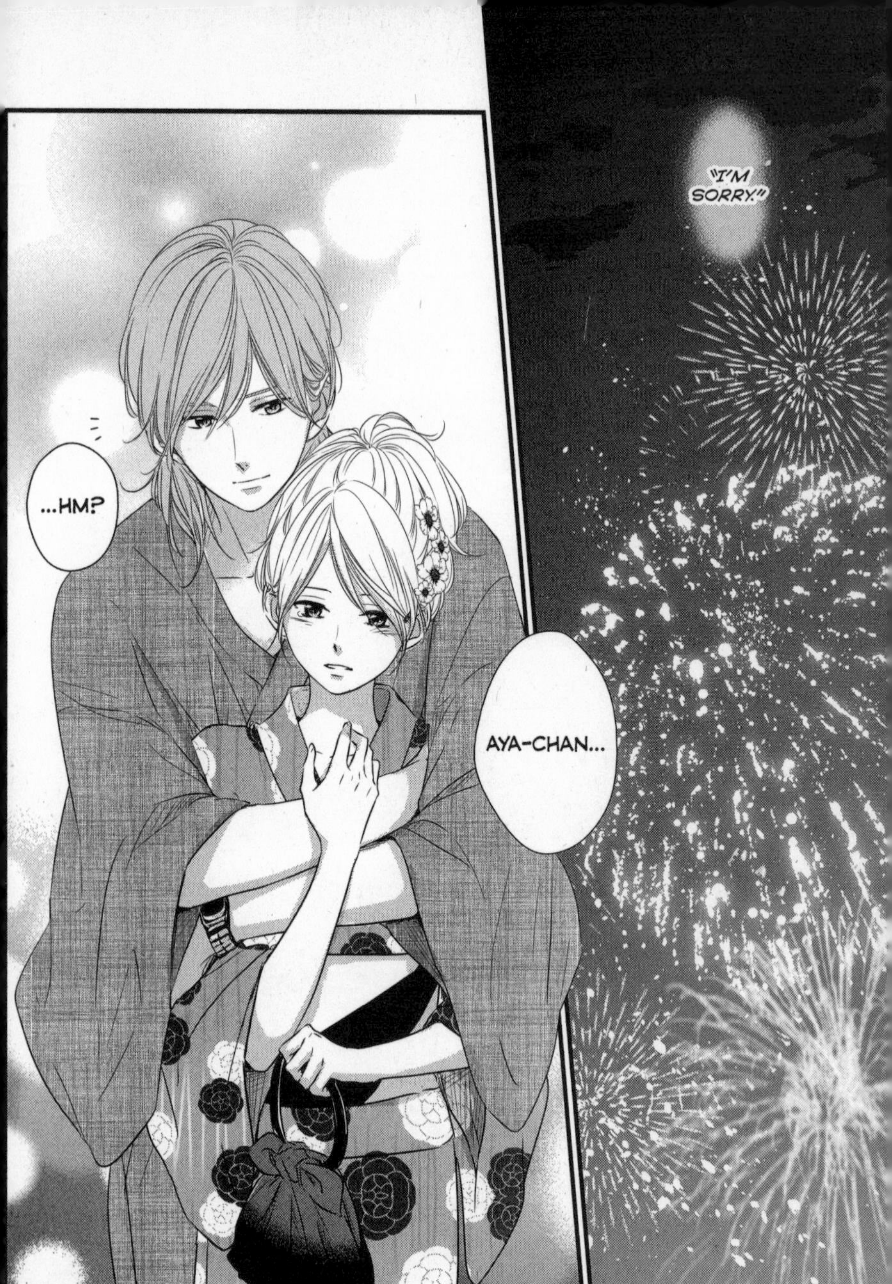
"I'M SORRY."
...HM?
AYA-CHAN...

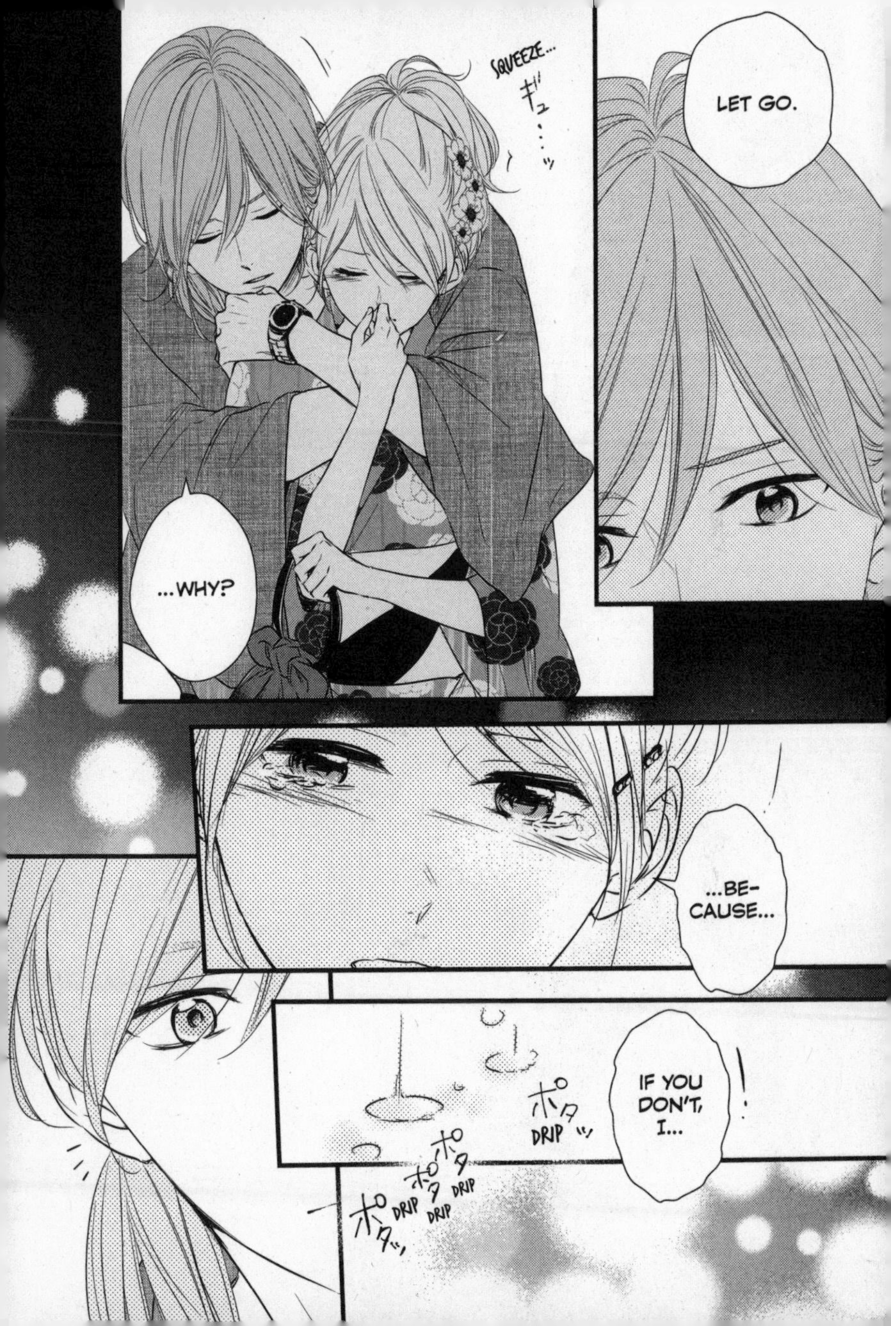
LET GO.
SQUEEZE...
ギュ・・・ッ
...WHY?
...BE-CAUSE...
IF YOU DON'T, I...
ポタッ
DRIP
ポタ
ポタ
ポタッ
DRIP
DRIP
DRIP

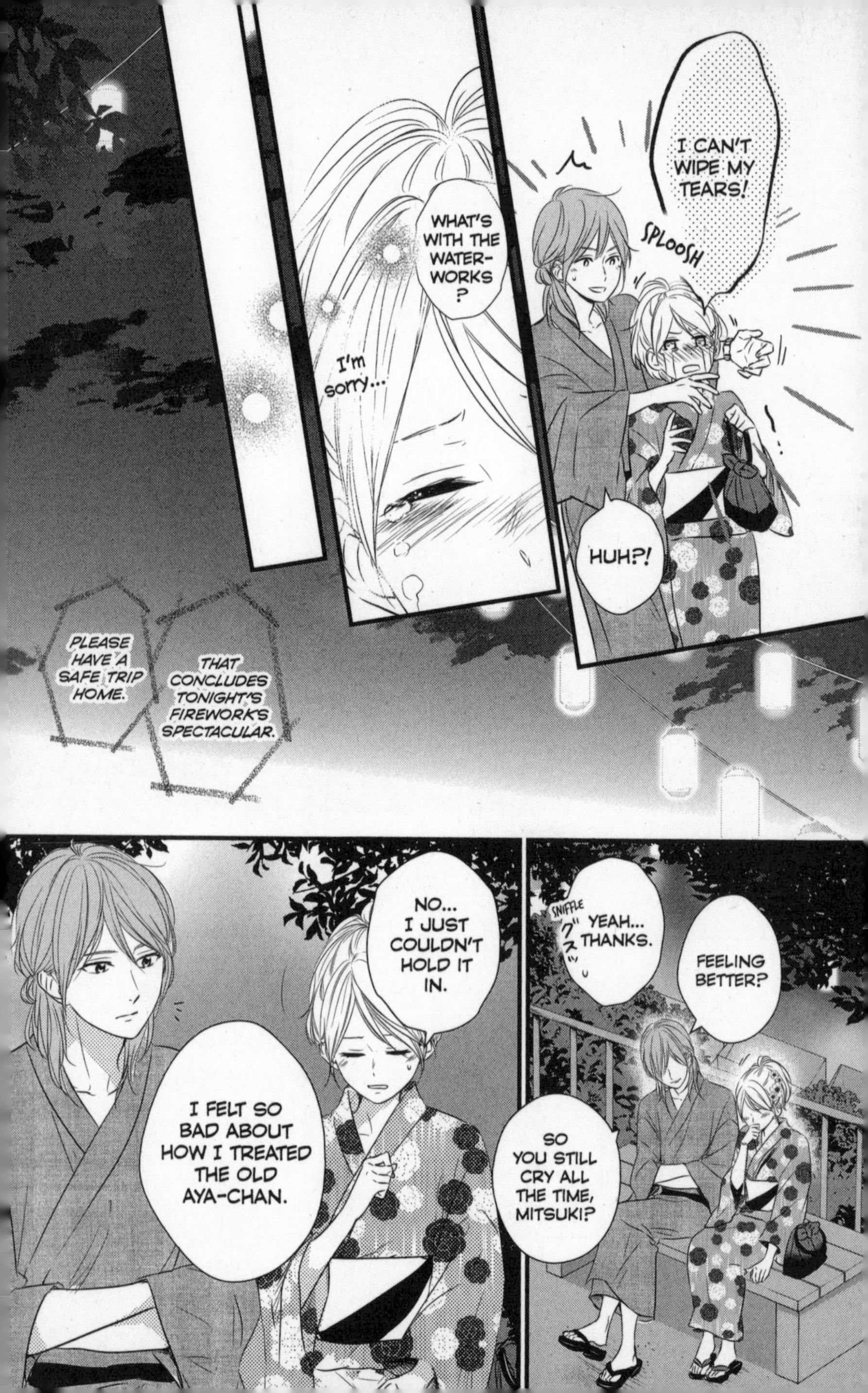
I CAN'T WIPE MY TEARS!
SPLOOSH
HUH?!
WHAT'S WITH THE WATER-WORKS?
I'm sorry...
THAT CONCLUDES TONIGHT'S FIREWORKS SPECTACULAR.
PLEASE HAVE A SAFE TRIP HOME.
FEELING BETTER?
SNIFFLE
YEAH... THANKS.
SO YOU STILL CRY ALL THE TIME, MITSUKI?
NO... I JUST COULDN'T HOLD IT IN.
I FELT SO BAD ABOUT HOW I TREATED THE OLD AYA-CHAN.

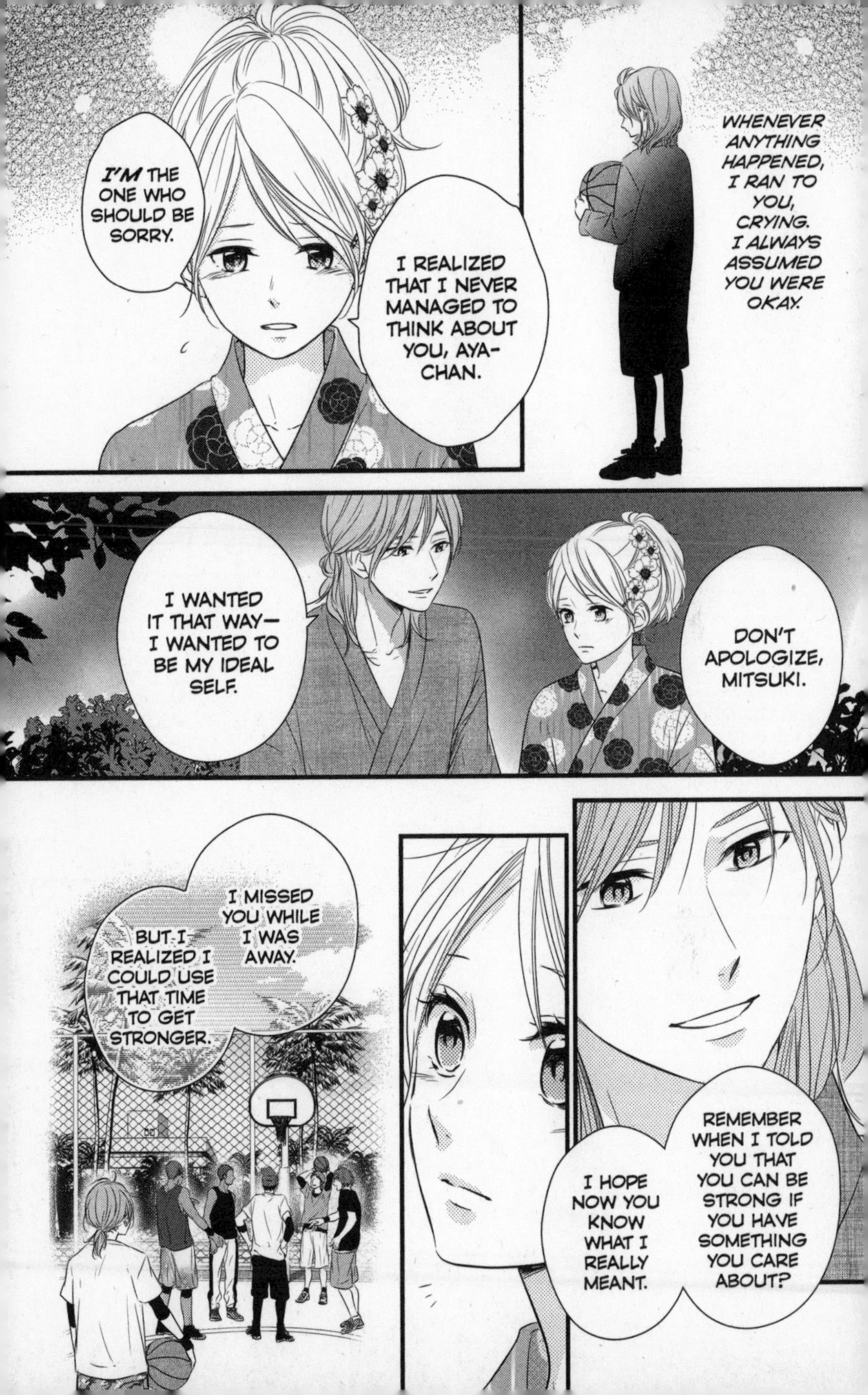
WHENEVER ANYTHING HAPPENED, I RAN TO YOU, CRYING. I ALWAYS ASSUMED YOU WERE OKAY.
I REALIZED THAT I NEVER MANAGED TO THINK ABOUT YOU, AYA-CHAN.
I'M THE ONE WHO SHOULD BE SORRY.
DON'T APOLOGIZE, MITSUKI.
I WANTED IT THAT WAY— I WANTED TO BE MY IDEAL SELF.
REMEMBER WHEN I TOLD YOU THAT YOU CAN BE STRONG IF YOU HAVE SOMETHING YOU CARE ABOUT?
I HOPE NOW YOU KNOW WHAT I REALLY MEANT.
I MISSED YOU WHILE I WAS AWAY.
BUT I REALIZED I COULD USE THAT TIME TO GET STRONGER.

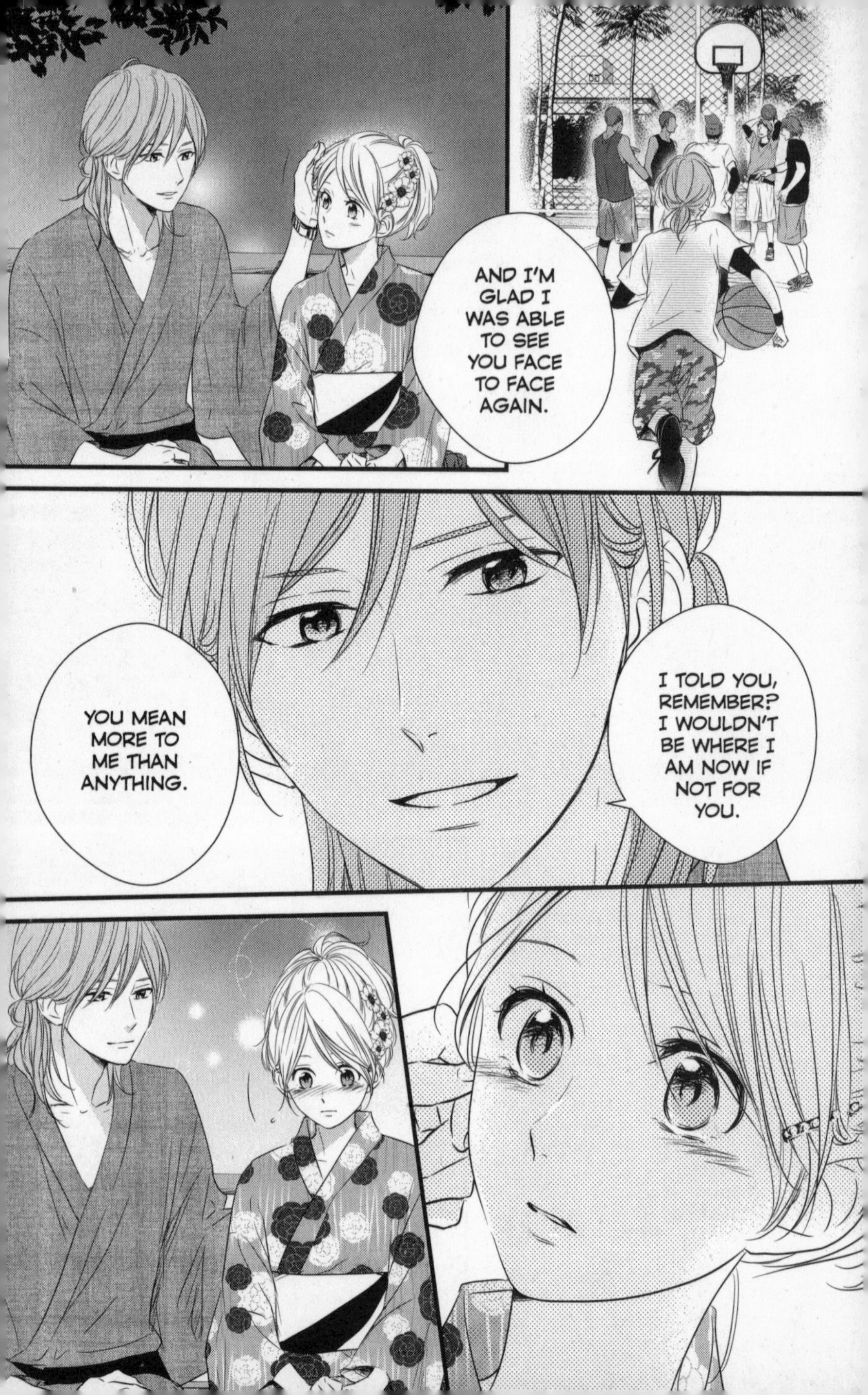
AND I'M GLAD I WAS ABLE TO SEE YOU FACE TO FACE AGAIN.
I TOLD YOU, REMEMBER? I WOULDN'T BE WHERE I AM NOW IF NOT FOR YOU.
YOU MEAN MORE TO ME THAN ANYTHING.

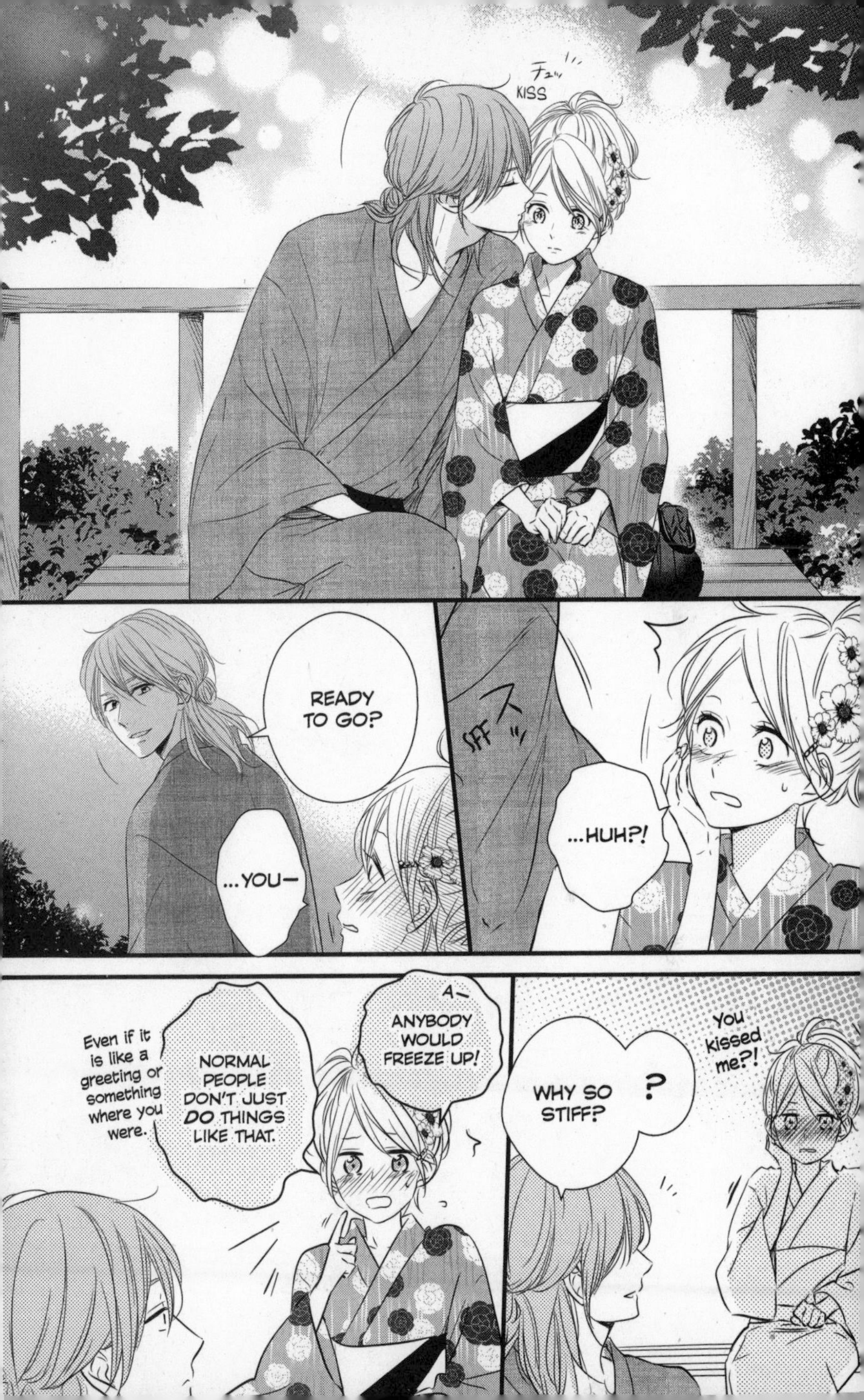
チュッ
KISS
SFF スッ
...HUH?!
READY TO GO?
...YOU—
You kissed me?!
WHY SO STIFF?
?
A— ANYBODY WOULD FREEZE UP!
NORMAL PEOPLE DON'T JUST *DO* THINGS LIKE THAT.
Even if it is like a greeting or something where you were.

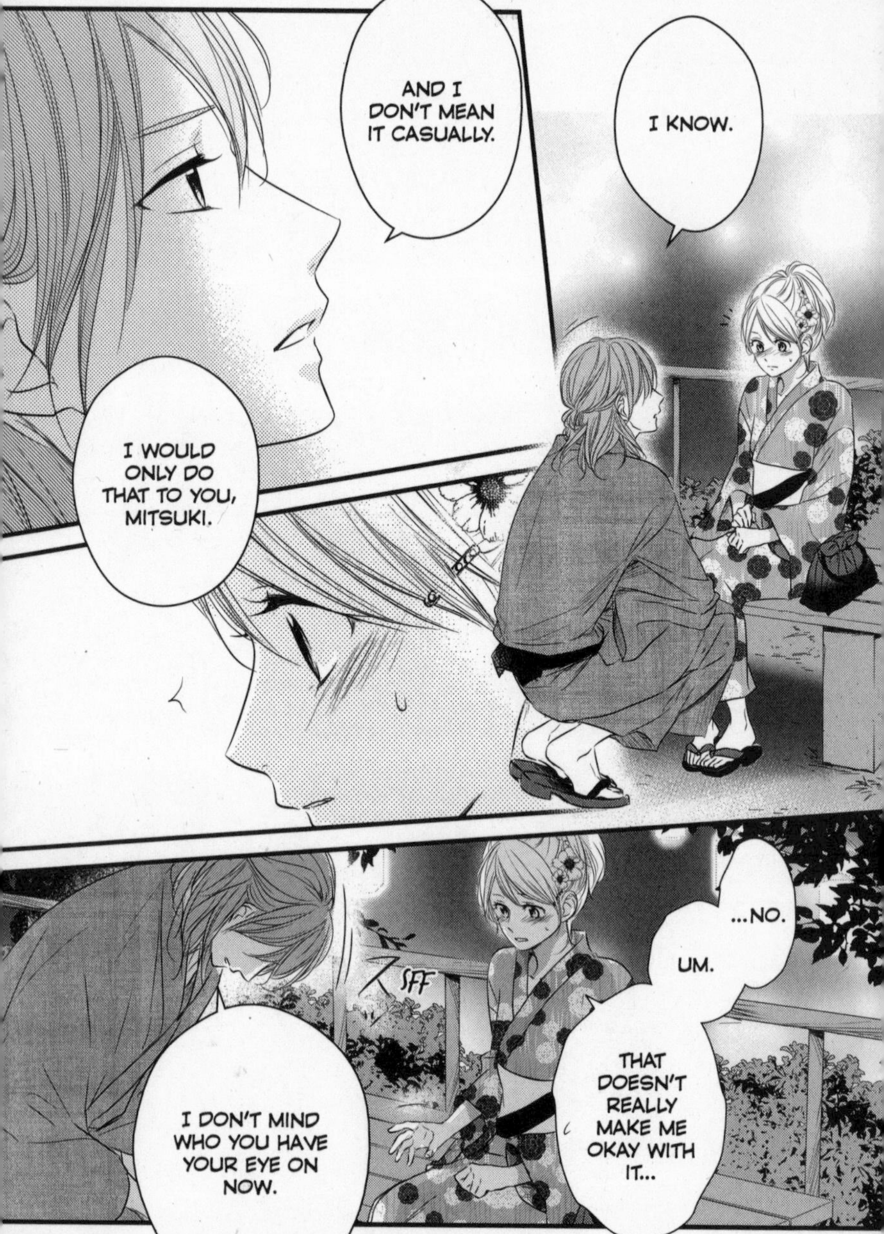
I KNOW.
AND I DON'T MEAN IT CASUALLY.
I WOULD ONLY DO THAT TO YOU, MITSUKI.
...NO.
UM.
THAT DOESN'T REALLY MAKE ME OKAY WITH IT...
SFF
I DON'T MIND WHO YOU HAVE YOUR EYE ON NOW.

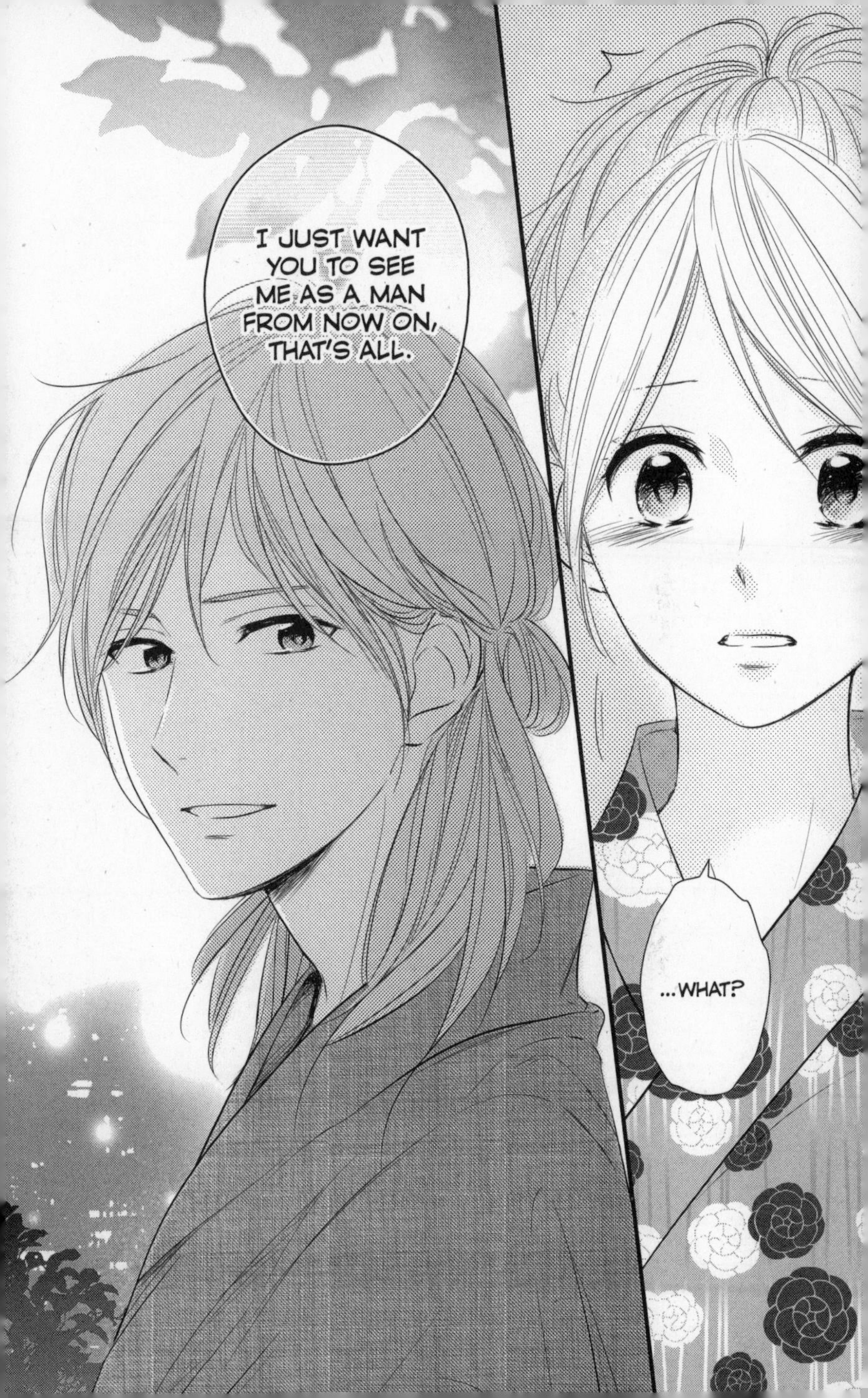
I JUST WANT YOU TO SEE ME AS A MAN FROM NOW ON, THAT'S ALL.
...WHAT?

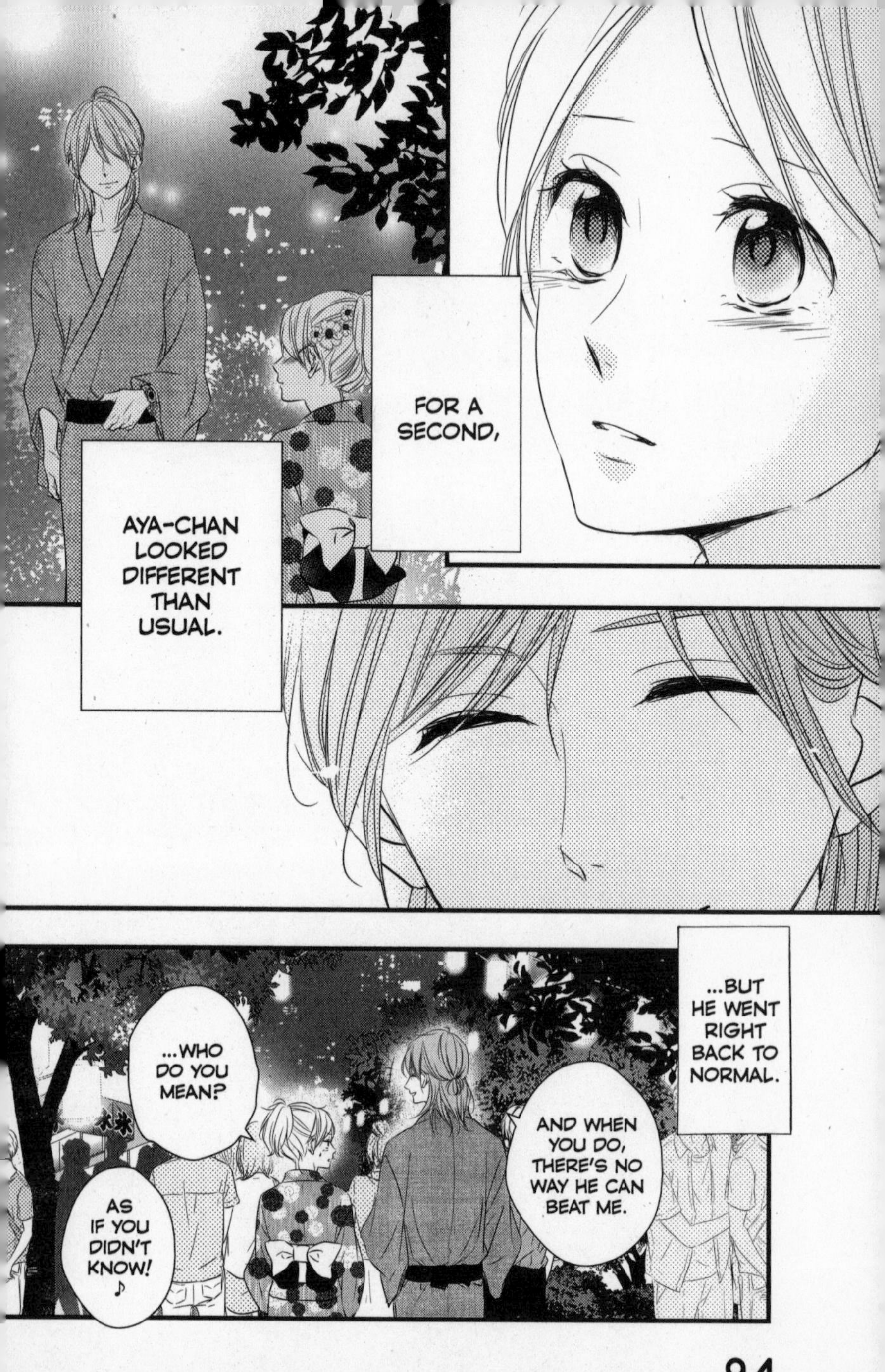

FOR A SECOND,
AYA-CHAN LOOKED DIFFERENT THAN USUAL.
...BUT HE WENT RIGHT BACK TO NORMAL.
AND WHEN YOU DO, THERE'S NO WAY HE CAN BEAT ME.
...WHO DO YOU MEAN?
AS IF YOU DIDN'T KNOW! ♪

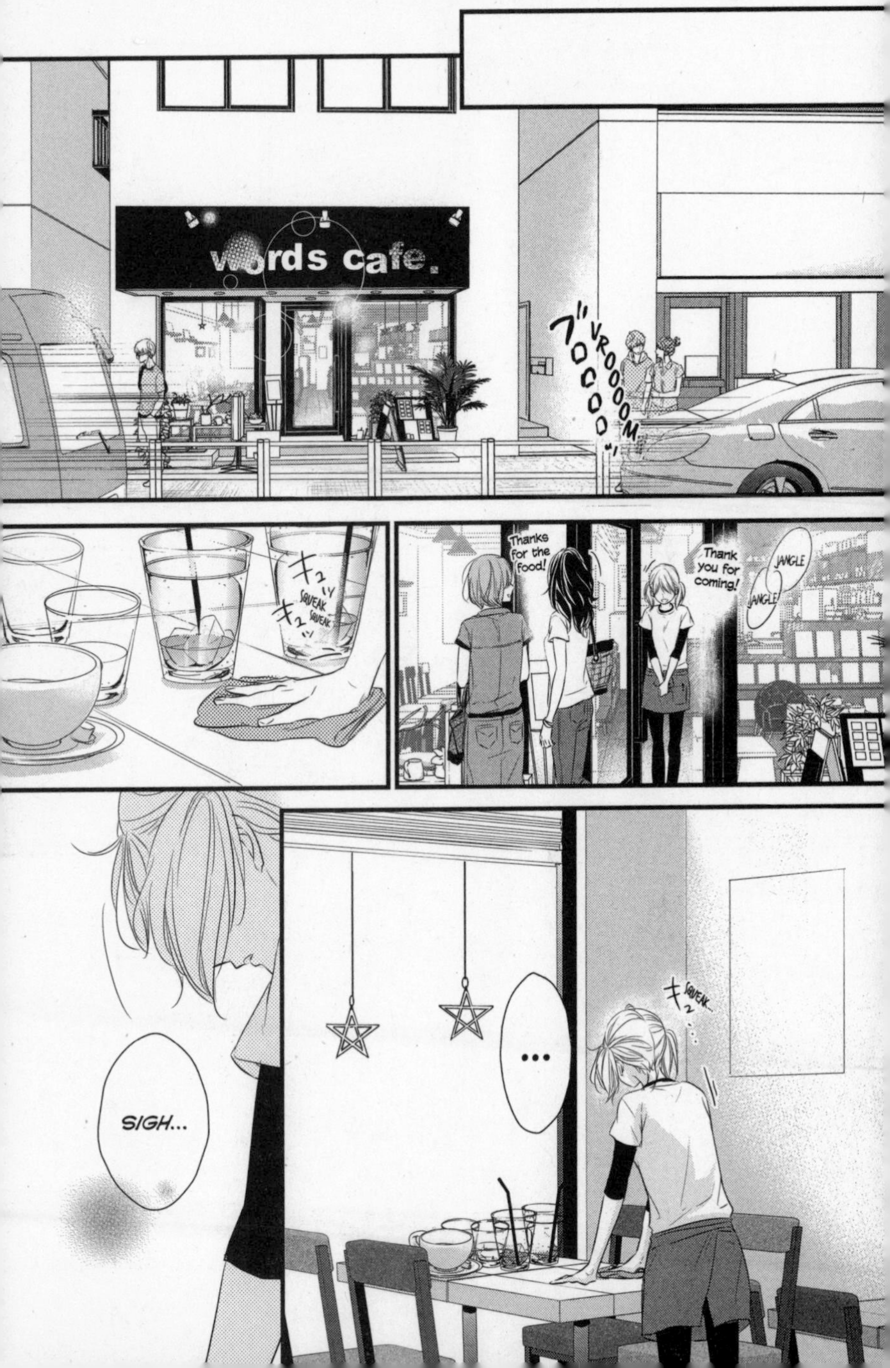

words cafe.
VROOOOOM
Thank you for coming!
JANGLE
JANGLE
Thanks for the food!
SQUEAK
SQUEAK
...
SQUEAK...
SIGH...

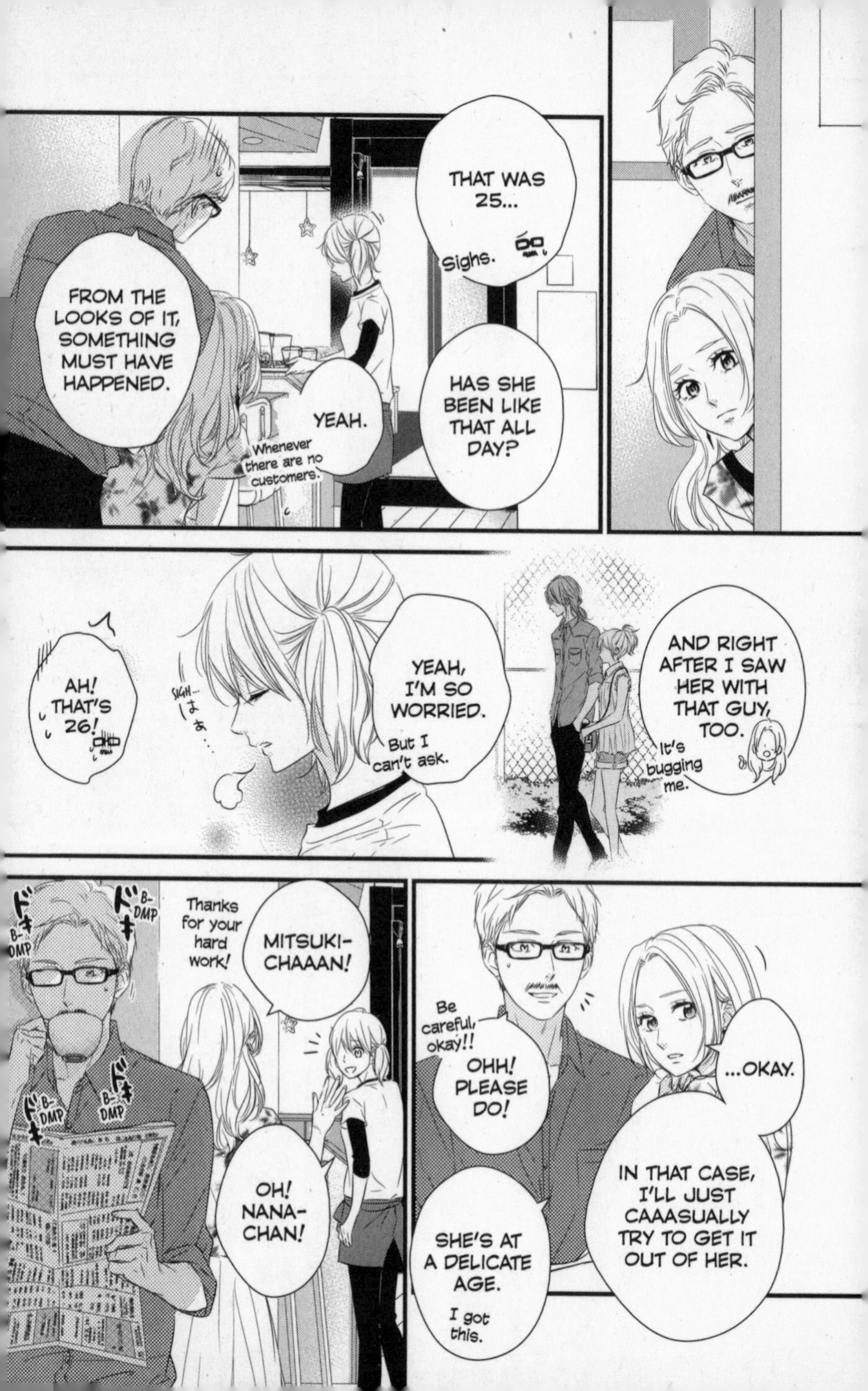
THAT WAS 25...
Sighs.
HAS SHE BEEN LIKE THAT ALL DAY?
YEAH.
Whenever there are no customers.
FROM THE LOOKS OF IT, SOMETHING MUST HAVE HAPPENED.
AND RIGHT AFTER I SAW HER WITH THAT GUY, TOO.
It's bugging me.
YEAH, I'M SO WORRIED.
But I can't ask.
SIGH... はぁ...
AH! THAT'S 26!
...OKAY.
IN THAT CASE, I'LL JUST CAAASUALLY TRY TO GET IT OUT OF HER.
SHE'S AT A DELICATE AGE.
I got this.
OHH! PLEASE DO!
Be careful, okay!!
MITSUKI-CHAAAN!
Thanks for your hard work!
OH! NANA-CHAN!
ドキ B-DMP
ドキ B-DMP
ドキ B-DMP
ドキ B-DMP

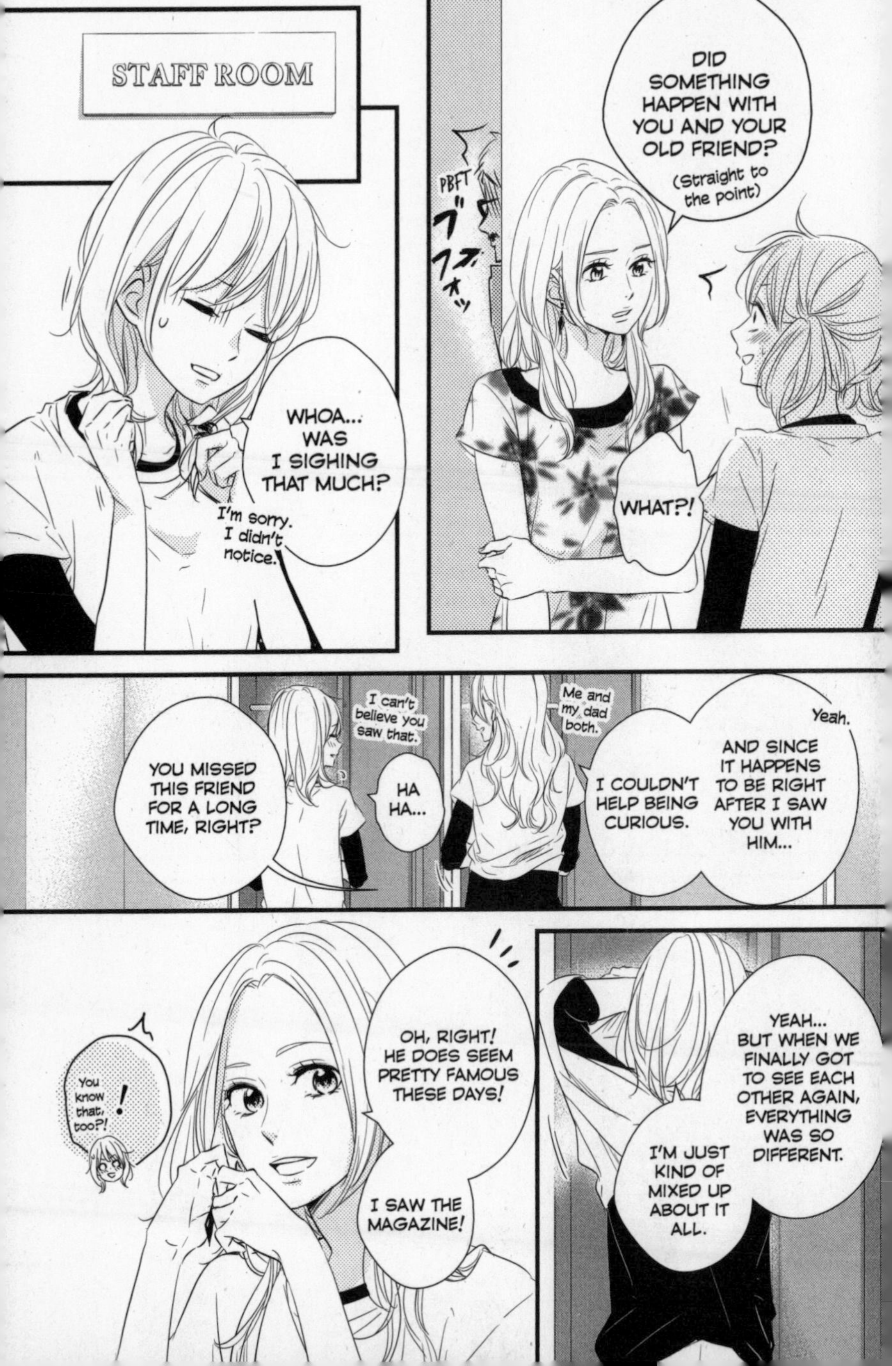
DID SOMETHING HAPPEN WITH YOU AND YOUR OLD FRIEND?
(Straight to the point)
PBFT
WHAT?!
STAFF ROOM
WHOA... WAS I SIGHING THAT MUCH?
I'm sorry. I didn't notice.
Yeah.
AND SINCE IT HAPPENS TO BE RIGHT AFTER I SAW YOU WITH HIM...
I COULDN'T HELP BEING CURIOUS.
Me and my dad both.
HA HA...
I can't believe you saw that.
YOU MISSED THIS FRIEND FOR A LONG TIME, RIGHT?
YEAH... BUT WHEN WE FINALLY GOT TO SEE EACH OTHER AGAIN, EVERYTHING WAS SO DIFFERENT.
I'M JUST KIND OF MIXED UP ABOUT IT ALL.
OH, RIGHT! HE DOES SEEM PRETTY FAMOUS THESE DAYS!
I SAW THE MAGAZINE!
You know that, too?!

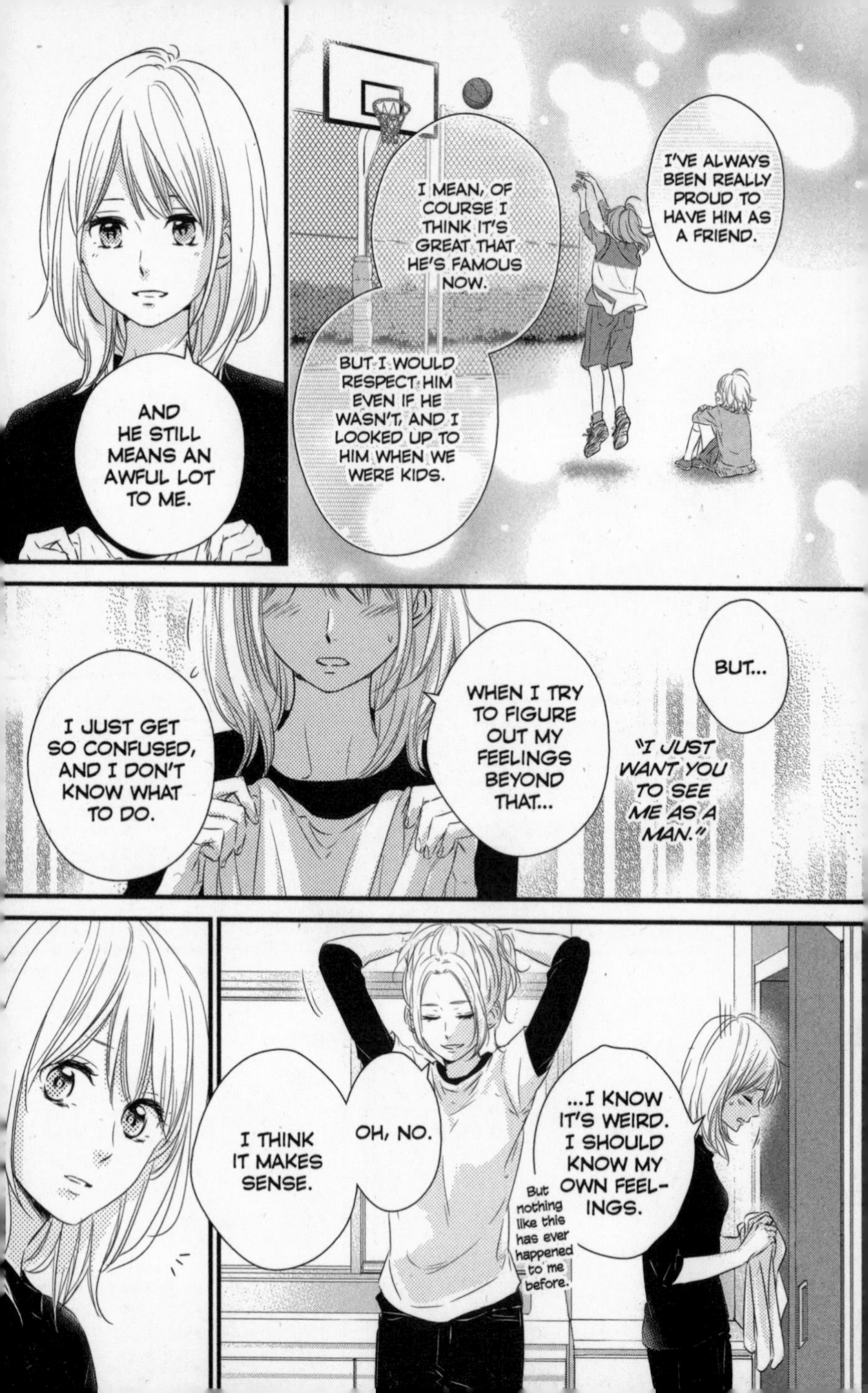
I'VE ALWAYS BEEN REALLY PROUD TO HAVE HIM AS A FRIEND.
I MEAN, OF COURSE I THINK IT'S GREAT THAT HE'S FAMOUS NOW.
BUT I WOULD RESPECT HIM EVEN IF HE WASN'T, AND I LOOKED UP TO HIM WHEN WE WERE KIDS.
AND HE STILL MEANS AN AWFUL LOT TO ME.
BUT...
"I JUST WANT YOU TO SEE ME AS A MAN."
WHEN I TRY TO FIGURE OUT MY FEELINGS BEYOND THAT...
I JUST GET SO CONFUSED, AND I DON'T KNOW WHAT TO DO.
...I KNOW IT'S WEIRD. I SHOULD KNOW MY OWN FEEL- INGS.
But nothing like this has ever happened to me before.
OH, NO.
I THINK IT MAKES SENSE.

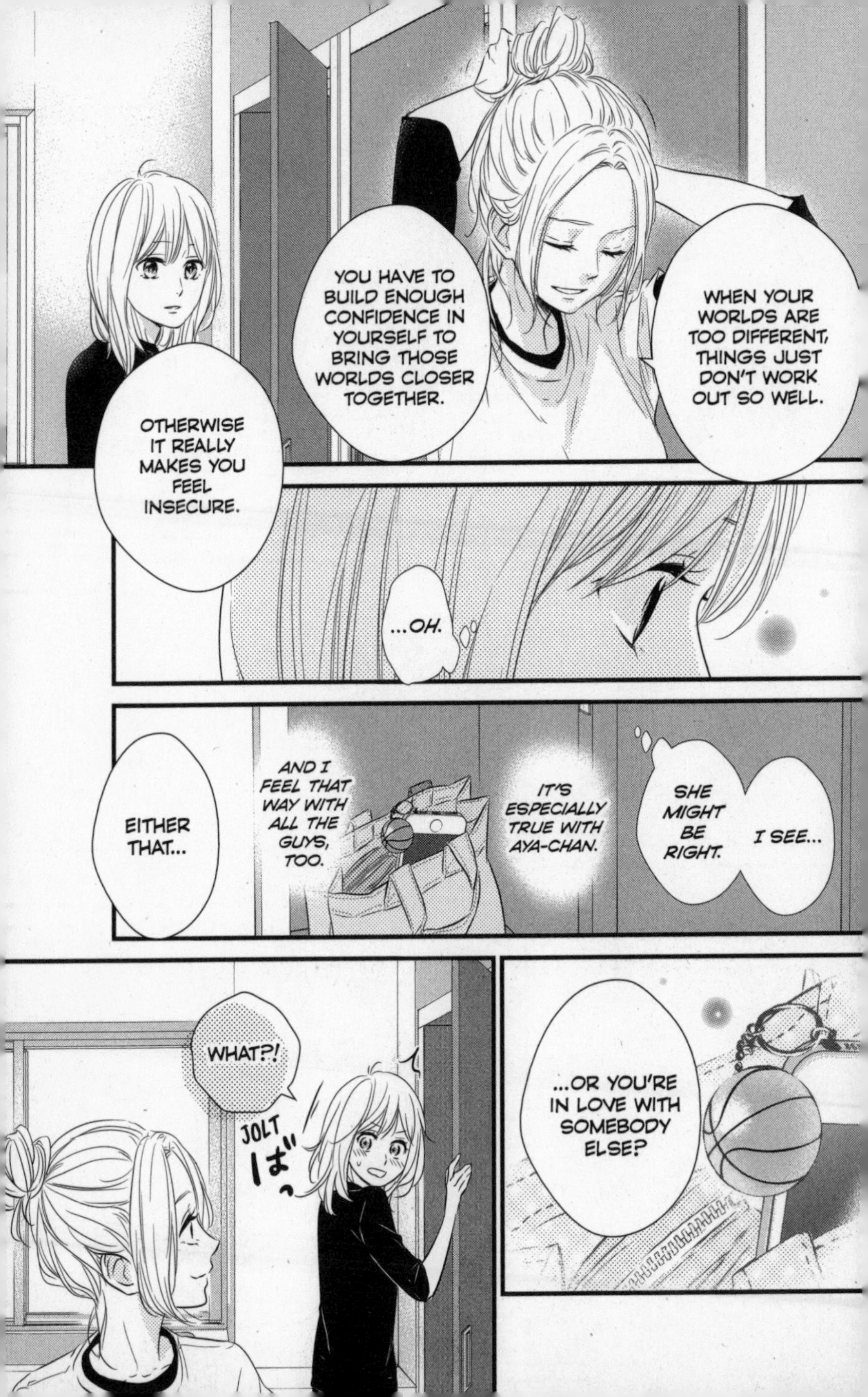

WHEN YOUR WORLDS ARE TOO DIFFERENT, THINGS JUST DON'T WORK OUT SO WELL.
YOU HAVE TO BUILD ENOUGH CONFIDENCE IN YOURSELF TO BRING THOSE WORLDS CLOSER TOGETHER.
OTHERWISE IT REALLY MAKES YOU FEEL INSECURE.
...OH.
I SEE...
SHE MIGHT BE RIGHT.
IT'S ESPECIALLY TRUE WITH AYA-CHAN.
AND I FEEL THAT WAY WITH ALL THE GUYS, TOO.
EITHER THAT...
...OR YOU'RE IN LOVE WITH SOMEBODY ELSE?
WHAT?!
JOLT
ばっ

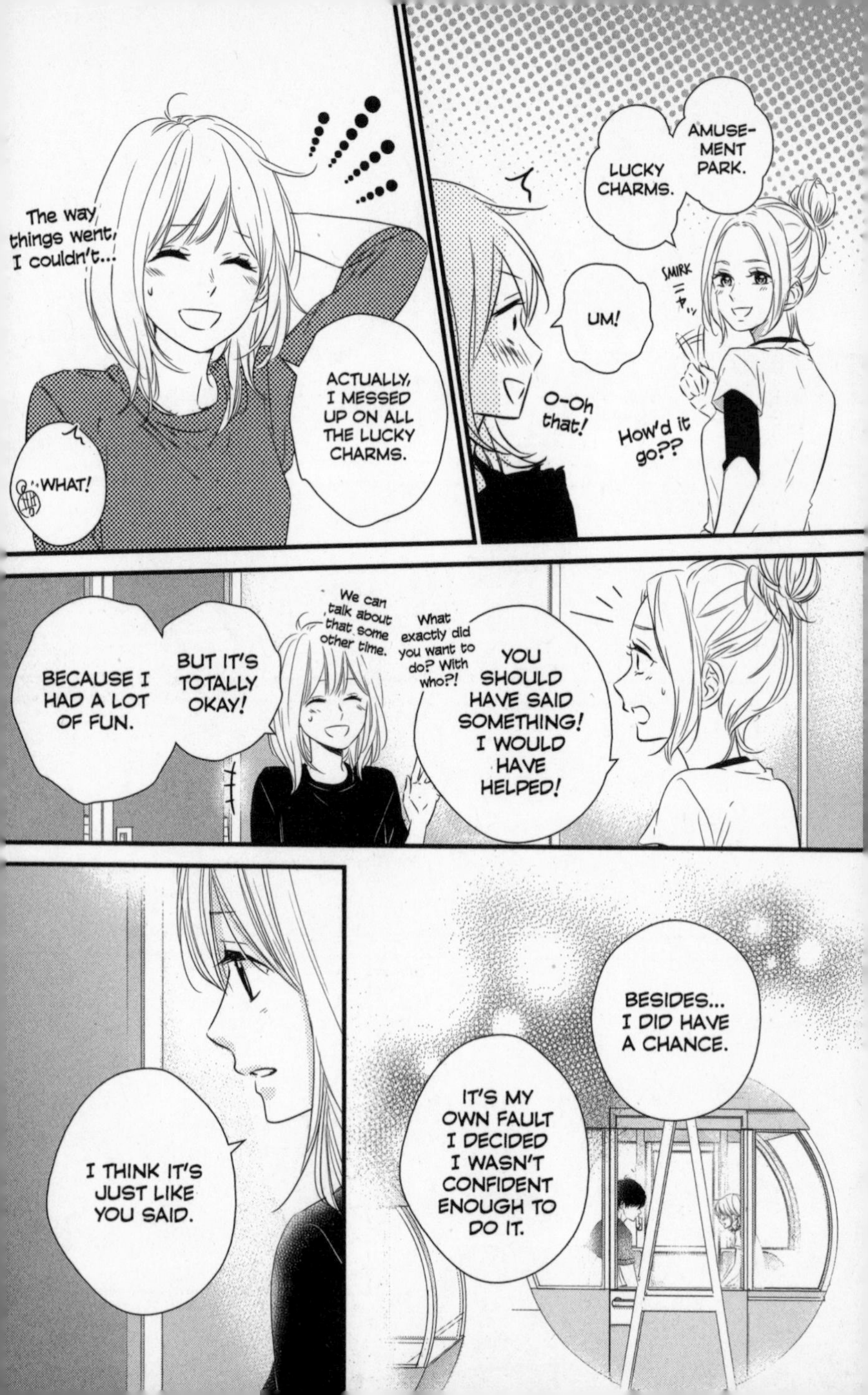
AMUSE-MENT PARK.
LUCKY CHARMS.
SMIRK
UM!
How'd it go??
O-Oh that!
The way things went, I couldn't...
ACTUALLY, I MESSED UP ON ALL THE LUCKY CHARMS.
WHAT!
YOU SHOULD HAVE SAID SOMETHING! I WOULD HAVE HELPED!
What exactly did you want to do? With who?!
We can talk about that some other time.
BUT IT'S TOTALLY OKAY!
BECAUSE I HAD A LOT OF FUN.
BESIDES... I DID HAVE A CHANCE.
IT'S MY OWN FAULT I DECIDED I WASN'T CONFIDENT ENOUGH TO DO IT.
I THINK IT'S JUST LIKE YOU SAID.

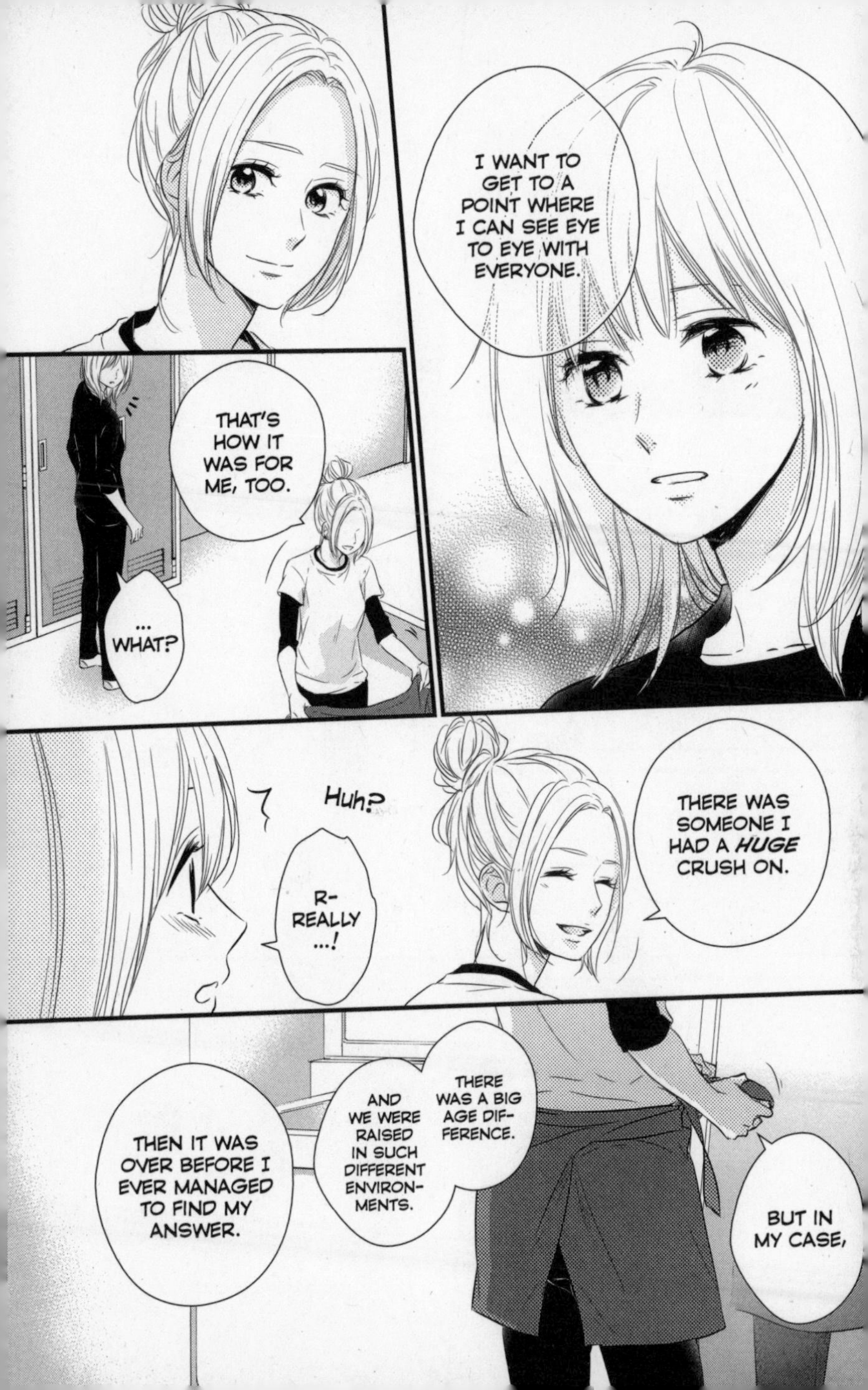
I WANT TO GET TO A POINT WHERE I CAN SEE EYE TO EYE WITH EVERYONE.
THAT'S HOW IT WAS FOR ME, TOO.
...WHAT?
THERE WAS SOMEONE I HAD A *HUGE* CRUSH ON.
Huh?
R-REALLY ...!
BUT IN MY CASE,
THERE WAS A BIG AGE DIF-FERENCE.
AND WE WERE RAISED IN SUCH DIFFERENT ENVIRON-MENTS.
THEN IT WAS OVER BEFORE I EVER MANAGED TO FIND MY ANSWER.

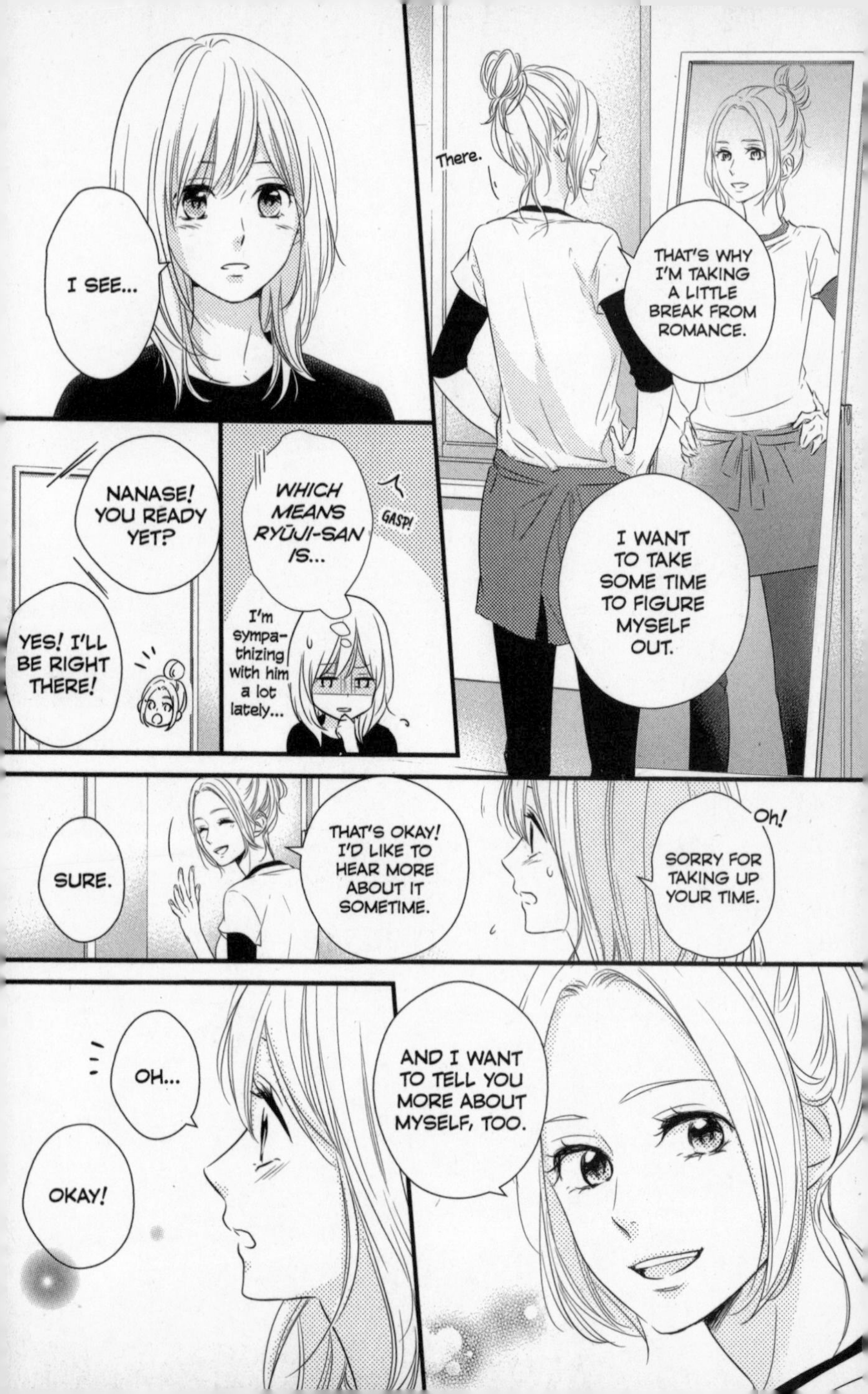
There.
THAT'S WHY I'M TAKING A LITTLE BREAK FROM ROMANCE.
I WANT TO TAKE SOME TIME TO FIGURE MYSELF OUT.
I SEE...
GASP!
WHICH MEANS RYŪJI-SAN IS...
I'm sympathizing with him a lot lately...
NANASE! YOU READY YET?
YES! I'LL BE RIGHT THERE!
Oh!
SORRY FOR TAKING UP YOUR TIME.
THAT'S OKAY! I'D LIKE TO HEAR MORE ABOUT IT SOMETIME.
SURE.
AND I WANT TO TELL YOU MORE ABOUT MYSELF, TOO.
OH...
OKAY!

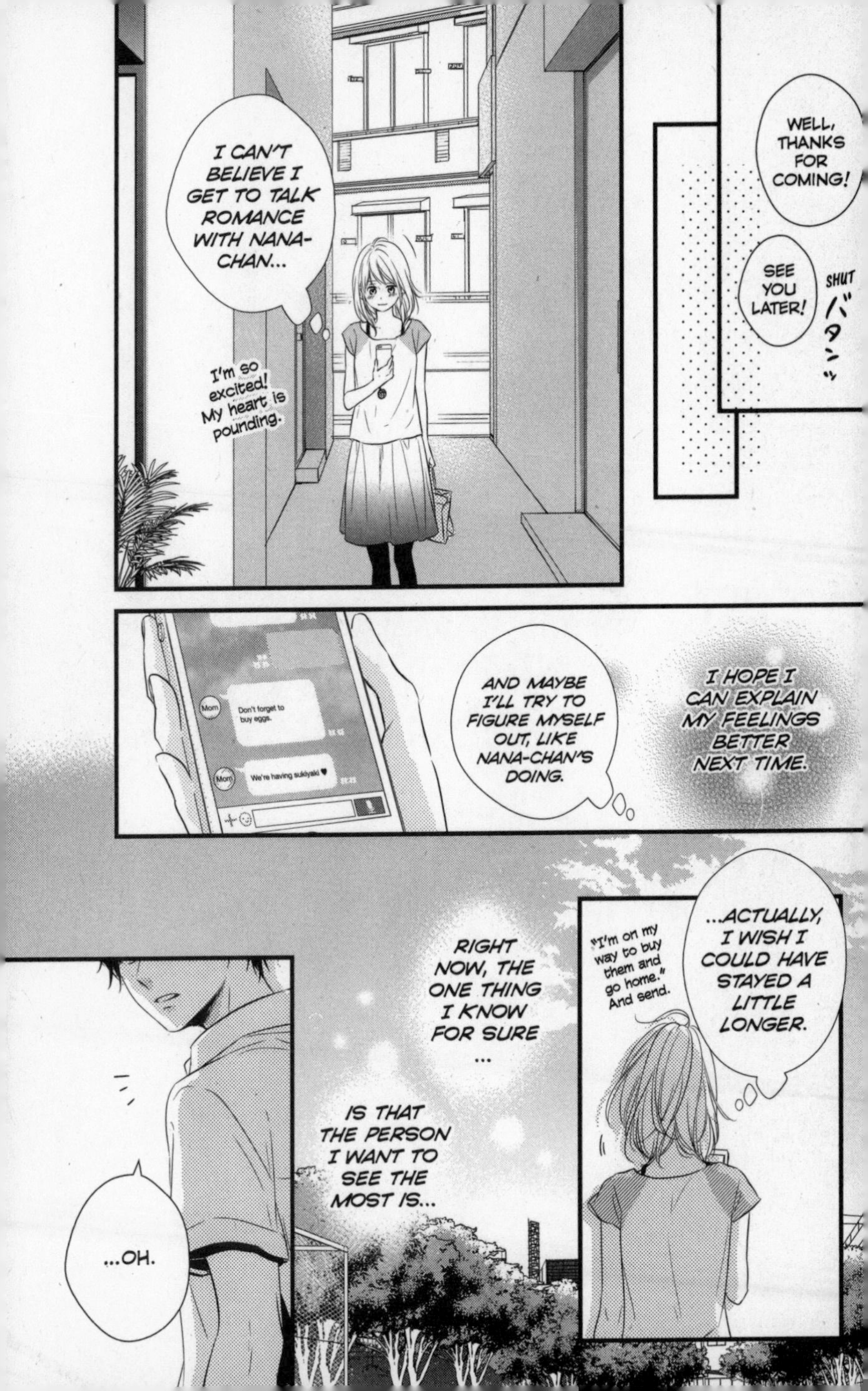
WELL, THANKS FOR COMING!
SEE YOU LATER!
SHUT
バタンッ
I CAN'T BELIEVE I GET TO TALK ROMANCE WITH NANA-CHAN...
I'm so excited! My heart is pounding.
I HOPE I CAN EXPLAIN MY FEELINGS BETTER NEXT TIME.
AND MAYBE I'LL TRY TO FIGURE MYSELF OUT, LIKE NANA-CHAN'S DOING.
Mom
Don't forget to buy eggs.
Mom
We're having sukiyaki ♥
...ACTUALLY, I WISH I COULD HAVE STAYED A LITTLE LONGER.
"I'm on my way to buy them and go home." And send.
RIGHT NOW, THE ONE THING I KNOW FOR SURE ...
IS THAT THE PERSON I WANT TO SEE THE MOST IS...
...OH.

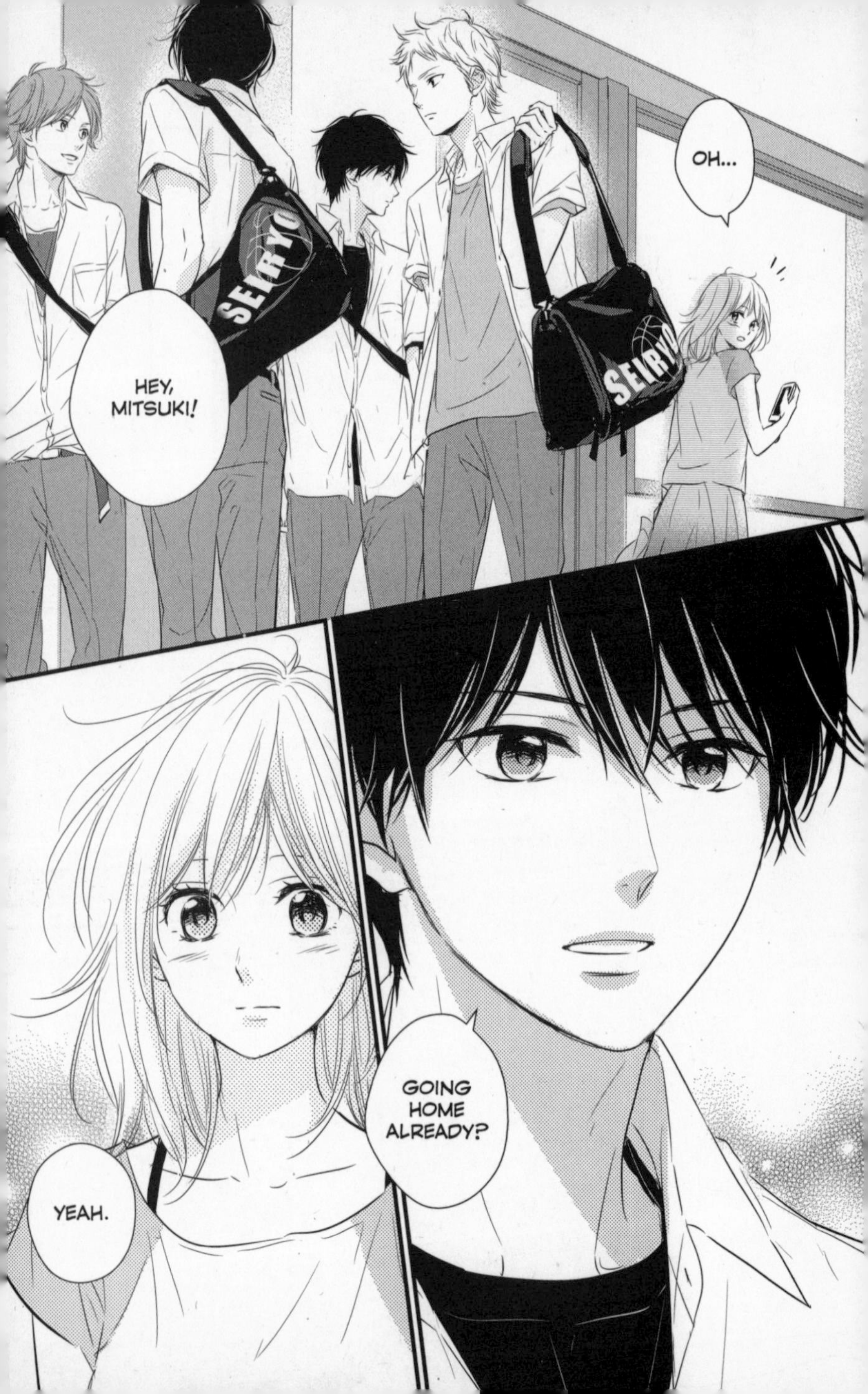
OH...
HEY, MITSUKI!
GOING HOME ALREADY?
YEAH.

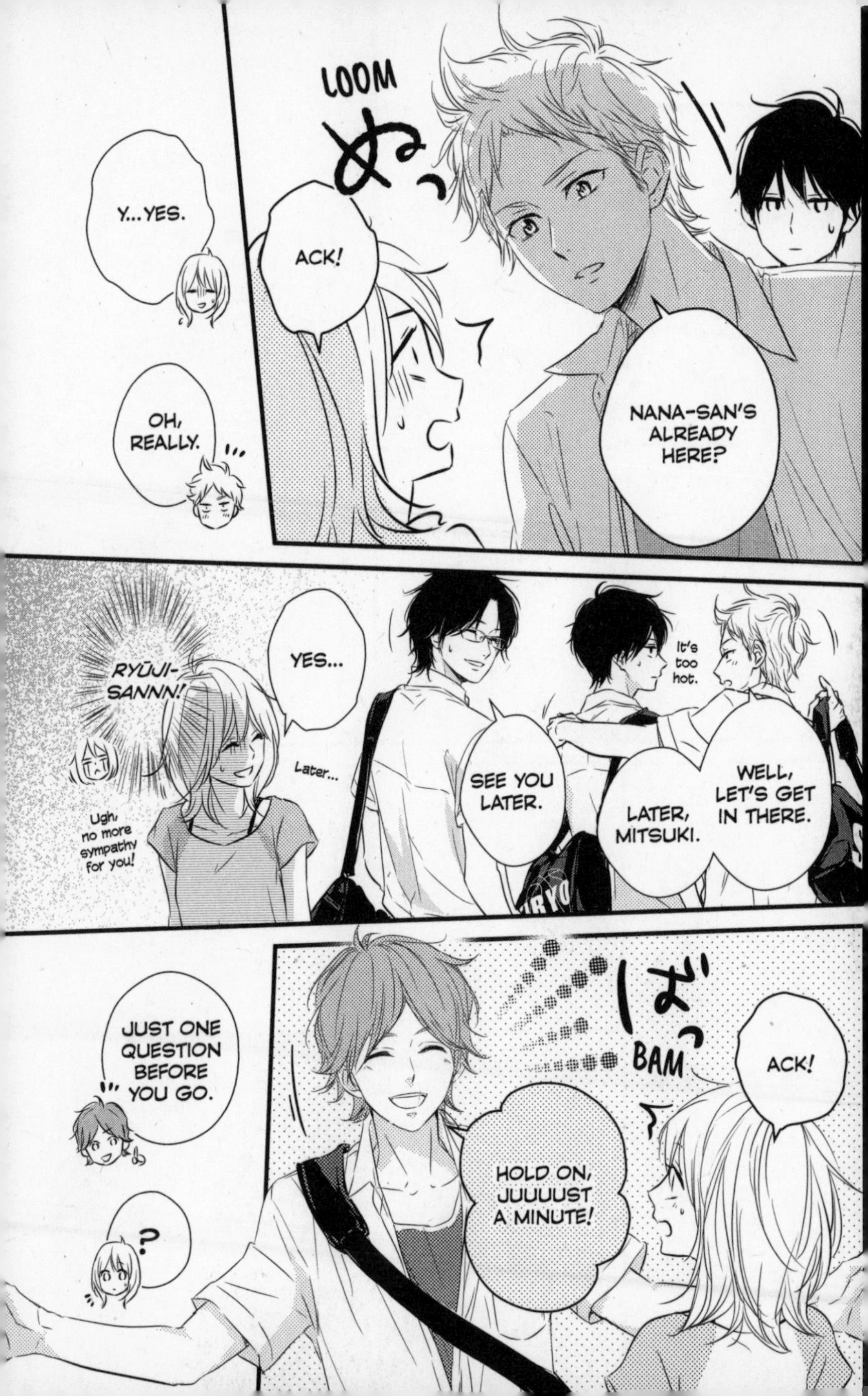
LOOM
ぬっ
ACK!
NANA-SAN'S ALREADY HERE?
Y...YES.
OH, REALLY.
WELL, LET'S GET IN THERE.
It's too hot.
LATER, MITSUKI.
SEE YOU LATER.
YES...
Later...
RYŪJI-SANNN!
Ugh, no more sympathy for you!
ばっ
BAM
ACK!
HOLD ON, JUUUUST A MINUTE!
JUST ONE QUESTION BEFORE YOU GO.
?

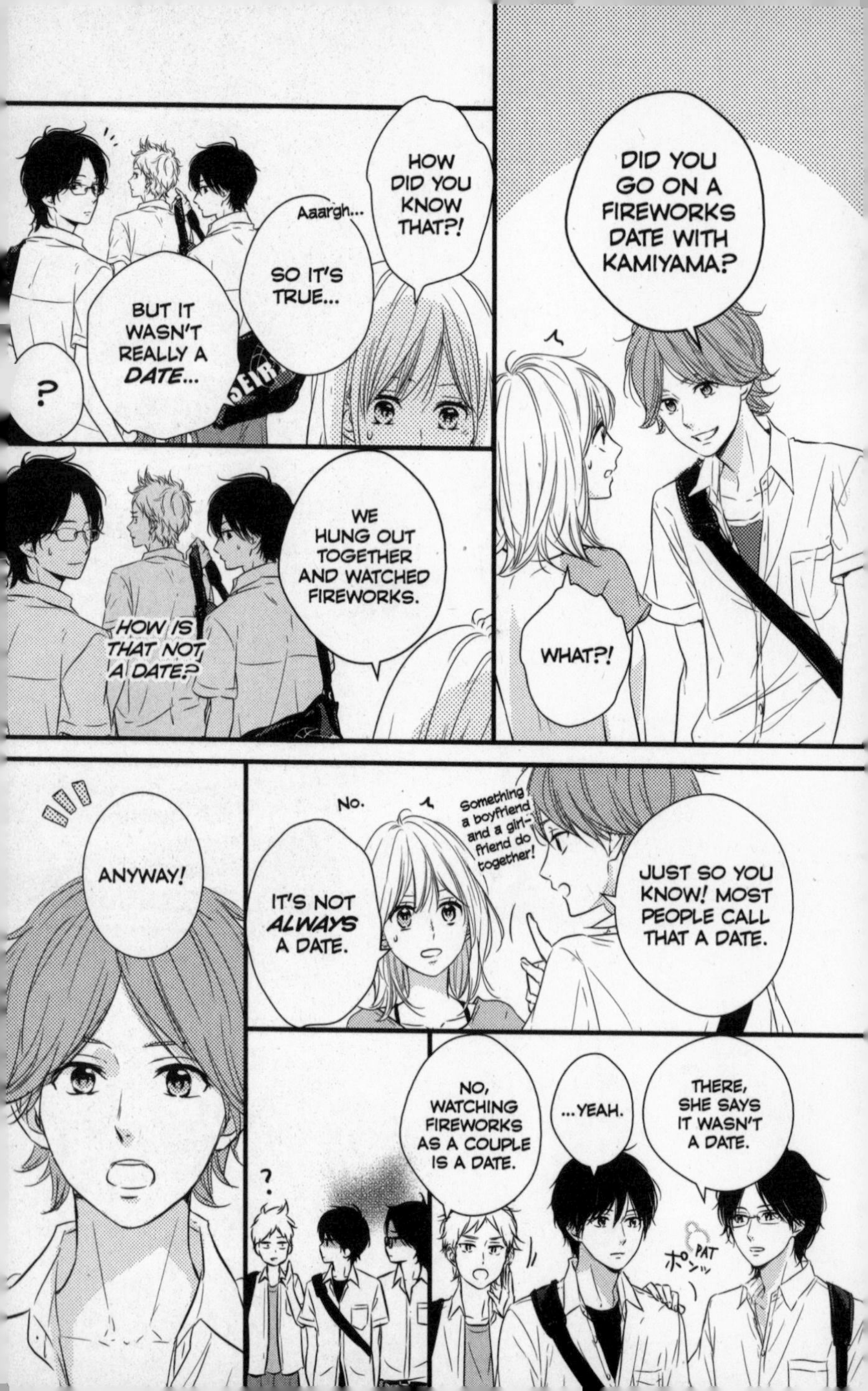
DID YOU GO ON A FIREWORKS DATE WITH KAMIYAMA?
WHAT?!
HOW DID YOU KNOW THAT?!
Aaargh...
SO IT'S TRUE...
BUT IT WASN'T REALLY A *DATE*...
?
WE HUNG OUT TOGETHER AND WATCHED FIREWORKS.
HOW IS THAT NOT A DATE?
JUST SO YOU KNOW! MOST PEOPLE CALL THAT A DATE.
Something a boyfriend and a girlfriend do together!
No.
IT'S NOT *ALWAYS* A DATE.
THERE, SHE SAYS IT WASN'T A DATE.
PAT
...YEAH.
NO, WATCHING FIREWORKS AS A COUPLE IS A DATE.
?
ANYWAY!

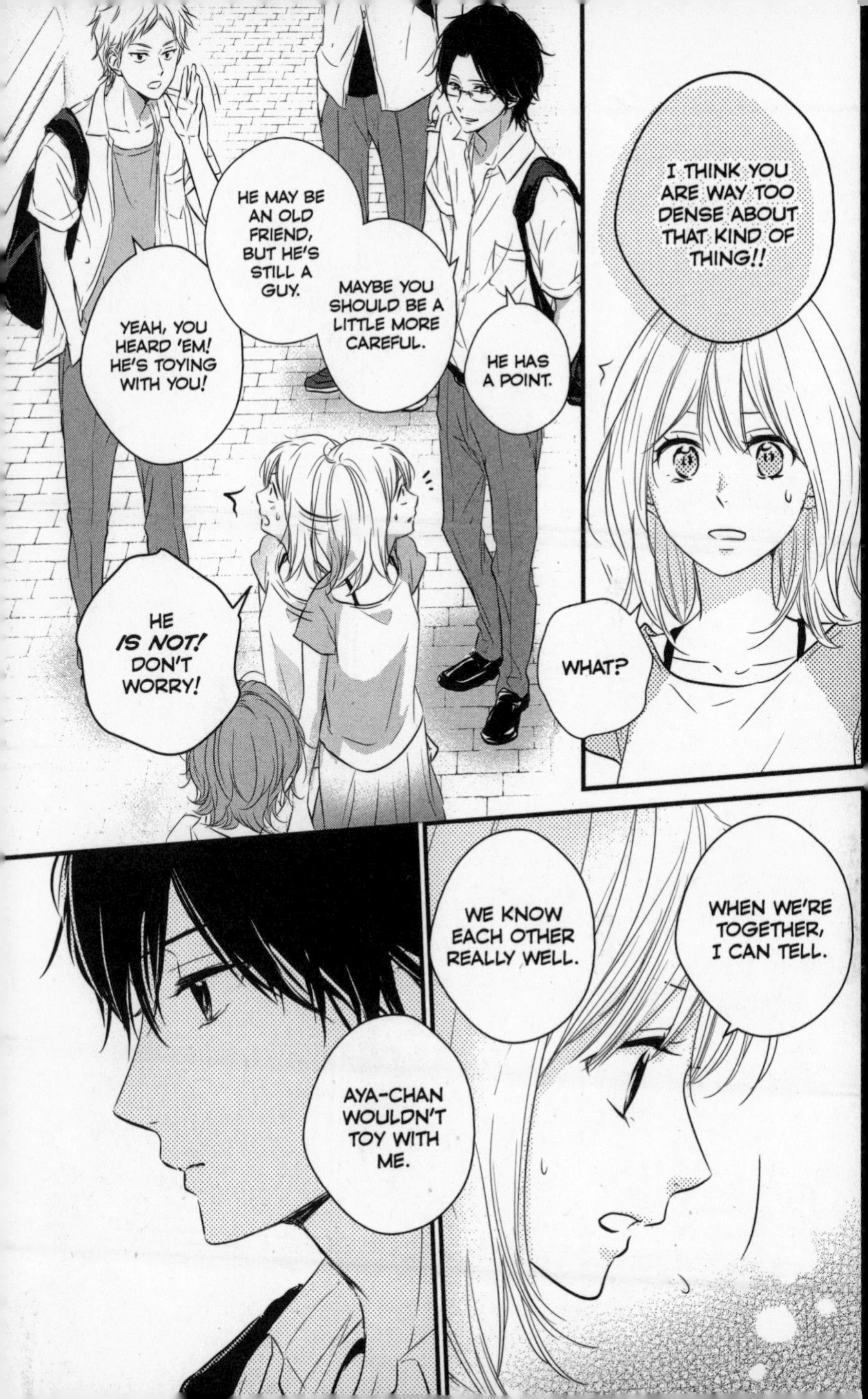
I THINK YOU ARE WAY TOO DENSE ABOUT THAT KIND OF THING!!
WHAT?
HE MAY BE AN OLD FRIEND, BUT HE'S STILL A GUY.
MAYBE YOU SHOULD BE A LITTLE MORE CAREFUL.
HE HAS A POINT.
YEAH, YOU HEARD 'EM! HE'S TOYING WITH YOU!
HE *IS NOT!* DON'T WORRY!
WHEN WE'RE TOGETHER, I CAN TELL.
WE KNOW EACH OTHER REALLY WELL.
AYA-CHAN WOULDN'T TOY WITH ME.

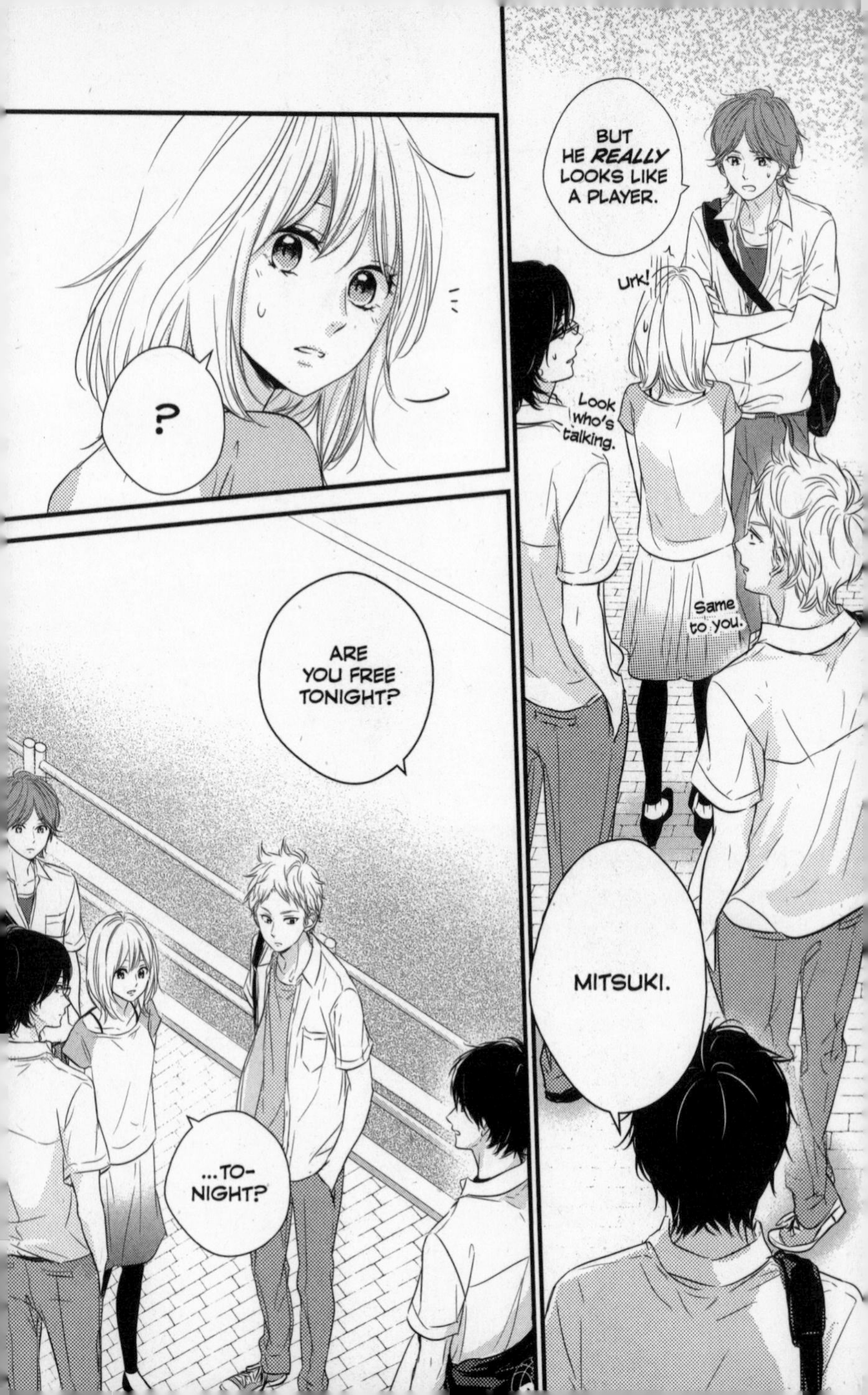
BUT HE *REALLY* LOOKS LIKE A PLAYER.
Urk!
Look who's talking.
Same to you.
MITSUKI.
?
ARE YOU FREE TONIGHT?
...TO-NIGHT?

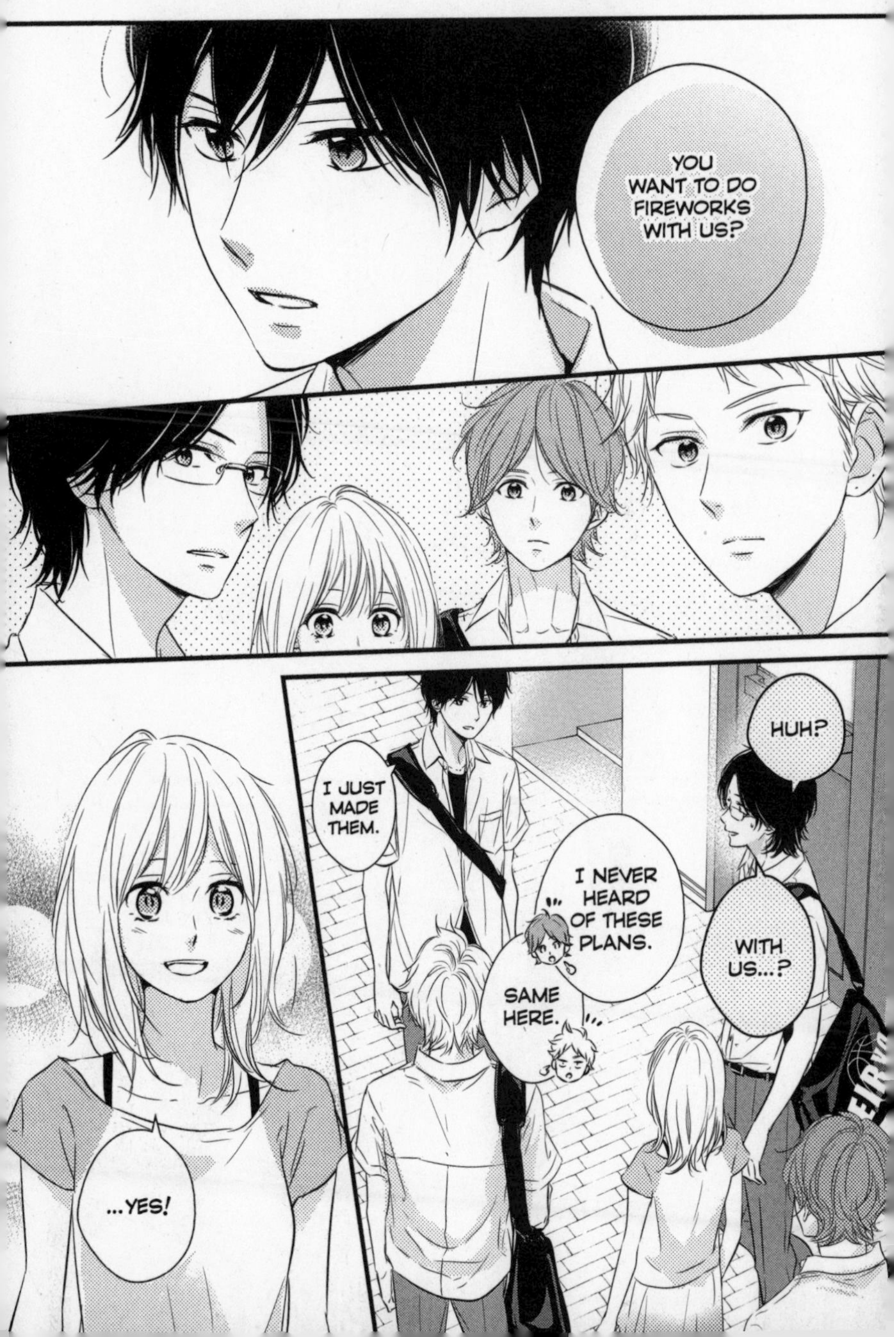
YOU WANT TO DO FIREWORKS WITH US?
HUH?
WITH US...?
I JUST MADE THEM.
I NEVER HEARD OF THESE PLANS.
SAME HERE.
...YES!

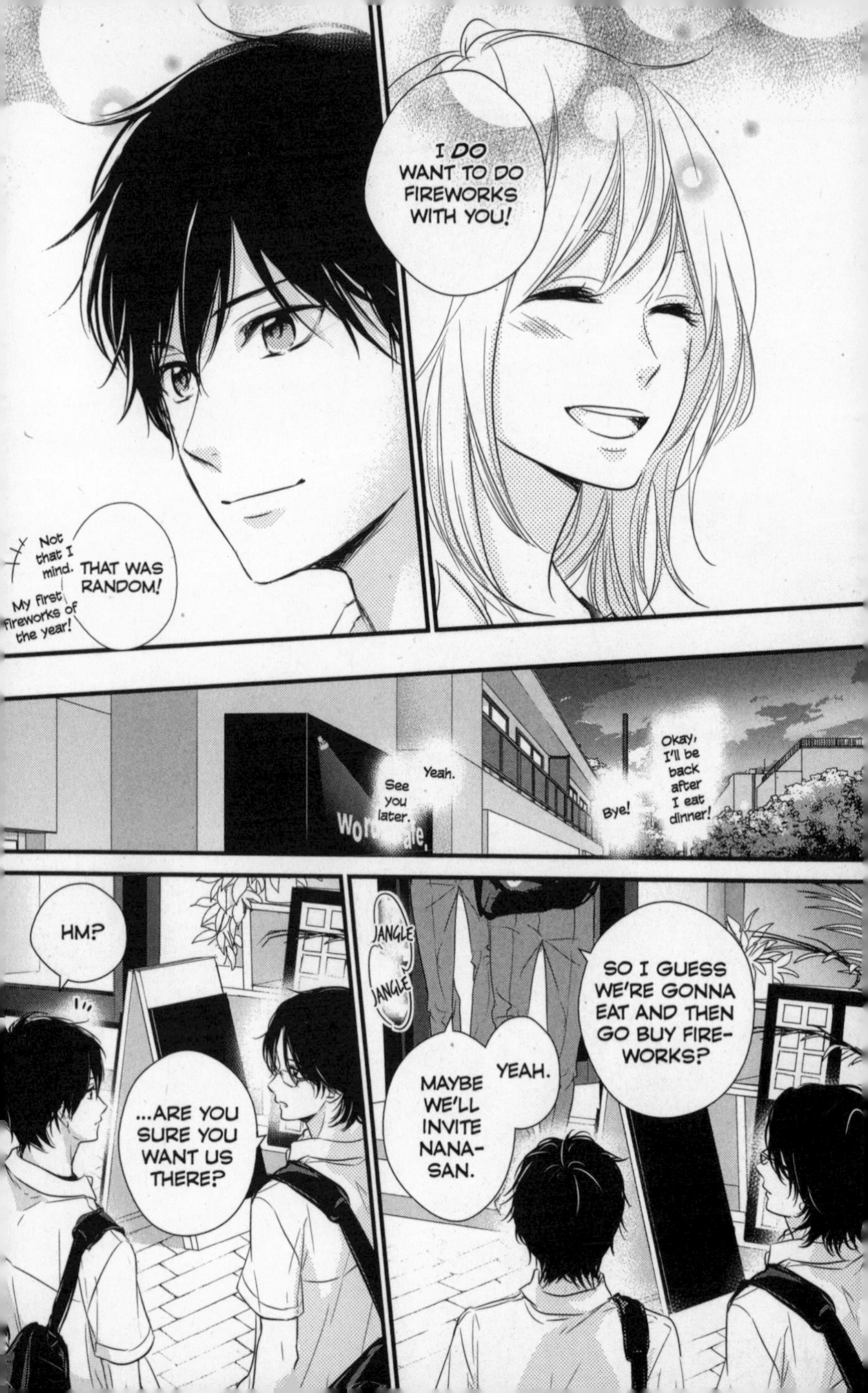
I DO WANT TO DO FIREWORKS WITH YOU!
THAT WAS RANDOM!
Not that I mind.
My first fireworks of the year!
Okay, I'll be back after I eat dinner!
Bye!
Yeah.
See you later.
SO I GUESS WE'RE GONNA EAT AND THEN GO BUY FIRE-WORKS?
YEAH.
MAYBE WE'LL INVITE NANA-SAN.
JANGLE
JANGLE
HM?
...ARE YOU SURE YOU WANT US THERE?

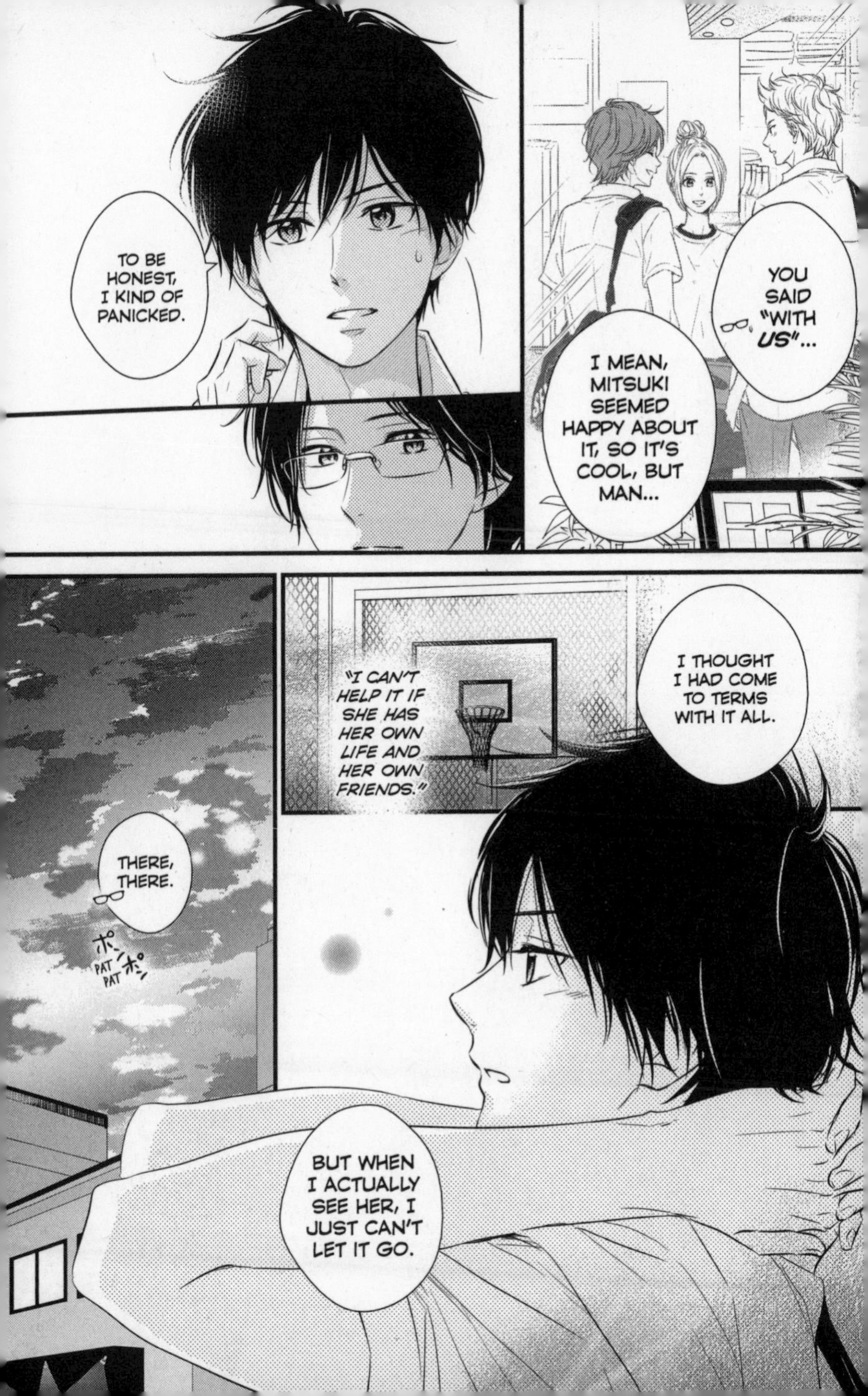
YOU SAID "WITH *US*"...
I MEAN, MITSUKI SEEMED HAPPY ABOUT IT, SO IT'S COOL, BUT MAN...
TO BE HONEST, I KIND OF PANICKED.
I THOUGHT I HAD COME TO TERMS WITH IT ALL.
"I CAN'T HELP IT IF SHE HAS HER OWN LIFE AND HER OWN FRIENDS."
BUT WHEN I ACTUALLY SEE HER, I JUST CAN'T LET IT GO.
THERE, THERE.
ポンポン
PAT PAT

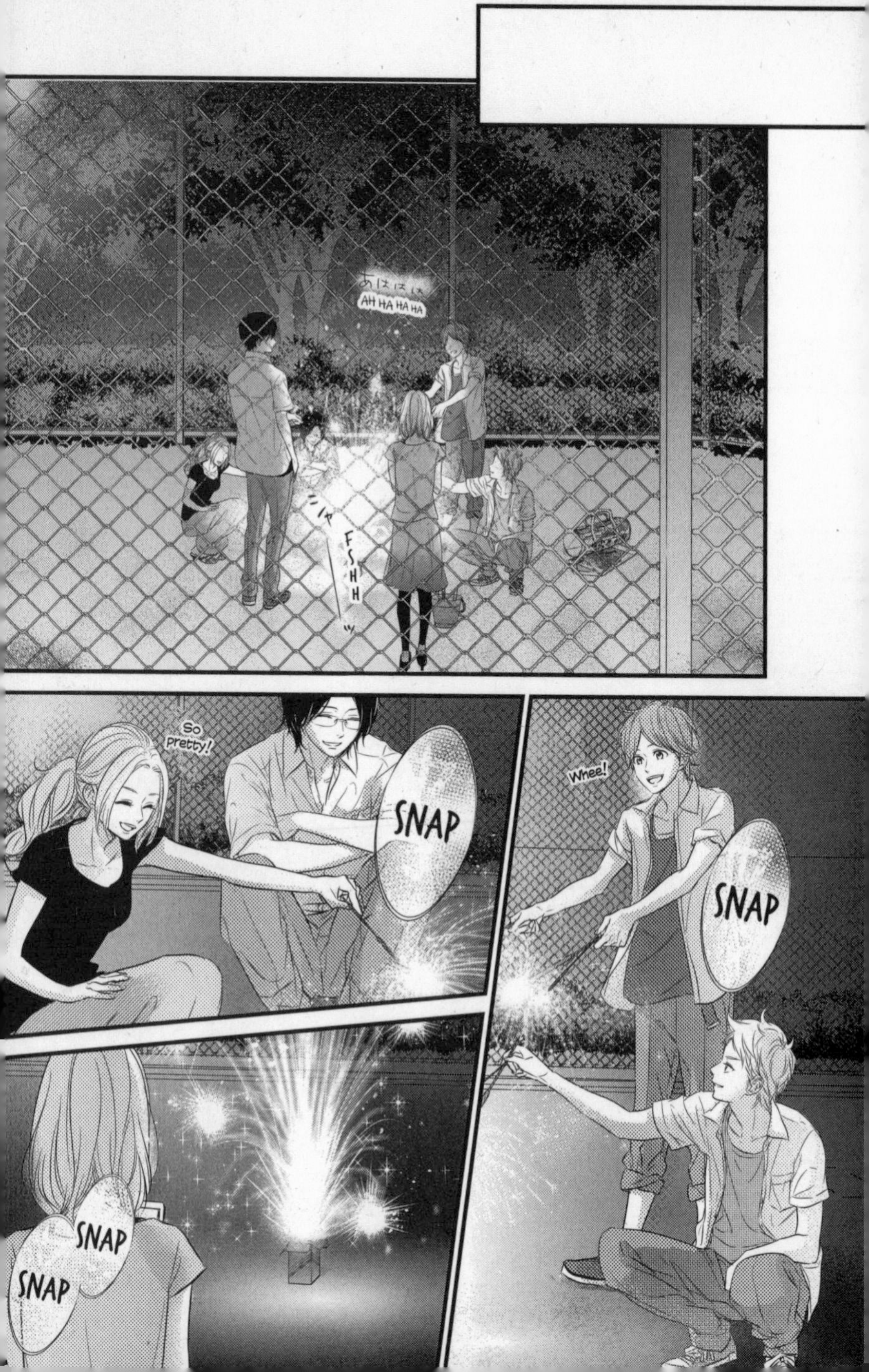
あははは
AH HA HA HA
FSHH
Whee!
SNAP
So pretty!
SNAP
SNAP
SNAP

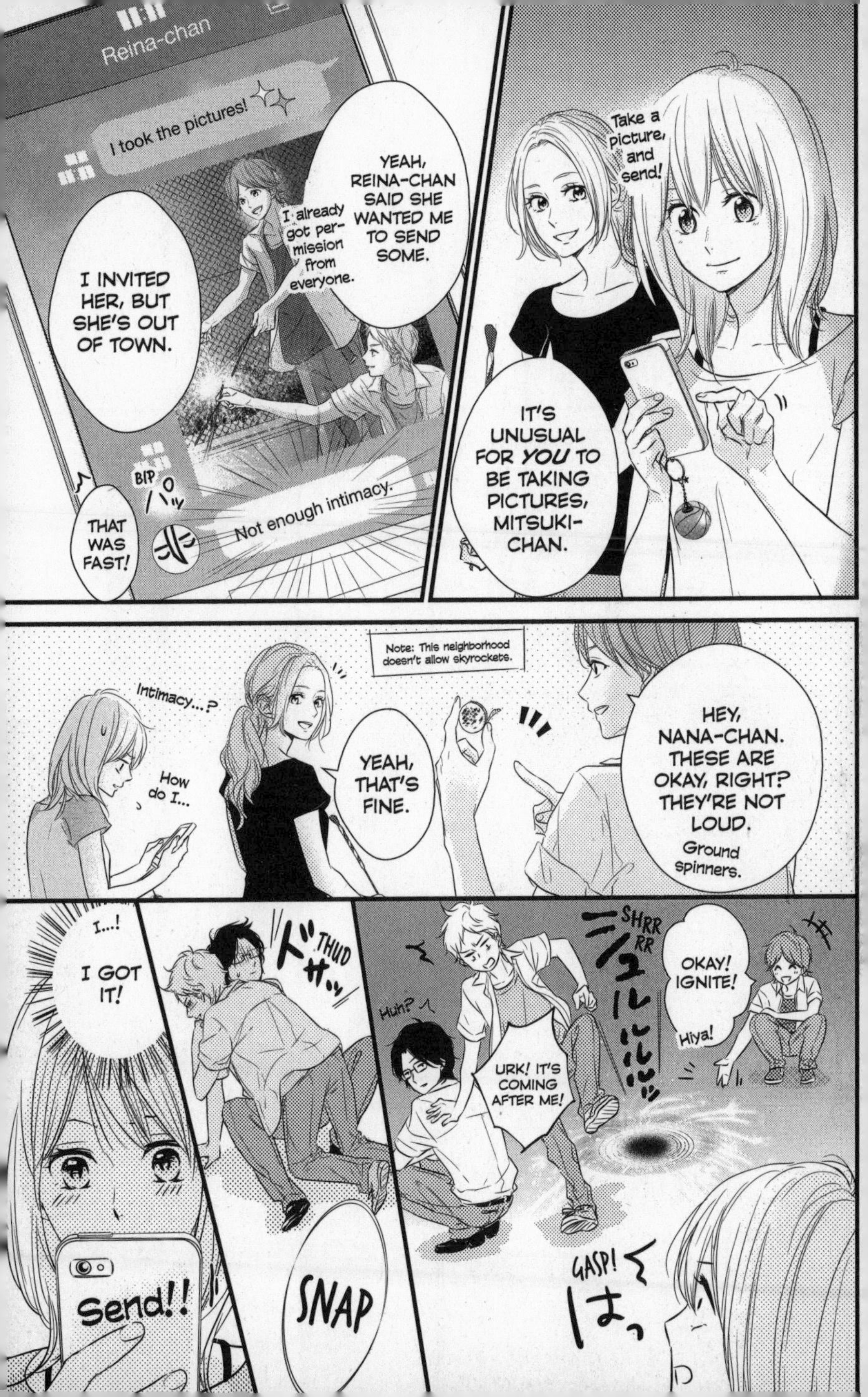

Take a picture, and send!
IT'S UNUSUAL FOR *YOU* TO BE TAKING PICTURES, MITSUKI-CHAN.
Reina-chan
I took the pictures!
YEAH, REINA-CHAN SAID SHE WANTED ME TO SEND SOME.
I already got permission from everyone.
I INVITED HER, BUT SHE'S OUT OF TOWN.
BIP
Not enough intimacy.
THAT WAS FAST!
HEY, NANA-CHAN. THESE ARE OKAY, RIGHT? THEY'RE NOT LOUD.
Ground spinners.
Note: This neighborhood doesn't allow skyrockets.
YEAH, THAT'S FINE.
Intimacy...?
How do I...
OKAY! IGNITE!
Hiya!
SHRRRR
URK! IT'S COMING AFTER ME!
Huh?
GASP!
THUD
SNAP
I...!
I GOT IT!
Send!!

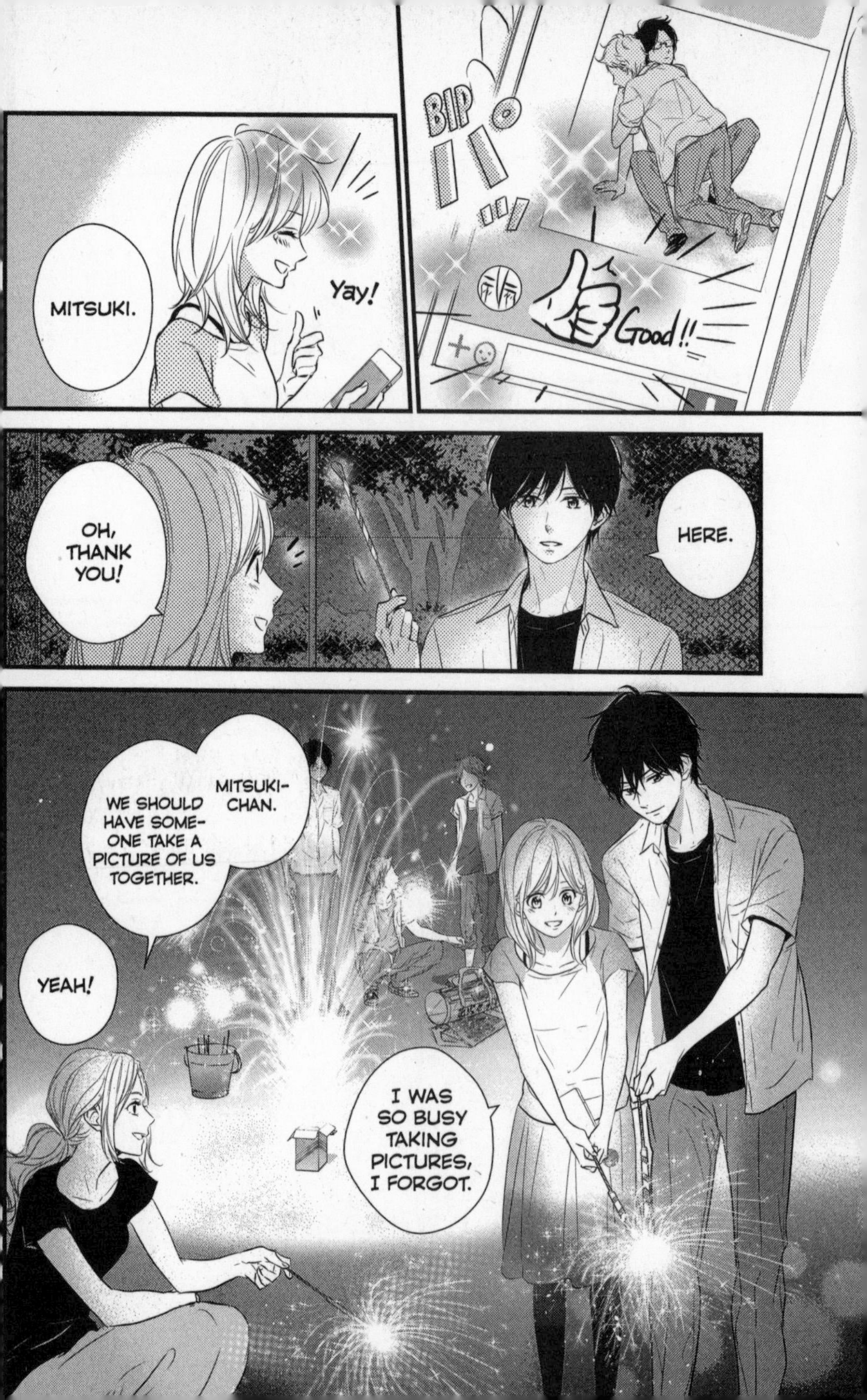
BIP
Good!!
Yay!
MITSUKI.
HERE.
OH, THANK YOU!
MITSUKI-CHAN.
WE SHOULD HAVE SOME-ONE TAKE A PICTURE OF US TOGETHER.
YEAH!
I WAS SO BUSY TAKING PICTURES, I FORGOT.

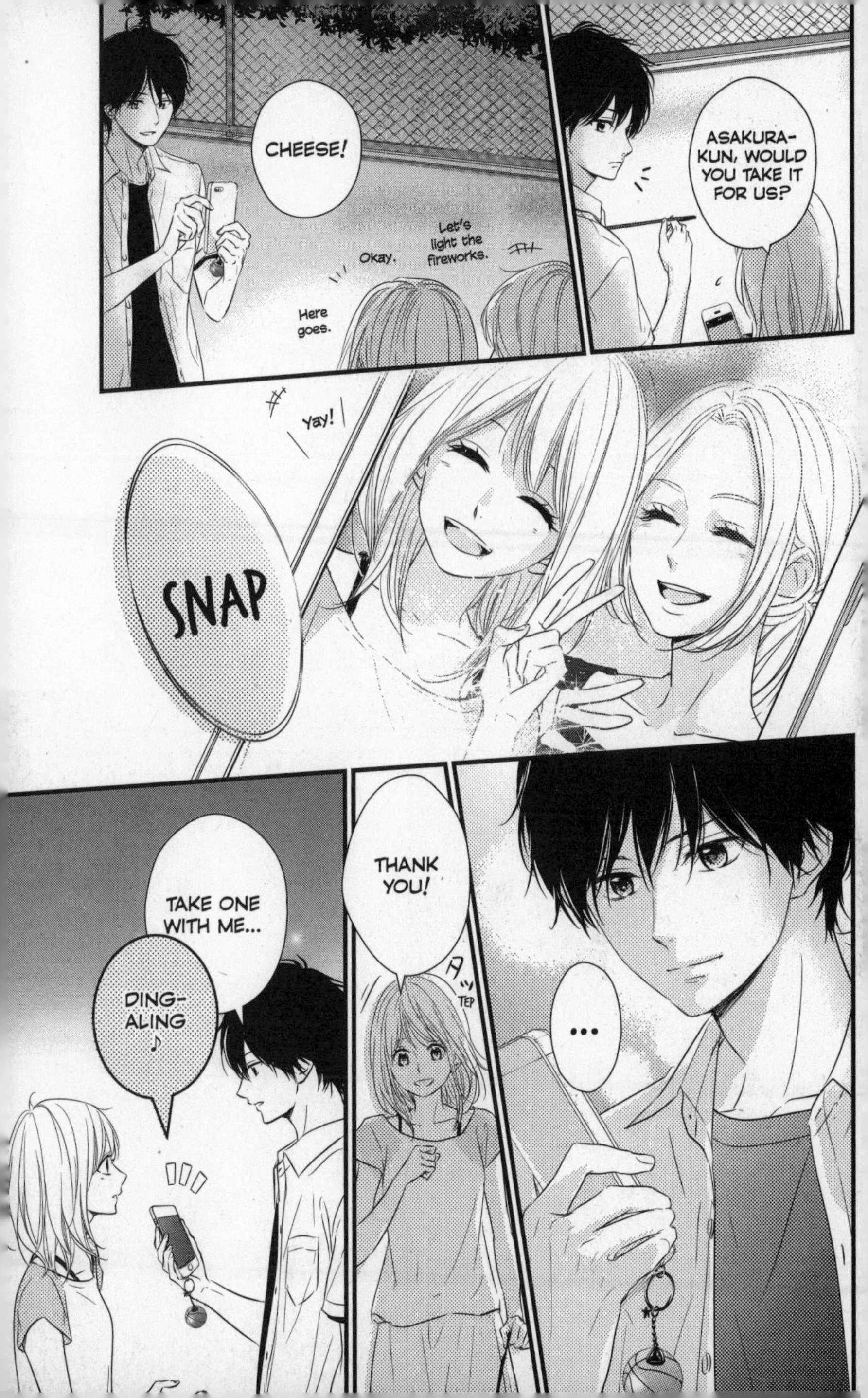
ASAKURA-KUN, WOULD YOU TAKE IT FOR US?
CHEESE!
Let's light the fireworks.
Okay.
Here goes.
Yay!
SNAP
...
THANK YOU!
TEP
TAKE ONE WITH ME...
DING-ALING ♪

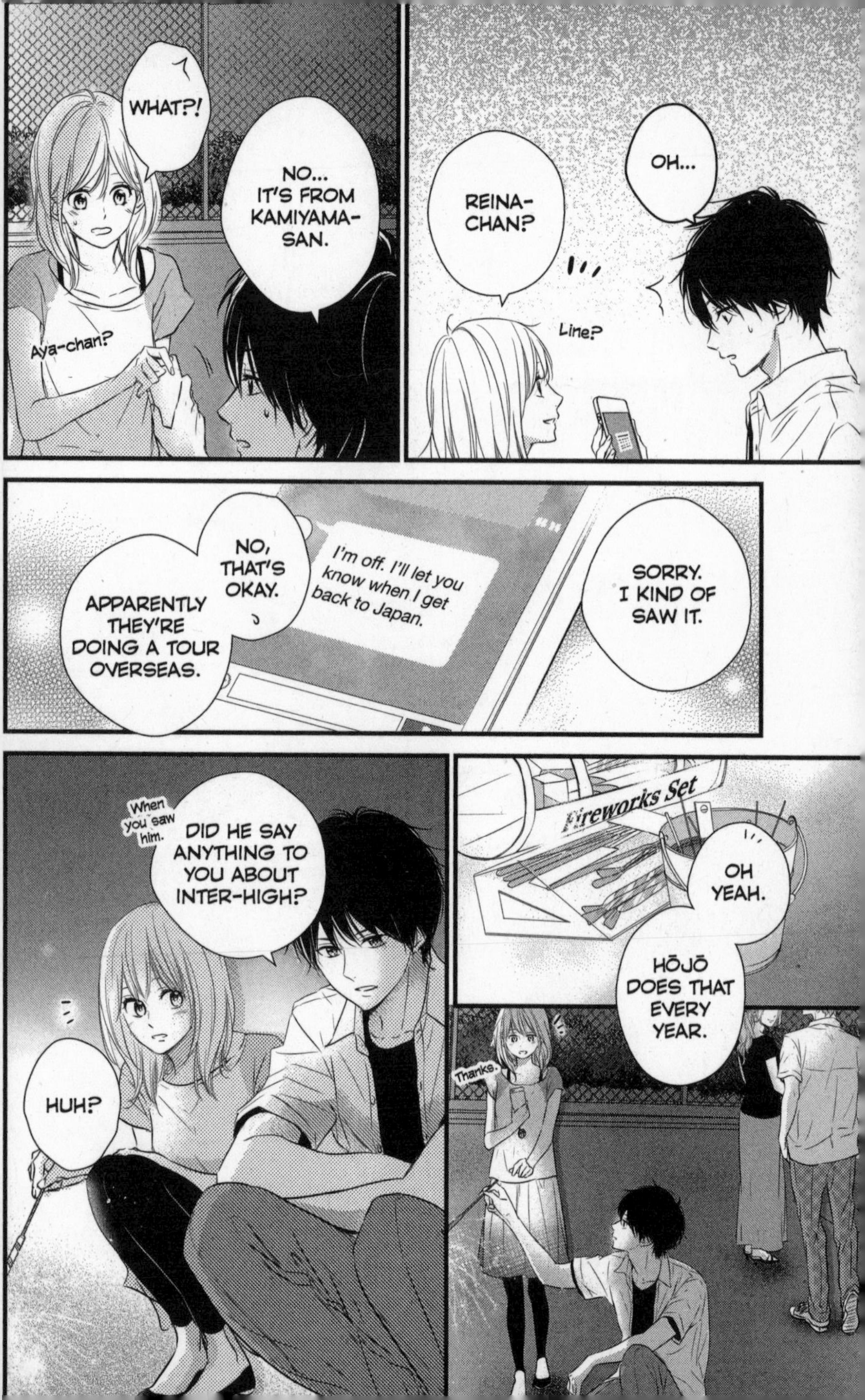
OH...
REINA-CHAN?
Line?
NO... IT'S FROM KAMIYAMA-SAN.
WHAT?!
Aya-chan?
SORRY. I KIND OF SAW IT.
I'm off. I'll let you know when I get back to Japan.
NO, THAT'S OKAY.
APPARENTLY THEY'RE DOING A TOUR OVERSEAS.
Fireworks Set
OH YEAH.
HŌJŌ DOES THAT EVERY YEAR.
Thanks.
When you saw him.
DID HE SAY ANYTHING TO YOU ABOUT INTER-HIGH?
HUH?

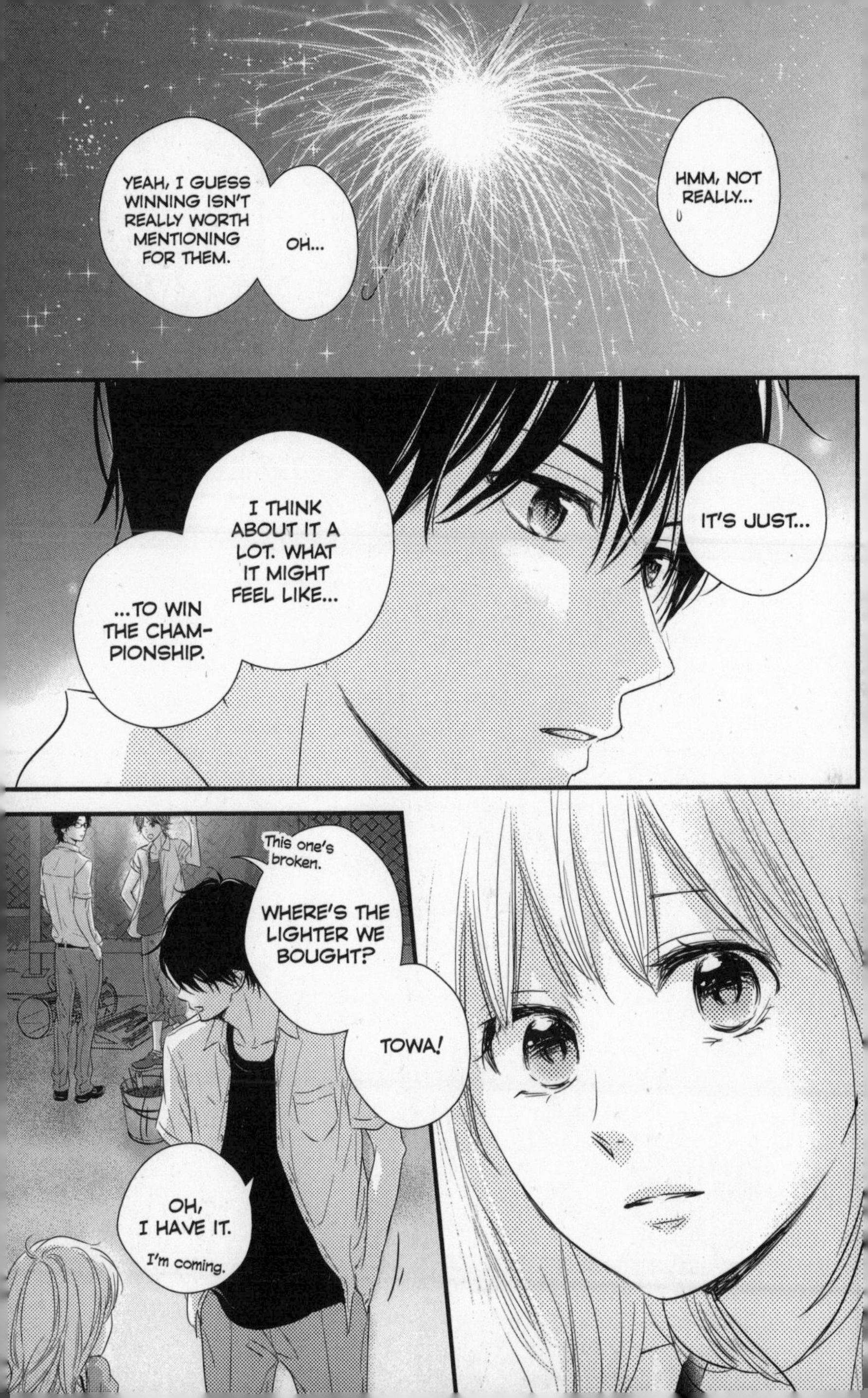
HMM, NOT REALLY...
OH...
YEAH, I GUESS WINNING ISN'T REALLY WORTH MENTIONING FOR THEM.
IT'S JUST...
I THINK ABOUT IT A LOT. WHAT IT MIGHT FEEL LIKE...
...TO WIN THE CHAMPIONSHIP.
This one's broken.
WHERE'S THE LIGHTER WE BOUGHT?
TOWA!
OH, I HAVE IT.
I'm coming.

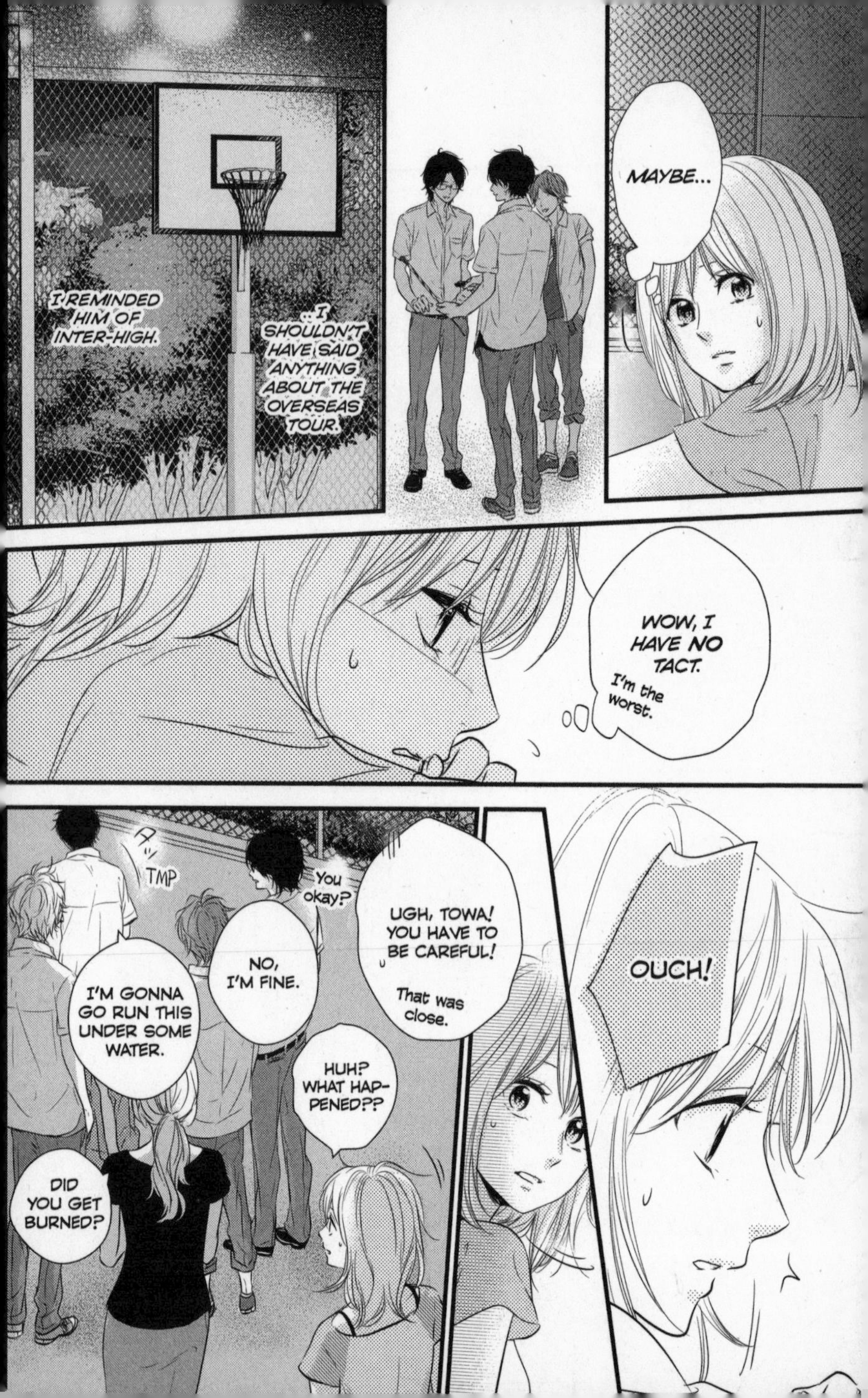
MAYBE...
I REMINDED HIM OF INTER-HIGH.
..I SHOULDN'T HAVE SAID ANYTHING ABOUT THE OVERSEAS TOUR.
WOW, I HAVE NO TACT.
I'm the worst.
OUCH!
UGH, TOWA! YOU HAVE TO BE CAREFUL!
That was close.
You okay?
タッ
TMP
NO, I'M FINE.
HUH? WHAT HAP-PENED??
I'M GONNA GO RUN THIS UNDER SOME WATER.
DID YOU GET BURNED?

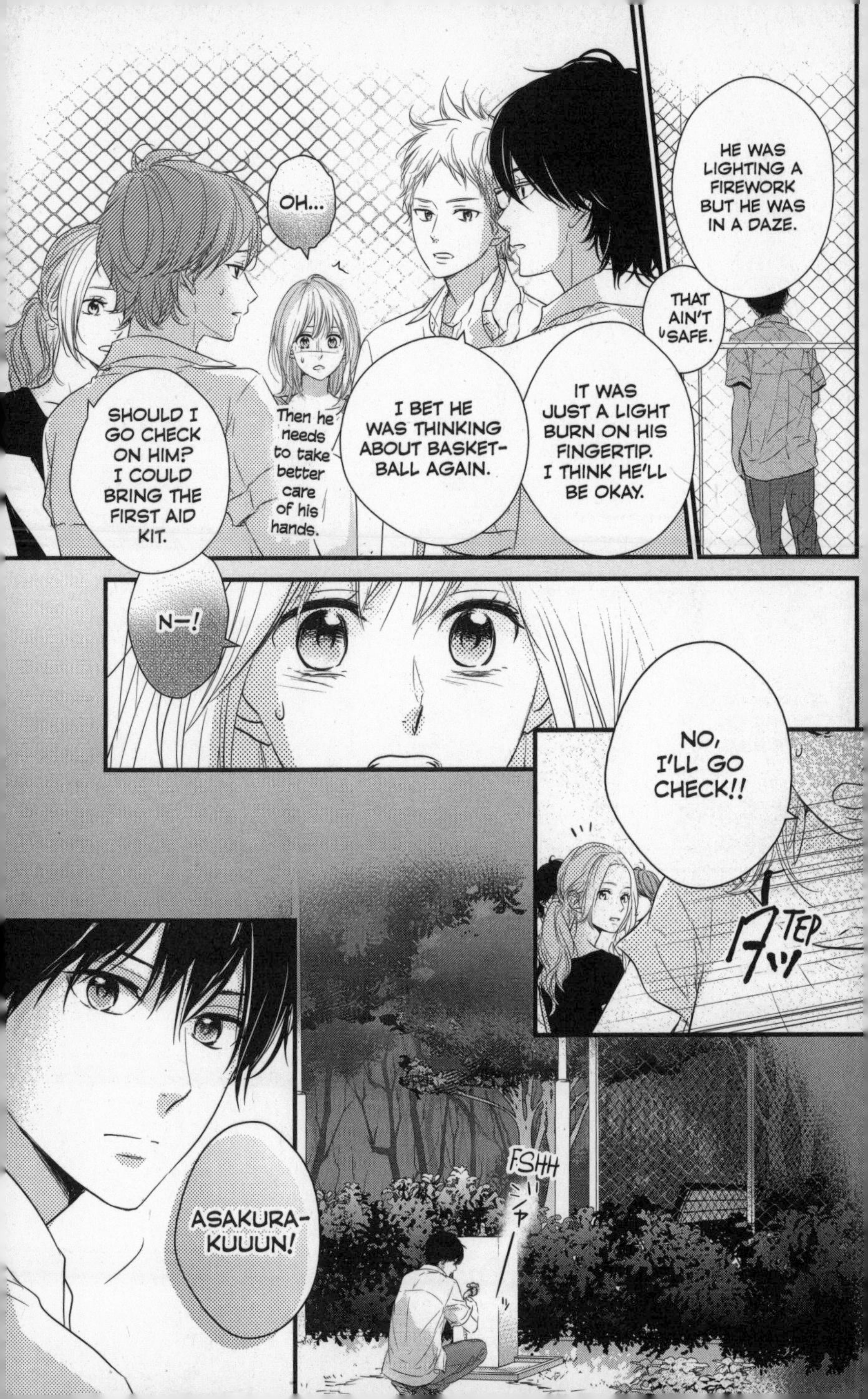
HE WAS LIGHTING A FIREWORK BUT HE WAS IN A DAZE.
THAT AIN'T SAFE.
IT WAS JUST A LIGHT BURN ON HIS FINGERTIP. I THINK HE'LL BE OKAY.
I BET HE WAS THINKING ABOUT BASKET-BALL AGAIN.
OH...
Then he needs to take better care of his hands.
SHOULD I GO CHECK ON HIM? I COULD BRING THE FIRST AID KIT.
N—!
NO, I'LL GO CHECK!!
TEP
FSHH
ASAKURA-KUUUN!

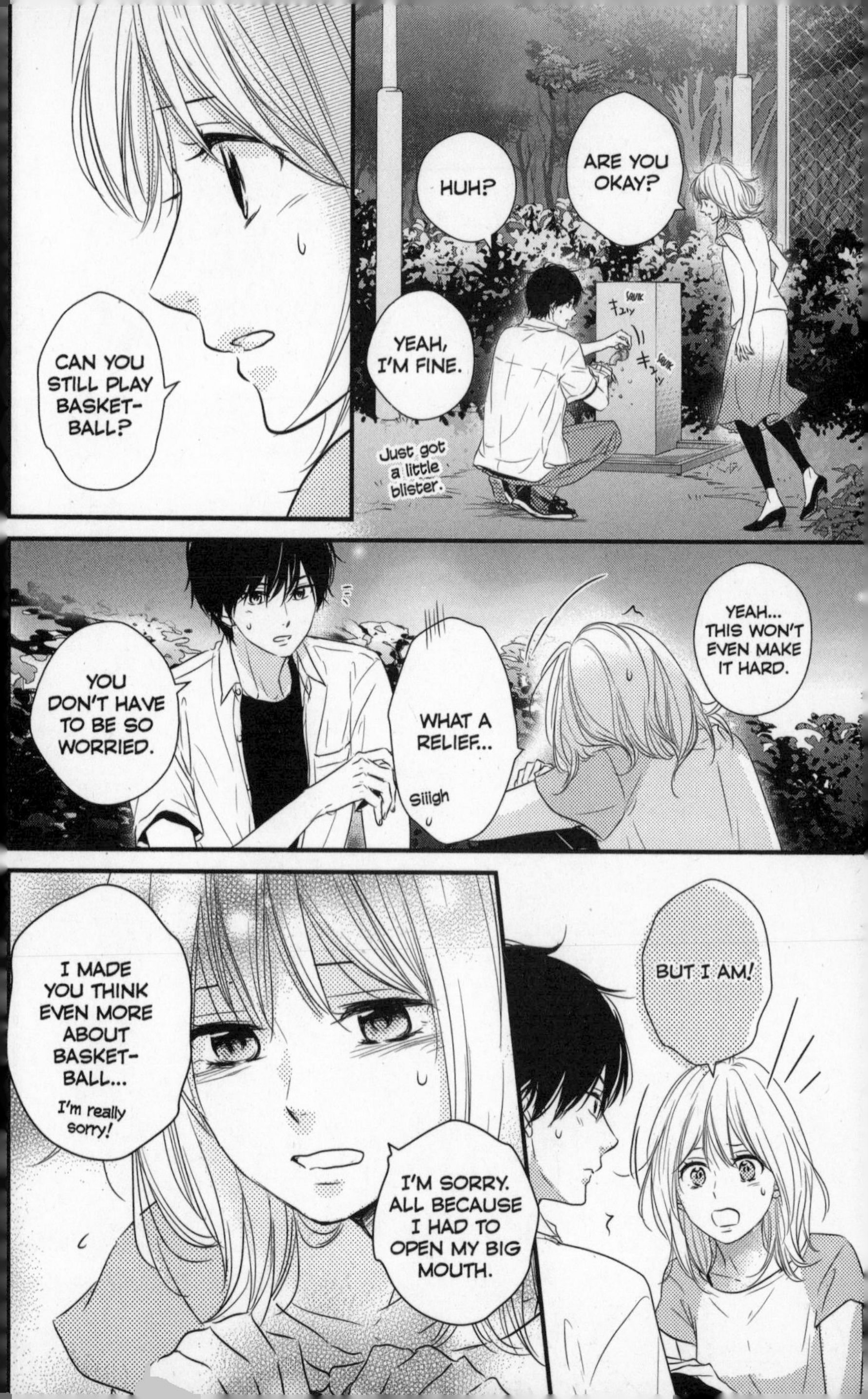
ARE YOU OKAY?
HUH?
YEAH, I'M FINE.
Just got a little blister.
CAN YOU STILL PLAY BASKET-BALL?
YEAH... THIS WON'T EVEN MAKE IT HARD.
WHAT A RELIEF...
Siiigh
YOU DON'T HAVE TO BE SO WORRIED.
BUT I AM!
I'M SORRY. ALL BECAUSE I HAD TO OPEN MY BIG MOUTH.
I MADE YOU THINK EVEN MORE ABOUT BASKET-BALL...
I'm really sorry!

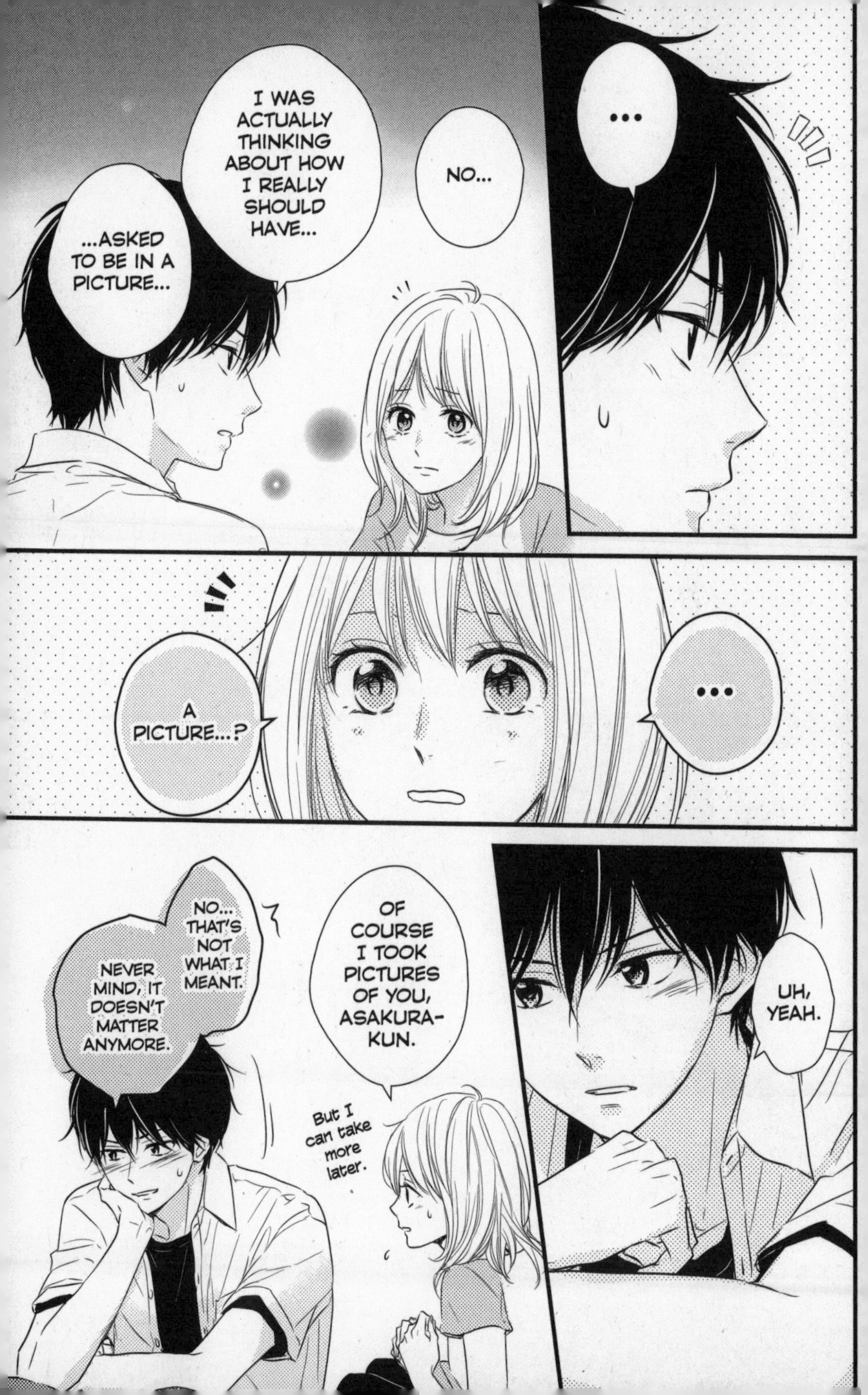
...
NO...
I WAS ACTUALLY THINKING ABOUT HOW I REALLY SHOULD HAVE...
...ASKED TO BE IN A PICTURE...
...
A PICTURE...?
UH, YEAH.
OF COURSE I TOOK PICTURES OF YOU, ASAKURA-KUN.
NO... THAT'S NOT WHAT I MEANT.
NEVER MIND, IT DOESN'T MATTER ANYMORE.
But I can take more later.

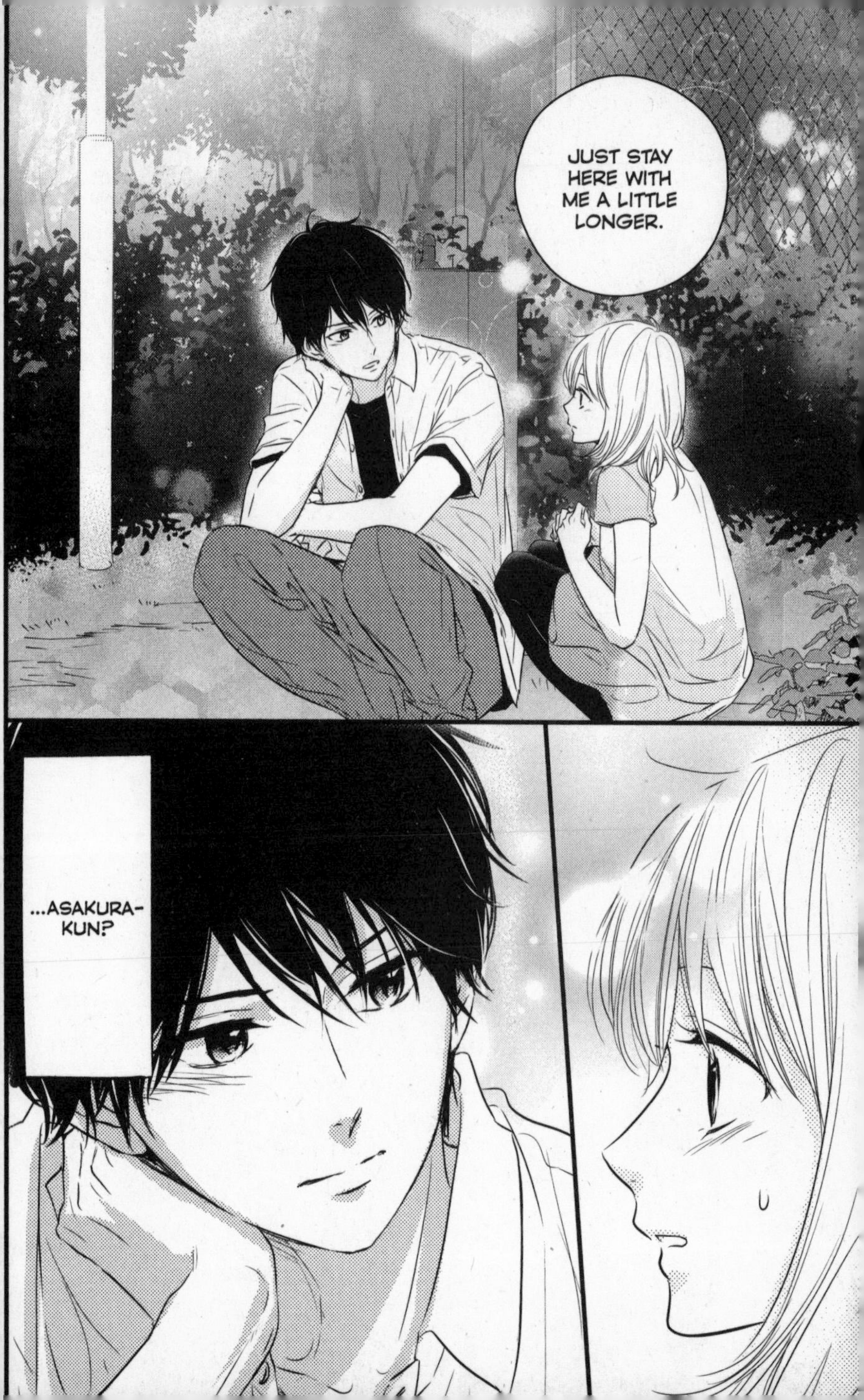
JUST STAY HERE WITH ME A LITTLE LONGER.
...ASAKURA-KUN?

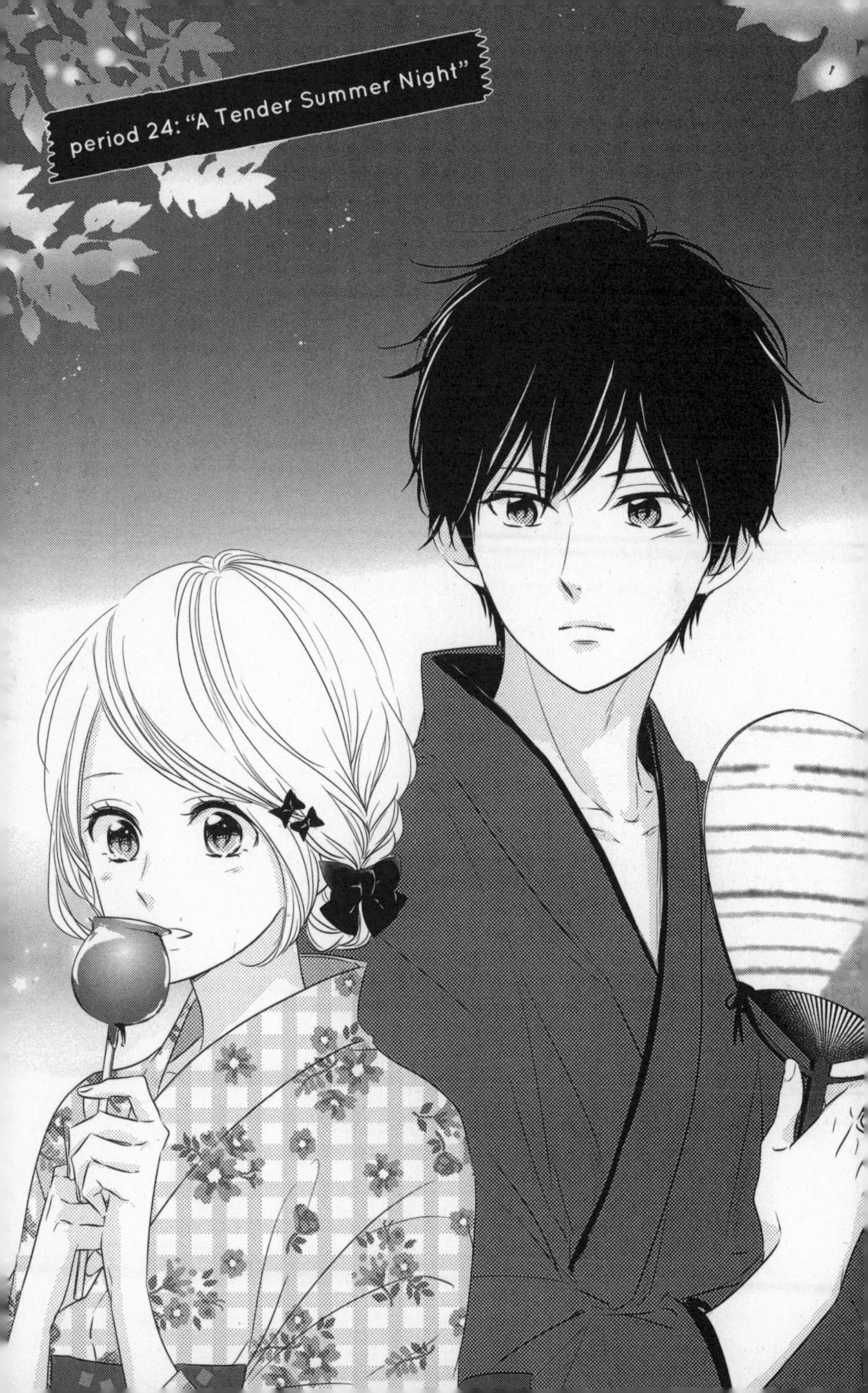
period 24: "A Tender Summer Night"

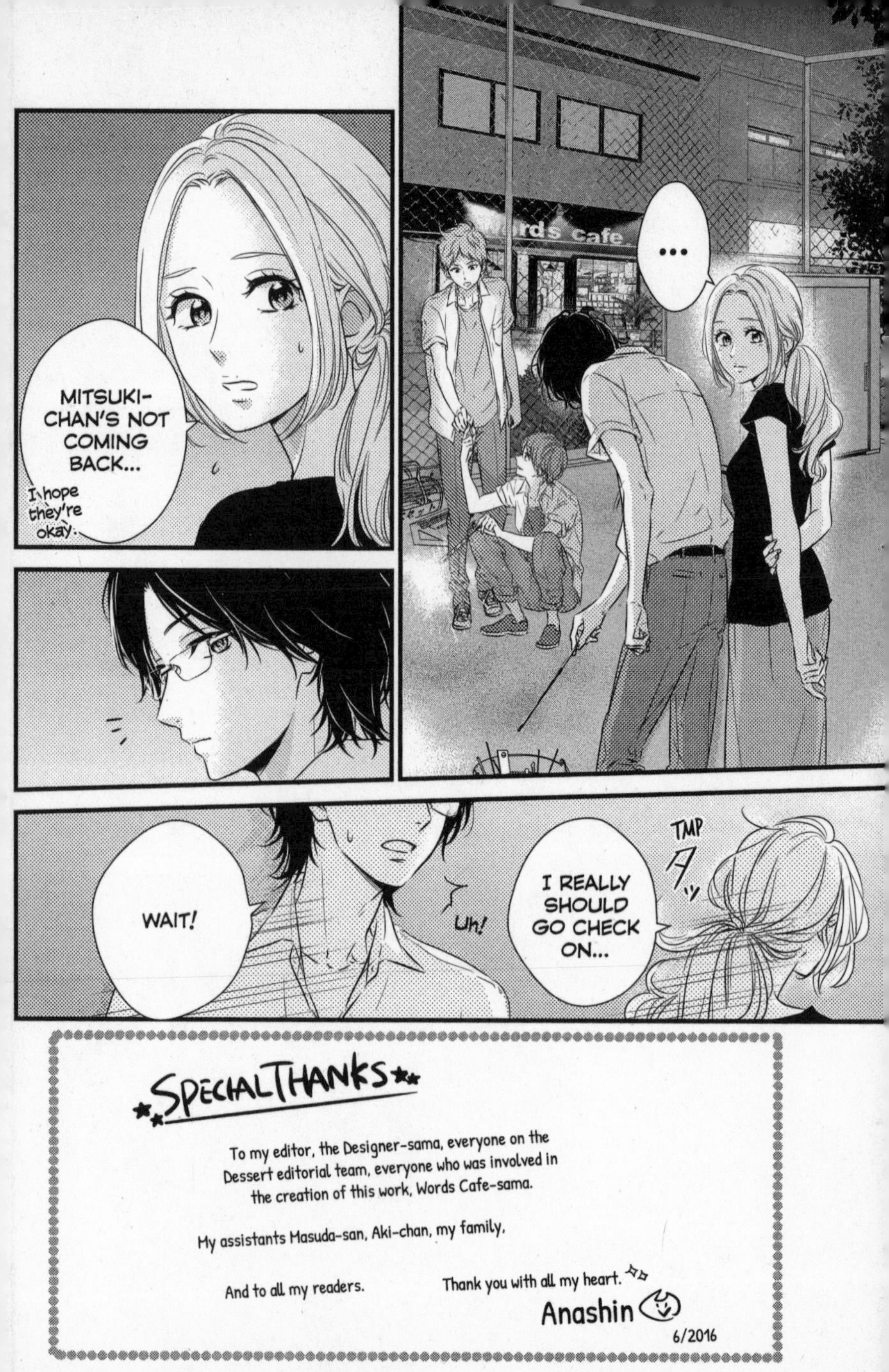
...
MITSUKI-CHAN'S NOT COMING BACK...
I hope they're okay.
TMP
I REALLY SHOULD GO CHECK ON...
Uh!
WAIT!

SPECIAL THANKS

To my editor, the Designer-sama, everyone on the Dessert editorial team, everyone who was involved in the creation of this work, Words Cafe-sama.

My assistants Masuda-san, Aki-chan, my family,

And to all my readers. Thank you with all my heart.

Anashin

6/2016

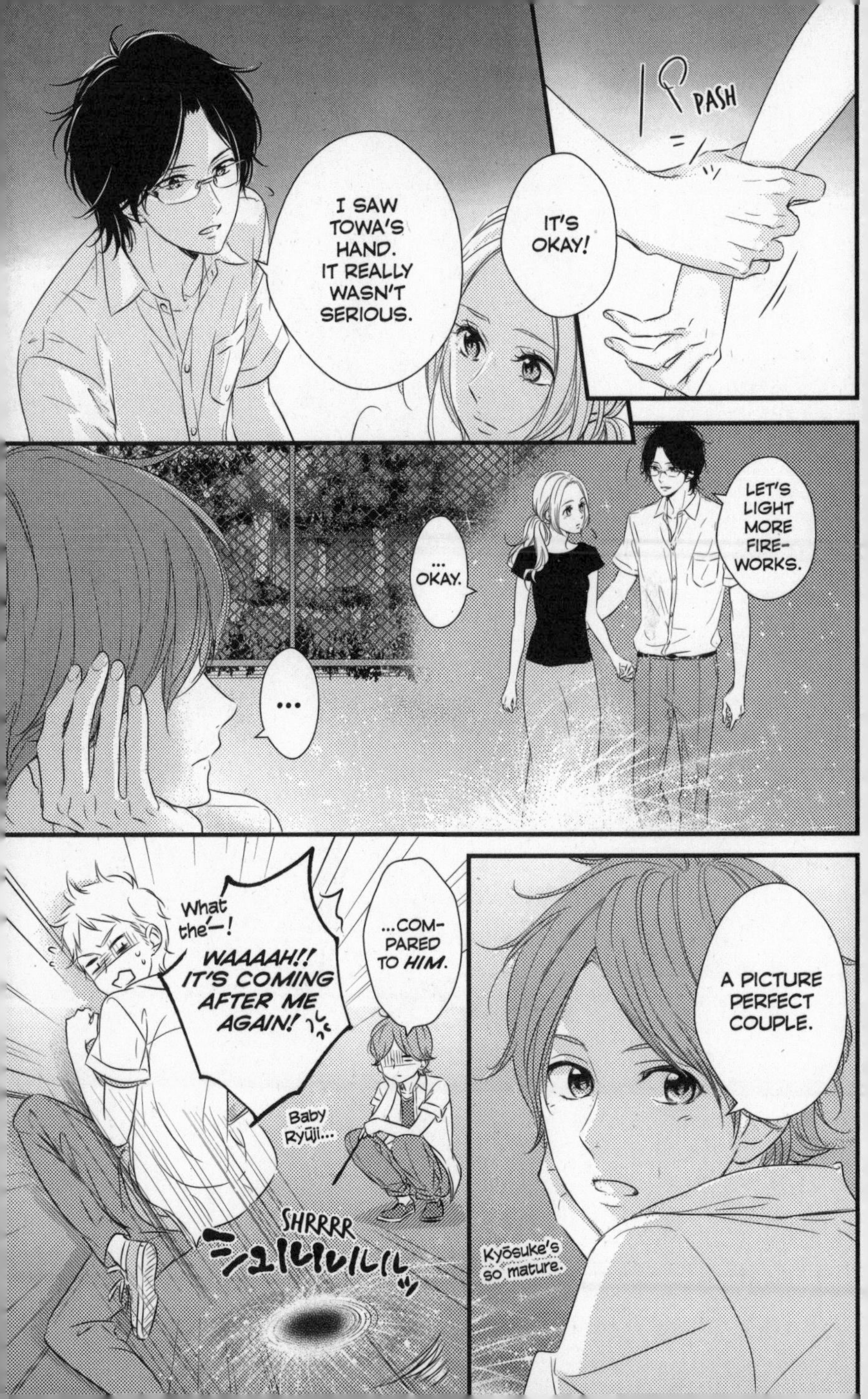
PASH
IT'S OKAY!
I SAW TOWA'S HAND. IT REALLY WASN'T SERIOUS.
LET'S LIGHT MORE FIRE-WORKS.
...OKAY.
...
A PICTURE PERFECT COUPLE.
Kyōsuke's so mature.
...COM-PARED TO HIM.
What the—!
WAAAAH!! IT'S COMING AFTER ME AGAIN!
Baby Ryūji...
SHRRRR

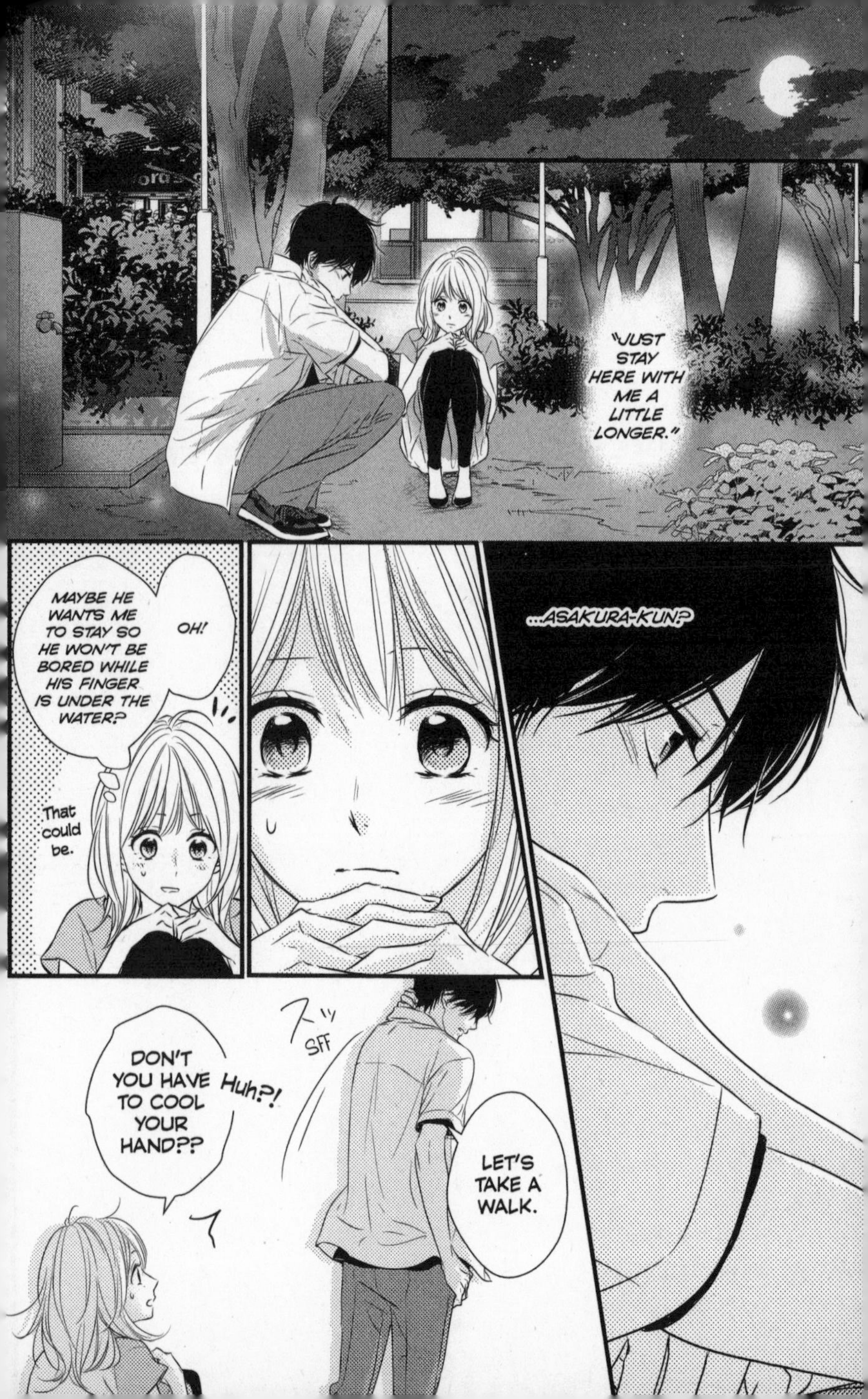
"JUST STAY HERE WITH ME A LITTLE LONGER."
...ASAKURA-KUN?
OH!
MAYBE HE WANTS ME TO STAY SO HE WON'T BE BORED WHILE HIS FINGER IS UNDER THE WATER?
That could be.
スッ
SFF
LET'S TAKE A WALK.
Huh?!
DON'T YOU HAVE TO COOL YOUR HAND??

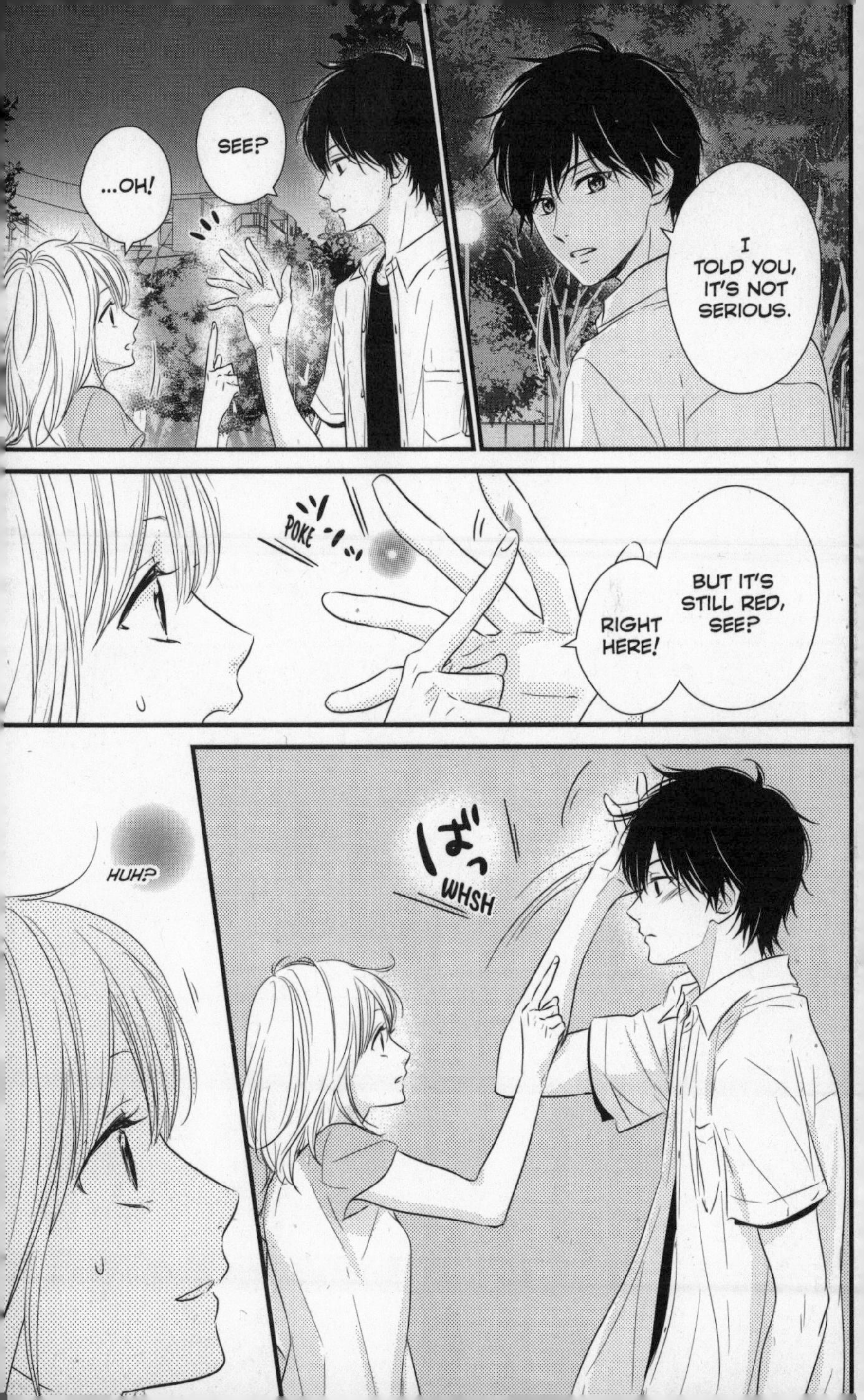
I TOLD YOU, IT'S NOT SERIOUS.
SEE?
...OH!
BUT IT'S STILL RED, SEE?
RIGHT HERE!
POKE
ばっ
WHSH
HUH?

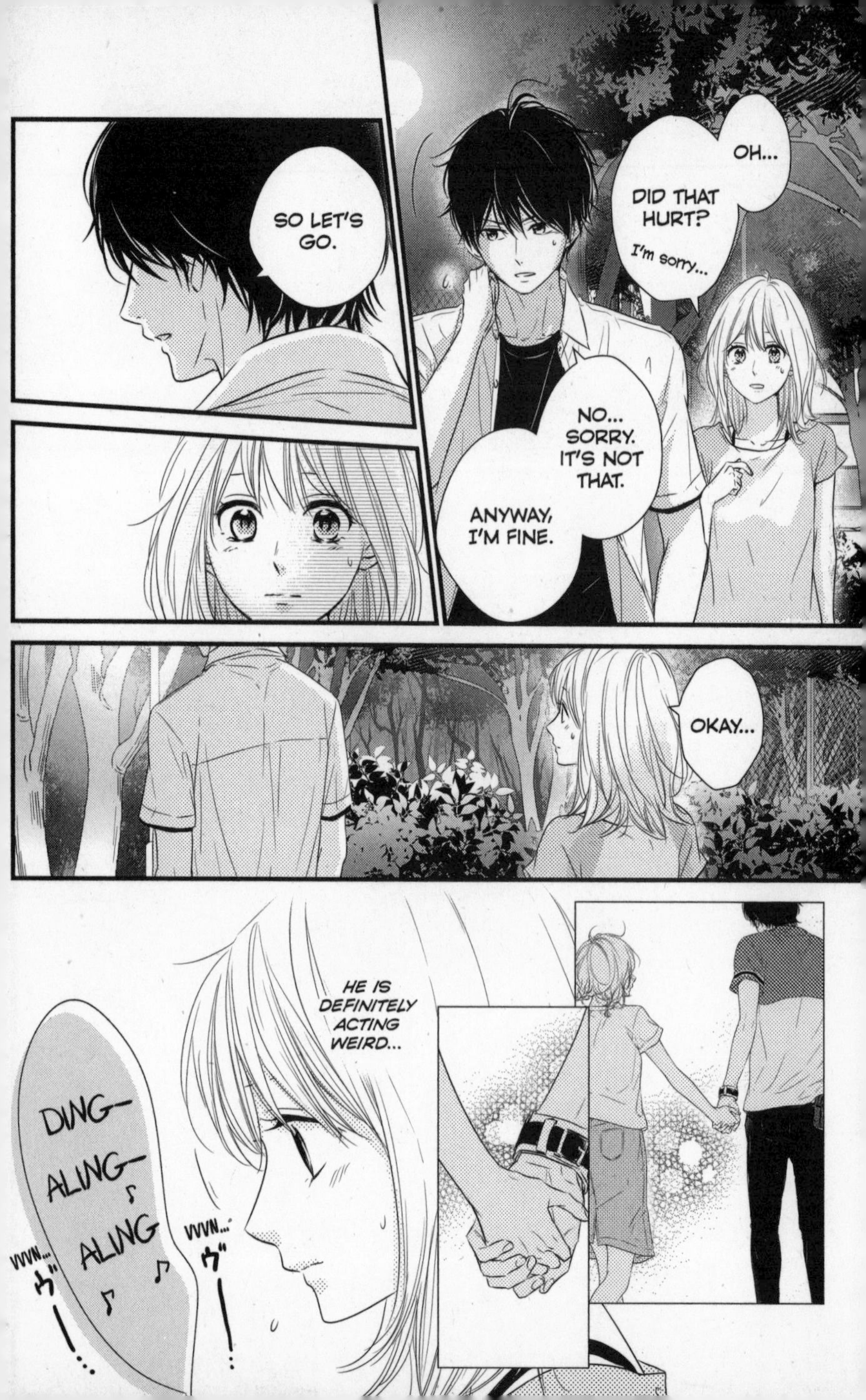
OH...
DID THAT HURT?
I'm sorry...
NO... SORRY. IT'S NOT THAT.
ANYWAY, I'M FINE.
SO LET'S GO.
OKAY...
HE IS DEFINITELY ACTING WEIRD...
VVVN... ヴー...
DING-ALING-ALING ♪
VVVN... ヴー...

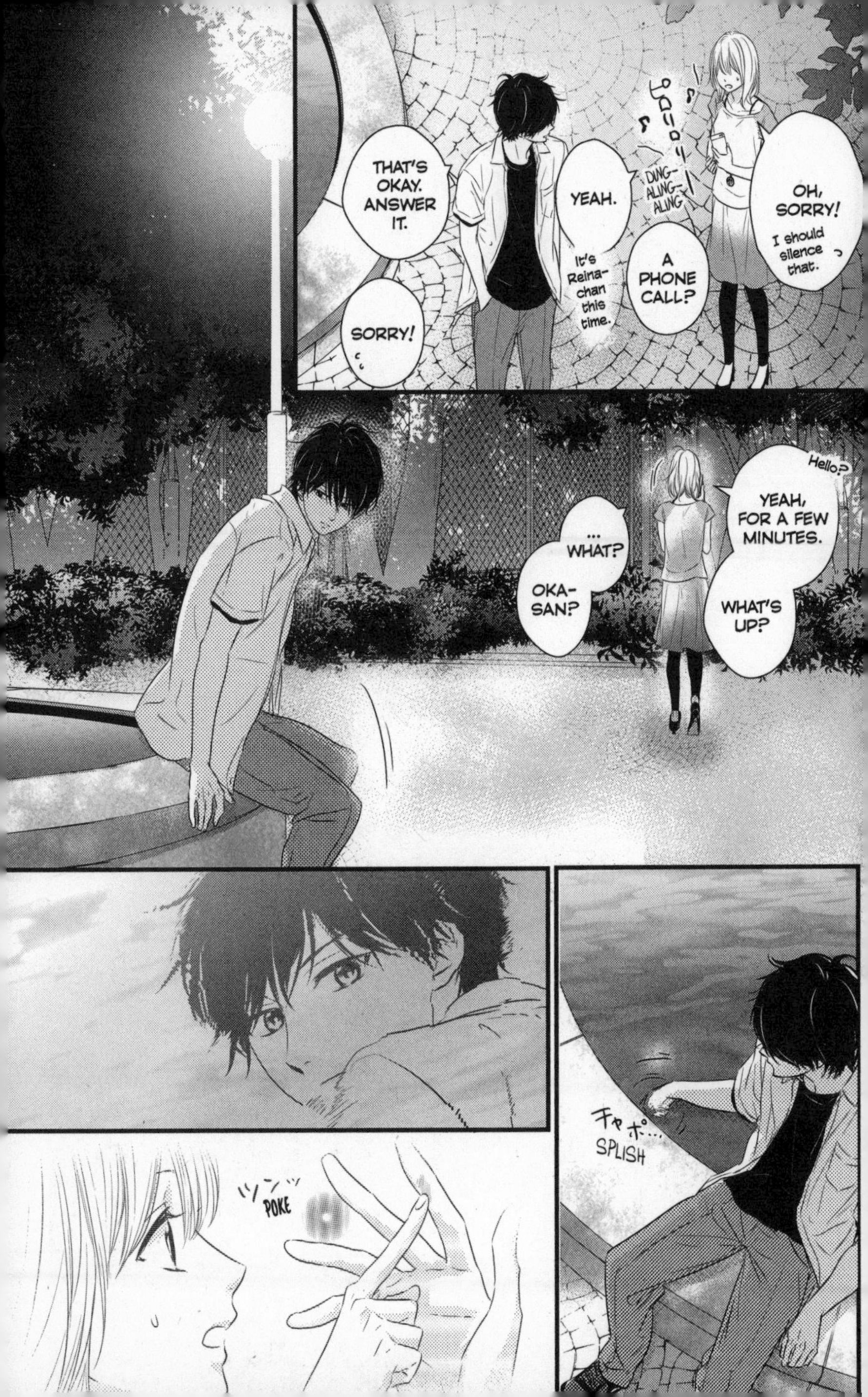
OH, SORRY!
I should silence that.
DING-ALING-ALING
A PHONE CALL?
YEAH.
It's Reina-chan this time.
THAT'S OKAY. ANSWER IT.
SORRY!
Hello?
YEAH, FOR A FEW MINUTES.
WHAT'S UP?
... WHAT?
OKA-SAN?
チャポ…
SPLISH
POKE

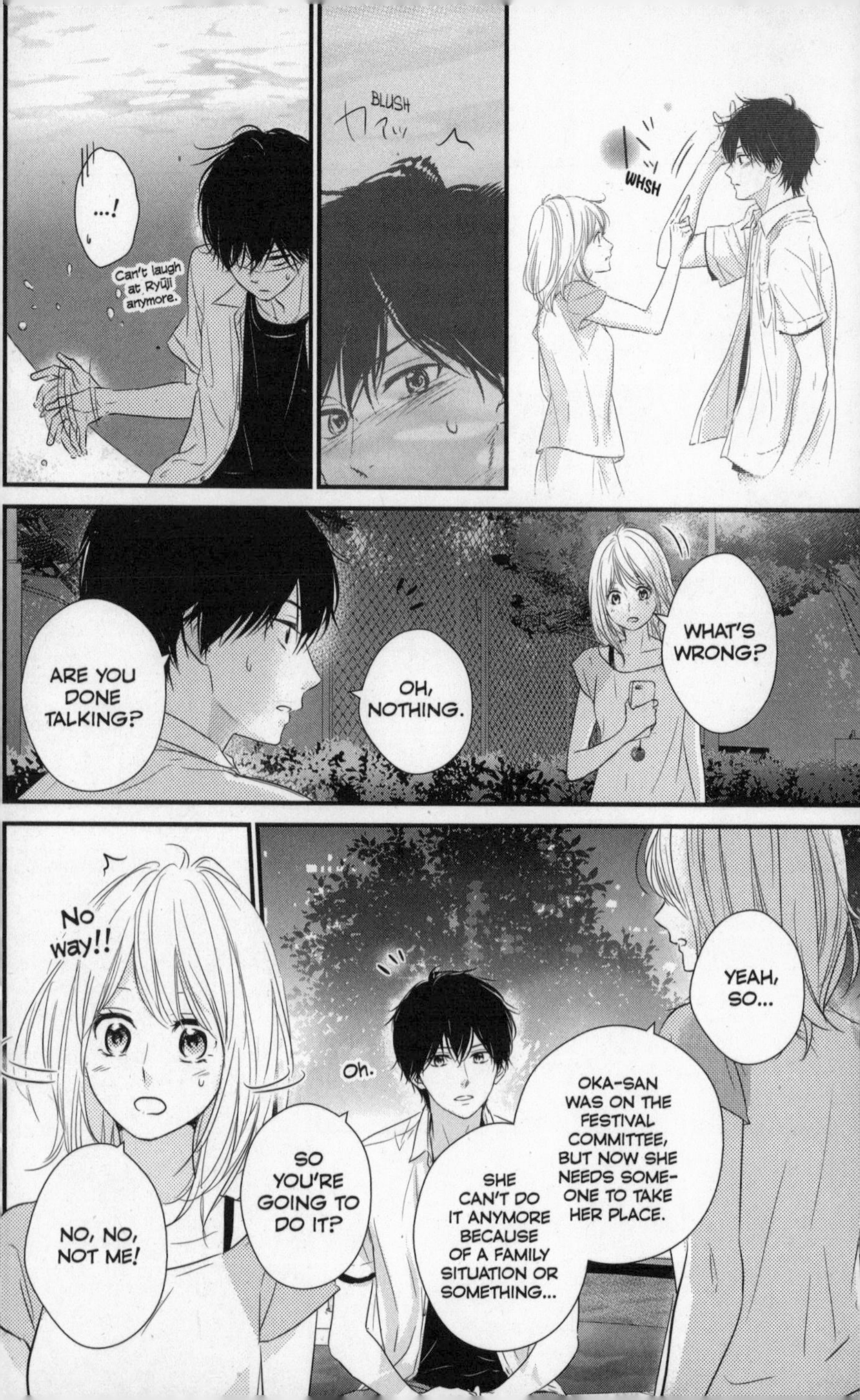
WHSH
BLUSH
...!
Can't laugh at Ryūji anymore.
WHAT'S WRONG?
OH, NOTHING.
ARE YOU DONE TALKING?
YEAH, SO...
OKA-SAN WAS ON THE FESTIVAL COMMITTEE, BUT NOW SHE NEEDS SOME-ONE TO TAKE HER PLACE.
SHE CAN'T DO IT ANYMORE BECAUSE OF A FAMILY SITUATION OR SOMETHING...
Oh.
SO YOU'RE GOING TO DO IT?
No way!!
NO, NO, NOT ME!

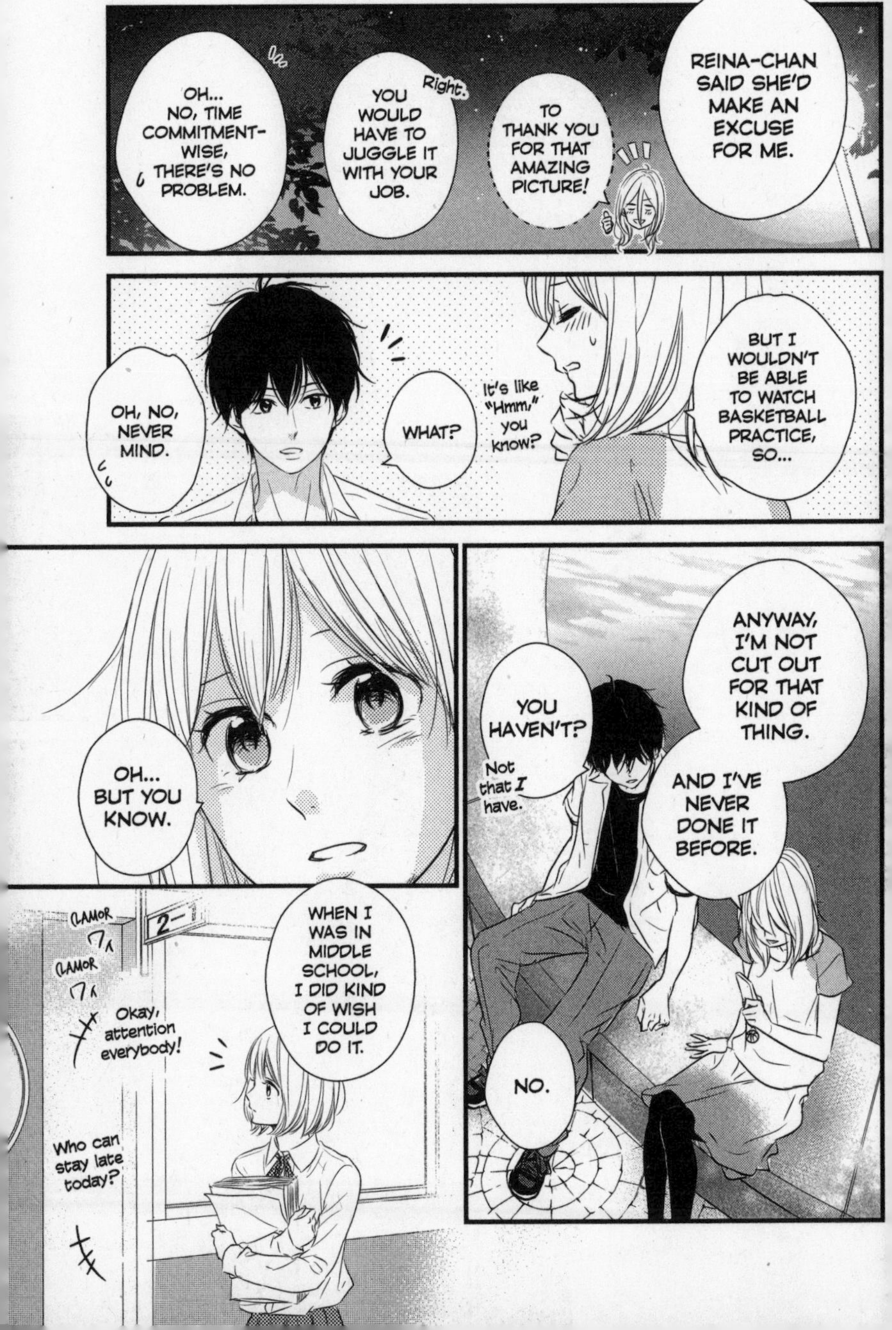
REINA-CHAN SAID SHE'D MAKE AN EXCUSE FOR ME.
TO THANK YOU FOR THAT AMAZING PICTURE!
Right.
YOU WOULD HAVE TO JUGGLE IT WITH YOUR JOB.
OH... NO, TIME COMMITMENT-WISE, THERE'S NO PROBLEM.
BUT I WOULDN'T BE ABLE TO WATCH BASKETBALL PRACTICE, SO...
It's like "Hmm," you know?
WHAT?
OH, NO, NEVER MIND.
ANYWAY, I'M NOT CUT OUT FOR THAT KIND OF THING.
AND I'VE NEVER DONE IT BEFORE.
YOU HAVEN'T?
Not that I have.
NO.
OH... BUT YOU KNOW.
WHEN I WAS IN MIDDLE SCHOOL, I DID KIND OF WISH I COULD DO IT.
CLAMOR
CLAMOR
Okay, attention everybody!
Who can stay late today?

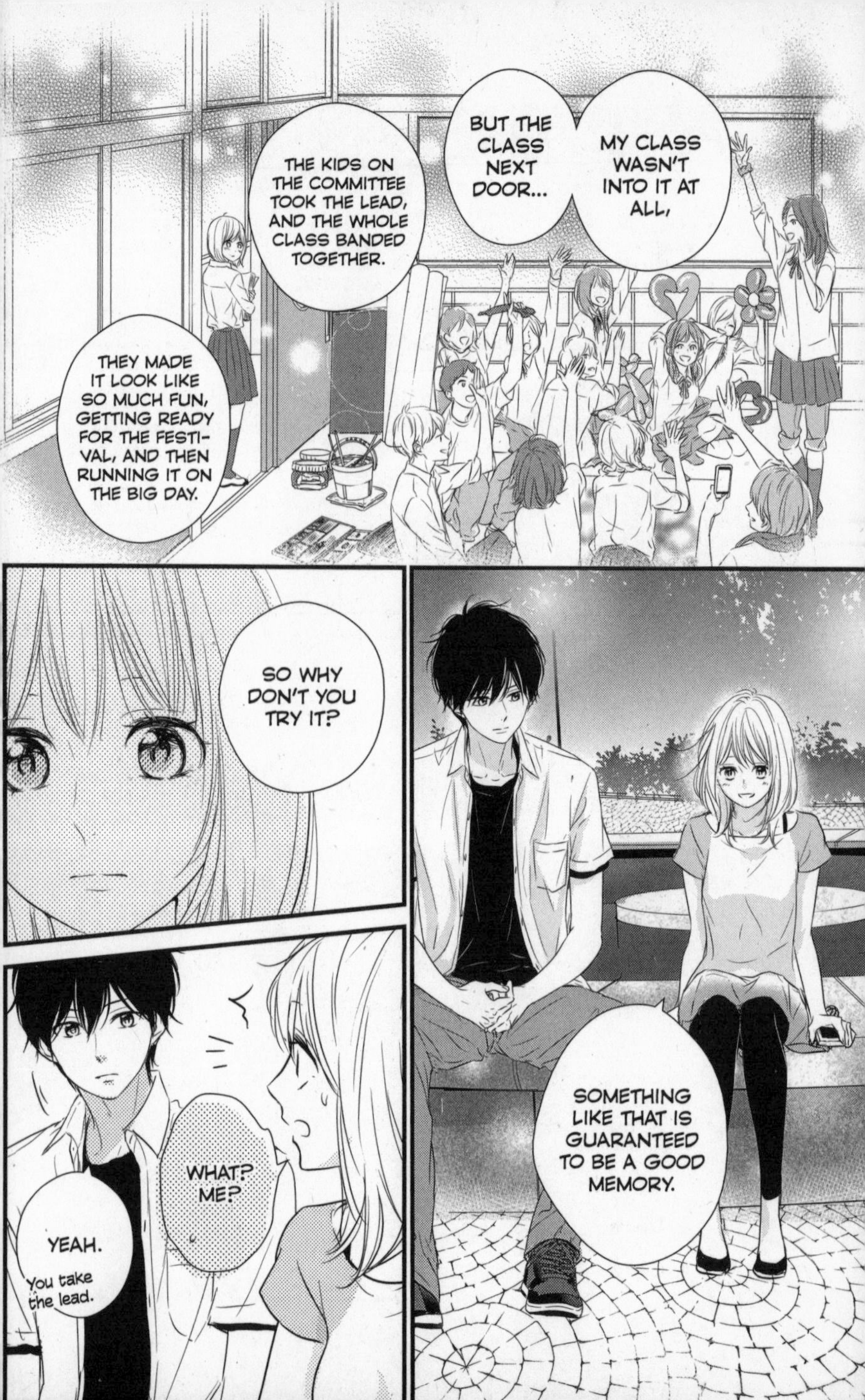
MY CLASS WASN'T INTO IT AT ALL,
BUT THE CLASS NEXT DOOR...
THE KIDS ON THE COMMITTEE TOOK THE LEAD, AND THE WHOLE CLASS BANDED TOGETHER.
THEY MADE IT LOOK LIKE SO MUCH FUN, GETTING READY FOR THE FESTI-VAL, AND THEN RUNNING IT ON THE BIG DAY.
SOMETHING LIKE THAT IS GUARANTEED TO BE A GOOD MEMORY.
SO WHY DON'T YOU TRY IT?
WHAT? ME?
YEAH.
You take the lead.

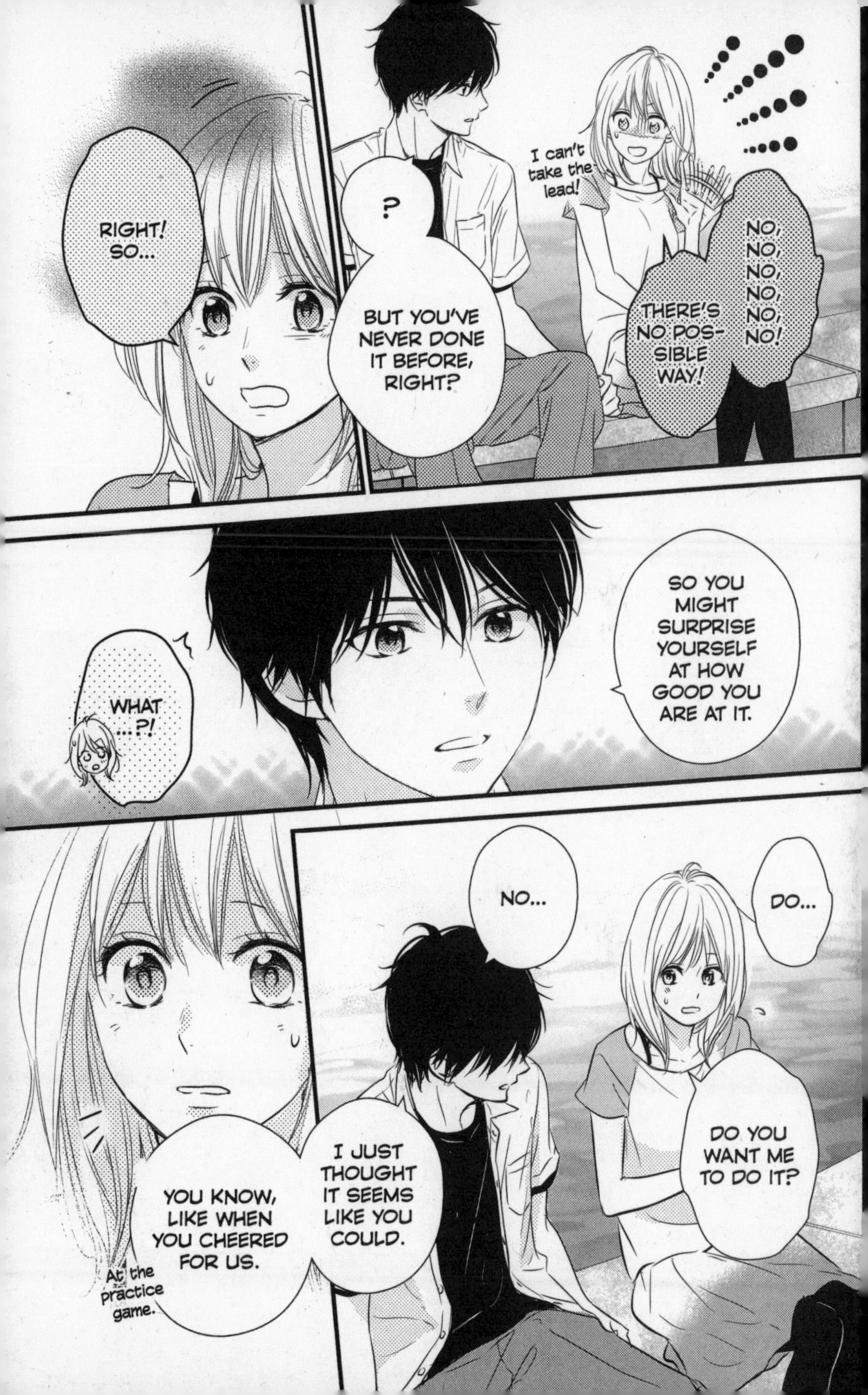
NO, NO, NO, NO, NO, NO!
THERE'S NO POS-SIBLE WAY!
I can't take the lead!
?
BUT YOU'VE NEVER DONE IT BEFORE, RIGHT?
RIGHT! SO...
SO YOU MIGHT SURPRISE YOURSELF AT HOW GOOD YOU ARE AT IT.
WHAT ...?!
DO...
NO...
DO YOU WANT ME TO DO IT?
I JUST THOUGHT IT SEEMS LIKE YOU COULD.
YOU KNOW, LIKE WHEN YOU CHEERED FOR US.
At the practice game.

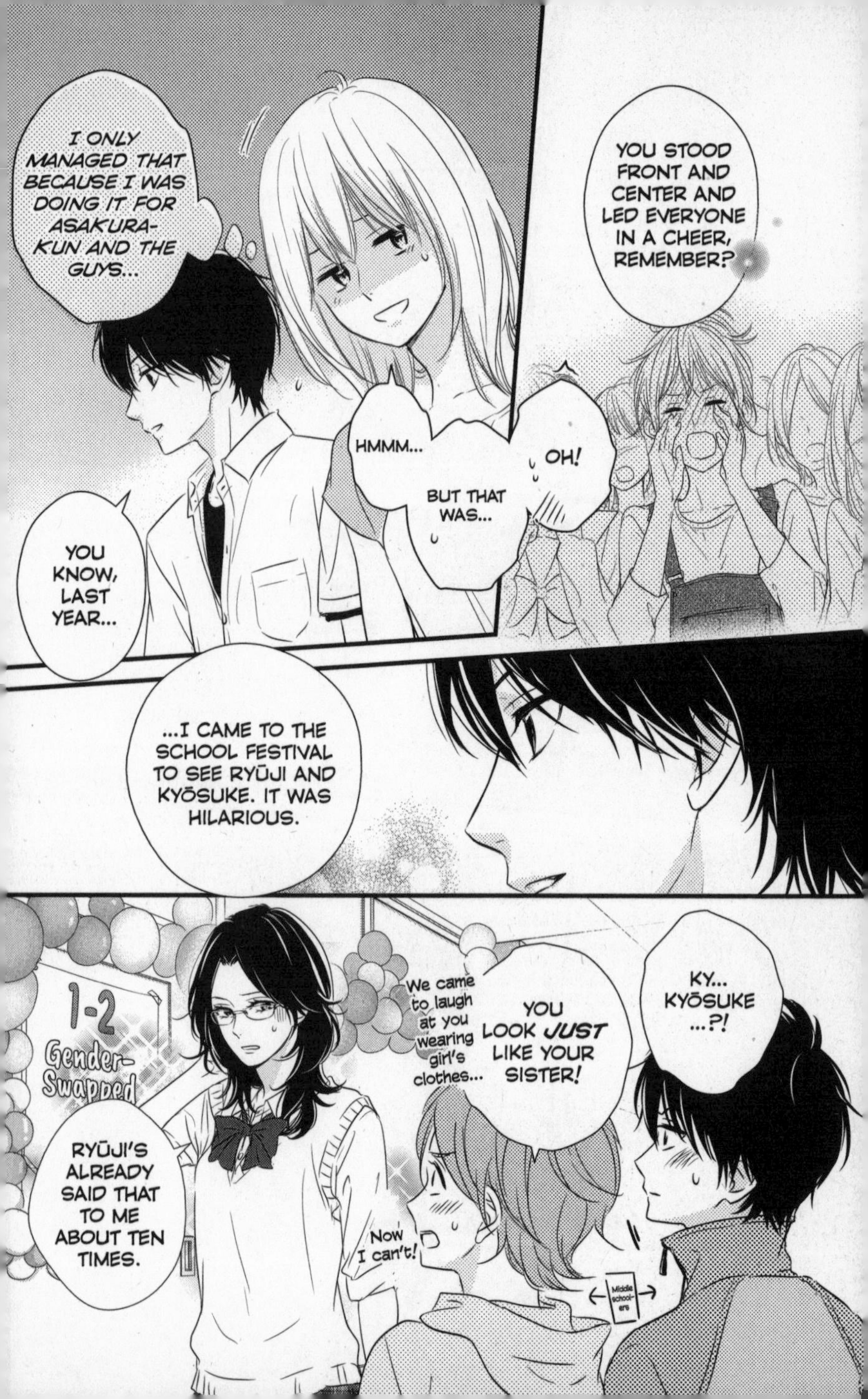
YOU STOOD FRONT AND CENTER AND LED EVERYONE IN A CHEER, REMEMBER?
HMMM...
OH!
BUT THAT WAS...
I ONLY MANAGED THAT BECAUSE I WAS DOING IT FOR ASAKURA-KUN AND THE GUYS...
YOU KNOW, LAST YEAR...
...I CAME TO THE SCHOOL FESTIVAL TO SEE RYŪJI AND KYŌSUKE. IT WAS HILARIOUS.
KY... KYŌSUKE ...?!
YOU LOOK *JUST* LIKE YOUR SISTER!
We came to laugh at you wearing girl's clothes...
Now I can't!
Middle schoolers
1-2
Gender-Swapped
RYŪJI'S ALREADY SAID THAT TO ME ABOUT TEN TIMES.

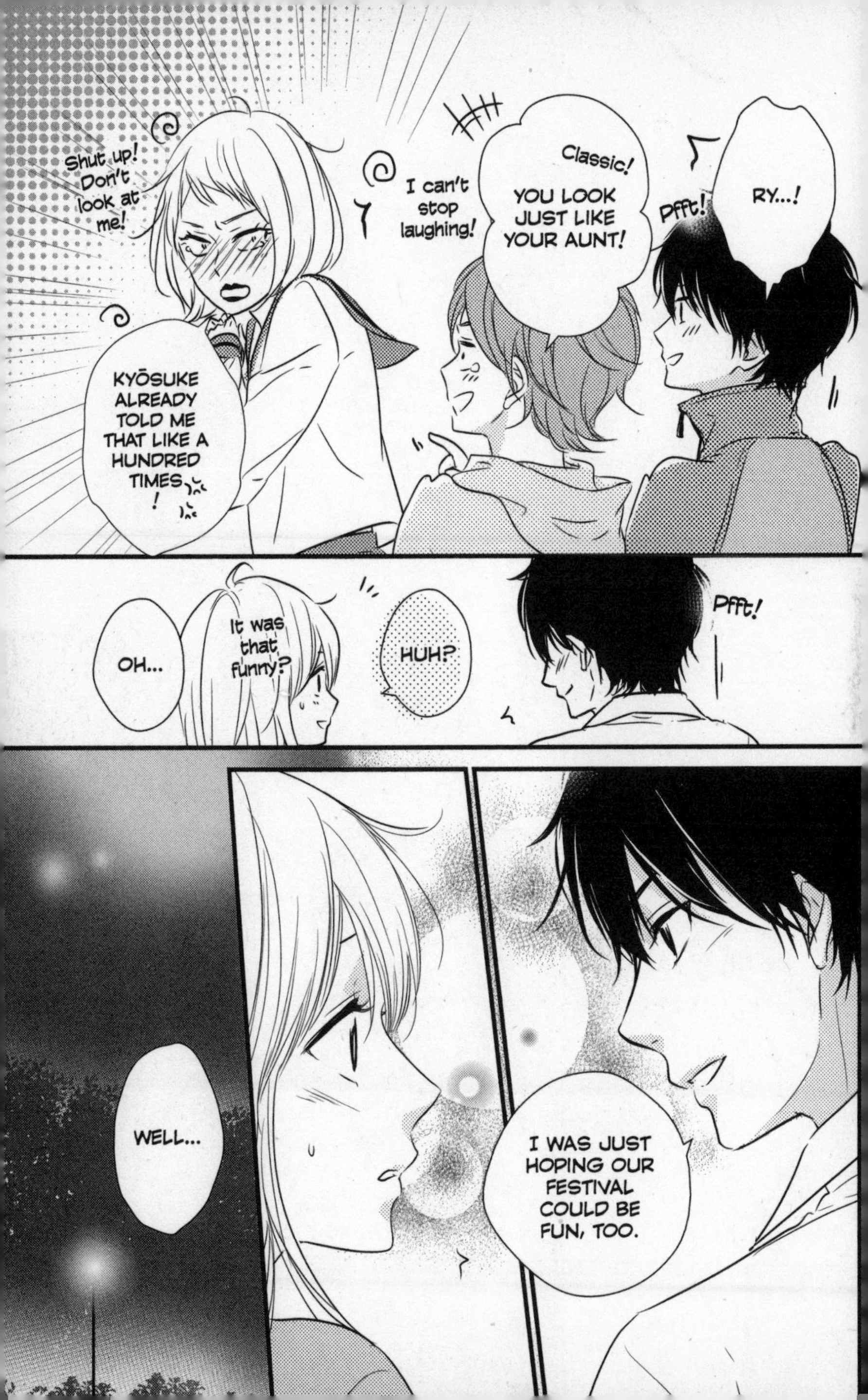
RY...!
Pfft!
Classic!
YOU LOOK JUST LIKE YOUR AUNT!
I can't stop laughing!
Shut up! Don't look at me!
KYŌSUKE ALREADY TOLD ME THAT LIKE A HUNDRED TIMES!
Pfft!
HUH?
It was that funny?
OH...
I WAS JUST HOPING OUR FESTIVAL COULD BE FUN, TOO.
WELL...

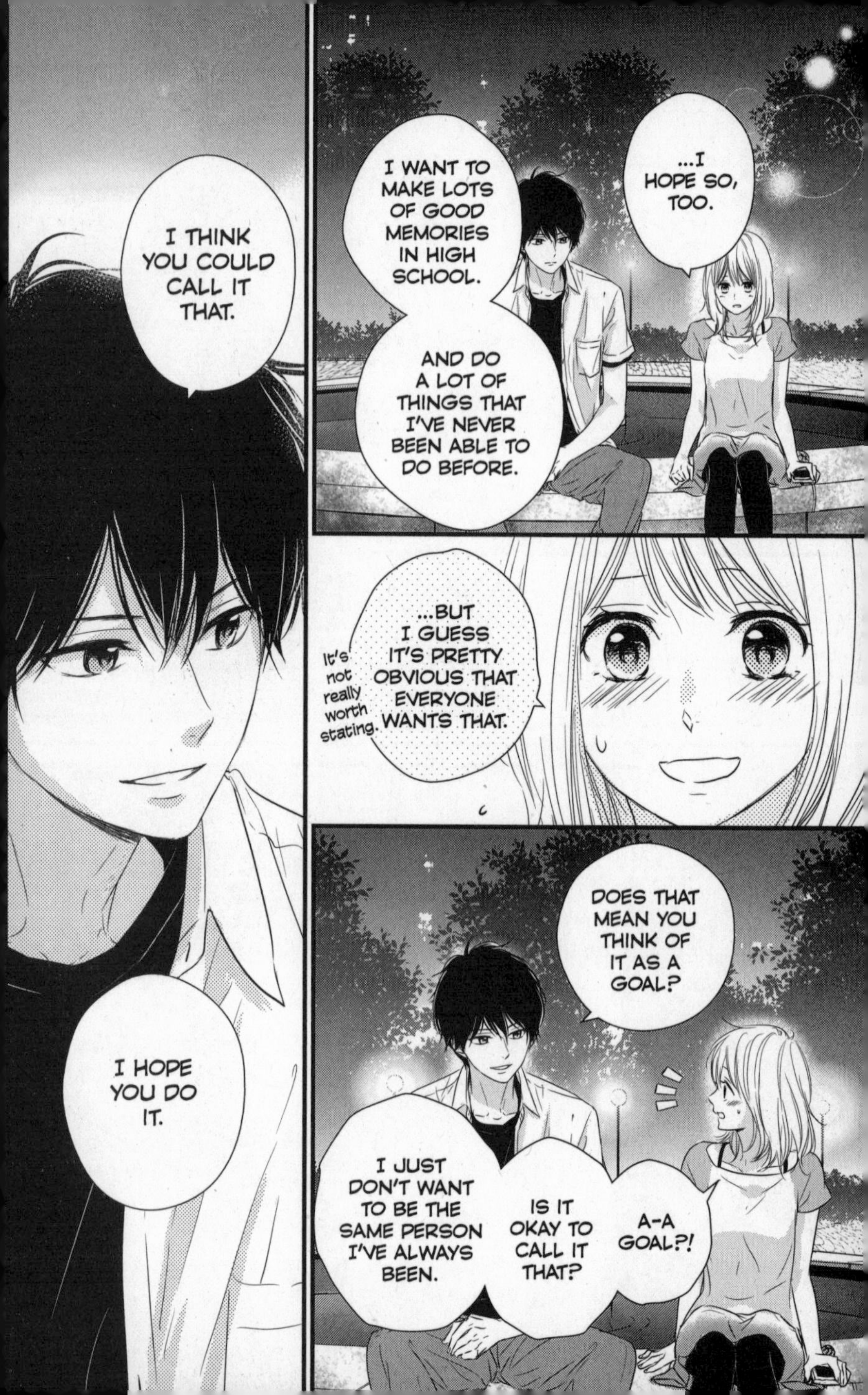
...I HOPE SO, TOO.
I WANT TO MAKE LOTS OF GOOD MEMORIES IN HIGH SCHOOL.
AND DO A LOT OF THINGS THAT I'VE NEVER BEEN ABLE TO DO BEFORE.
...BUT I GUESS IT'S PRETTY OBVIOUS THAT EVERYONE WANTS THAT.
It's not really worth stating.
DOES THAT MEAN YOU THINK OF IT AS A GOAL?
A-A GOAL?!
IS IT OKAY TO CALL IT THAT?
I JUST DON'T WANT TO BE THE SAME PERSON I'VE ALWAYS BEEN.
I THINK YOU COULD CALL IT THAT.
I HOPE YOU DO IT.

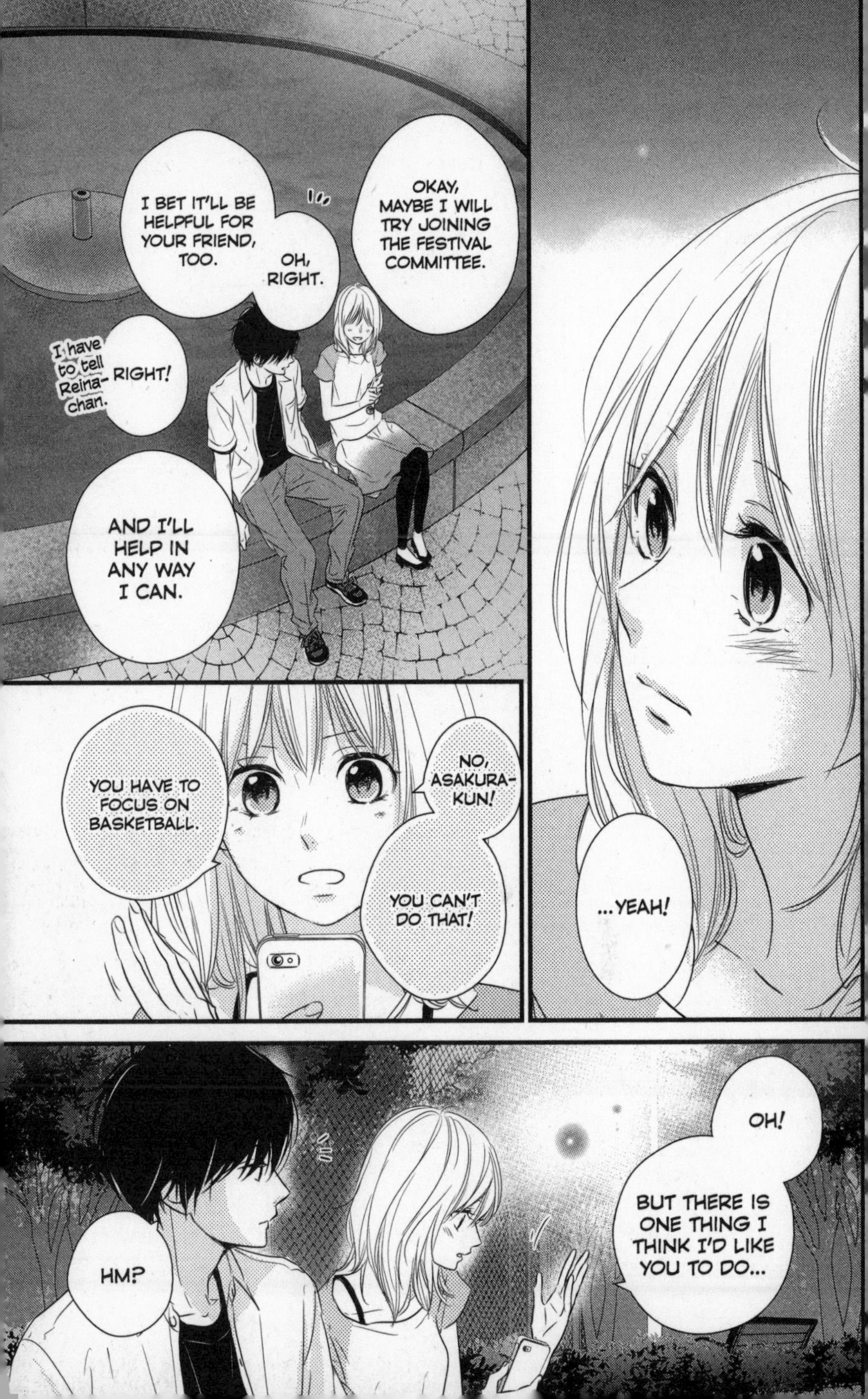
...YEAH!
OKAY, MAYBE I WILL TRY JOINING THE FESTIVAL COMMITTEE.
I BET IT'LL BE HELPFUL FOR YOUR FRIEND, TOO.
OH, RIGHT.
RIGHT!
I have to tell Reina-chan.
AND I'LL HELP IN ANY WAY I CAN.
NO, ASAKURA-KUN!
YOU CAN'T DO THAT!
YOU HAVE TO FOCUS ON BASKETBALL.
OH!
BUT THERE IS ONE THING I THINK I'D LIKE YOU TO DO...
HM?

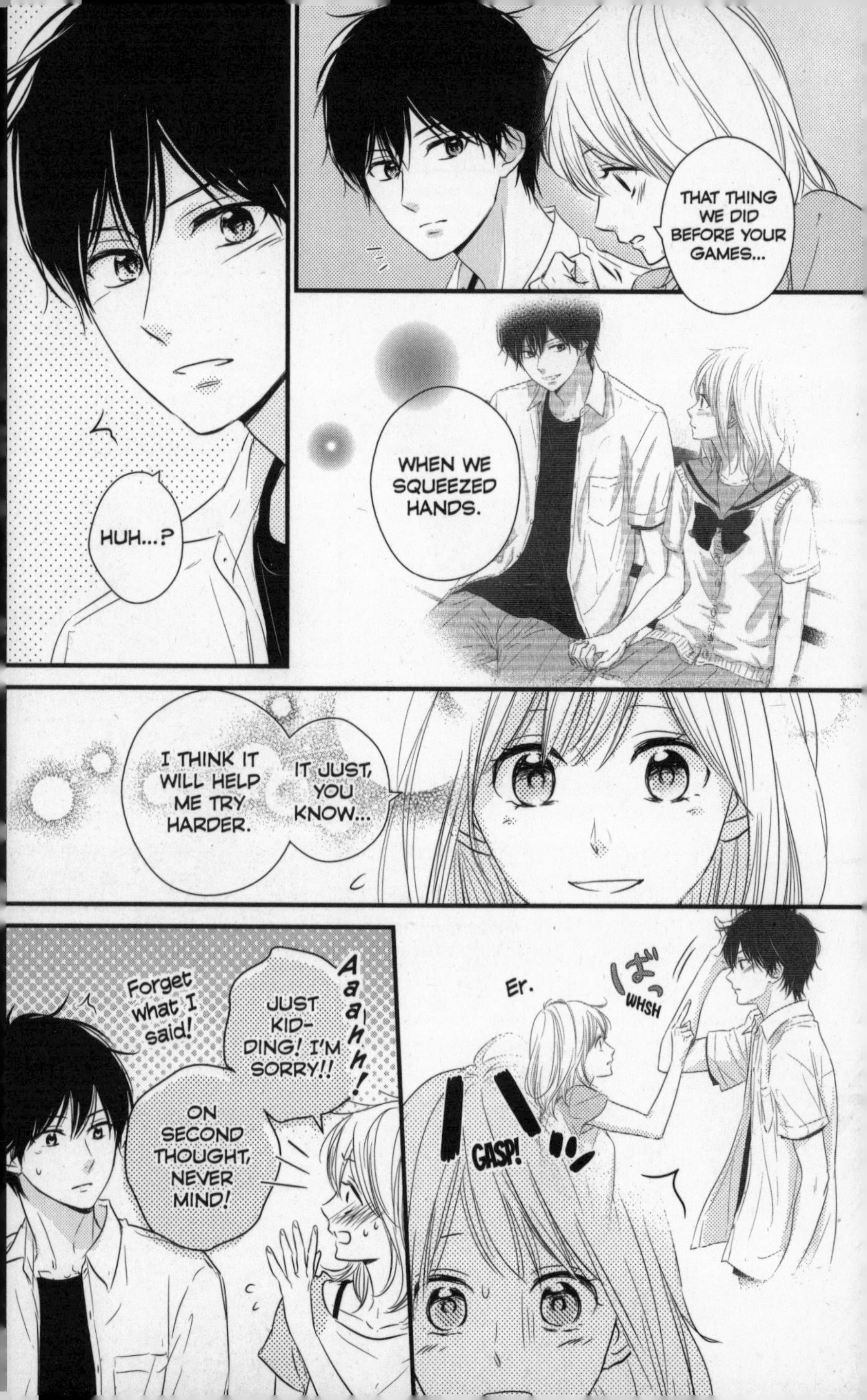
THAT THING WE DID BEFORE YOUR GAMES...
WHEN WE SQUEEZED HANDS.
HUH...?
IT JUST, YOU KNOW...
I THINK IT WILL HELP ME TRY HARDER.
Er.
WHSH
GASP!
Aaahh!
JUST KID-DING! I'M SORRY!!
Forget what I said!
ON SECOND THOUGHT, NEVER MIND!

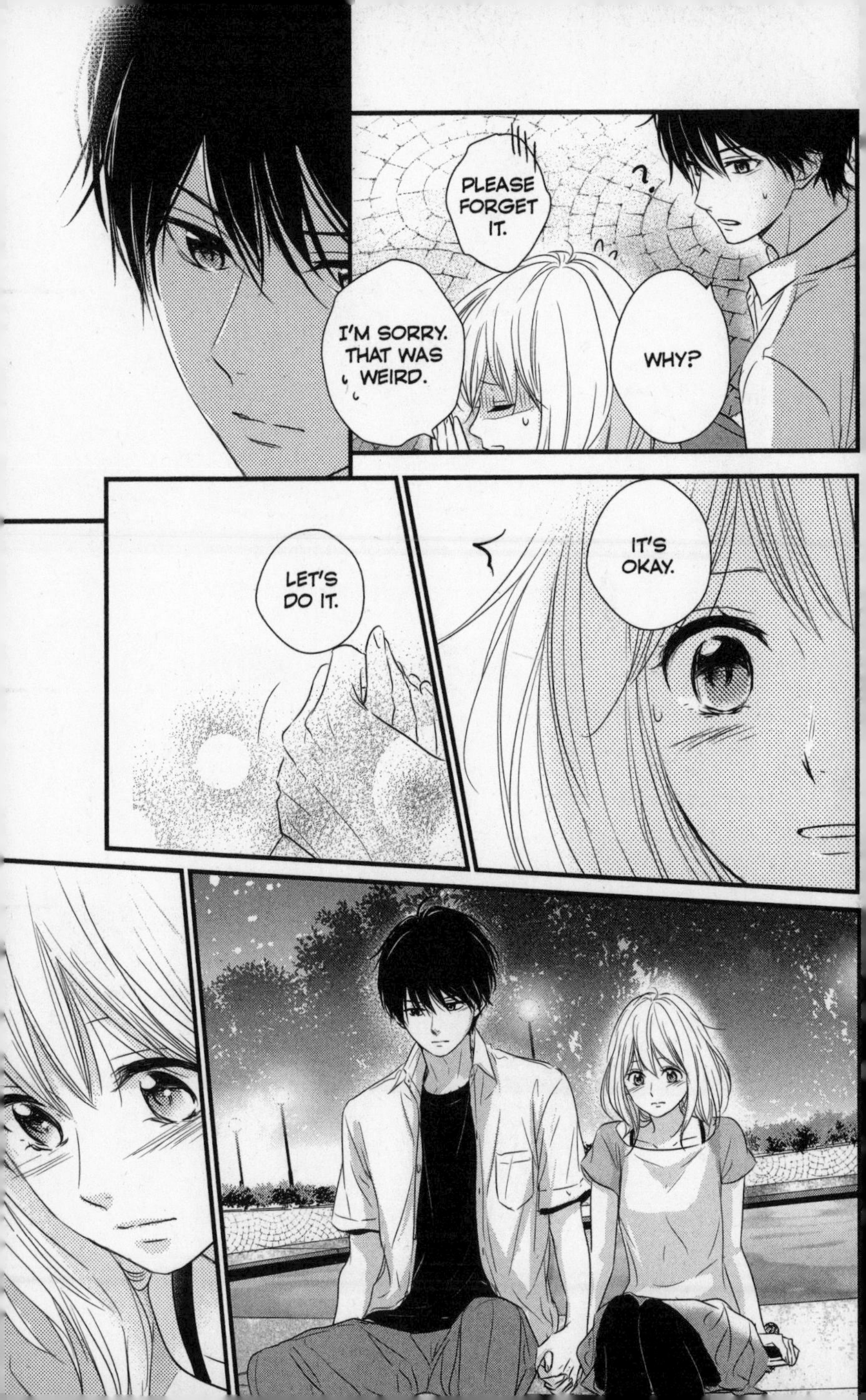
I'M SORRY. THAT WAS WEIRD.
PLEASE FORGET IT.
WHY?
IT'S OKAY.
LET'S DO IT.

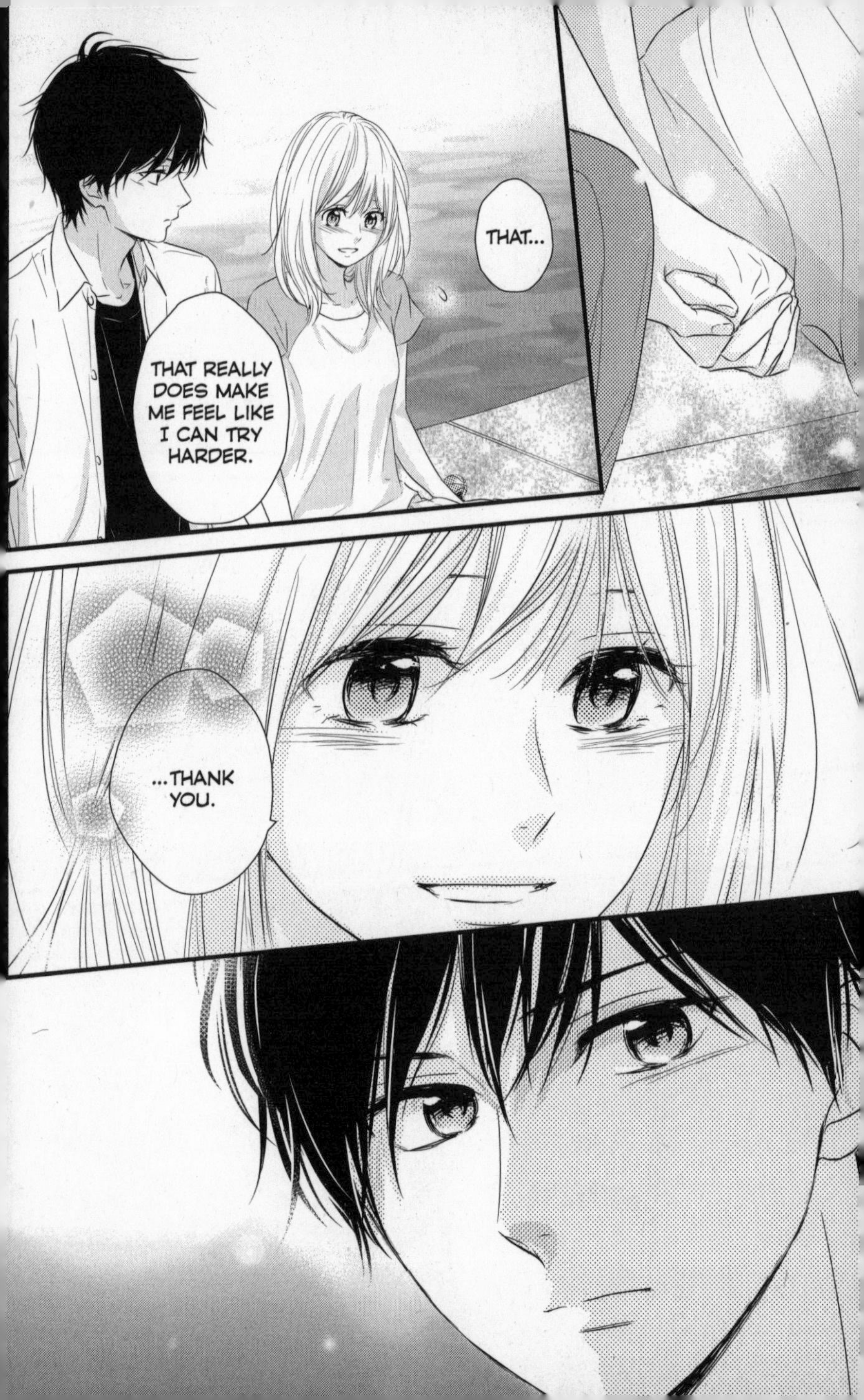
THAT...
THAT REALLY DOES MAKE ME FEEL LIKE I CAN TRY HARDER.
...THANK YOU.

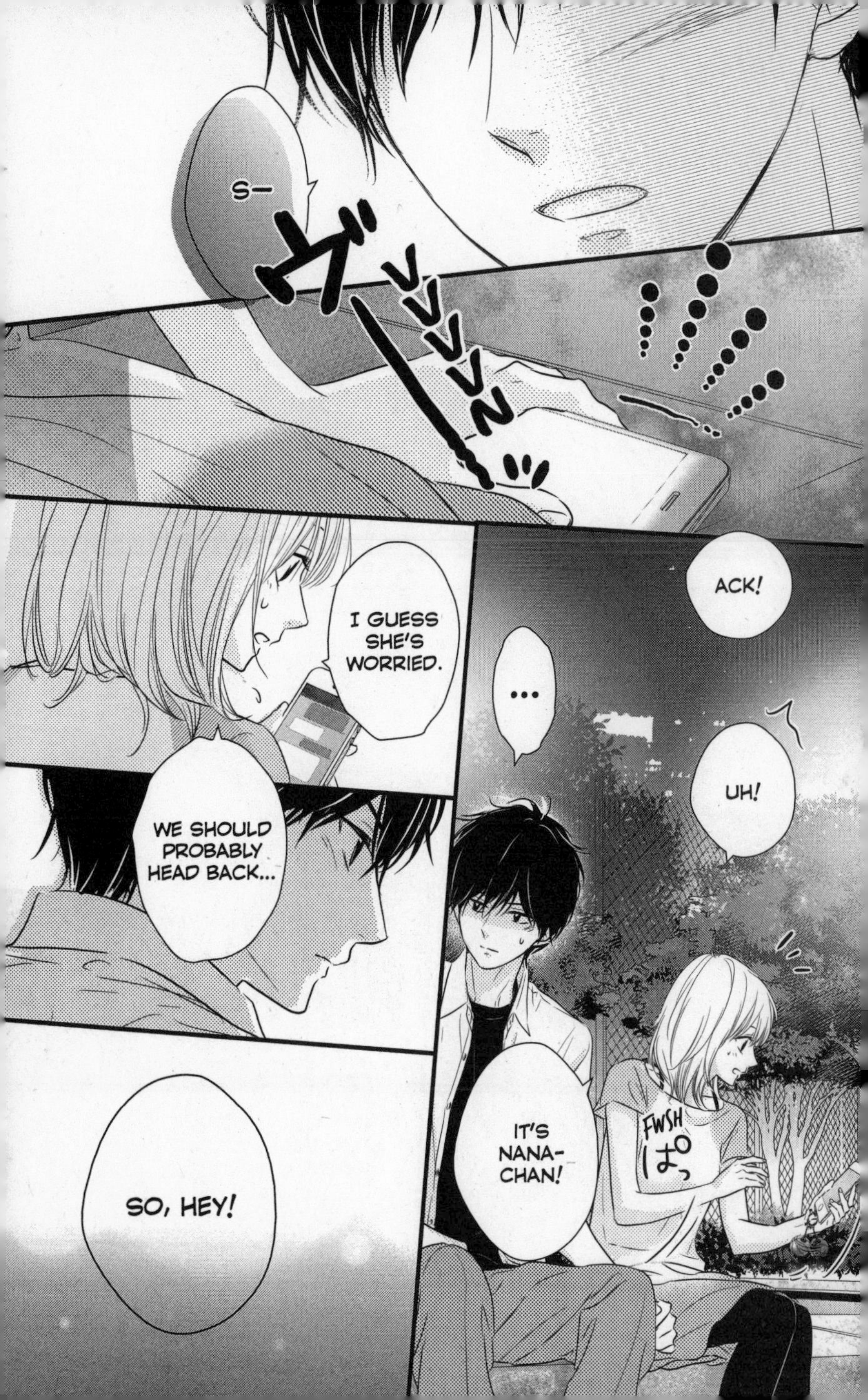
S—
VVVVVZ
ACK!
...
UH!
FWSH ぱっ
IT'S NANA-CHAN!
I GUESS SHE'S WORRIED.
WE SHOULD PROBABLY HEAD BACK...
SO, HEY!

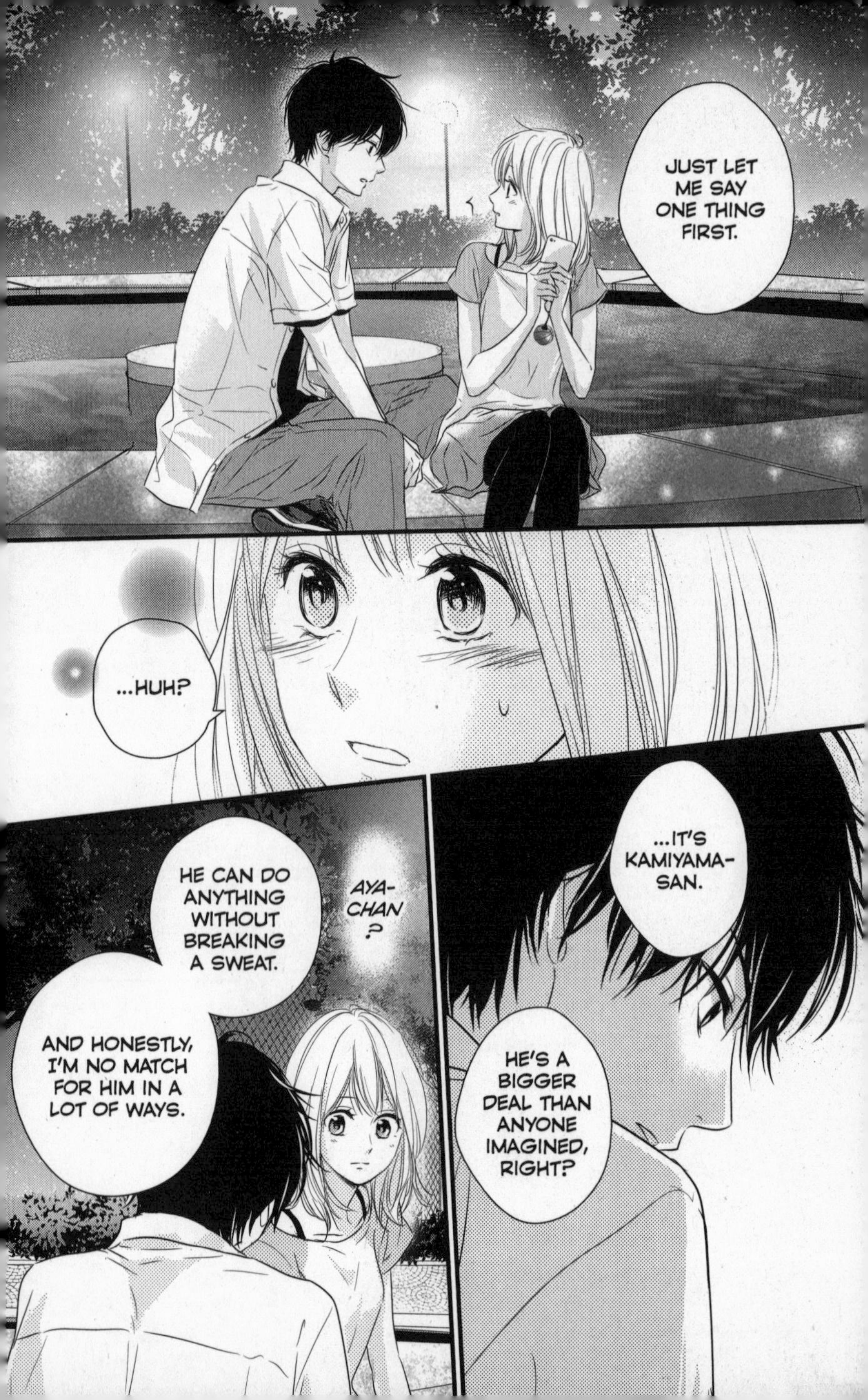
JUST LET ME SAY ONE THING FIRST.
...HUH?
...IT'S KAMIYAMA-SAN.
HE'S A BIGGER DEAL THAN ANYONE IMAGINED, RIGHT?
AYA-CHAN?
HE CAN DO ANYTHING WITHOUT BREAKING A SWEAT.
AND HONESTLY, I'M NO MATCH FOR HIM IN A LOT OF WAYS.

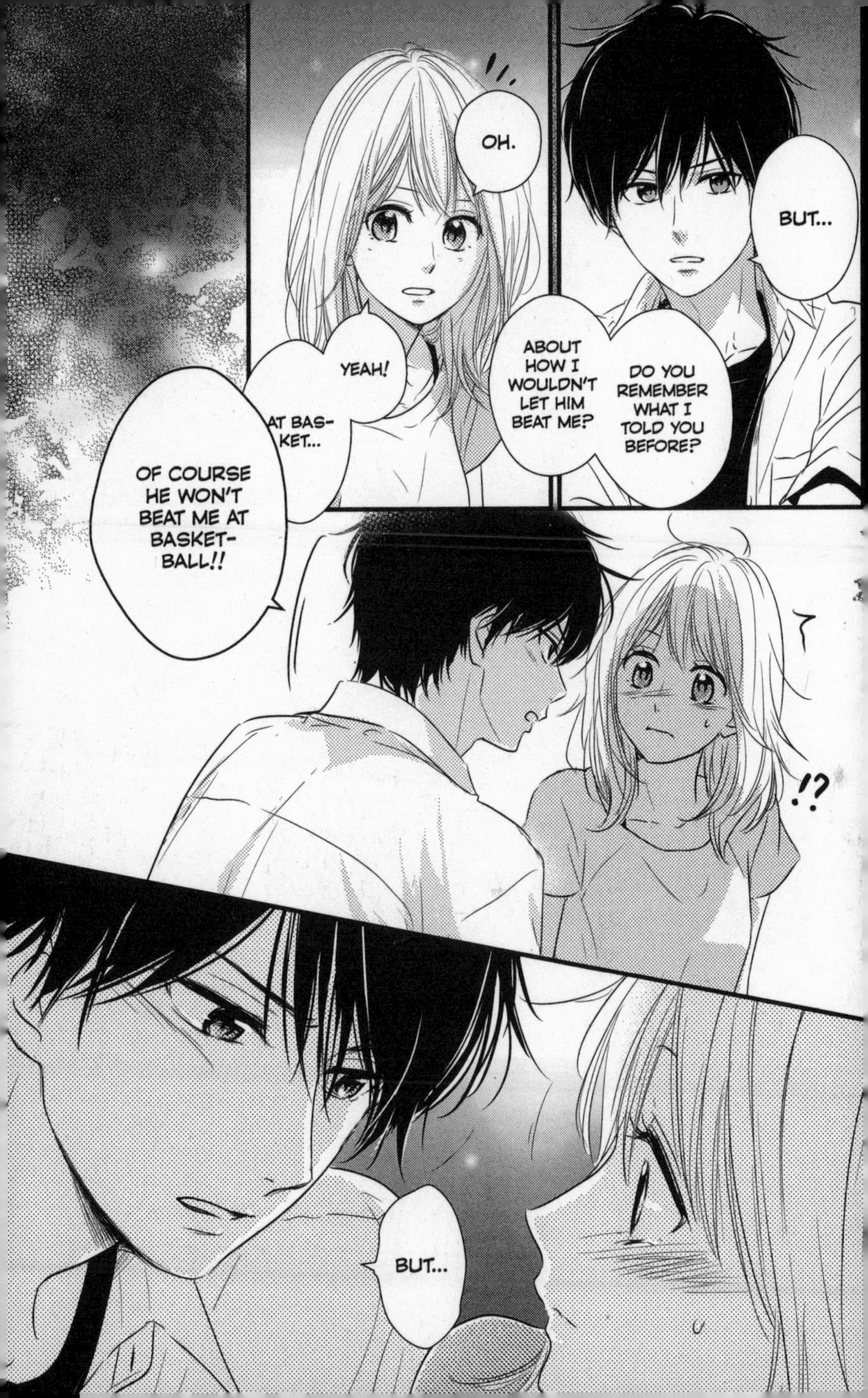
BUT...
DO YOU REMEMBER WHAT I TOLD YOU BEFORE?
ABOUT HOW I WOULDN'T LET HIM BEAT ME?
OH.
YEAH!
AT BASKET...
OF COURSE HE WON'T BEAT ME AT BASKETBALL!!
!?
BUT...

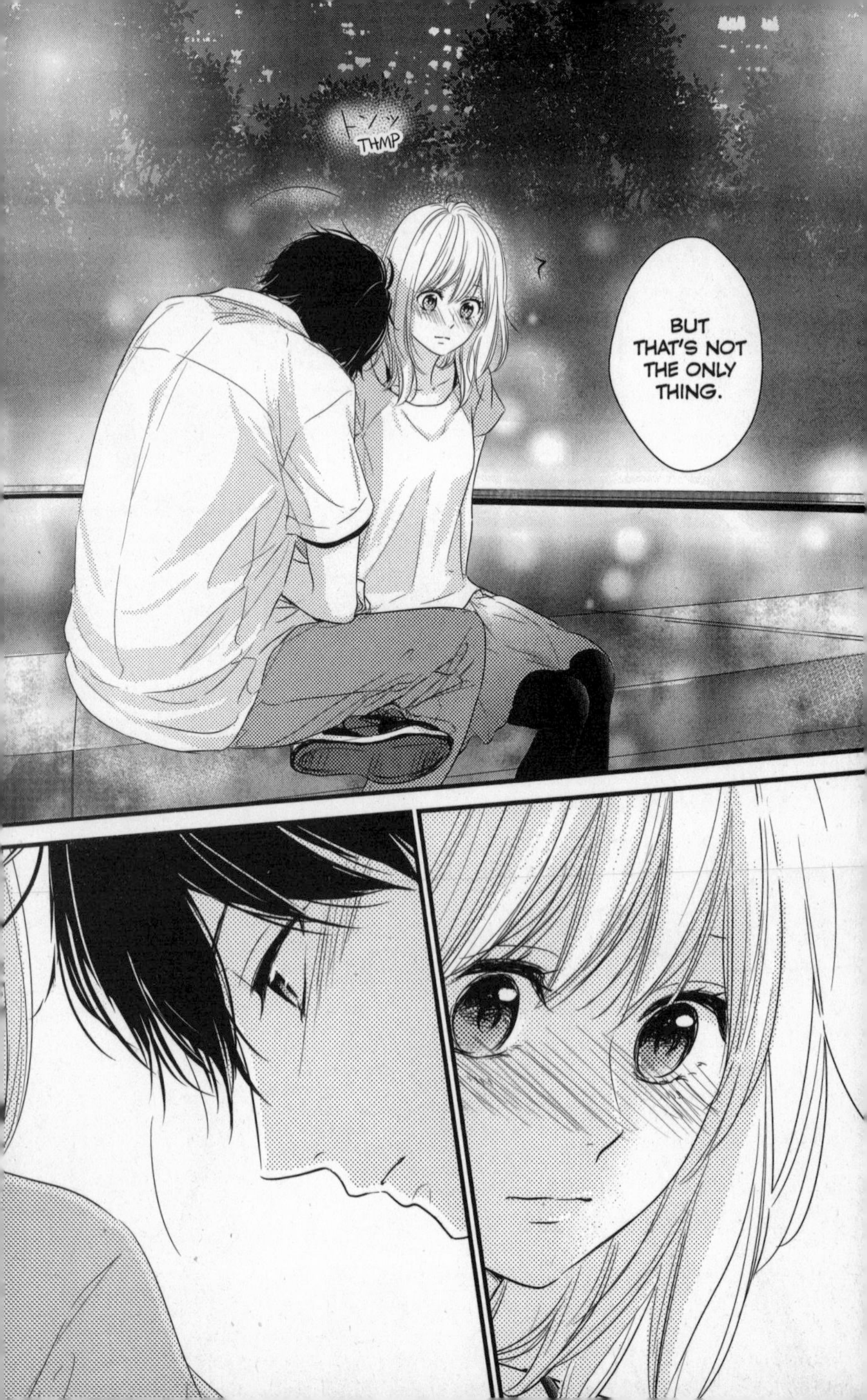
トンッ
THMP
BUT THAT'S NOT THE ONLY THING.

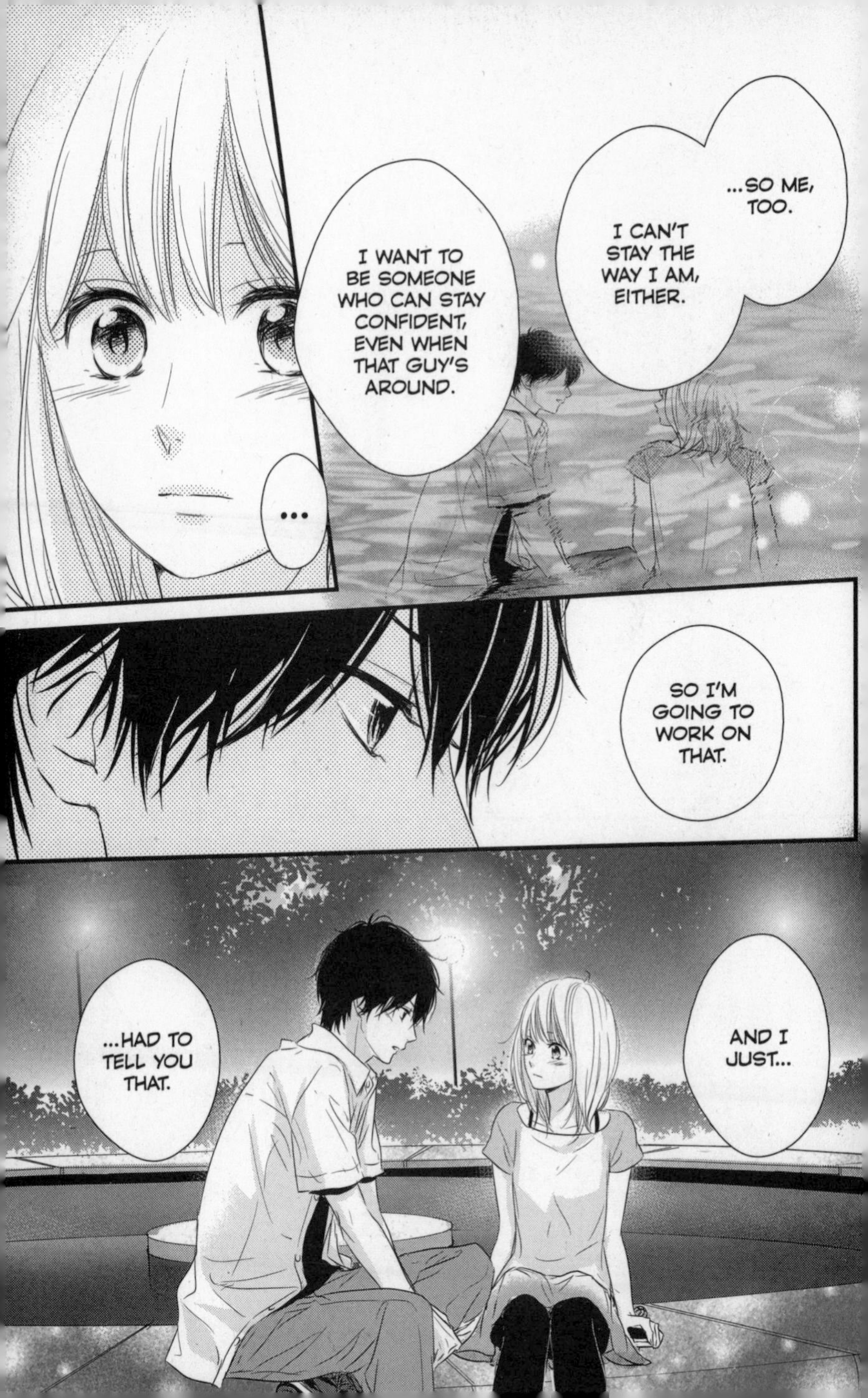
...SO ME, TOO.
I CAN'T STAY THE WAY I AM, EITHER.
I WANT TO BE SOMEONE WHO CAN STAY CONFIDENT, EVEN WHEN THAT GUY'S AROUND.
...
SO I'M GOING TO WORK ON THAT.
AND I JUST...
...HAD TO TELL YOU THAT.

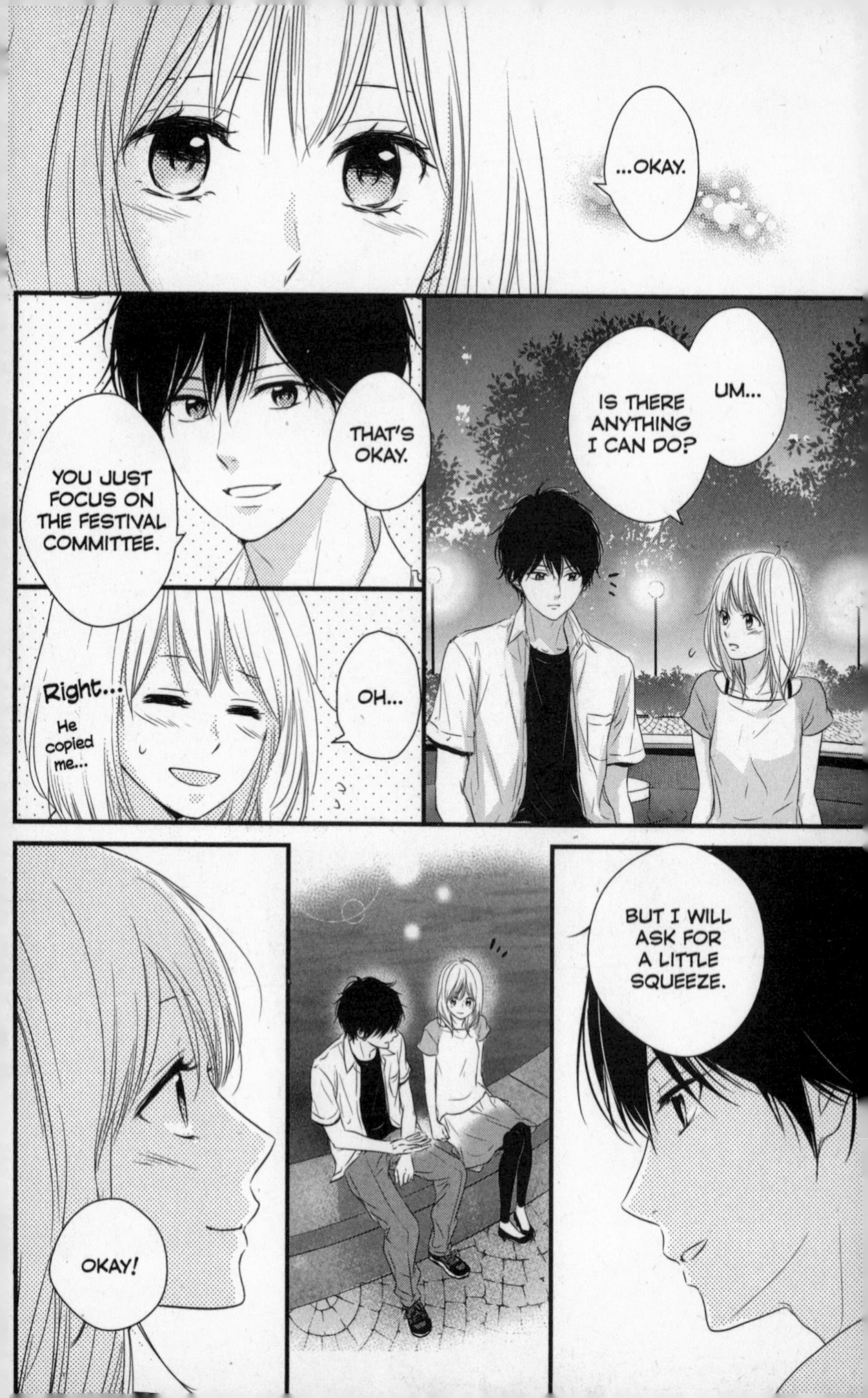

...OKAY.
UM...
IS THERE ANYTHING I CAN DO?
THAT'S OKAY.
YOU JUST FOCUS ON THE FESTIVAL COMMITTEE.
OH...
Right...
He copied me...
BUT I WILL ASK FOR A LITTLE SQUEEZE.
OKAY!

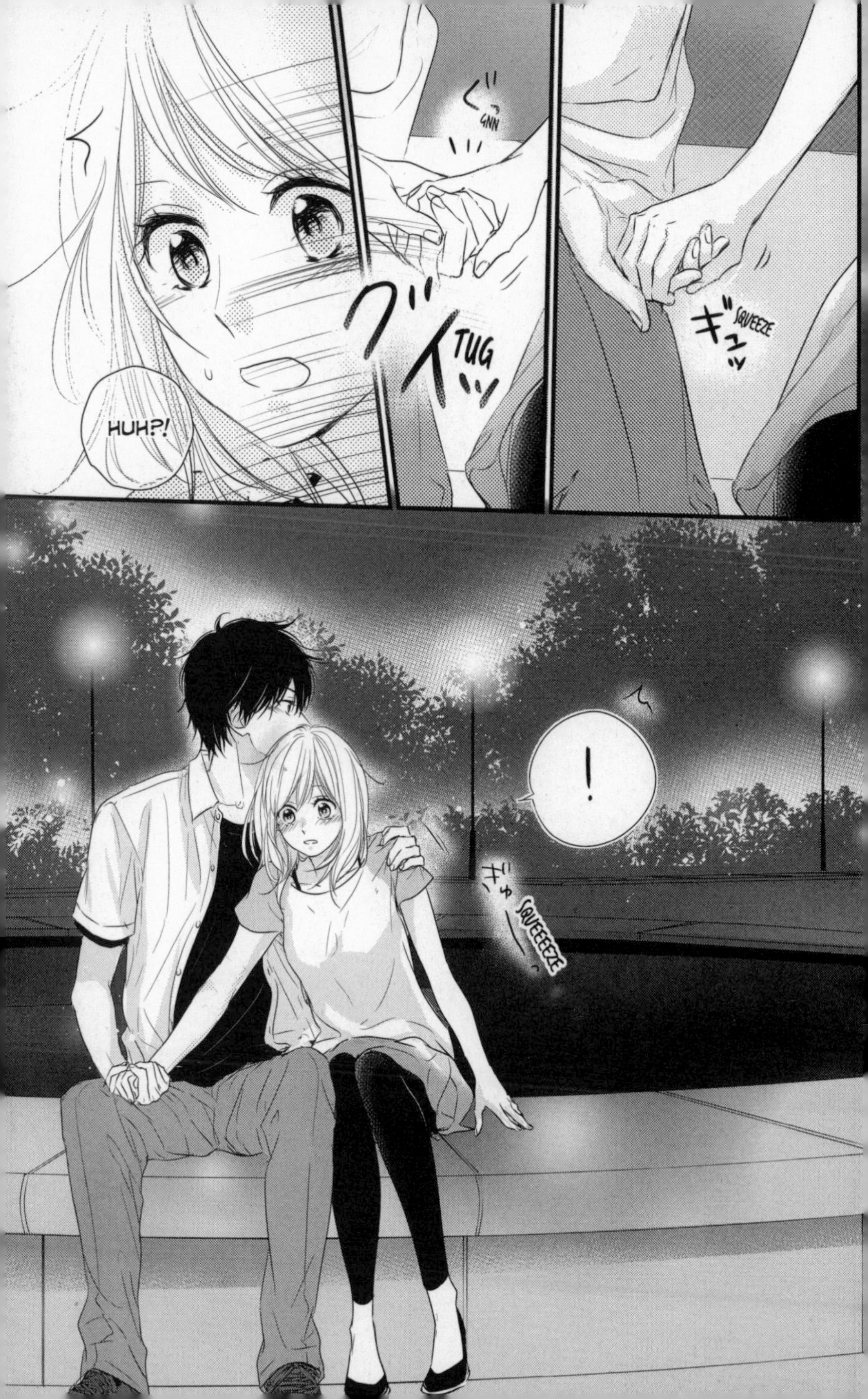
ギュッ
SQUEEZE
ぐっ
GNN
グイッ
TUG
HUH?!
!
ぎゅーっ
SQUEEEEEZE

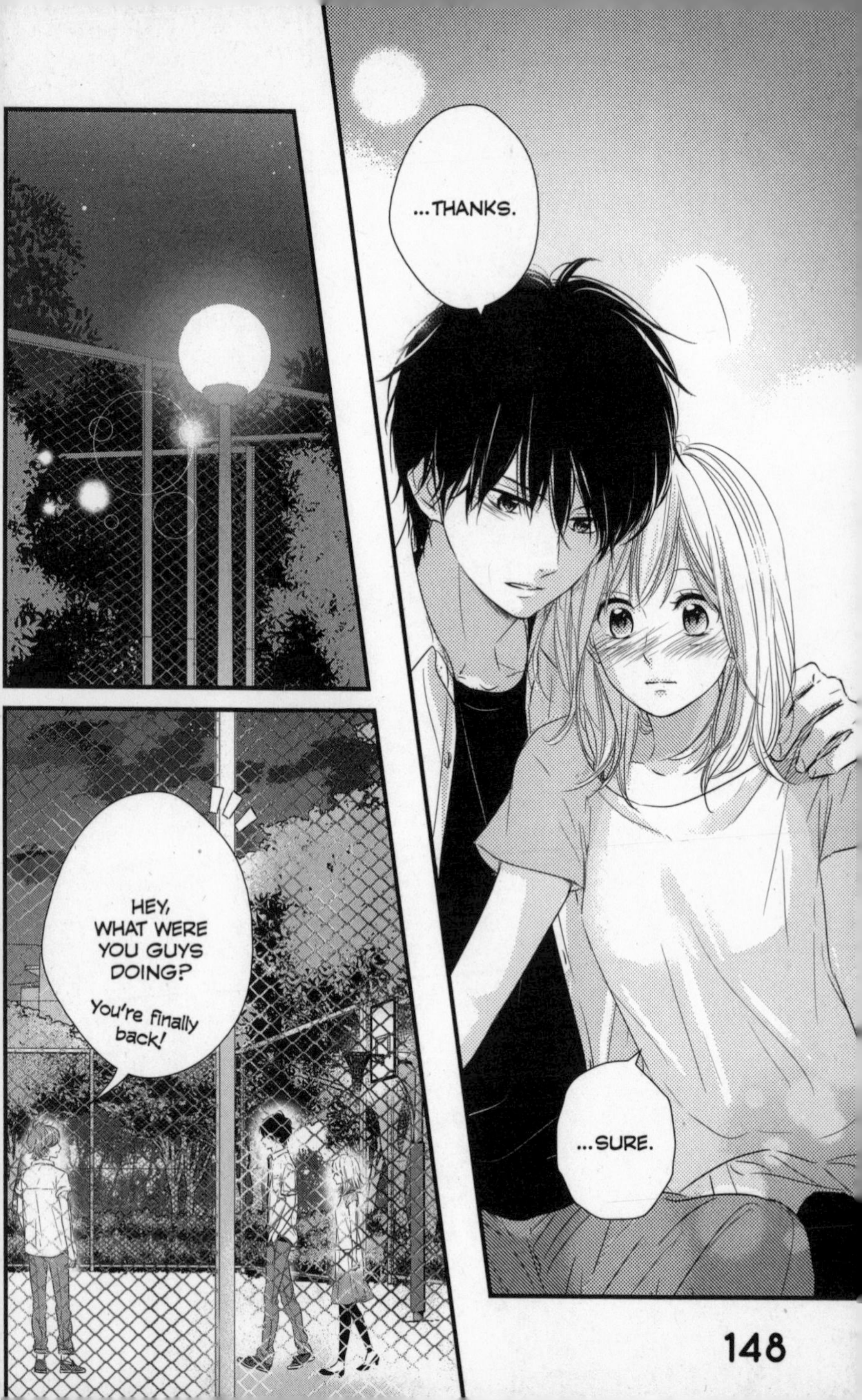
...THANKS.
...SURE.
HEY, WHAT WERE YOU GUYS DOING?
You're finally back!

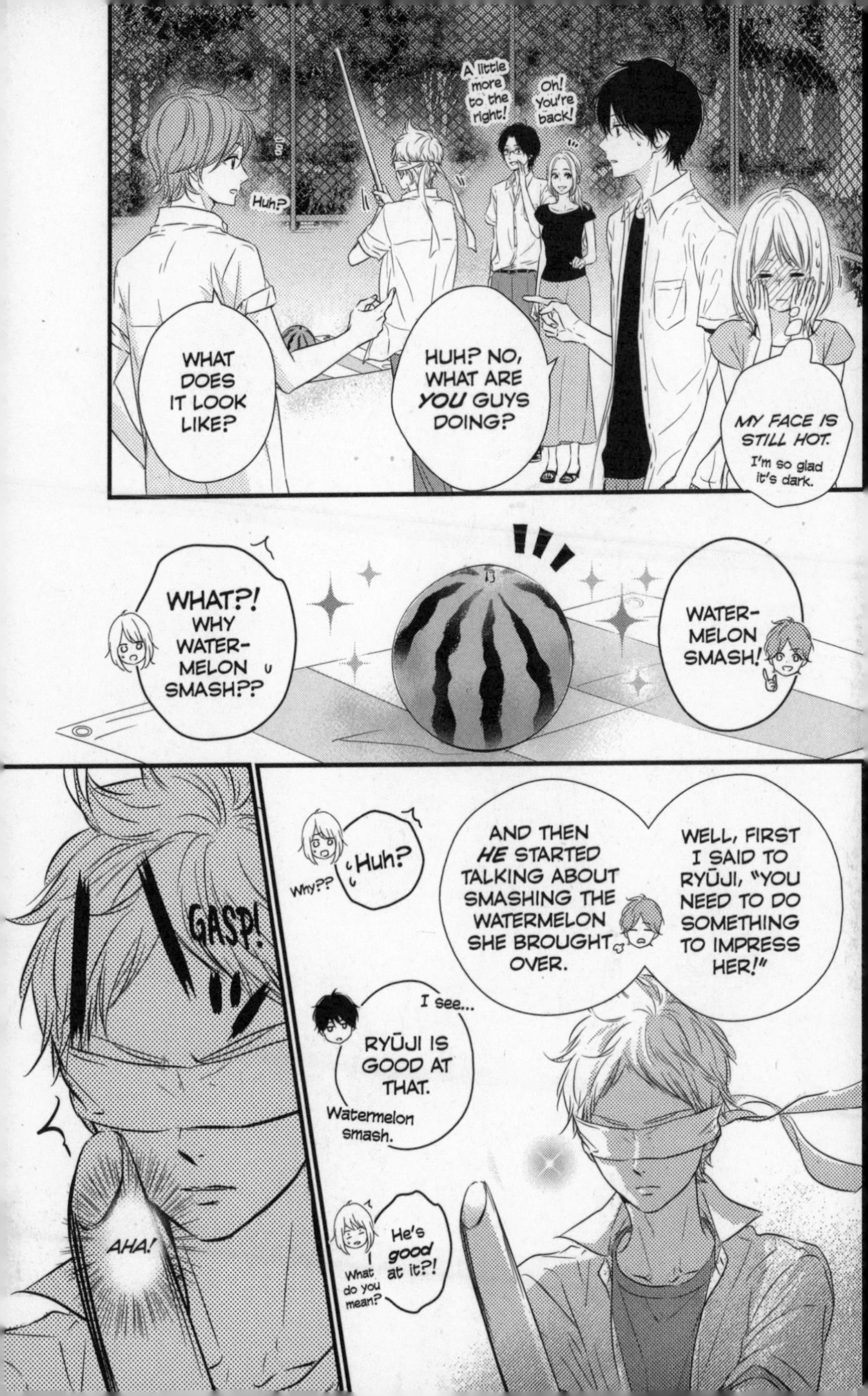
Oh! You're back!
A little more to the right!
MY FACE IS STILL HOT.
I'm so glad it's dark.
HUH? NO, WHAT ARE *YOU* GUYS DOING?
Huh?
WHAT DOES IT LOOK LIKE?
WATER-MELON SMASH!
WHAT?! WHY WATER-MELON SMASH??
WELL, FIRST I SAID TO RYŪJI, "YOU NEED TO DO SOMETHING TO IMPRESS HER!"
AND THEN *HE* STARTED TALKING ABOUT SMASHING THE WATERMELON SHE BROUGHT OVER.
Huh?
Why??
I see...
RYŪJI IS GOOD AT THAT.
Watermelon smash.
He's *good* at it?!
What do you mean?
GASP!
AHA!

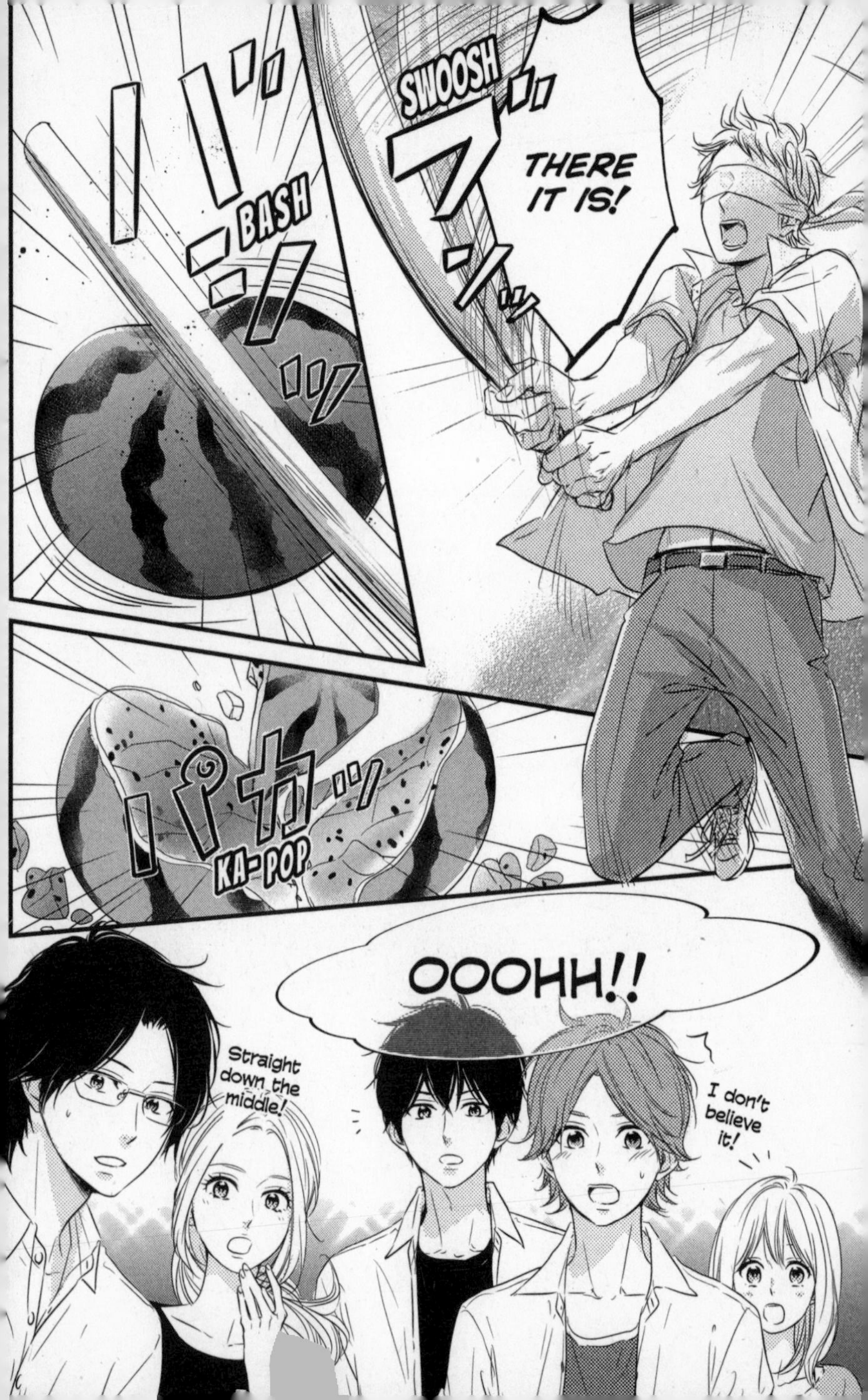
SWOOSH
THERE IT IS!
BASH
KA-POP
OOOHH!!
I don't believe it!
Straight down the middle!

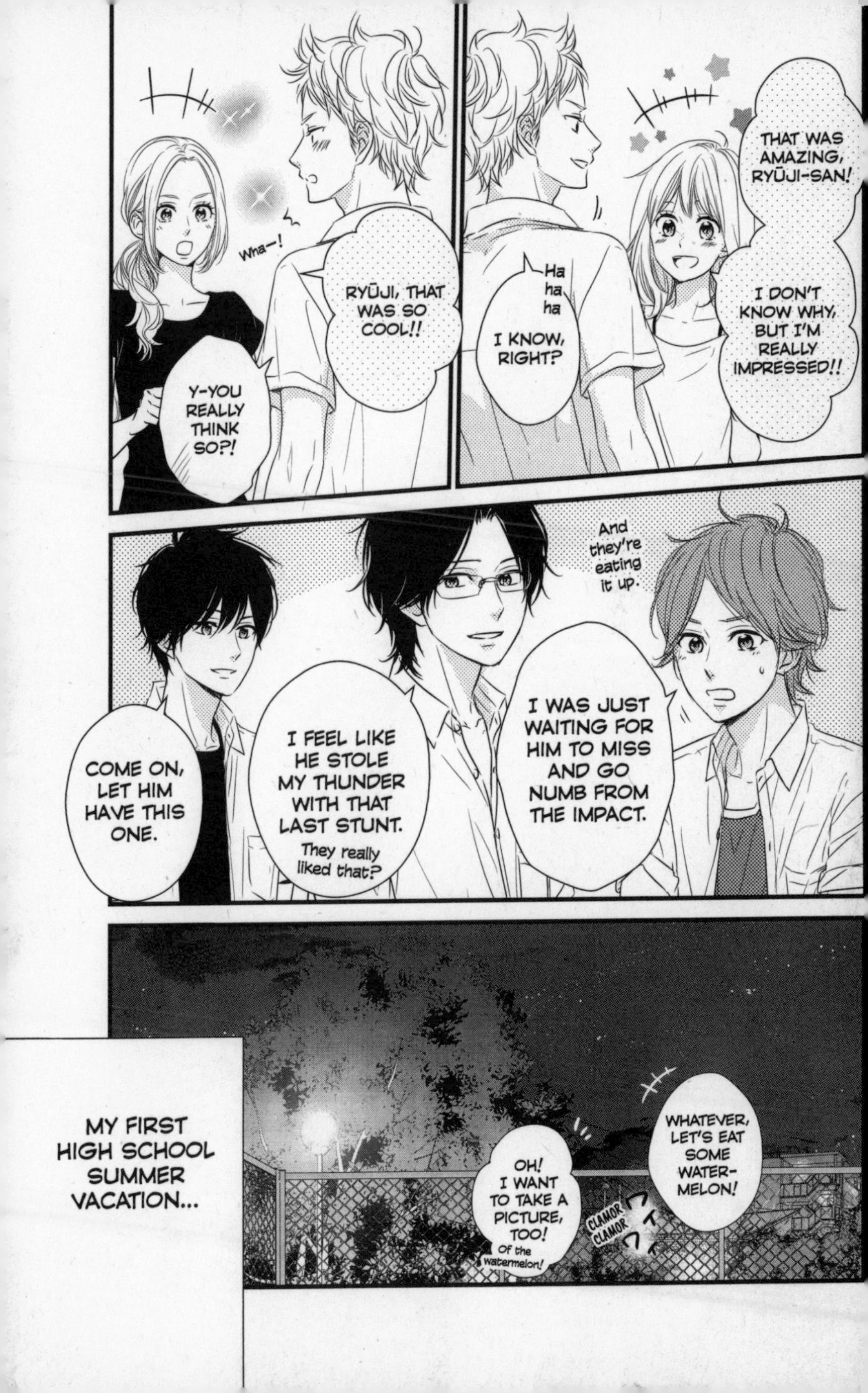
THAT WAS AMAZING, RYŪJI-SAN!
I DON'T KNOW WHY, BUT I'M REALLY IMPRESSED!!
Ha ha ha
I KNOW, RIGHT?
RYŪJI, THAT WAS SO COOL!!
Wha—!
Y-YOU REALLY THINK SO?!
And they're eating it up.
I WAS JUST WAITING FOR HIM TO MISS AND GO NUMB FROM THE IMPACT.
I FEEL LIKE HE STOLE MY THUNDER WITH THAT LAST STUNT.
They really liked that?
COME ON, LET HIM HAVE THIS ONE.
WHATEVER, LET'S EAT SOME WATER-MELON!
CLAMOR CLAMOR
OH! I WANT TO TAKE A PICTURE, TOO!
Of the watermelon!
MY FIRST HIGH SCHOOL SUMMER VACATION...

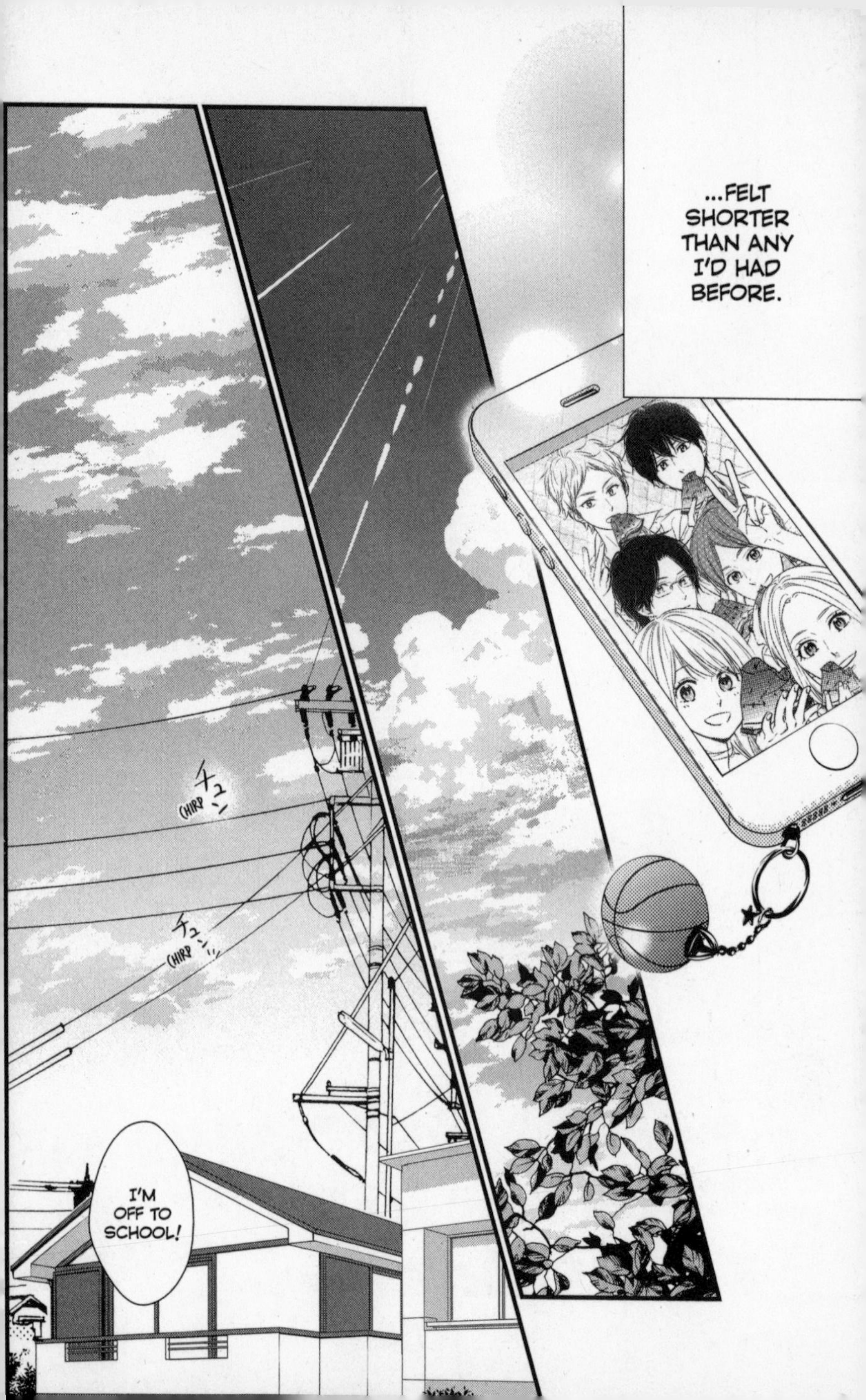
...FELT SHORTER THAN ANY I'D HAD BEFORE.
チュン
CHIRP
チュンッ
CHIRP
I'M OFF TO SCHOOL!

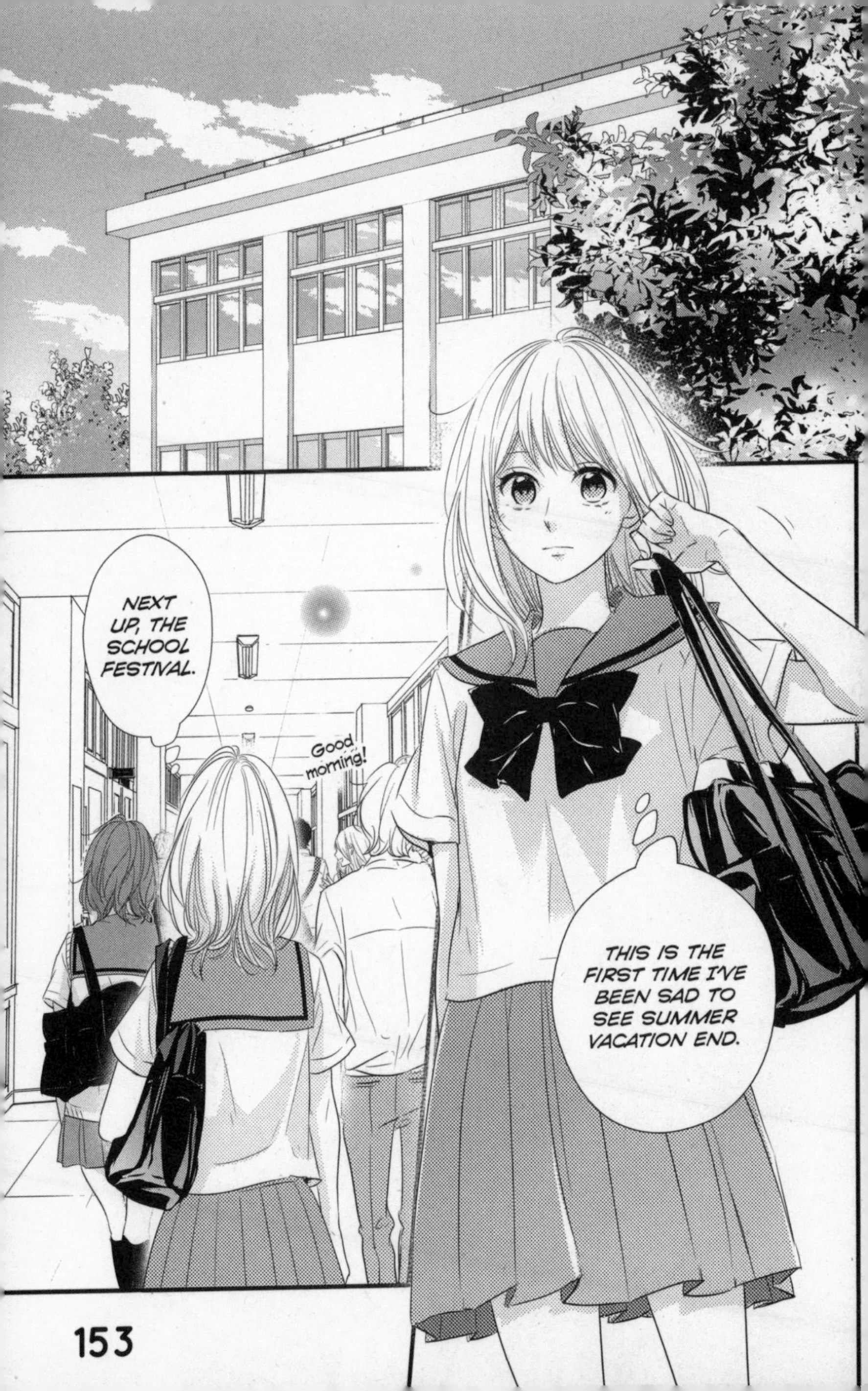
THIS IS THE FIRST TIME I'VE BEEN SAD TO SEE SUMMER VACATION END.
Good morning!
NEXT UP, THE SCHOOL FESTIVAL.

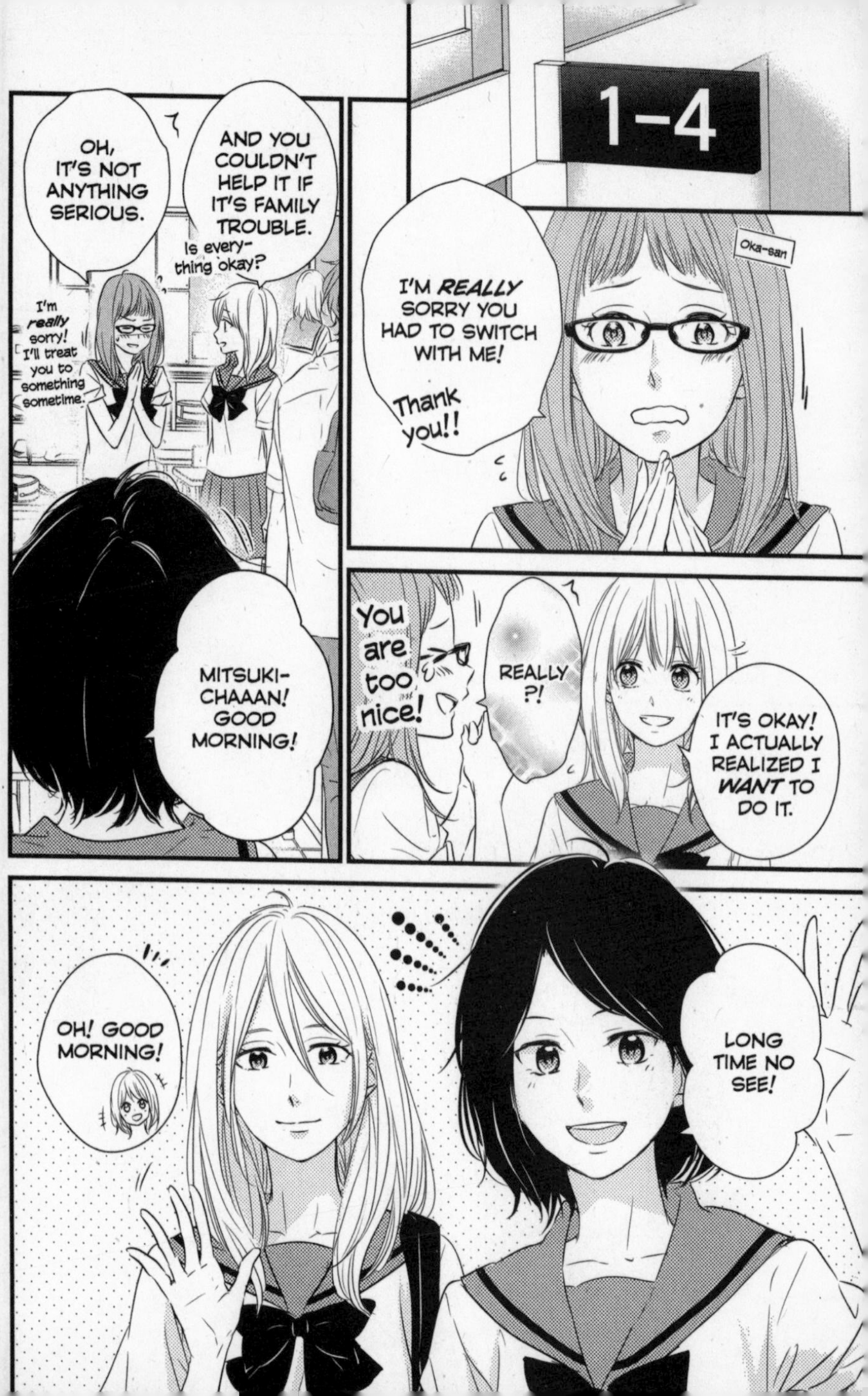
1-4
Oka-san
I'M *REALLY* SORRY YOU HAD TO SWITCH WITH ME!
Thank you!!
IT'S OKAY! I ACTUALLY REALIZED I *WANT* TO DO IT.
REALLY?!
You are too nice!
AND YOU COULDN'T HELP IT IF IT'S FAMILY TROUBLE.
OH, IT'S NOT ANYTHING SERIOUS.
Is every-thing okay?
I'm *really* sorry! I'll treat you to something sometime.
MITSUKI-CHAAAN! GOOD MORNING!
LONG TIME NO SEE!
OH! GOOD MORNING!

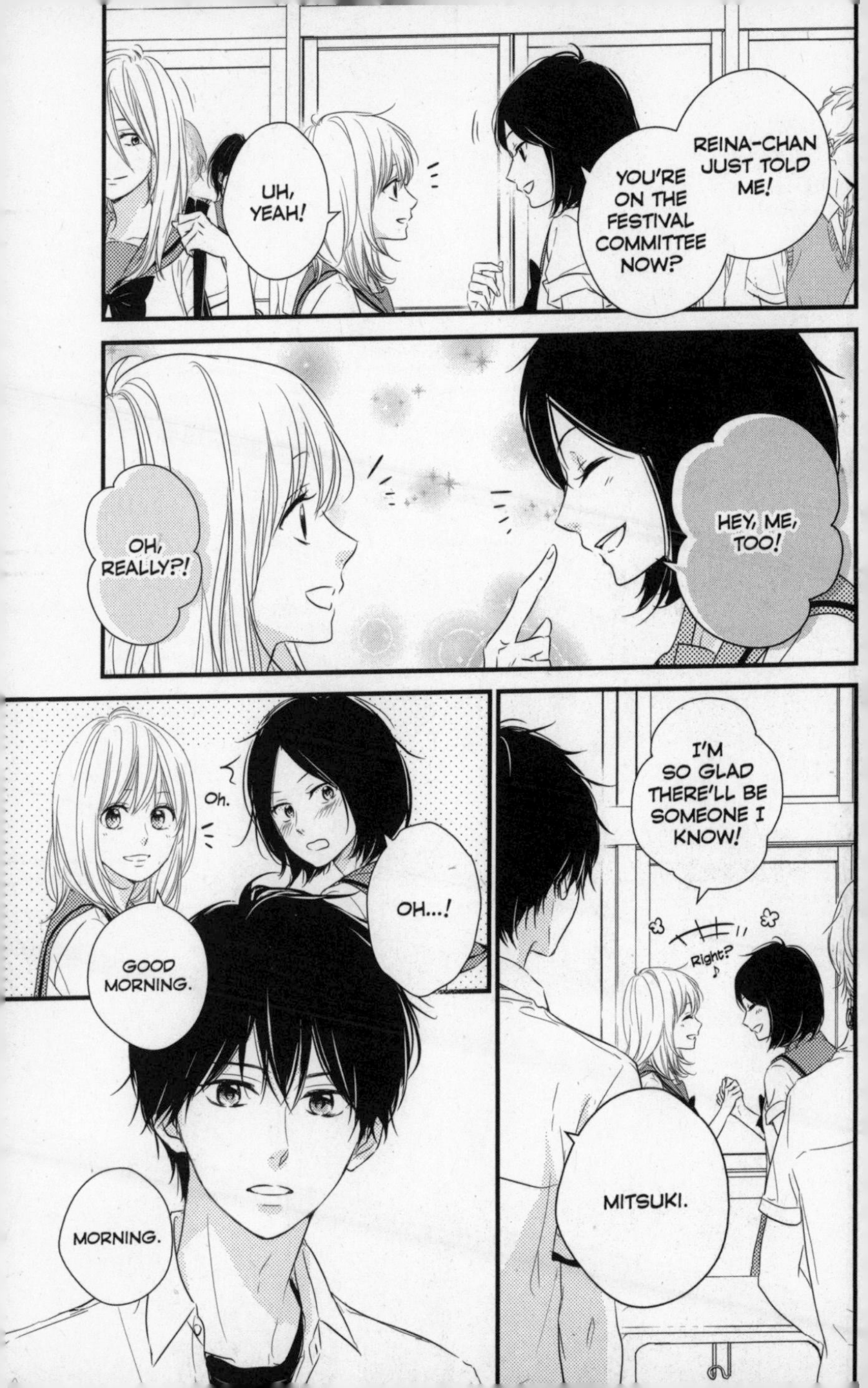
REINA-CHAN JUST TOLD ME!
YOU'RE ON THE FESTIVAL COMMITTEE NOW?
UH, YEAH!
HEY, ME, TOO!
OH, REALLY?!
I'M SO GLAD THERE'LL BE SOMEONE I KNOW!
Right? ♪
MITSUKI.
Oh.
OH...!
GOOD MORNING.
MORNING.

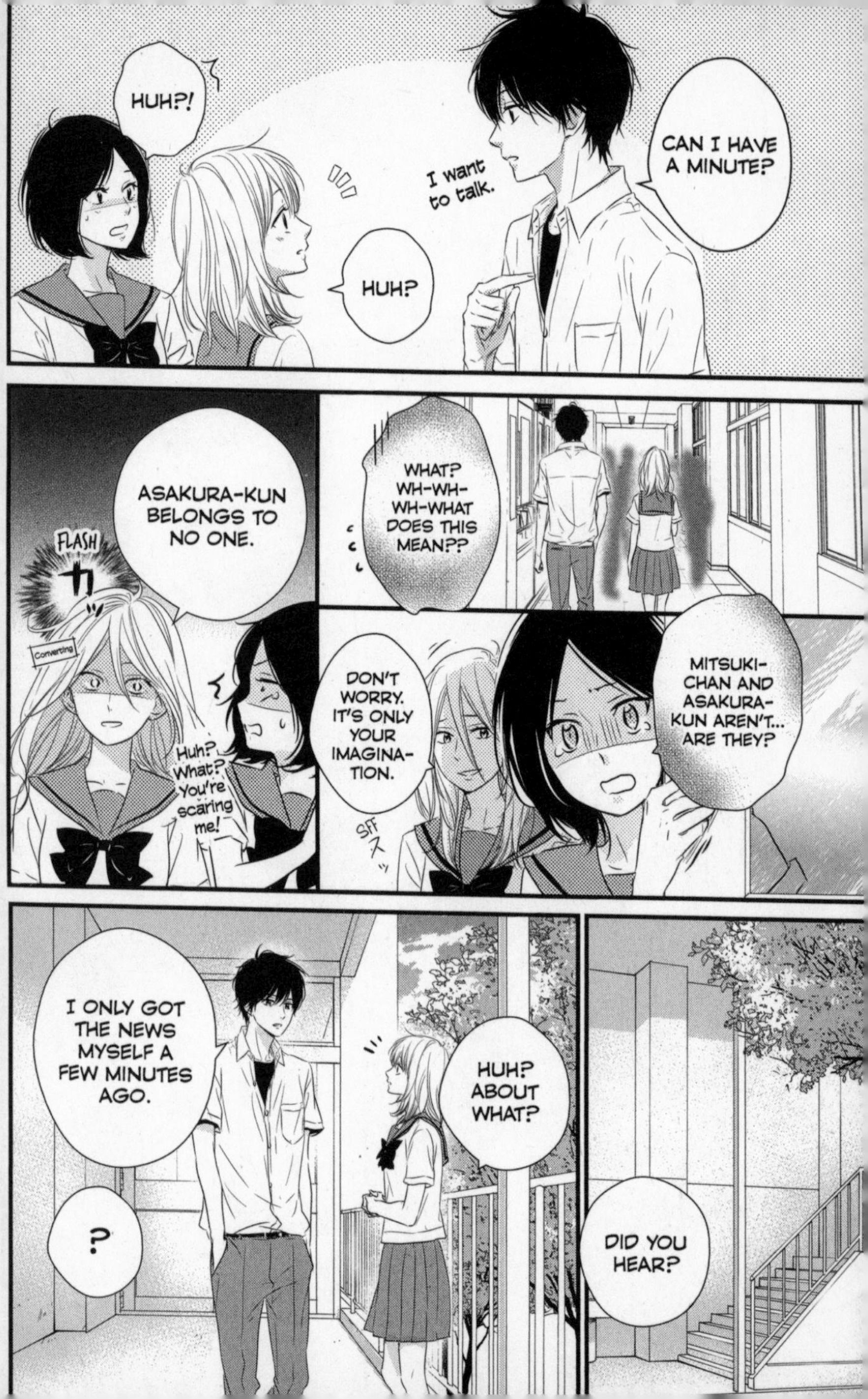
CAN I HAVE A MINUTE?
I want to talk.
HUH?
HUH?!
WHAT? WH-WH-WH-WHAT DOES THIS MEAN??
MITSUKI-CHAN AND ASAKURA-KUN AREN'T... ARE THEY?
DON'T WORRY. IT'S ONLY YOUR IMAGINATION.
SFF
ASAKURA-KUN BELONGS TO NO ONE.
FLASH
Converting
Huh? What? You're scaring me!
DID YOU HEAR?
HUH? ABOUT WHAT?
I ONLY GOT THE NEWS MYSELF A FEW MINUTES AGO.
?

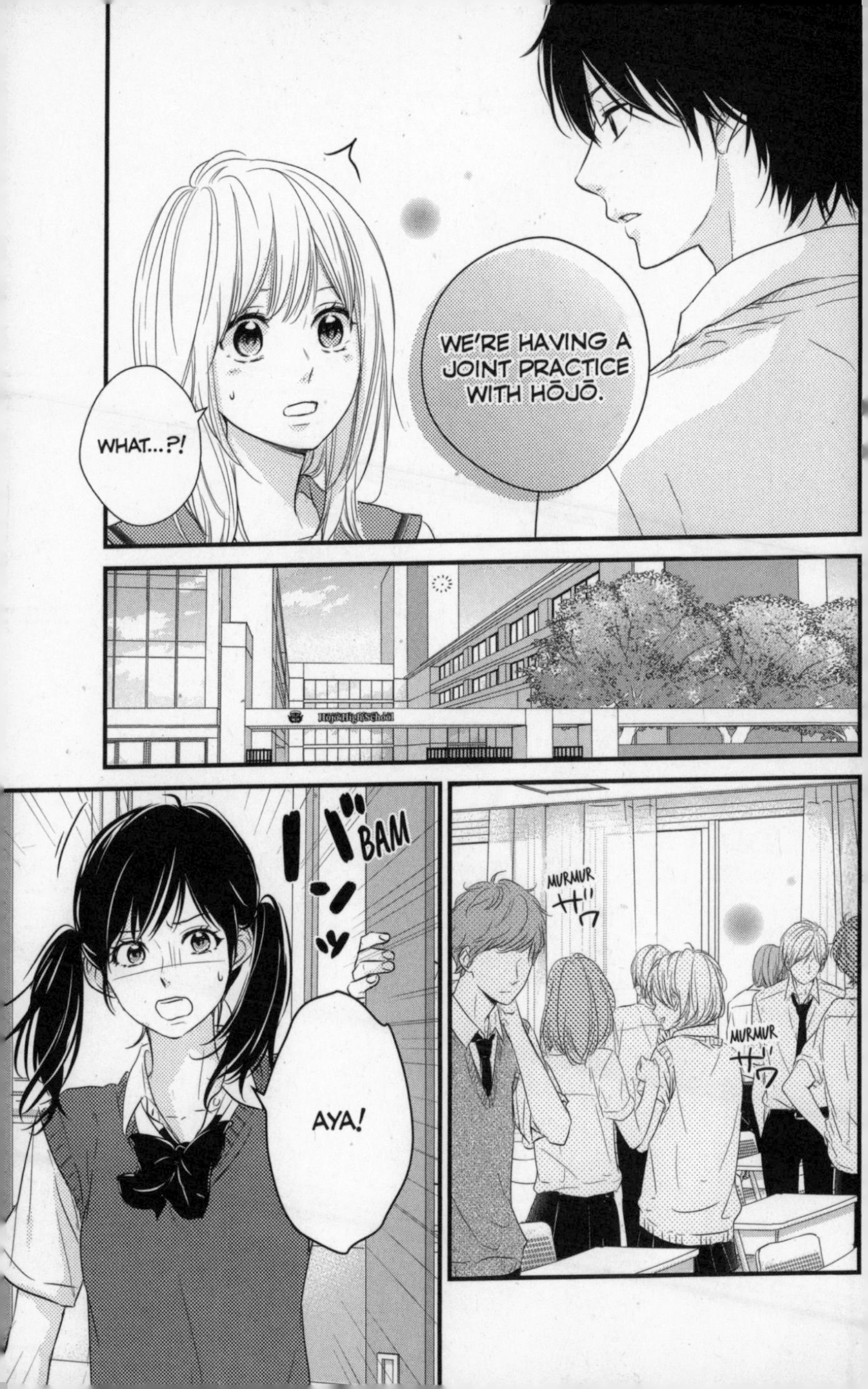
WE'RE HAVING A JOINT PRACTICE WITH HŌJŌ.
WHAT...?!
MURMUR ザワ
MURMUR ザワ
バンッ BAM
AYA!

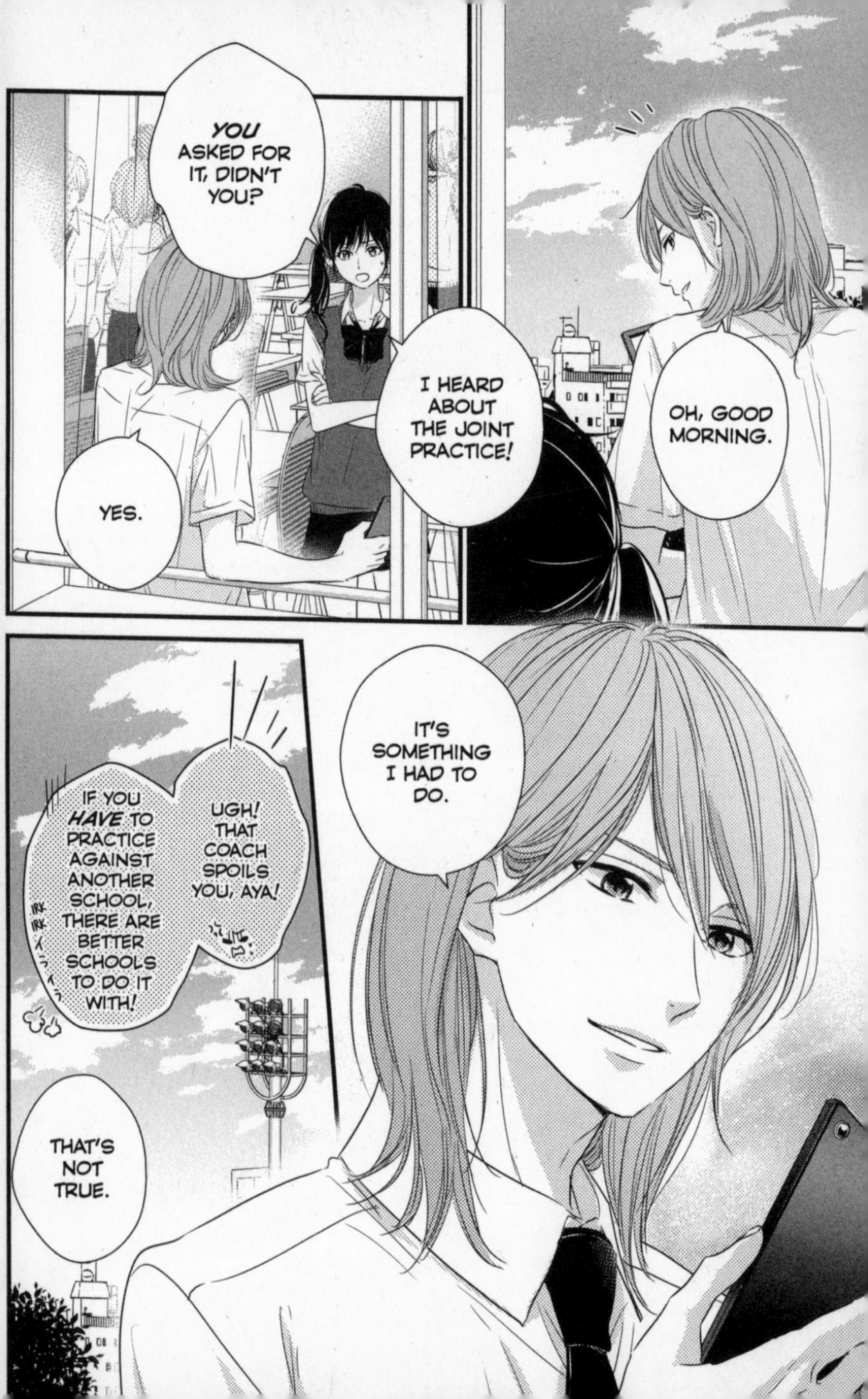

OH, GOOD MORNING.
I HEARD ABOUT THE JOINT PRACTICE!
YOU ASKED FOR IT, DIDN'T YOU?
YES.
IT'S SOMETHING I HAD TO DO.
UGH! THAT COACH SPOILS YOU, AYA!
IF YOU HAVE TO PRACTICE AGAINST ANOTHER SCHOOL, THERE ARE BETTER SCHOOLS TO DO IT WITH!
IRK IRK
THAT'S NOT TRUE.

I'M SURE THERE ARE THINGS TO BE GAINED FROM THIS.
ABC
DEF
JKL
MNO
TUV
Give Asakura-kun a message for me.
ACK!
!
"I'm declaring war. I can't wait. ^^"
AYA-CHAN...
...SAYS HE DECLARES WAR.
It's just a joint practice, isn't it?

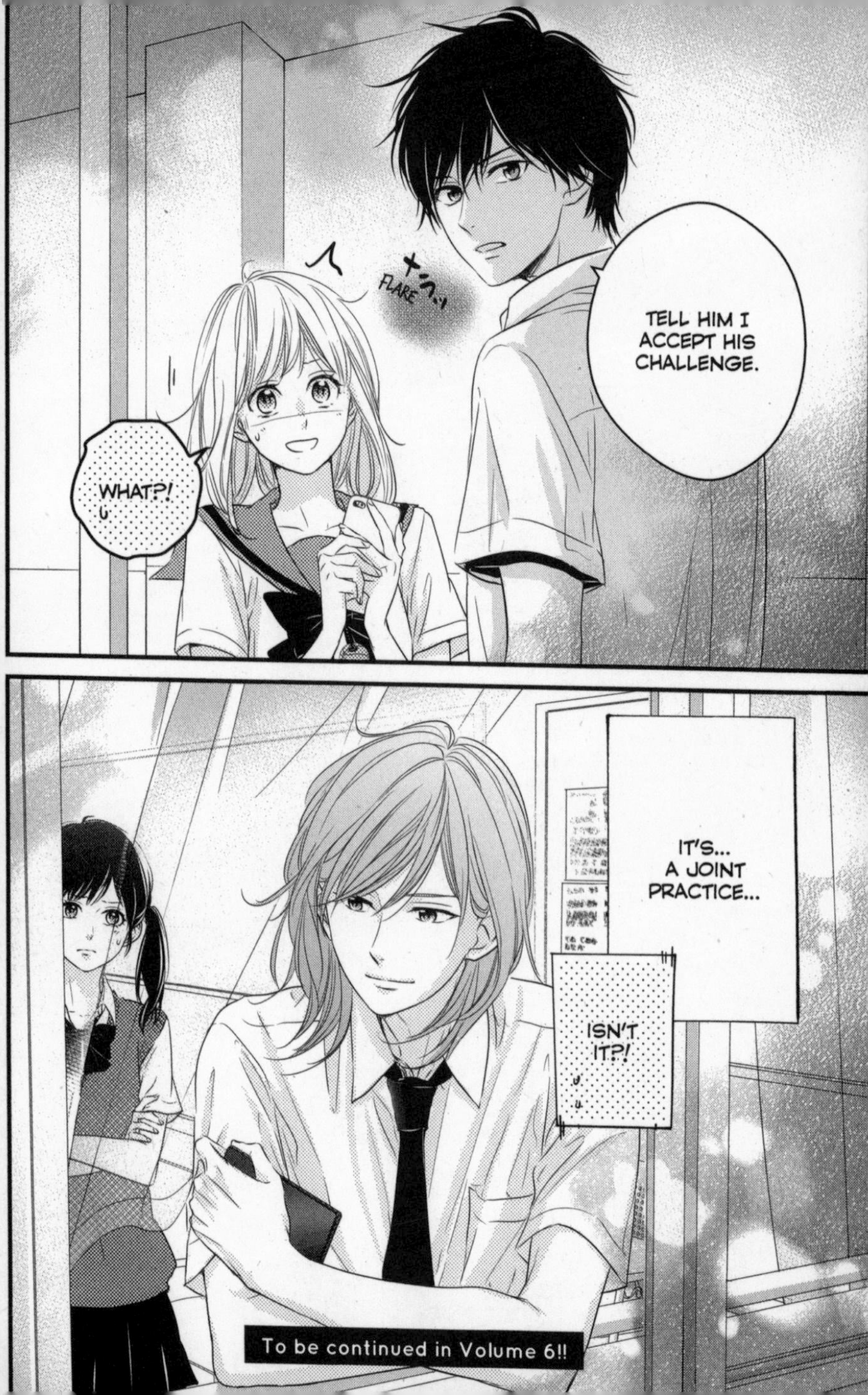
TELL HIM I ACCEPT HIS CHALLENGE.
FLARE
WHAT?!
IT'S... A JOINT PRACTICE...
ISN'T IT?!
To be continued in Volume 6!!

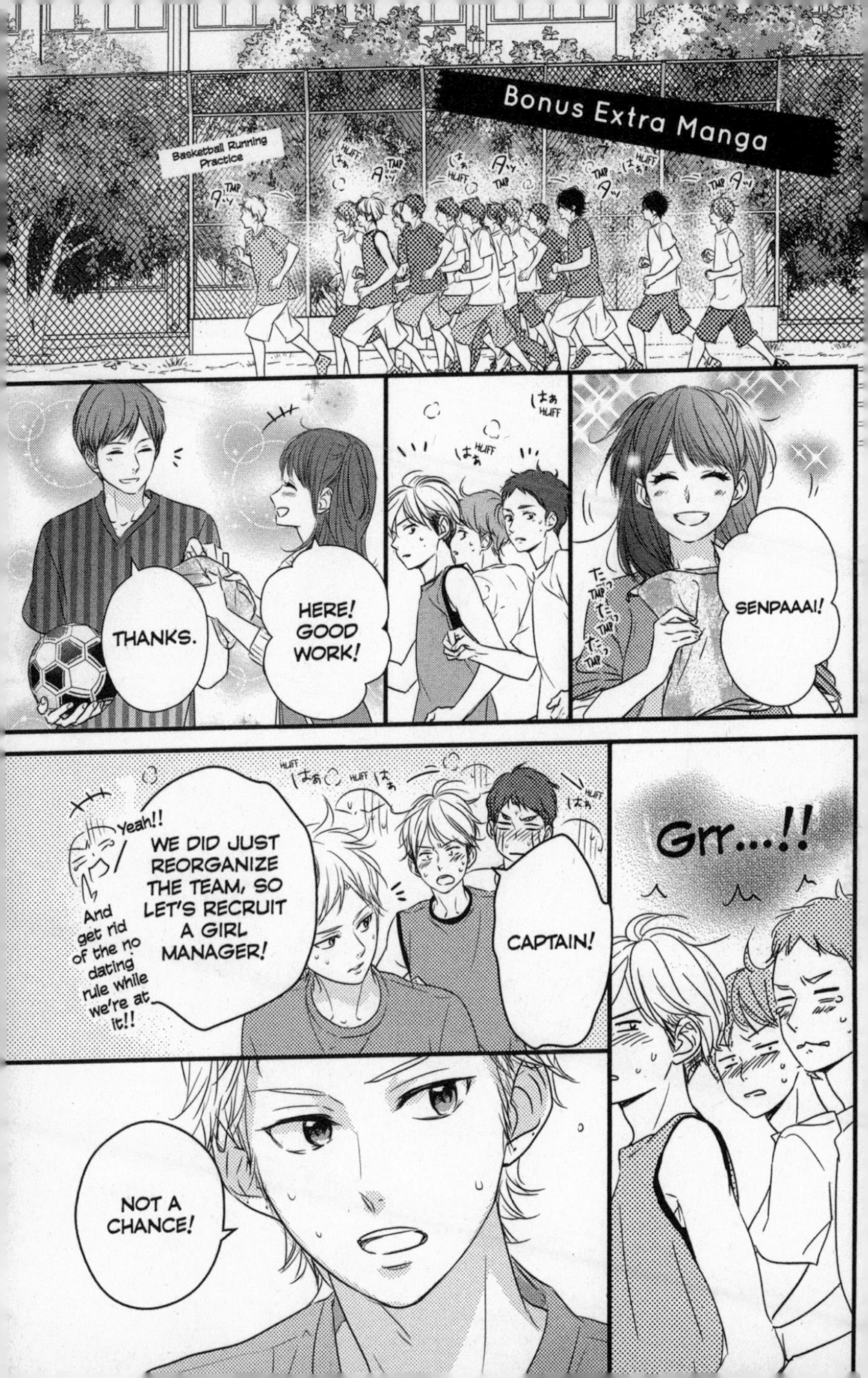

Bonus Extra Manga
Basketball Running Practice
HUFF
TMP
SENPAAAI!
TMP
HUFF
HERE! GOOD WORK!
THANKS.
Grr...!!
HUFF
CAPTAIN!
WE DID JUST REORGANIZE THE TEAM, SO LET'S RECRUIT A GIRL MANAGER!
Yeah!!
And get rid of the no dating rule while we're at it!!
NOT A CHANCE!

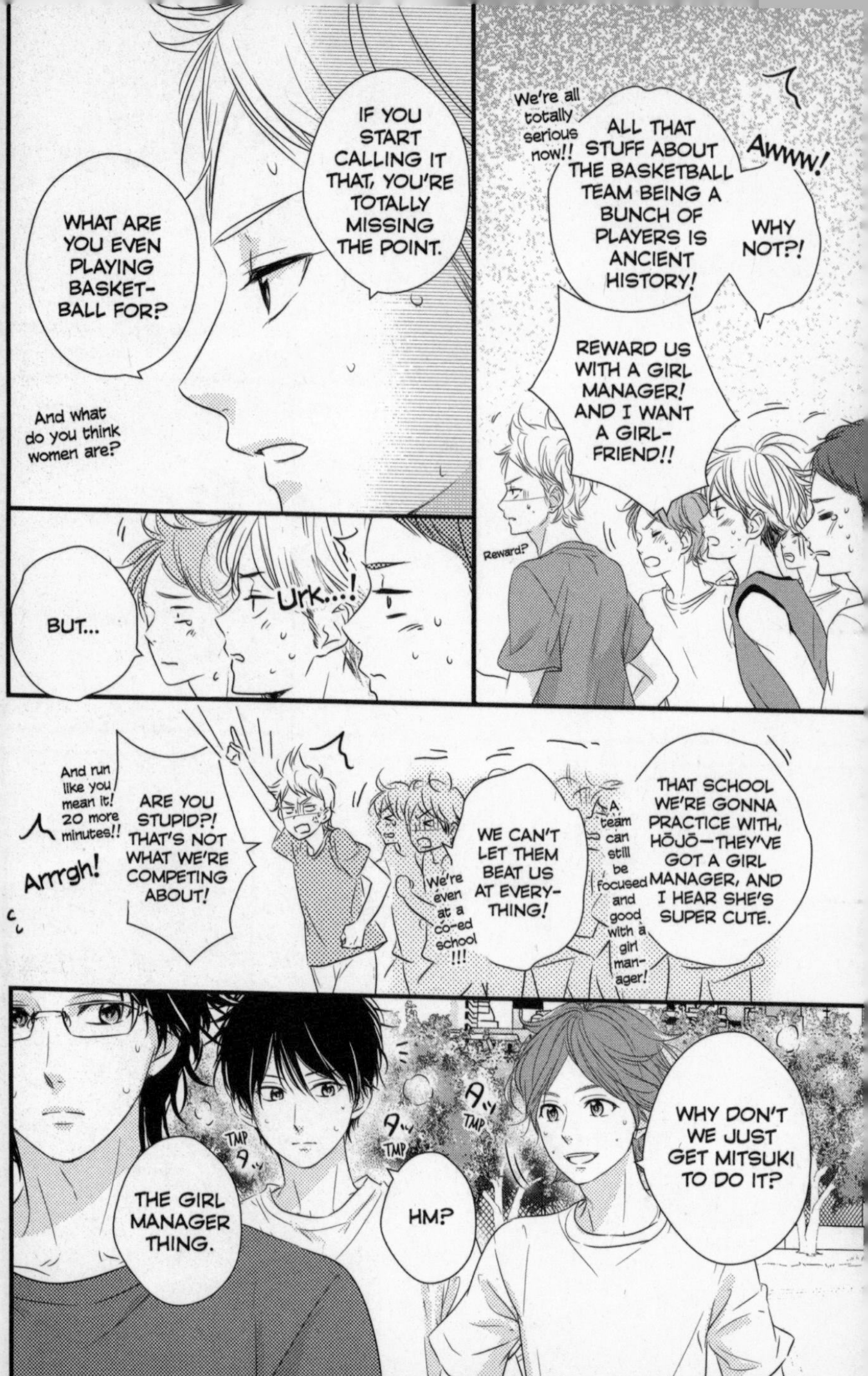
Awww!
WHY NOT?!
ALL THAT STUFF ABOUT THE BASKETBALL TEAM BEING A BUNCH OF PLAYERS IS ANCIENT HISTORY!
We're all totally serious now!!
REWARD US WITH A GIRL MANAGER! AND I WANT A GIRL-FRIEND!!
Reward?
IF YOU START CALLING IT THAT, YOU'RE TOTALLY MISSING THE POINT.
WHAT ARE YOU EVEN PLAYING BASKET-BALL FOR?
And what do you think women are?
Urk...!
BUT...
THAT SCHOOL WE'RE GONNA PRACTICE WITH, HŌJŌ—THEY'VE GOT A GIRL MANAGER, AND I HEAR SHE'S SUPER CUTE.
A team can still be focused and good with a girl man-ager!
WE CAN'T LET THEM BEAT US AT EVERY-THING!
We're even at a co-ed school!!!
ARE YOU STUPID?! THAT'S NOT WHAT WE'RE COMPETING ABOUT!
And run like you mean it! 20 more minutes!!
Arrrgh!
WHY DON'T WE JUST GET MITSUKI TO DO IT?
TMP
TMP
HM?
TMP
THE GIRL MANAGER THING.

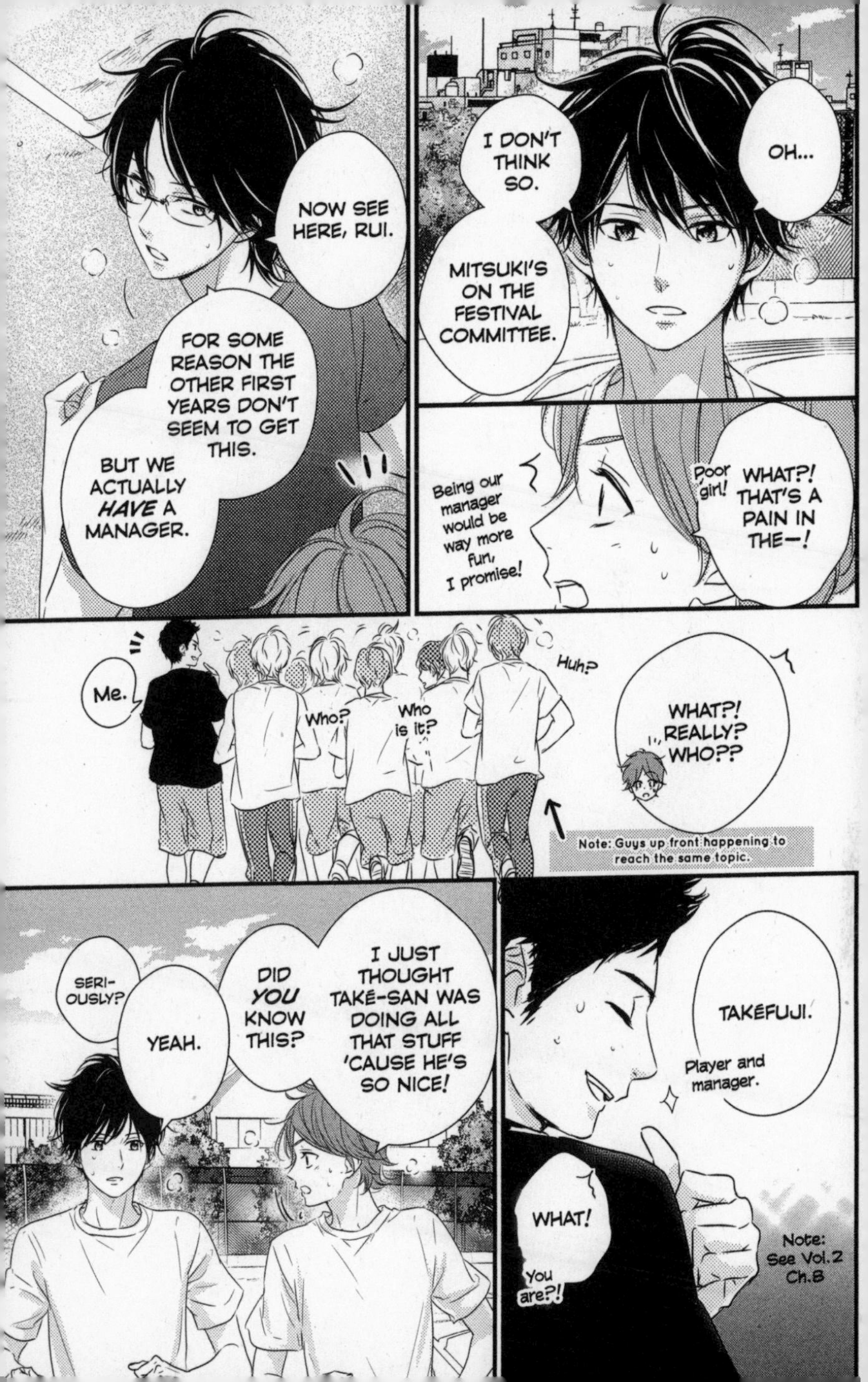
OH...
I DON'T THINK SO.
MITSUKI'S ON THE FESTIVAL COMMITTEE.
WHAT?! THAT'S A PAIN IN THE—!
Poor girl!
Being our manager would be way more fun, I promise!
NOW SEE HERE, RUI.
FOR SOME REASON THE OTHER FIRST YEARS DON'T SEEM TO GET THIS.
BUT WE ACTUALLY *HAVE* A MANAGER.
WHAT?! REALLY? WHO??
Huh?
Note: Guys up front happening to reach the same topic.
Who is it?
Who?
Me.
TAKÉFUJI.
Player and manager.
WHAT!
You are?!
Note: See Vol.2 Ch.8
I JUST THOUGHT TAKÉ-SAN WAS DOING ALL THAT STUFF 'CAUSE HE'S SO NICE!
DID *YOU* KNOW THIS?
SERIOUSLY?
YEAH.

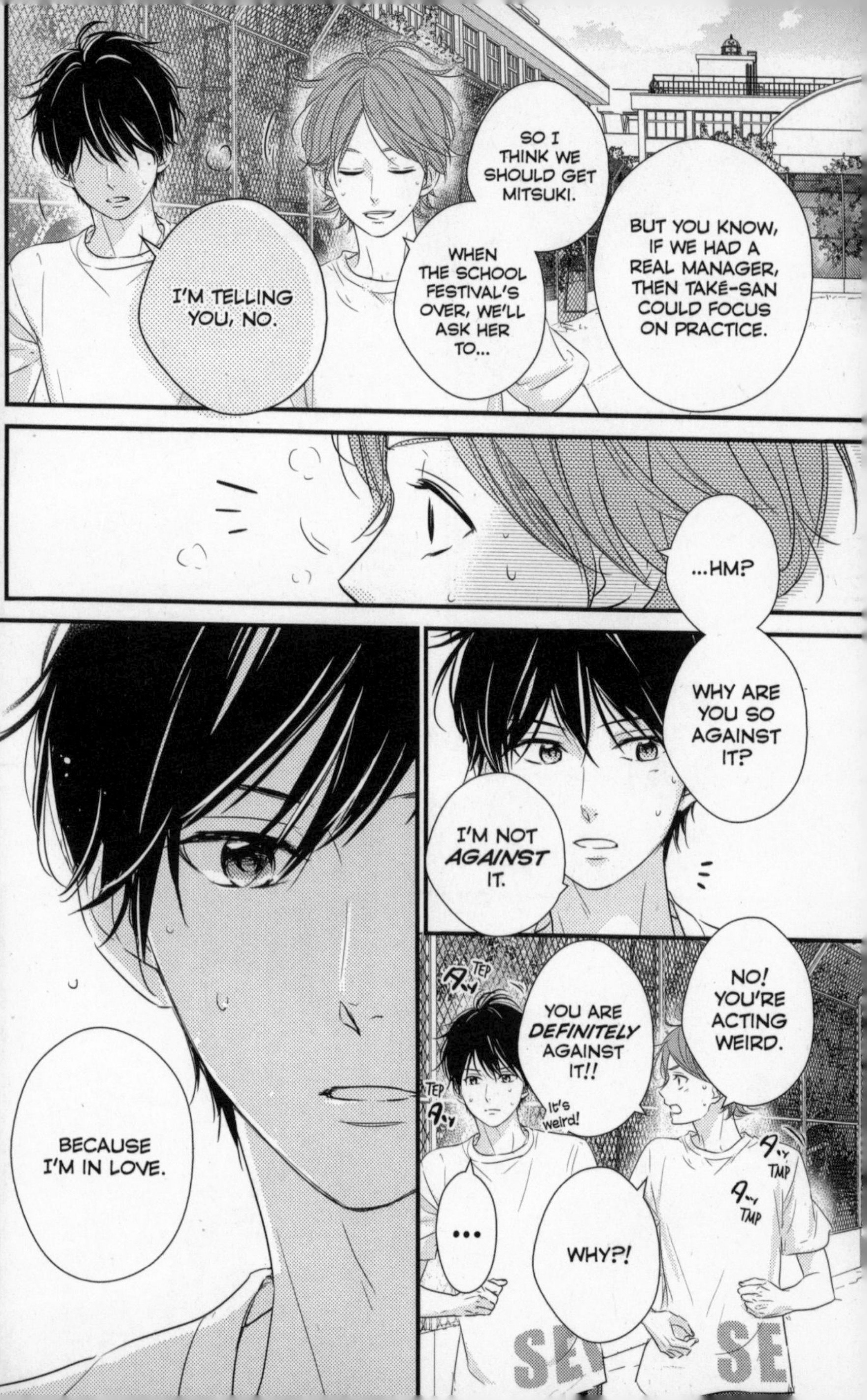
BUT YOU KNOW, IF WE HAD A REAL MANAGER, THEN TAKÉ-SAN COULD FOCUS ON PRACTICE.
SO I THINK WE SHOULD GET MITSUKI.
WHEN THE SCHOOL FESTIVAL'S OVER, WE'LL ASK HER TO...
I'M TELLING YOU, NO.
...HM?
WHY ARE YOU SO AGAINST IT?
I'M NOT *AGAINST* IT.
NO! YOU'RE ACTING WEIRD.
YOU ARE *DEFINITELY* AGAINST IT!!
TEP
TEP
It's weird!
TMP
TMP
WHY?!
...
BECAUSE I'M IN LOVE.

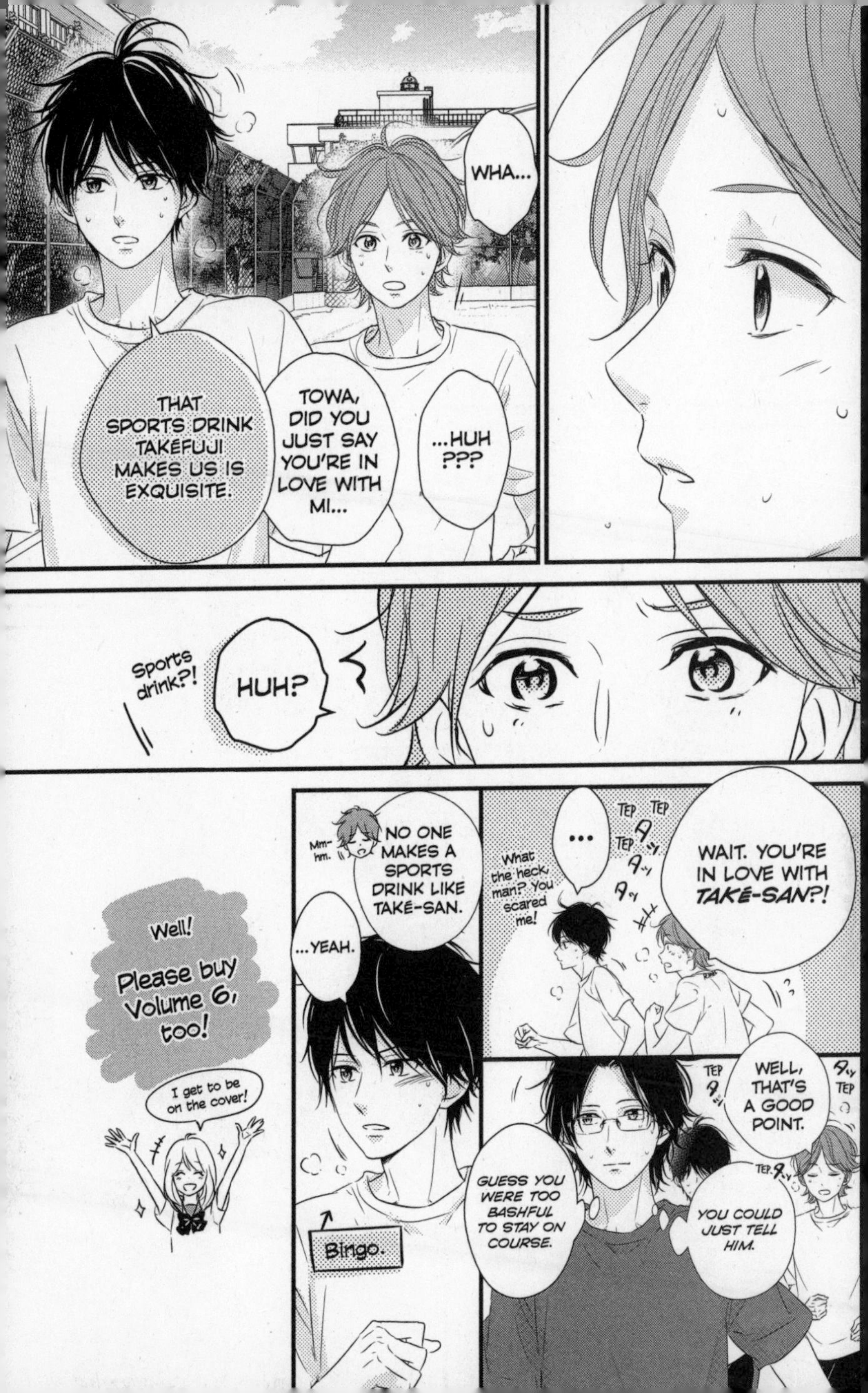

WHA...
...HUH ???
TOWA, DID YOU JUST SAY YOU'RE IN LOVE WITH MI...
THAT SPORTS DRINK TAKÉFUJI MAKES US IS EXQUISITE.
HUH?
Sports drink?!
WAIT. YOU'RE IN LOVE WITH TAKÉ-SAN?!
TEP TEP
TEP
...
What the heck, man? You scared me!
TEP
WELL, THAT'S A GOOD POINT.
TEP
TEP
YOU COULD JUST TELL HIM.
GUESS YOU WERE TOO BASHFUL TO STAY ON COURSE.
NO ONE MAKES A SPORTS DRINK LIKE TAKÉ-SAN.
Mm-hm.
...YEAH.
Bingo.
Well! Please buy Volume 6, too!
I get to be on the cover!

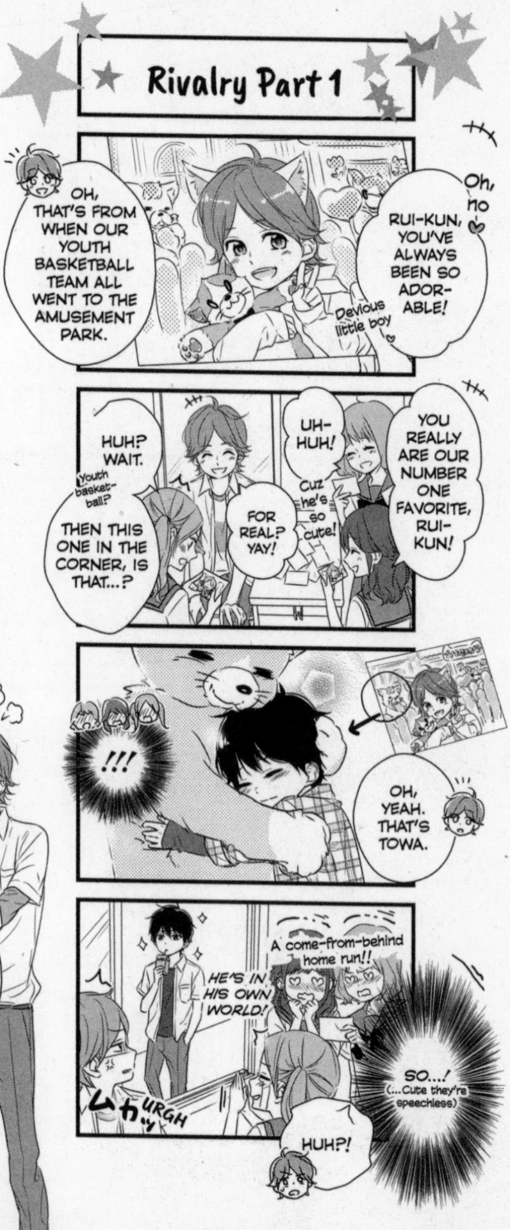
Rivalry Part 1
Oh, no ♡
RUI-KUN, YOU'VE ALWAYS BEEN SO ADOR-ABLE!
Devious little boy ♡
OH, THAT'S FROM WHEN OUR YOUTH BASKETBALL TEAM ALL WENT TO THE AMUSEMENT PARK.
YOU REALLY ARE OUR NUMBER ONE FAVORITE, RUI-KUN!
UH-HUH!
Cuz he's so cute!
FOR REAL? YAY!
HUH? WAIT.
Youth basket-ball?
THEN THIS ONE IN THE CORNER, IS THAT...?
OH, YEAH. THAT'S TOWA.
!!!
A come-from-behind home run!!
HE'S IN HIS OWN WORLD!
SO...!
(...Cute they're speechless)
URGH
HUH?!
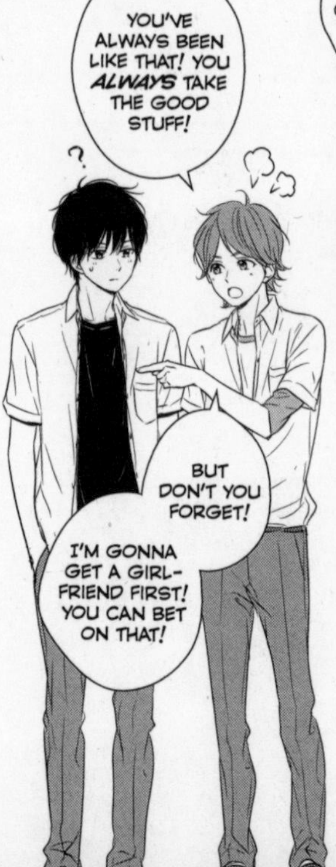
YOU'VE ALWAYS BEEN LIKE THAT! YOU *ALWAYS* TAKE THE GOOD STUFF!
BUT DON'T YOU FORGET!
I'M GONNA GET A GIRL-FRIEND FIRST! YOU CAN BET ON THAT!

Rivalry Part 2

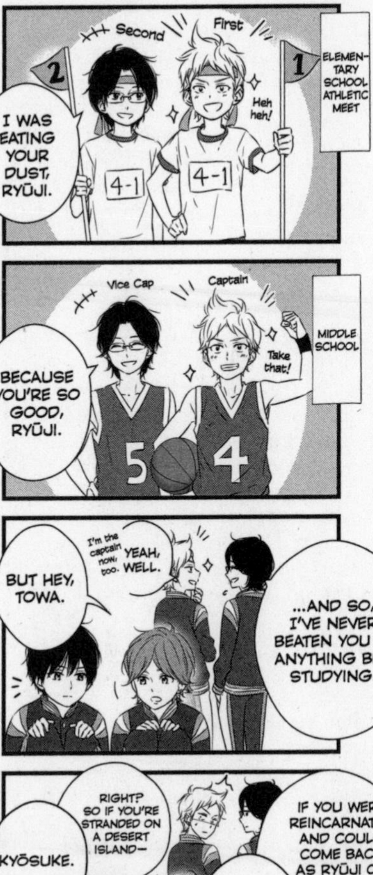
ELEMENTARY SCHOOL ATHLETIC MEET
First
Heh heh!
Second
I WAS EATING YOUR DUST, RYŪJI.
MIDDLE SCHOOL
Captain
Take that!
Vice Cap
BECAUSE YOU'RE SO GOOD, RYŪJI.
...AND SO, I'VE NEVER BEATEN YOU AT ANYTHING BUT STUDYING.
YEAH, WELL.
I'm the captain now, too.
BUT HEY, TOWA.
IF YOU WERE REINCARNATED AND COULD COME BACK AS RYŪJI OR KYŌSUKE, WHO WOULD YOU—
KYŌSUKE.
RIGHT? SO IF YOU'RE STRANDED ON A DESERT ISLAND—
KYŌSUKE.
AT LEAST LET HIM FINISH THE QUESTION!

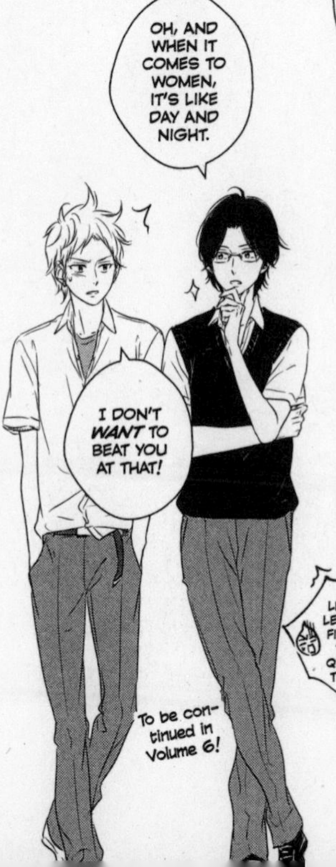
OH, AND WHEN IT COMES TO WOMEN, IT'S LIKE DAY AND NIGHT.
I DON'T *WANT* TO BEAT YOU AT THAT!
To be continued in Volume 6!

Translation Notes

Summer spectacular, page 70

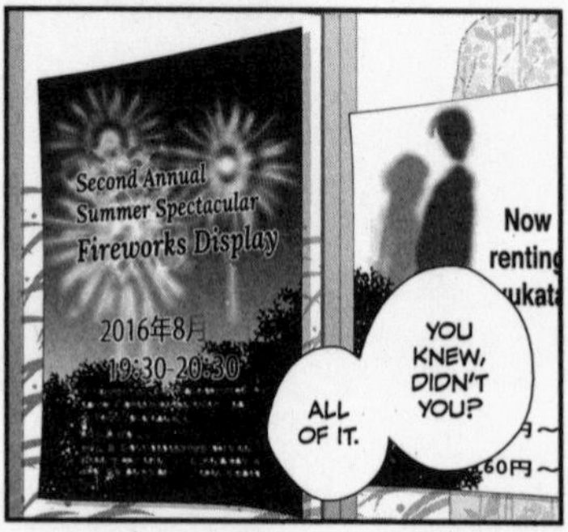
Second Annual
Summer Spectacular
Fireworks Display
2016年8月
19:30-20:30
Now
YOU KNEW, DIDN'T YOU?
ALL OF IT.

To be more precise, the term used is *nōryō*, which roughly means "obtain coolness." The term is used for events that are designed to help people forget the heat of the summer and enjoy their lives again. This particular event may also be a way to help the local kimono vendors, because festivals and fireworks shows are an excellent opportunity to wear a traditional summer kimono, the yukata.

School festival, page 132

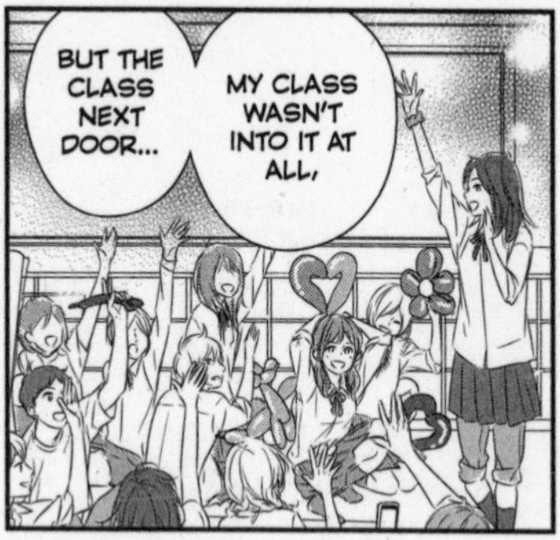
MY CLASS WASN'T INTO IT AT ALL,
BUT THE CLASS NEXT DOOR...

In Japan, schools will hold yearly festivals to display the students' artistic, intellectual, and business skills. These festivals are often called *bunkasai*, meaning "culture festival," to differentiate them from *taiikusai*, or "athletic festivals," in which students show off their athletic prowess. Classes and clubs will set up displays outside or in their classroom that can be anything from a restaurant to a haunted house.

Watermelon smash, page 149

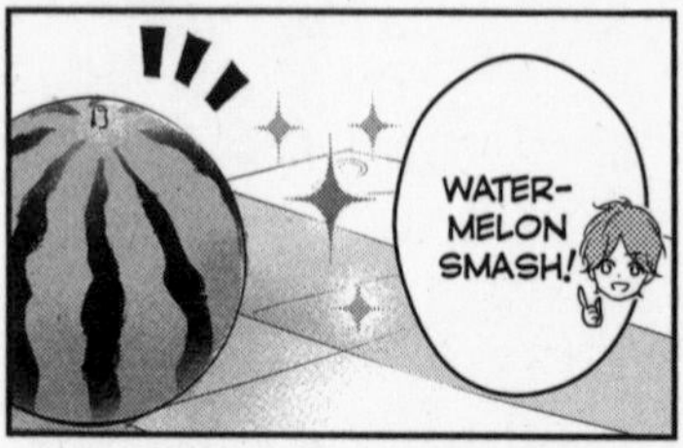
WATER-MELON SMASH!

This is a common summer game in Japan with a simple objective: to smash a watermelon. The watermelon will be set on a towel on the ground, and the players will take turns being blindfolded and spun around three times. They will then take a wooden stick and try to find and smash the watermelon. Often those watching will offer advice that will lead the player in the right (or wrong) direction. Whoever breaks the watermelon open wins.

Waiting for Spring

WAITING FOR SPRING

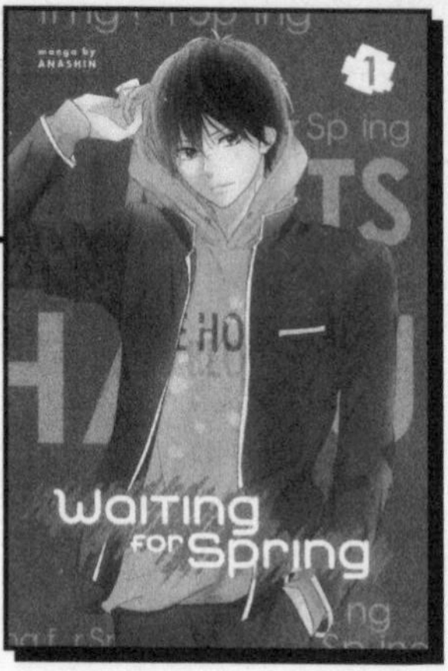
manga by ANASHIN
1
Waiting for Spring

A sweet romantic story of a soft-spoken high school freshman and her quest to make friends. For fans of earnest, fun, and dramatic shojo like *Kimi ni Todoke* and *Say I Love You*.

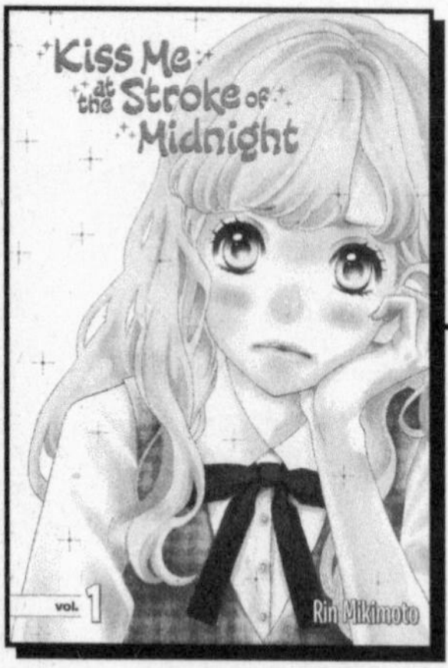
Kiss Me at the Stroke of Midnight
vol. 1
Rin Mikimoto

KISS ME AT THE STROKE OF MIDNIGHT

An all-new Cinderella comedy perfect for fans of *My Little Monster* and *Say I Love You*!

LOVE AND LIES

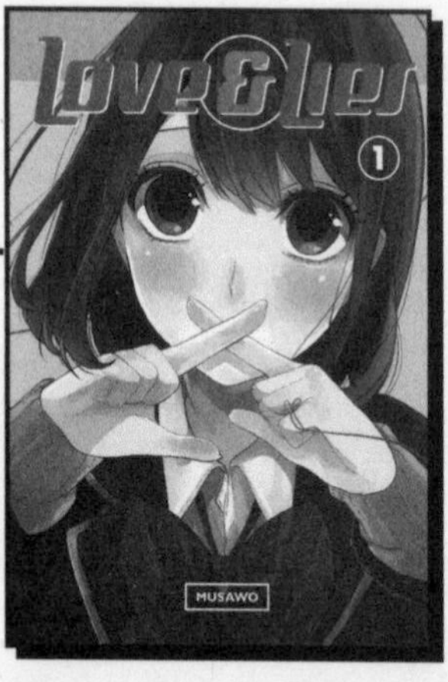
Love&lies
1
MUSAWO

Love is forbidden. When you turn 16, the government will assign you your marriage partner. This dystopian manga about teen love and defiance is a sexy, funny, and dramatic new hit! Anime now streaming on Anime Strike!

KC KODANSHA COMICS

17 years after the original *Cardcaptor Sakura* manga ended, CLAMP returns with more magical adventures from a beloved manga classic!

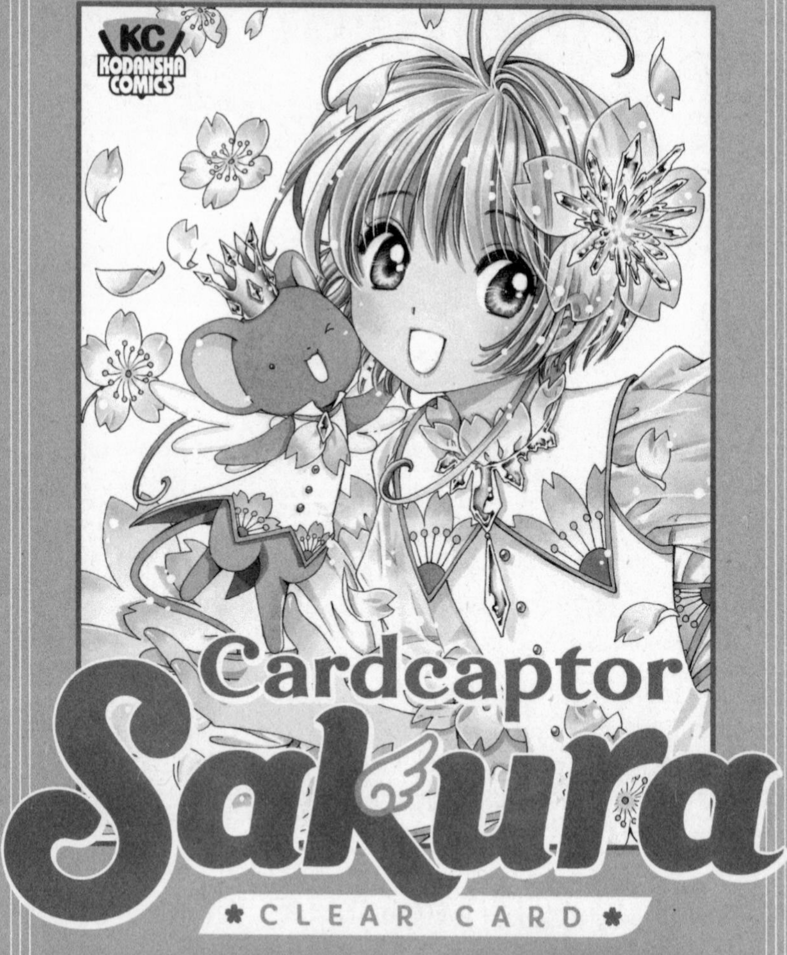
KC
KODANSHA COMICS
Cardcaptor
Sakura
CLEAR CARD

Sakura Kinomoto's about to start middle school, and everything's coming up cherry blossoms. Not only has she managed to recapture the scattered Clow Cards and make them her own Sakura Cards, but her sweetheart Syaoran Li has moved from Hong Kong to Tokyo and is going to be in her class! But her joy is interrupted by a troubling dream in which the cards turn transparent, and when Sakura awakens to discover her dream has become reality, it's clear that her magical adventures are far from over...

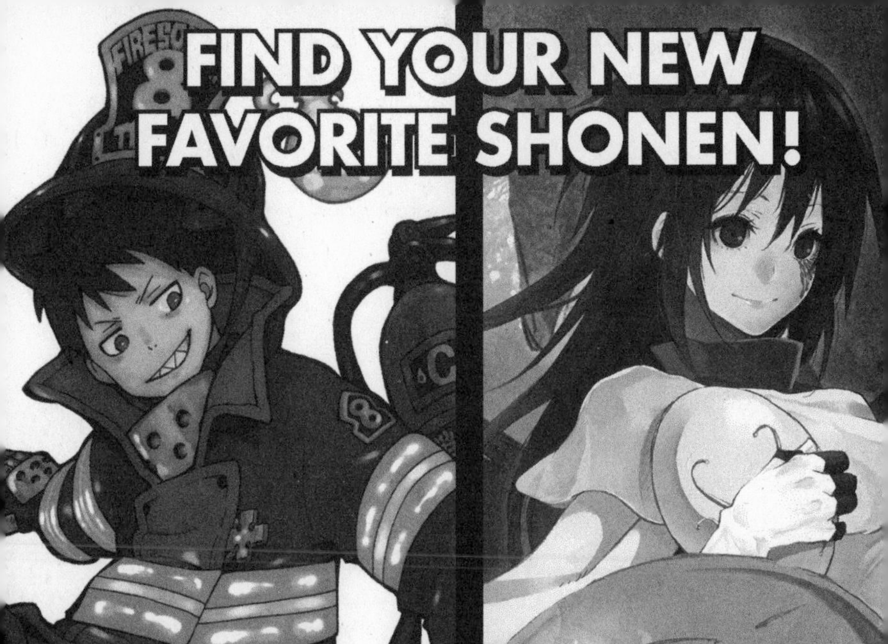
FIND YOUR NEW
FAVORITE SHONEN!
FIRE FORCE
THAT TIME I GOT REINCARNATED AS A
SLIME
KC
KODANSHA
COMICS

A Kodansha Comics Trade Paperback Original
Waiting for Spring volume 5 copyright © 2016 Anashin
English translation copyright © 2018 Anashin

Published in the United States by Kodansha Comics, an imprint of Kodansha USA Publishing, LLC, New York.

Publication rights for this English edition arranged through Kodansha Ltd, Tokyo.

ISBN 978-1-63236-586-6

Printed in the United States of America.

www.kodanshacomics.com

9 8 7 6 5 4 3 2 1
Translation: Alethea and Athena Nibley
Lettering: Sara Linsley
Editing: Haruko Hashimoto
Kodansha Comics edition cover design by Phil Balsman